The
AIR FORCE
INTEGRATES

1945–1964
Second Edition

ALAN L. GROPMAN

To Muhammad
With respect
Alan Gropman

SMITHSONIAN INSTITUTION PRESS
Washington and London

Designer: Martha Sewall

Library of Congress Cataloging-in-Publication Data
Gropman, Alan L., 1938–
    The Air Force integrates, 1945–1964 / Alan L. Gropman.—2nd ed.
        p.   cm.
    Originally published: Washington, D.C. : Office of Air Force History, 1978.
    Includes bibliographical references and index.
    ISBN 1-56098-999-8 (alk. paper)
        1. United States. Air Force—Afro-Americans—History.   2. Sociology, Military—
United States—History—20th century.   3. United States—Race relations.   I. Title.
UG834.A37G76   1998
358.4′008996073—dc21   98-13699

British Library Cataloguing-in-Publication Data available

Manufactured in the United States of America
05 04 03 02 01 00 99 98   5 4 3 2 1

⊗ The paper used in this publication meets the minimum requirements of the American
National Standard for Information Sciences—Permanence of Paper for Printed Library
Materials ANSI Z39.48-1984.

Contents

Preface

he U.S. Air Force racially integrated to improve its military effectiveness—not because of altruism or political direction but because of the desire to become a more potent combat force. This was a significant race relations lesson 20 years ago when the Office of Air Force History published *The Air Force Integrates: 1945–1964,* my account of how that service racially integrated. It may be an even more important message today as race relations sour in the United States and as the propensity of young black men to serve in the military declines to its lowest point since the Defense Department began, more than 20 years ago, to measure interest in enlisting.

The Air Force Integrates: 1945–1964 is based on my dissertation that completed my work for a Ph.D. at Tufts University in 1975. During the next three years I reshaped the dissertation, resulting in the 1977 monograph. The volume you now hold in your hands is a revised edition of *The Air Force Integrates.* The current work omits the complete rendition of numerous air force regulations printed as appendix II of the earlier version. All of the original illustrations (which were mostly head shots of prominent figures in the story) have been deleted. This edition contains 31 new photographs that do more than simply decorate the story—they add substance to the narrative. I have also corrected minor errors of fact and updated the language. Research since 1977, moreover, caused me to revise my approach to President Harry S Truman. I have been less generous to Truman in this revised edition. The bibliography has been brought up-to-date in this preface, which lists recent books that bear on the subject of blacks in the military. Finally, the preface very briefly carries the story of blacks in the air force into the mid-1990s.

The thesis of the original work has worn well: essentially, the air force integrated itself when its senior leaders came to the conclusion that segregation had wrecked air force efficiency and hindered effectiveness. After taking into account the post–World War II Zeitgeist and probing the effects of Harry S Truman's motivations and his election-campaign-inspired Executive Order 9981, I concluded that the air force deputy chief of staff for personnel (with encouragement from the service secretary and the air force assistant secretary) carried this reform to fulfillment because he found racial segregation to be inefficient and unnecessary. Reviews of *The Air Force Integrates, 1945–1964*, papers delivered in scholarly forums, and numerous roundtable discussions with other historians who have studied the era have reinforced this key proposition. The Smithsonian Institution Press believes it appropriate to reissue the work because the fundamental theme remains important; the original volume has been out of print for more than a decade and was never easy to obtain even when it was in print.

Why does this account begin in 1945 and end in 1964? The former year is a good starting point to tell the story of air force racial integration because in that year, despite the heroic and often uniquely successful performance of America's first black pilots—the Tuskegee Airmen—the U.S. Army Air Forces, direct ancestor of the U.S. Air Force, was completely segregated. That is, the black aviators had proved themselves equal to whites, but the army air forces (AAF) remained segregated nevertheless.

The latter year marked the passage of the most comprehensive civil rights act in the United States since Reconstruction. By 1964 the air force had completely desegregated, and the enactment of the landmark bill that year helped to ensure that black airmen would not be humiliated in the communities in which they were stationed.

Air force racial integration was complete by 1964, but gains have been made by blacks since that time. This preface will sketch in that information, largely through the use of statistics. For just one example, the Air Force Academy, established in 1954, graduated only one black cadet in 1964, but from the mid-1970s to the mid-1990s it commissioned more than 1,000. The story, therefore, needs to be brought up-to-date.

Contents of the Monograph

In 1945 the U.S. Army Air Forces was a totally racially segregated institution; its personnel policies were ruled by prejudices inherited from previous decades. Twenty years later, its successor armed force, the U.S. Air Force, had terminated all forms of racial segregation and had undertaken—as had its sibling services—to end all forms of discrimination on and off base. This narrative concentrates on the development of the air force from racial segregation to integration and, beyond that, to equal opportunity, especially pertaining to off-base housing, education, and entertainment.

I analyzed two key elements to establish a baseline for this assessment: first, the military writings of the interwar period (1919–39) that debated the best use of black soldiers, and second, the AAF's wartime treatment of an uprising of several hundred black officers in April 1945 at Freeman Field, Indiana. Transcripts of telephone conversations of the commander at Freeman Field, the commander of First Air Force and members of his staff, and various senior officials in the Pentagon clearly reveal the racial biases of the officer corps. The army and its air forces of the period from 1919 to 1945 were not racially enlightened, but then neither was the United States of America. The armed forces of that era should not be regarded independent of the U.S. social-racial context.

The interwar period was miserable for black Americans. The war years were certainly not golden for black America, except perhaps by comparison with the wretched decades preceding the war. Segregation was practiced in the North and the South, *de facto* in the former and *de jure* in the latter. Blacks who moved north during World War II to seek employment in war industries and to escape the bigotry that denied them the right to vote, that severely hampered their serving on juries, that discouraged their participation in public education, and that sanctioned the lynching of blacks found no warm welcome in northern metropolises such as Detroit, Chicago, or New York. Yet life in the North was obviously better because laws and customs did not deny blacks the right to vote or to go to nonsegregated schools, and blacks by the hundreds of thousands demonstrated their approval of the relatively better life outside the South by moving north and west. The military racism detailed in the early chapters of this book, then, fits the appalling U.S. racial milieu. The racist 1925 Army War College report (detailed in chapter 1), a story that was told many times during the interwar period, was based on literature then commonly found in the United States.

The first two chapters here outline the intolerance of the military bureaucracy and also the inability of the military leaders to see beyond their prejudices in the period between World War II and air force independence in September 1947. The serious racial altercations at MacDill Army Air Field and Fort Worth Army Air Field in 1946 and 1947 (described in chapter 2) demonstrate how racially unenlightened the army and its air forces were after World War II. Blacks at these two bases had serious grievances, but when the AAF leadership sought causes for the unrest that had resulted in a three-day riot at MacDill and in a similar but less dramatic upset at Fort Worth, they blamed Communist influences. They overlooked other factors such as overcrowded living conditions, rigid maintenance of racial segregation, and gross inequities in treatment, especially in the terms of discharge. After receiving notification of discharge, whites could wait out the period between the announcement of discharge and the actual date at home. Blacks, on the other hand, were required to spend the period working at hard labor building a commercial airport!

The military racial climate was not entirely negative during or immediately after World War II. There were tentative signs in 1945 and 1946 that the army was beginning to reevaluate its rigid racial policies, as indicated by the report of the Gillem Board (also covered in chapter 2). But the generally cold reception that Lt. Gen. Alvan Gillem's recommendations received from army and AAF leadership demonstrates that those services were not willing in 1945 and 1946 to diverge from the racial climate in the country.

Change came to the military—and this is the thesis of the book—when leaders realized that the military would benefit by altering its racial policies and practices. Once that decision was made, the services brooked little opposition, within or without, in making the racial reform. We can suppose that there was bigotry to be overcome in the uniformed force, and we know that many politicians, some quite powerful in Congress, were hostile to racial integration. Chapter 3 discusses the implementation of racial integration and the overcoming of opposition inside and outside the air force.

A handful of senior air force officers recognized that segregation was an inefficient personnel policy that brought no advantage to the service. They knew, furthermore, that there was a causal relationship between segregation and racial disturbances. Indeed, there were numerous racial altercations during World War II, and at the center of each of them was differential treatment of blacks and whites. In the air force, the person who understood this best was Lt. Gen. Idwal Edwards, Air Force Deputy Chief of Staff for Personnel. He deserves to be remembered as the person most responsible for integrating the air force. Secretary Stuart Symington, Assistant Secretary Eugene Zuckert, Chief of Staff Gen. Carl Spaatz, and Vice Chief of Staff Lt. Gen. Hoyt Vandenberg made up the handful of men who, with Edwards, made this new personnel arrangement work.

These men, especially Edwards, Symington, and Zuckert, understood that segregation was in fact discrimination, which lowered morale. More serious was the effect that segregation had on the air force overall. Given the state of most blacks in a bigoted United States, the problems created by apartheid in the larger society were concentrated within the services. For example, unequal schools shortchanged blacks and caused low aptitude, common in black units. Thus large black units would necessarily perform at a lower level than white units. Similarly, most blacks were poor. Poverty bred, then and now, destructive social pathologies that inclined black units toward a higher incidence of disciplinary problems. Because of segregation, furthermore, Edwards was not permitted to transfer qualified blacks who were surplus in black units to white units that might be short in these specialties. Likewise, he could not transfer surplus whites into black units that were short of needed people. Such restrictions were personnel folly.

The few leaders who integrated the air force, furthermore, recognized that there was no scientific basis for segregation. That is, they realized that segregation was not based on racial inferiority but was founded instead on prejudice. They had seen the Tuskegee Airmen in World War II create a fighter group that was uniquely successful in its defense of bombers. They knew that blacks who had the same aptitude as whites and were given the same training as whites were as productive as whites. They had authorized studies in 1945 and 1947 that had proved that racism—here, the concept that blacks were inherently inferior to whites—was a false doctrine.

However, these few senior officers (especially the uniformed ones) were not particularly sensitive to the political, educational, and social problems faced by black Americans. These officers were not eager to help blacks solve their larger problems within a bigoted United States. This is especially true of Generals Spaatz, Vandenberg, and Edwards. They were, however, intensely interested in improving the air force. Chapter 3 details the roles played by General Edwards and his uniformed and civilian superiors in integrating the air force.

Desegregation came to the air force in May 1949 largely because of military pragmatism. Two words in the previous sentence need to be decoded. "Desegregation" is a better word to use than "integration" at this point in the story. When the air force abolished all black units, it desegregated itself, deciding no longer to assign people by race. But integration implies a level of cohesion going beyond merely assigning people according to capability. It took some years to achieve that level of bonding. The other word needing explanation is the adverb "largely." No complex effect has a single cause, and the decision to abandon a race-based personnel system that had been practiced in the military on and off since 1775 and continuously since the Civil War certainly was not induced by a single element. My research, however, indicates that the pragmatic concerns of the air force senior leadership were the overwhelming factors in the equation.

Since President Truman's well-known Executive Order 9981 calling for equal opportunity in the armed forces is a rival claimant to promoting racial integration, I spent some time investigating its origins and the president's motives. I recognize how slippery dealing with motives can be. It seems clear from the evidence, however, that Truman's purposes were overwhelmingly political. He was animated by a fierce desire to win the election of 1948 and was advised by some of the best political minds in the country to issue the executive order, promulgated in late July 1948, to win the black bloc vote. Memos to the president stated that he needed the black vote to win the election. Serious students of the Truman presidency find Executive Order 9981 to have been inspired by the election campaign. Truman indeed won the black vote, which carried him back to the White House.

Truman, on the other hand, had always demonstrated a respect and consideration for the "little man" and had supported anti-lynching legislation. He had served in the artillery in World War I and was appalled by the violence that black servicemen faced in the South when returning from both World Wars I and II. He also appointed a civil rights committee to explore reforms that would benefit blacks. Finally, he openly campaigned for the black vote in 1948, speaking in Harlem and on the steps of the Lincoln Memorial—an especially symbolic location—about civil rights matters. But Truman was also a lifelong social segregationist. He did not believe in school racial integration, he objected to the 1954 *Brown* decision, and he certainly was vocal in his opposition to social integration. His executive order, moreover, called not for racial integration but only for equal opportunity. He did not appoint the Fahy Committee to oversee military racial practices until after he was safely elected. And he put the Fahy Committee out of business before the army and the marine corps integrated and while the navy was practicing only the barest tokenism.

I considered other factors, too. There is no question, for example, that the times had changed. The bitter fruits of racism in Germany and elsewhere during World War II made all Americans pay more attention to the sins of America's past and present. U.S. propaganda during World War II emphasized the notion that there was only one America. The political climate was changing. The move of millions of blacks to the North during and after the war was beginning to influence the political stands taken by northern politicians.

But I don't want to get carried away by these alterations. Race-baiting Theodore Bilbo was still in the Senate, and the South was solidly racist. Witness that Gov. Strom Thurmond bolted from the Democratic Party in 1948 and ran for president against Truman because of the president's support for civil rights for blacks: Thurmond carried several states. Most of chapter 3 deals with the political milieu and with my argument on the primary forces underlying the decision to integrate racially. Factoring all this into the equation, I still come to the conclusion that air force integration occurred when it did because of Idwal Edwards and others' pragmatic drive to enhance the service's effectiveness. The reader will have to judge whether or not I am convincing.

Racial integration (as opposed to desegregation) did not advance rapidly in the air force in the mid-1950s. Only very slowly did blacks rise to senior leadership positions, either officer or enlisted. In May 1949 when the air force began the integration process, 0.5 percent of the officer corps was black, and in

1951 when the air force had eliminated the last all-black unit, blacks made up 0.6 percent of the officer corps. The percentage of black officers did not reach 1 percent until 1954, the year of the *Brown* school integration decision. When the Civil Rights Act of 1964 became law, only 1.5 percent of the air force officer corps was black.

Enlisted men, furthermore, were rarely promoted to supervisory ranks in the noncommissioned officer corps. In 1949, with an enlisted force that was 6 percent black, only 1.8 percent of the E-7 master sergeants (then the top enlisted rank) were black. In 1954, with an enlisted force that was 8.7 percent black, only 1.9 percent of the E-7s were black. In 1962 two new supervisory enlisted ranks were added—E-8 and E-9—but only 0.8 percent of the E-9 chief master sergeants were blacks. (Today the number is 17.8 percent, and blacks make up 17.2 percent of the enlisted force.)

More serious yet, the air force paid little attention to the difficulty experienced by blacks off the post—in the North and the South. Chapter 4 highlights these problems. Black troops could get into serious trouble when they tried to take their integrated, on-base experience off the post. For example, civilian bus companies often had permission to pick up people while circulating on a military post, and while on base, they could not enforce local segregation rules. Once the bus crossed the line onto civilian turf, though, blacks had to move to the back of the bus in those locales that required it. Those airmen who refused to move to the back of the bus not only got into trouble with local sheriffs but also found that their violation of local laws received no support from the air force and that their transgressions reflected badly on them in their official air force record.

It is an error, however, to think that blacks were most humiliated or suffered most in the South during this period of strict segregation. Black airmen sustained greater pain living in the rural North in states such as Maine, North and South Dakota, and northern Michigan. In the South, black airmen had black communities for support. In the rural North, at bases like Dow Air Force Base and Loring Air Force Base in Maine and Minot Air Force Base in North Dakota, no such comforts were to be found, and the local population was often highly bigoted and usually hostile. Blacks had no social life off the base and faced gross discrimination in terms of housing, employment opportunities for themselves (moonlighting) or their dependents, and social recreation. Chapter 4 deals with the air force reticence in addressing these problems.

The era of John F. Kennedy and Lyndon B. Johnson marked a time of greatly increased interest (at least at the highest level, that of the commander in chief) in helping blacks overcome residual prejudices in the services and also of support for improving their lot in civilian communities. The account of Kennedy's Gesell

Committee and the effect its report had on the armed services is detailed in chapter 5.

The Air Force Integrates was published in late 1977. The decade and a half between 1964 and that year was distinguished by the changes that came about in the services because of the race riots that occurred in all the services in the late 1960s and early 1970s. The disorder that most affected the air force was the three-day disturbance in May 1971 at Travis Air Force Base. Immediately after the Travis Air Force Base riot, all the services conferred on the race problems that were seriously affecting mission accomplishment, and out of those discussions came the establishment of the Defense Race Relations Institute, located at Patrick Air Force Base in Florida. These matters are discussed in the epilogue. My original work concluded with the thought that the services should not abandon this organization (today called the Defense Equal Opportunity Management Institute) until the general society from which it draws its members has solved the race problem. I have seen nothing in the past 20 years to make me alter that advice.

The Defense Equal Opportunity Management Institute trains people to recognize discrimination—sexual, ethnic, religious, and racial—and then to work at the unit level to eliminate it. The armed services perform their mission based on unit cohesion, and the officers and enlisted personnel who graduate from the Defense Equal Opportunity Management Institute are educated and trained to see themselves as central to the military mission (not as social workers): their charge is to keep the service united. They do not see equal opportunity as an end but as a means to an end, and that end is unit effectiveness. That, after all, is the theme of this book: the air force integrated to make a better, more efficient, more effective air force.

Bringing the Air Force Story Up-to-Date

What has changed since the original volume was published? The appendixes demonstrate the growth in the numbers of blacks in the air force over the 20-year period from 1945 to 1964. Those facts can now be brought up-to-date.

I remarked earlier that the Air Force Academy commissioned one black officer in 1964, the year of the landmark Civil Rights Act. But the first blacks commissioned by the academy in Colorado graduated in the previous year, and there were 3. There were 4 in 1965 and 0 in 1966. The numbers do not begin to show significant increases until after the recognition by the services in 1971 that more had to be done to promote equal opportunity actively if smooth race relations were to be perpetuated. The list below gives the numbers of blacks graduating from the Air Force Academy between 1963 and 1997.

1963: 3	1972: 13	1981: 43	1990: 64
1964: 1	1973: 17	1982: 53	1991: 61
1965: 4	1974: 17	1983: 59	1992: 75
1966: 0	1975: 17	1984: 74	1993: 72
1967: 1	1976: 31	1985: 68	1994: 48
1968: 6	1977: 27	1986: 70	1995: 62
1969: 6	1978: 30	1987: 62	1996: 70
1970: 8	1979: 36	1988: 60	1997: 43
1971: 9	1980: 37	1989: 55	

The year 1976 is the first year that the effects of an increased recruiting program can be seen. I was part of this recruiting effort, which began in 1972 with the goal to let blacks know that the Air Force Academy was indeed interested in increasing its number of black cadets. Standards remained the same, but the academy increased its efforts to spread the word and actively talk to blacks about the benefits of an academy education and an air force career.

Another dramatic increase can be seen in the percentage of blacks in both the enlisted and the officer forces. In the previous volume I cut off the figures in 1972 for the officers and 1970 for the enlisted personnel. In 1972 blacks made up 1.7 percent of the officer corps. In 1995 the figure was 5.63 percent, an increase of more than 200 percent. The enlisted force was 11.67 percent black in 1970 and was 16.92 percent black in 1995. The following table gives the figures for the years between 1973 and 1995.

	Percentage of Black Officers	Percentage of Black Enlisted Personnel
1973	1.95	13.40
1974	2.23	14.22
1975	2.61	14.55
1976	2.84	14.64
1977	3.23	14.59
1978	3.61	14.82
1979	4.23	15.74
1980	4.66	16.33
1981	4.83	16.65
1982	5.04	17.05
1983	5.27	17.00

Continued on next page

	Percentage of Black Officers	Percentage of Black Enlisted Personnel
1984	5.34	16.95
1985	5.38	17.14
1986	5.34	17.29
1987	5.35	17.32
1988	5.44	17.57
1989	5.52	17.38
1990	5.61	17.65
1991	5.72	17.36
1992	5.74	17.14
1993	5.68	16.89
1994	5.68	16.82

In 1995 blacks were 12.1 percent of the civilian population between the ages of 18 and 44; thus blacks made up a significantly higher percentage of the air force than they did of the general U.S. population (this is true of the other services as well, with the army having the highest percentage of blacks).

Most dramatic of the changes that have occurred in the air force over the past 20 years is the vast growth in the number of blacks in supervisory ranks. Whites are supervised by blacks in the military more than in any other job or profession in the world. I have already noted the more than 200 percent increase in black officers in the past 23 years. Let us now compare the enlisted rank structure of blacks in 1970 with that of 1996.

	1970 (%)	1996 (%)
E-1	18.3	15.2
E-2	14.8	15.7
E-3	11.8	14.7
E-4	10.7	14.5
E-5	14.7	19.2
E-6	10.1	19.8
E-7	6.2	20.0
E-8	4.4	18.4
E-9	3.9	17.8

This chart shows that the percentage of black senior supervisors grew over a 26-year period by more than 300 percent. It also signifies that blacks reenlist at higher percentages than whites. This is revealed by the fact that blacks make up about 15 percent of the first three enlisted grades but about 18 percent of the three highest enlisted grades. Blacks have a higher reenlistment rate in all services because the services practice true equal opportunity and because one gets responsibility and authority with rank regardless of race.

The year 1970 is a good one from which to measure progress because in that year the air force introduced the Weighted Airman Promotion System in order to remove subjectivity and bias from the enlisted promotion system. Under this program, points are awarded for time in service, time in grade, decorations, enlisted performance reports, and most important, scores on two objective tests—the Specialty Knowledge Test and the Promotion Fitness Examination. These two examinations amount to as much of the point total as all other factors combined. Now black airmen competed under a color-blind point system, and their promotion rate increased dramatically.

The officer growth, though not as spectacular in actual numbers, is even more spectacular in percentage increases. In 1970 there was one black general officer; in 1996 there were 9. The percentage of black generals was 0.2 percent (1 of 429 generals) in 1970 and 3.3 percent in 1996 (9 of 275). Whereas only 0.4 percent of the colonels in 1970 were black (25 of 6,133), 2.6 percent were in 1996 (103 of 4,022). No other big business in the United States, or anywhere else in the world, has a higher percentage of black executives. The army's officer figures in 1996, incidentally, are double those of the air force, and the officer percentages in the marine corps and the navy are about the same as in the air force. No black had reached four-star rank in the air force by 1970, and the one black general in the service that year retired as a lieutenant (three-star) general. Since then there have been three black four-star generals, and all three were commanders of major commands: North American Air Defense Command; Air Force Systems Command; and Air Force Air Education and Training Command.

Recent Bibliography

Let me suggest a few books that address the subject of blacks in the military and that have been published since *The Air Force Integrates*. People seeking a complete history of how all the armed forces racially integrated should consult Morris J. MacGregor, Jr.'s *Integration of the Armed Forces, 1940–1965* (Washington, D.C.: Center of Military History, 1980). This massive account gives the status of all the services, including the Coast Guard, in the World War II period, deals effectively with the political background of the late 1940s and early 1950s, and describes in great detail the integration process, demonstrating how each service uniquely approached this matter.

For a general background on the subject of blacks in the U.S. military, read Bernard C. Nalty's *Strength for the Fight: A History of Black Americans in the Military* (New York: Free Press, 1986). Nalty's history covers the subject from the colonial wars through Vietnam and deals realistically with the racial problems the services faced in the late 1960s and early 1970s. Nalty and MacGregor teamed to produce a 13-volume compendium of documents that is indispensable to understanding the role blacks played in U.S. wars and the conditions under which they served. See *Blacks in the United States Armed Forces: Basic Documents* (Wilmington, Del.: Scholarly Resources, 1977).

Those wanting to discover why the air force led the way among the services in racial integration need to understand the Tuskegee Airmen. Four volumes, in addition to the ones listed in the bibliography, should be consulted. Robert Jakeman's *The Divided Skies: Establishing Segregated Flight Training at Tuskegee, Alabama, 1934–1942* (Tuscaloosa: University of Alabama Press, 1992), lays out the racial and domestic politics that caused the AAF to train black pilots in the midst of one of the most hostile locations in the United States. This was an unfortunate choice. Alan Osur's *Blacks in the Army Air Forces during World War II* (Washington: Office of Air Force History, 1977) is a pioneer work. This monograph details how and why the AAF brought blacks on board during the war when it did not want blacks under any circumstances. Before mid-1941 the AAF had no blacks. Osur's account is valuable in explaining how blacks made a major contribution in a service that did not want them. (The marine corps also had no blacks in 1941 and wanted none, but blacks went much further in the AAF than in the World War II marine corps, and the navy in 1941 relegated blacks to service only in the mess corps.) The best volume dealing with the unique success of the Tuskegee Airmen, who wrote an enviable record in the skies over North Africa, Italy, and Germany, is Stanley Sandler's *Segregated Skies: All-Black Combat Squadrons of WWII* (Washington, D.C.: Smithsonian Institution Press, 1992). Sandler focuses on achievement and not on treatment, something rare in most accounts dealing with blacks. The Tuskegee Airmen flew 200 escort missions in 1944 and 1945, to some of the most heavily defended targets in the Third Reich, and never lost a B-17 or a B-24 bomber to an enemy fighter, a unique achievement. Sandler's carefully documented history is necessary reading. Finally, James C. Warren recently published a study—*The Freeman Field Mutiny* (San Raphael, Calif.: Donna Ewald, 1995)—describing the events at Freeman Field in April 1945 that resulted in the wholesale replacement of the white command structure in the 477th Bombardment Group (Medium). General Edwards was well aware of the situation at Freeman Field, and this altercation influenced him greatly. Warren's book is essential reading if one wants to understand this event.

Acknowledgments

Let me end by thanking those many people who helped me with this work in both the 1970s and the 1990s. I was truly blessed with a wonderful display of cooperation and encouragement. My commander when I began the dissertation, Dr. Alfred F. Hurley, Head of the History Department at the Air Force Academy, financed my first research trip, calling it "seed money," and read the first draft of the first chapter. He gave me a semester leave from my teaching duties to pursue my research. Dr. David MacIsaac and Dr. John Guilmartin read chapters 1 and 2 and told me to press on. William Cunliffe, of the Modern Military Branch at the National Archives, and his colleagues Edward Reese and Virginia Jezierski (known to all as Mrs. Jerri) saved me a great deal of time and were endlessly helpful and friendly. Charles F. Cooney, of the Library of Congress, was similarly useful. Charles Ohrvall, of the Truman Library, and Joan Howard, of the Eisenhower Library, were indispensable, and Sylvia Turner, of the Kennedy Library, was also cooperative.

Without the staff assistance provided by the Albert F. Simpson Historical Research Center, Maxwell Air Force Base, Alabama, this study would not have seen the light of day. Marguerite Kennedy (known to all as Margo), Chief of the Historical Reference Branch, opened all the doors, and James N. Eastman, Jr., Chief of the Historical Research Branch, kept them open. Morris J. MacGregor, Jr., a historian with the U.S. Army's Center for Military History, assisted me countless times at every stage of my work, from the time I was finishing my Ph.D. coursework at Tufts, through the dissertation process, and into publishing *The Air Force Integrates*. Nobody else did more to shape my thinking. Two of the Tuskegee Airmen, Louis Purnell and Spann Watson, were exceptionally interested in my study, were extraordinarily generous with me, and were primary sources for much that is found in chapters 1, 2, and 3. Both have become lifelong friends. I am also indebted to the late James C. Evans, who provided me with invaluable background information. Betty Fogler, of the U.S. Air Force Academy Library, Interlibrary Loan, obtained material for me from throughout the United States while I was stationed at the academy and also sent me material while I was stationed in Germany.

The help and encouragement I received from the Tufts University history faculty cannot be overstated. Professor Russell E. Miller supervised my dissertation and supported my studies from the time of my arrival at Tufts as a graduate student in 1959. No other individual has so influenced my growth as a historian. Without his advice and the generosity of his time, I might never have completed my dissertation. Professor Daniel Mulholland was second reader on my master's thesis and my dissertation. For more than six years he remained firmly in my corner. Also Professors George Marcopoulis, Aubrey Parkman, and Robert Taylor always took an interest in all my projects.

The Office of Air Force History secured a grant of money from Air Staff funds for my research and provided necessary services. I can never hope to repay men such as Dr. Murray Green, Dr. Charles Hildreth, William Mattson, Lawrence Paszek, Max Rosenberg, David Schoem, and Herman Wolk. After I completed my dissertation, two historians helped me turn it into a book. Carl Berger read it and made many valuable recommendations. Dr. Stanley L. Falk, Chief Historian, also read it and offered valuable criticism and was most responsible for turning my project into a book. Readers will recognize that it took some intrepidity for the U.S. Air Force Chief Historian to publish a work as critical of the air force as this is. His only criteria were truth and objectivity.

Dr. Von Hardesty recommended that the Smithsonian Institution Press republish my monograph, and over the 15 years we have known each other he has proved to be a sensitive and helpful historian and friend. His partner on the "Black Wings" exhibit, Dr. Dominick Pisano, was also exceptionally helpful. Col. Steven Randolph has, for more than 25 years, been a valued critic and friend. I am most grateful to Dr. Mark Hirsch and Dr. Peter Cannell for their decision to reissue and revise the book and for all of the assistance I received from them and their staffs. The Smithsonian Institution Press hired D. Teddy Diggs to edit the revised manuscript; the readers—and I, of course—owe her a great deal.

I also owe much to my family. Over the years many people seemed never to tire (although they must have) of hearing how the air force integrated and what that meant for the larger society. My family put up with much distraction and a great deal of travel both during and after the writing. My daughter, Elizabeth Chang, copyedited the first manuscript and saved me from much embarrassment. My sons, Robert and Michael, enjoyed listening to my stories. My wife, Jackie, supplied love in addition to encouragement. I thank them all.

n April 1945 more than 100 black officers forcefully protested segregated facilities and discriminatory policies at Freeman Field, Indiana. They were arrested by their white commanders for mutiny. This significant but little known event,[1] which occurred in the closing year of World War II, is important in the history of the army air forces because no other event better illustrates the attitude of its white military leadership toward blacks. To understand the factors which precipitated the revolt, it is essential to review army racial policies formulated during the 1920s and 1930s. These policies, based upon racist premises, affected black and white relations for decades that followed. It should be stressed, however, that the military leadership between the two world wars was no more bigoted than other segments of American society. But that knowledge brought little comfort to those who had to endure the system. Without admitting that it had succumbed to racist theories, the military leadership had in fact adopted the racist hyperbole popular in the interwar years.

Interwar Black Personnel Policy

When World War I began in August 1914, the U.S. Army had no plans to employ the vast reservoir of black manpower should the nation become involved in the European conflict. Following America's entrance into the war in April 1917, the army did undertake to recruit black troops totaling about 400,000. Most black soldiers served in the Services of Supply, while others were formed into two infantry divisions and saw action in combat in France. Their effectiveness, however, was a controversial issue after the war. The question of the future use of black personnel was subsequently studied by ten Army War College classes.[2] Essentially, these students reaffirmed decisions made by Gen. John J. Pershing, the army chief of staff, in 1922.

In that year Pershing implemented the recommendation of a staff study which suggested that only the four historically black combat regiments, the 9th and 10th Cavalries and the 24th and 25th Infantries, be manned in the regular army and that segregated National Guard units be maintained and used as army corps reserve commanders saw fit. The authors of the staff study believed that blacks had to be employed in a combat role. They stated, "To follow the policy of exempting the Negro population of this country from combat service means that the white population on which the future of the country depends, would suffer the brunt of the loss, the Negro none." The black American, they continued, was "a citizen of the United States, entitled to all of the rights of citizenship and subject to all the obligations of citizenship." They believed, however, that "no Negro officer should command a white officer."[3] The 1922 plan was no improvement over prewar policies, mainly because it did not call for the establishment of a cadre to train a larger number of blacks. The Army War College, perhaps recognizing this shortcoming, time and again searched for a better plan. What emerged on each occasion was a muddled program of black quotas reflecting racist policies.

A typical study was the Army War College's "Memorandum for the Chief of Staff" of 30 October 1925 titled "The Use of Negro Manpower in War."[4] Signed by Maj. Gen. H. E. Ely, Army War College commandant, this report was the product of "several years study by the faculty and student body of the Army War College." It concluded that black men believed themselves inferior to white men, that they were by nature subservient, and that they lacked initiative and resourcefulness. Blacks, furthermore, were fair laborers but were considered inferior as technicians and fighters.[5] According to this report, blacks were also very low in the scale of human evolution. "The cranial cavity of the Negro is smaller than the white; his brain weighing 35 ounces contrasted with 45 for the white." If any blacks did score well on intelligence tests, the reason given was that they possessed a "heavy strain of white blood."[6]

Black officers, the report claimed, lacked not only the mental capacity to command but courage as well. Their interest was seen as not to fight for their country but solely to advance their racial interests. Worst of all, according to the report, the black "soldier utterly lacked confidence in his colored officer." The black "officer was still a Negro, with all the faults and weaknesses of character inherent in the Negro race, exaggerated by the fact that he wore an officer's uniform."[7]

The compilers of this study also believed that blacks had a profoundly superstitious nature and possessed abundant moral and character weaknesses. The writers declared: "Petty thieving, lying, and promiscuity are much more common among Negroes than among whites. Atrocities connected with white women have been the cause of considerable trouble among Negroes." Most damning of all, according to the report blacks were deemed cowardly. "In physical courage," it stated, "it must be admitted that the American Negro falls well back of the white man and possibly behind all other races."[8]

The memorandum also argued that racial segregation was dictated by inherited inferiority. The black supposedly possessed "physical, mental, moral and other psychological characteristics" that "made it impossible for him to associate socially with any except the lowest class of whites." The sole exceptions to this were "the Negro concubines who have sometimes attracted men who, except for this association, were considered high class." Typical of those army officials who came before and who would come later, these white officers believed that black "social inequality makes the close association of whites and blacks in military organization inimicable to harmony and efficiency."[9]

In endorsing the memorandum, General Ely concluded that the study was based on the need for military efficiency and was "eminently fair to both the Negro and the white man."[10] His views, however, must not be taken out of context. The 1920s were uneasy years for American blacks as well as for other racial and ethnic minorities. After World War I and the Bolshevik Revolution, fear gripped America, and the country turned inward, rejecting anyone who looked, acted, or spoke differently. This was the decade that produced restrictive immigration legislation and saw the Ku Klux Klan win sufficient public and official acceptance to parade down Washington's Pennsylvania Avenue. Even pragmatic career military men succumbed to the pervading atmosphere and the storm of hate.[11]

It was against this background that the faculty and students casually denigrated the fighting performance of blacks. In a section of the study dealing with black service in previous wars, the writers only perfunctorily praised the courage and successes of black servicemen. They ignored or deliberately overlooked the fact that more than 10 percent of Union army troops during the closing years of the Civil War were black. Indeed, black soldiers won 38 Medals of Honor between 1863 and 1898—during the Civil, Indian, and Spanish-American Wars. Such facts were not mentioned in the Army War College study.[12]

Confronted by such points of view, blacks found it difficult to enter the army. By 1937 there were only 6,500 blacks in an army of 360,000 men, constituting 1.8 percent of the total. The attitude of the army air corps was worse: it would not accept blacks in any capacity.[13] The air corps maintained this posture until the early 1940s, when political pressures forced it to modify its stand. Blacks had not been permitted to join the American air service during World War I, although a black American, Eugene Jacque Bullard, flew in combat with the Lafayette Flying Corps.[14] The belief that blacks were unsuitable for air duty remained unchanged up to the early years of World War II.

World War II Personnel Policy

After the war began in September 1939, the army undertook to reformulate its black policy. At the time, the army had only the four regular black regiments. With the start of hostilities in Europe, the question arose whether to increase the number of black units. The black community criticized the army for not acting expeditiously. The response was that the army was not a free agent in these matters, that it was only following the will of the majority. The army's chief of personnel stated: "The War Department is not an agency which can solve national questions relating to the social or economic position of the various racial groups composing our Nation. The War Department administers the laws affecting the military establishment; it cannot act outside the law, nor contrary to the will of the majority of the citizens of the nation."[15]

The army's view throughout the war was that its primary concern was only to maintain a fighting machine and that it was not interested in changing social customs. It also reasoned that segregation was not discriminatory. After all, the Supreme Court had ruled on numerous occasions that segregation was not discrimination per se. The army, in a phrase, would maintain separate but equal facilities.[16] Long into the war and well after it, the army contended: "Segregation is required, discrimination is prohibited."[17]

In the fall of 1940, after Germany had conquered France and the Low Countries, the army further outlined a program for black military employment. Blacks would be recruited for the expanded army in a strength proportional to that of the national population. Black units were to be established in each major army branch; black reserve officers were to be assigned only to black units; and blacks would be able to attend Officers Candidate School (OCS), a privilege previously denied them. Regarding segregation, an official statement declared: "The policy of the War Department is not to intermingle colored and white personnel in the same regimental organizations. This policy has proven satisfactory over a long period of years and to make changes would produce situations destructive to morale and detrimental to the preparation for national defense." The policy statement also announced that blacks were "being given aviation training as pilots, mechanics and technical specialists. This training will be accelerated. Negro aviation units will be formed as soon as the necessary personnel have been trained."[18]

Black efforts to enter aviation units became one of the "most widespread and widely publicized of all the prewar public pressure campaigns affecting the Negro and the Army."[19] Throughout the 1930s the National Association for the Advancement of Colored People (NAACP) and black newspapers had pressured the War Department without success. The answer in 1931 to a request that blacks be used in at least service units drew an air corps response that it required "men of technical and mechanical experience and ability. As a rule, the colored man has not been attracted to this field in the same way or the same extent as the white man."[20]

In 1939 Congress attempted to force the hand of the air corps by calling for the establishment of black civilian pilot training schools, a branch of a broader civilian program. These schools were created to provide a cadre of flyers should the United States become involved in the war. The air corps did sponsor several black flying schools but took none of the graduates. Beginning with the fall of that year, the Civilian Pilot Training Program established several black flight schools and permitted some blacks to train in integrated northern flying schools. During the first year, 91 blacks (out of a class of 100) passed, achieving a record on par with that of the whites. The air corps remained reluctant, however, to accept any of these graduates into its ranks, arguing that the congressional legislation did not require it to employ them but simply to establish the schools.[21] It pointed out that blacks and whites could not be mixed and, since no provision had been made to create black air corps squadrons, they could not enlist because there were no units to which they could be assigned.[22] Yet, one should not minimize the genuine concern some air corps leaders expressed about interracial problems. For example, they foresaw a problem should a black pilot execute a forced landing at a "white" base. Such an incident raised the question: Where, then, could he eat or sleep? What would white enlisted men do if ordered by a black pilot to service his aircraft? These were serious questions in 1940.

Throughout 1939 and 1940, the air corps refused to alter its stand. By early 1941, however, feeling pressure from politicians eager to garner the black bloc vote (especially President Franklin D. Roosevelt) and threatened with lawsuits from enterprising blacks, the air corps established one pursuit squadron with 47 black officers and 429 black enlisted men.[23] Tuskegee was selected as the most suitable location for segregated training. The air corps created a Jim Crow air force at the headquarters of black accommodation. Black leaders and the black press were unimpressed with this meager concession. But they temporarily muzzled their discontent because they believed that criticism might halt further opportunities for black pilots. On 22 March 1941 the 99th Pursuit Squadron was activated, and the following year saw the activation of the 100th Pursuit Squadron.[24] Most of the pilots of these two squadrons were initially trained by the Civilian Pilot Training Program, which produced more than 2,000 black pilots during World War II.[25]

The Tuskegee Airmen were created partly because President Franklin D. Roosevelt, who was running for a third term, needed to shore up his waning support among black voters in the 1940 election.[26] Certainly, the air corps did not want blacks, and neither did Secretary of War Henry L. Stimson. He wrote in his diary that "leadership is not embedded in the Negro race" and making blacks commissioned officers was to court "disaster." He also predicted that blacks would fail as aviators.[27] Roosevelt as well was no activist on civil rights matters, but the Republican candidate, Wendell L. Willkie, pressed determinedly for the black vote. Roosevelt, seeking to counter Willkie's appeal, promised to create black flying units and promoted Benjamin O. Davis, Sr., to brigadier general, the first black to hold that rank.[28] The president also appointed William Hastie as Stimson's civilian aide on black affairs. For these and other reasons, Roosevelt won a majority of the black vote.[29] Having gained these advantages, most blacks were eager to agitate for the right to fight in combat so that they might make future demands based on their military accomplishments. Most black Americans considered their quest as a struggle on two fronts: first, to fight America's enemies abroad, and second, to help guarantee a victory against the black's enemies at home.[30]

Henry H. (Hap) Arnold, commanding general of the U.S. Army Air Forces, believed that creating black officers would introduce an impossible social problem, that is, black officers would command white enlisted men.[31] To avoid the above situation, Arnold built a tightly segregated black component of the air corps, labeled the "Spookwaffe" by some of its black members. Segregation, however, and the policy for all components of the army to take a quota of blacks crippled intelligent personnel policies. The technically oriented air corps had a need for better-educated personnel, but most blacks did not score as well as most whites on aptitude tests. The average score on the Army General Classification Test (AGCT)— which measured educational achievement and level—was 107 for whites, whereas blacks averaged 79. Only 15 percent of the whites were in the lowest two categories, IV and V, compared with 80 percent of the blacks.

One solution the air corps implemented to correct the social and quota problems was to set up aviation squadrons. Each base was allotted approximately 400 blacks who were assigned to these catchall laboring units. There were more than 250 such squadrons in 1944. Blacks were also assigned to segregated truck companies, medical and quartermaster detachments, and air base defense units. Although more than 16 percent of the blacks scored in the highest three categories of the AGCT and had abilities far beyond those called for in menial tasks, they also were assigned to laboring units without regard for occupational specialties, educational backgrounds, tested aptitudes, or any other classification method. Blacks were assigned according to the numbers received and space availability.[32] Such segregated units at once encountered serious difficulties. Segregation implied that in a black unit of 200 men, almost one-half of them would fall in the lowest aptitude category, while another 70 would score in the next lowest. In comparable white units, 16 generally were in the lowest aptitude level and fewer than 50 classified in the next lowest. White units could spread out their less-endowed soldiers, while the black units concentrated them.[33] Almost 50 percent of all servicemen in class V did not comprehend such words as "discipline, individual, outpost, maintain, and observation," and fewer than a quarter of the men understood "barrage, cadre, counter-clockwise, personnel, exterior and ordnance." These were commonplace words appearing in announcements on bulletin boards and in manuals.[34]

Black units were often poorly trained and frequently led by officers who also were of comparatively low quality. Although the air corps accepted its quota, no more than 6.1 percent of its force was black.[35] The vast majority of these were enlisted men. Their difficulties will be examined in chapter 2.

The Tuskegee Airmen

In March 1941, the first blacks were accepted into the air corps for flight training. It is probably safe to say that the military leadership considered this at best an unwanted, unnecessary experiment and at worst an unwarranted political intrusion. Tuskegee Army Air Field was established on 23 July 1941, and training began the following 1 November. There were 13 men in the first class: 1 officer and 12 flying cadets. The officer was Benjamin O. Davis, Jr., a West Point graduate, 35th of 276 in the class of 1936, who had been "silenced" during his stay at the military academy because he was black.[36] During the war years, Tuskegee trained 650 single-engine pilots, 217 twin-engine pilots, and 60 auxiliary pilots and also graduated five pilots from Haiti.[37]

This training, accomplished in Jim Crow fashion, disturbed William Hastie, Secretary Stimson's civilian aide on black affairs. Air corps segregation policies and insensitive discriminatory acts later forced Hastie to resign. Stimson and Assistant Secretary of War John J. McCloy viewed him as a representative of the NAACP, and they actually kept Hastie ignorant of matters on blacks. The final blow came with the creation of a Special Troop Policies Committee, headed by McCloy (the McCloy Committee). It was formed without Hastie's knowledge and, more significantly, excluded him from its membership.[38]

Hastie and the black press regularly criticized the Tuskegee airfield program with its white command element. The best Hastie could say about the Tuskegee location was that it was uneconomical; and he was unhappy with the Tuskegee Institute for accepting and monopolizing black pilot training and with the air corps for lodging black flying training in Alabama. He believed Tuskegee and the air corps were involved in an unholy alliance to keep blacks segregated.[39] Hastie admitted, however, that the air corps gave blacks the best of facilities and instructors, but the *Pittsburgh Courier* denied even that.

In a five-part series of articles in 1944, the *Courier,* the leading black newspaper in the country, with the largest circulation, attacked Tuskegee Army Air Field as a "citadel to the theory that there can be segregation without discrimination." The newspaper held that whites were there chiefly to "advance themselves without re-

gard to the damage done to the general morale of Negro Army personnel." The
Courier complained that whites did not associate with blacks and that no officer,
including Col. Noel Parrish, who assumed command of Tuskegee Army Air Field
in December 1942 and remained in command throughout the war, belonged to the
officers' club. There was even a hint that airplane accidents might have been caused
through the deliberate sabotage of aircraft.[40]

Tuskegee's safety record belied sabotage, and Colonel Parrish had membership
in the club. In fact, Parrish socialized in an open and relaxed manner with blacks,
and when he was promoted from chief of training to commander, Truman K. Gibson, Hastie's assistant and his successor, reported that morale at Tuskegee improved.[41] After the war, Parrish was probably the first white of any stature to advocate integration. He argued, "Unless some deliberate break in the expensive and
inefficient shell of segregation is made now, the next emergency will find the Air
Force embarrassingly unprepared for the large scale employment of Negro manpower. As operations and logistics advance into the atomic age, the personnel policies of the Civil War become increasingly burdensome."[42]

Parrish understood much better than his white contemporaries that segregation
was the prime cause of low morale among blacks. He quoted Rayford W. Logan of
Howard University, Washington, D.C., who stated, "However segregation may be
rationalized, it is essentially the denial of belonging." Parrish knew that segregated
units were "no darker on the top than other units," and that this had to appear to
the blacks as a "trick." Black units were "regarded as gift horses to be ridden by
white men with Negroes doing the shoveling."[43] Morale problems, then, were unlikely to end when the pilots graduated from Tuskegee.

Following graduation, the 99th Pursuit Squadron encountered difficulties ob-
taining an overseas combat mission. Successive deployment dates passed, and in
the interim the 99th flew training missions to remain proficient. The air corps
could find no place for the unit because no one, apparently, wanted it. It remained
stateside for a year before being ordered to North Africa, and as they departed, the
black airmen knew that upon their performance "depended the future of Negroes
in military aviation."[44] The 99th arrived in North Africa in April 1943 and flew its
first combat mission on 2 June over Pantelleria. A week later the unit made its first
enemy contact. It scored its first kill in July, but no more enemy aircraft were de-
stroyed until January 1944. General Arnold was unhappy with this dry spell, as was
Col. William W. Momyer.[45]

Momyer, commander of the 33d Fighter Group, of which the 99th was a part,
reported in September 1943 that the 99th had unsatisfactory air discipline and had
not yet acquired the ability to work and fight as a team. He claimed that its for-
mations disintegrated under fire, and he condemned its lack of aggressiveness. He
wanted the unit removed from combat.[46]

Momyer's recommendation was endorsed favorably as it moved up through the chain of command. One general officer remarked, "The Negro type has not the proper reflexes to make a first-class fighter pilot." Lt. Gen. Carl Spaatz, commanding general, Northwest African Air Forces, endorsed the report, telling Arnold that the 99th had been given a fair test. Arnold then recommended that the 99th be removed from an active combat role, that the 332d Fighter Group (upon attaining combat-ready status) also be sent to a noncombat area, and that the proposed training program to create a black bombardment group be abandoned. It was clear to the command element that the blacks had failed their test.[47]

Arnold, however, was aware of the political implications of barring blacks from combat and asked Gen. George Marshall, the army chief of staff, to secure Roosevelt's approval before abandoning them. Marshall asked Army G-3 (Operations) to study the role of blacks in combat, both in the air and on the ground, because he needed more information. G-3 advised that the evidence was inconclusive and recommended that the 332d be sent to the Mediterranean for a true test. Truman Gibson argued that the negative comments by Momyer and others were unfair, since many white units also responded poorly when first thrust into battle and the 99th also had no combat veterans to leaven the unit. Its flight leaders were neophytes because of segregation. Col. Benjamin O. Davis, Jr., 99th commander, on temporary duty to the United States, further refuted Momyer's allegations. Davis admitted that the 99th had adjustment difficulties but added that only once had the unit dispersed under fire and even then it had not fled but had continued to fight man-to-man, though in a disorganized fashion. The more combat missions the 99th flew, Davis argued, the more aggressive it became. Davis's testimony plus the report of G-3 bought more time for the squadron, and by January 1944 the 99th had so improved its capabilities that the original Momyer report was shelved and no action was taken. In January 1944, the 99th (now attached to the 79th Fighter Group) scored well over Anzio. On 27 January, 15 of the Tuskegee airmen engaged more than 16 German Focke-Wulf 190s, destroying six and damaging four. Later in the day, the unit added three more kills.[48]

At the end of the month, the 332d Fighter Group began to arrive, with Davis as its commander. In July, the group received the P-51 for long-range escort duty, and on the 18th the 332d shot down 11 aircraft. On 24 March 1945, the 332d flew a 1,600-mile round trip to Berlin on escort duty, bagging three German jet fighters. The group's record on escort duty remained unparalleled. It never lost an American bomber to enemy aircraft. During its combat career, the 332d was awarded several unit combat decorations.[49]

Though the 99th and 332d had problems, they did win a measure of glory. Their difficulties, however, were minimal when contrasted with the obstacles confronting the newly activated 477th Bombardment Group (Medium). Arnold tried to abort this unit before it was born, and the group never entered into battle, although it had been in existence sufficient time to have fought. Its history constitutes a significant chapter in U.S. military race relations and, far more important, vividly demonstrates the racial attitudes of the army air forces (AAF) leadership.

The 477th Bombardment Group (M) (Colored)

Because bomber squadrons required many more crew members than fighter units, the 477th was confronted with severe manning problems. By 1943 there were 199,637 blacks in the AAF,[50] a number that was insufficient to man rapidly a four-squadron B-25 group and continue to supply personnel replacements to the 332d. The air corps could not locate qualified blacks in sufficient numbers with the same aptitudes as whites to man the ground support or flying organizations. For pilot and navigator training, therefore, as well as for ground technical training, the AAF was required to accept blacks with significantly lower aptitude scores. Black candidates for pilot, navigator, and bombardier training could enter with an aptitude score of four or less on a nine-point scale, while whites were required a score of seven.[51] But lowering the aptitude requirements for black units ultimately proved harmful. If aptitude testing had any validity, and the air corps had made a science of testing,[52] then one must assume that black flying units had to be below the proficiency level of the white units. The 477th Bombardment Group was activated on 15 January 1944 without a backlog of trained personnel and was doomed from the outset. Up to this time, the AAF had never had black navigators and bombardiers. Consequently, it became necessary either to establish a completely separate navigator and bombardier facility like Tuskegee or to maintain ad hoc segregation at an established navigator and bombardier school. The latter solution was adopted.[53] In the autumn of 1943 it was decided that creation of such a bombardment group was feasible. Col. Robert R. Selway, Jr., a 1924 graduate of West Point, was selected to lead the 477th Bombardment Group (M) (Colored).[54]

Selway began to form the unit in mid-January 1944 at Selfridge Army Air Field, Michigan. White supervisory personnel were drawn from the combat theaters as well as from stateside units. Blacks came from Tuskegee and the combat theaters. By mid-February there were 200 men in the group, including the first contingent of black enlisted technicians. Its personnel strength increased slowly because only Tuskegee could train black pilots and the Alabama complex also furnished replacements for the 332d in Italy. By 5 May, more time than it normally took to train a white B-25 unit, only half of the officer complement had arrived, and the outfit was acutely short of navigators and bombardiers.[55]

On the same day, the 477th—without advance notice—was ordered to board trains and moved to Godman Field, Kentucky, adjoining Fort Knox. The official unit history states that the move was made to take advantage of "better atmospheric conditions for flying" and that the housing and maintenance facilities at Godman were "adequate."[56] A more plausible explanation for the move appears to have been an attempt to disassociate the men from "racial agitators" in Detroit. Selfridge had four times the hanger space as Godman Field, seven times the acreage, more and longer runways, five times the gasoline capacity, and better flying weather. Godman could not house the entire group because of insufficient hanger and apron space, and its runways had deteriorated and could barely handle bombers. Godman Field also lacked an air-to-ground gunnery range.[57] The black press objected to the move and was particularly vocal about sending the men into the South.[58]

Although the 477th was authorized 128 navigators and navigator-bombardiers, by 14 October—nine months after the unit's creation—only 23 had arrived. By the same date, only half of the authorized 176 pilots had been assigned. They flew repeated routine proficiency missions but undertook no combat crew training. Theirs was an unusually safe flying unit. The first aircraft accident, a landing mishap during a squall, came after the 14,000-flying-hour mark. Twice Maj. Gen. Frank O. D. Hunter, First Air Force commander, commended the unit for its "exceptionally low accident rate."[59]

Between mid-October 1944 and mid-January 1945, 84 new bombardiers and 60 new pilots arrived, but not all bombardiers had received formal navigator training. This had to be accomplished before they could perform as navigator-bombardiers. At the end of 1944, navigation training continued apace and the 477th had enough qualified specialists to undertake combat crew training. But as the winter weather closed in, flyable hours at Godman were reduced to 40 percent of normal, because of "low ceilings, icing . . . and increased smoke." Yet, the flying performance of the group was impressive. In its first year, the 477th flew 17,875 hours with two minor accidents, neither of which was attributable to crew error.[60]

The AAF attempted to solve the problem of Godman's inadequate facilities with another move of the unit to Freeman Field, near the town of Seymour in southern Indiana in March 1945. This move disrupted training and precipitated severe morale problems. Fort Knox, adjoining Godman, had been a better location because it had a sizable civilian black population nearby. The town of Seymour lacked this advantage, and according to the unit historian, most of its residents would not "accept or intermingle with the colored troops . . . socially or in their daily business. . . . Some local grocery stores refused to sell their groceries to wives of colored officers and restaurant owners also refused service."[61]

The Freeman Field Mutiny

More significant was the mutiny which occurred in April 1945. The official unit history remains silent about the causes of the revolt. A "sudden interruption of progress in the training program occurred on the 24th of April when sudden orders to return to Godman were received."[62] Godman, which was notorious for its lack of space and inadequate flying facilities, could not accommodate all of the group's aircraft, and a number of airplanes had to be left at Freeman. Only gradually did the 477th recover from the latest move, and between mid-April and mid-July 1945 the group experienced five accidents with 11 fatalities. The unit lost all of its effectiveness and did not become combat-ready before the war's end because its combat training was subordinated to the question of who could enter the base officers' club!

The black officers viewed the return to Godman as proof that the AAF would sacrifice training to maintain segregation. They claimed the right to enter any officers' club, a position guaranteed by army regulations. The white hierarchy, however—particularly Colonel Selway and General Hunter—refused to permit blacks to use club facilities that the group commander had reserved for white personnel.

Hunter's views were clearly established, and perhaps knowledge of his stand helped to provoke the mutiny and other altercations. He wrote in December 1944: "Racial friction will exist in a marked degree if colored and white pilots are trained together. . . . It is considered more consistent with the war aims to procure maximum efficiency in white combat crew training and handle the Negro problem to the best of our ability, on as a few bases as it may be concentrated, [than] to lower the quality of combat training on all bases in an effort to appease certain agitators. . . . The doctrine of social equality cannot be forced on a spirited young pilot preparing for combat."[63]

Earlier in 1943, Hunter had created a storm over a segregated officers' club, at Selfridge Army Air Field, Michigan. He had ordered that the single officers' club on the base be used solely by whites, and he declared that blacks would have to wait until one was built for them. Offended by this announcement, many black officers entered the club and were arrested. Much to Hunter's chagrin, the incident led to an official reprimand for Col. William Boyd, the base's white commander. Hunter then called Lt. Gen. Barney M. Giles, chief of air staff, Headquarters, U.S. Army Air Forces, in Washington to ask that the reprimand be aimed at himself for ordering the segregation.[64] When forced later to endorse the reprimand, Hunter tried to mitigate its intent by stating that Boyd had simply carried out orders. But such a mitigation would embarrass the AAF headquarters, and Giles told Hunter's chief of staff when that the reprimand could contain no such mitigating comments. Giles also apologized for the mess that Hunter and Boyd were in, stating that he had condoned segregation and "backed them 100% on this thing."[65] A few days later, Giles informed Hunter, "I told Gen. Arnold how you felt about it, that you didn't want anybody in your command taking the rap for something you condoned." He also told Hunter that Arnold had been sympathetic: "I told General Arnold that we wouldn't let them join the club and he approved."[66]

The reprimand given to Boyd was sharply worded:

1. Investigation by the Office of the Inspector General has disclosed that racial discrimination against colored officers . . . was due to your conduct in denying to colored officers the right to use the Officer's Club. . . . Such action is in violation of Army Regulations and explicit War Department instructions on this subject.
2. As a commissioned officer of the Regular Army of many years standing you must have had knowledge that your conduct in this respect was highly improper. Not only does your conduct indicate a lack of good judgment, but it also tends to bring criticism upon the military service. . . .
3. You are hereby formally reprimanded and admonished that any future action on your part will result in your being subjected to the severe penalties prescribed by the Articles of War.[67]

The reprimand of Boyd demonstrates that Hunter was not a free agent in dealing with blacks in his command, but he persisted. The following May 1944, Hunter called Brigadier General Harper at the Pentagon to find out if orders were going to be issued that "the colored and white will be on 100% equal footing socially." He was told: "Not at all. There will be no orders on it." Hunter replied, "Well now, by golly, that's what they're raising all this hell about at Selfridge." But he was assured that the dispute at Selfridge was over a lack of equal facilities, that segregation was not the issue. Hunter, however, knew differently. He demanded issuance of explicit orders for the War Department authorizing separate clubs and the right to handle any disturbances without interference from the Pentagon. He was told to make sure he provided equal facilities, for if he did that, he would have "complied with what the War Department had in mind."[68]

But the latter statement was in error because since December 1940, Army Regulation 210-10 had outlawed segregated officers' clubs. It stated: "No officer clubs, messes, or similar organization of officers will be permitted by the post commander to occupy any part of any public building . . . unless such club, mess, or other organization extends to all officers on the post the right to full membership."[69] The blacks cited the regulation as their justification for protesting segregation at Selfridge and later at Freeman.

Hunter was aware that blacks hated segregation, but his prejudices were too fixed to have that fact alter his attitude. Also, some officers in the Pentagon continued to labor under the false impression that blacks favored segregation so long as black facilities were equal. Here again War Department literature clearly disputed this thinking. War Department Pamphlet 20-6, *Command of Negro Troops,* issued in February 1944, maintained that the "idea of racial segregation is disliked by almost all Negroes and downright hated by most. White people and Negro . . . fail to have a common understanding of the meaning of segregation. . . . The protesting Negro . . . knows from experience that separate facilities are rarely equal, and that too often racial segregation rests on a belief in racial inferiority."[70]

The issue of segregated officers' clubs, however, was only one cause of the 1945 mutiny. Black airmen also had other grievances which ignited their anger. For example, they found themselves caught up in a white promotion mill. Thus no black could outrank a white. When a white was promoted out of a job, another took his place. The notion prevailed that no black, "no matter how competent, could perform assigned duties better than any white man no matter how incompetent."[71] Added to the endless and frustrating manning problems, inadequate flight facilities, disruptive unit moves, and the discouraging promotion policy was a segregated officers' club structure. The combination finally produced an explosion.

Selway sought to avoid the officers' club problem at Godman by having whites join the all-white officers' club at Fort Knox, leaving the Godman club all-black. Since Fort Knox could extend membership to whomever it wished, and since no black officers were assigned to Fort Knox, it was suggested that there were no grounds for black complaints.[72] Colonel Selway notified the blacks before the move to Freeman Field that there would be two separate (but equal) officers' clubs at the new post. Race was supposedly not involved: one club would be for supervisors and the other for trainees.[73] But all whites were designated supervisors, and all blacks were designated trainees.

As blacks arrived at Freeman, they protested the violation of Army Regulation 210-10. On 10 March 1945, Selway called Hunter and told him he was going to close the club at Freeman until he was assured that his orders were legal. Hunter asked, "What club?" Selway said, "The one that belongs to the white officers." Hunter disagreed: "Oh no, I wouldn't do that. As far as I'm concerned if you've gotten out orders assigning one club to the OTU [Officers Training Unit] Group and one club to the permanent party personnel, and don't say anything about color, race, or creed you've complied with my orders. . . . I'd be delighted for them to commit enough actions that way so I can court-martial some of them." The issue was clear to Colonel Selway: the blacks were demanding social equality, and he was not going to grant it. He concluded the conversation by informing Hunter that spies within the black units were keeping him informed.[74]

Following this and similar discussions, General Hunter's intelligence section sent a white agent to Freeman to evaluate the situation. His 31 March report was alarming: "The primary location of discontent and most likely location of any possible uprising is at the Freeman Air Base. The colored officers and colored enlisted men located there are in the majority thus giving them the psychological feeling of superiority over the white personnel, and the white personnel . . . resent said attitude." Some whites made "disgruntled remarks" in the presence of blacks, but all those put in the report had been made at the white officers' club. They included, for example, the following statements:

c. "If one of them makes a crack at my wife, laughs or whistles at her, like I saw them do to some white girls downtown, so help me, I'll kill him."

d. "I killed two of them in my home town, and it wouldn't bother me to do it again."

e. "I went to the show on this base my first and last time because I'm afraid I'll get into trouble some night when they start making remarks about the white actors and actresses: besides that, the smell in the show is terrible."

h. "Their club is better than ours. Why don't they stay in their place."

i. "That isn't just what they are looking for. What they want to do is stand at the same bar with you, and be able to talk with your wife. They are insisting on equality."[75]

The black press was also alert to the crisis. The *Indianapolis Recorder* reported on 17 March 1945 that the men were "incensed at . . . segregation" at Freeman and the officers were "staging an organized protest" by boycotting "Jim Crow facilities."[76] A *Pittsburgh Courier* headline read: "Bombardiers disgusted at Freeman Field Bias." The newspaper reported that the blacks had been threatened with severe penalties if they did not obey segregation rulings. It cited paragraph 19 of Army Regulation 210-10 as the basis for the black complaint.[77]

On 5 April the first major events of the mutiny occurred. On that day 100 officers arrived at Freeman Field from Godman to begin their combat crew training. Selway was told that these new officers were planning to descend in groups upon the white officers' club, and he ordered the provost marshal to "exclude any trainee personnel under penalty of arrest." At 9:15 P.M. four black officers tried to enter. On being told they could not, they left without incident. A half hour later 19 black officers attempted to enter the club and were blocked by the provost marshal, standing with outstretched arms. Two officers "forcibly pushed the Provost Marshal through the doorway." One was heard to remark, "Well, let me go in and get arrested." All 19 entered, had their names taken, were arrested, and were confined to quarters. Less than a half hour later three more blacks tried to enter and were sent away. Then minutes later, another group of 14 gained entry and were arrested. The incidents continued until the club was closed for the night.[78] Three blacks of the 61 arrested actually used force to enter. Only they were tried some months later.[79]

When Hunter learned of these actions, he called the deputy chief of air staff, Brig. Gen. Ray L. Owens, in Washington. He reported: "Out at Freeman Field . . . a bunch of these colored officers forced their way into the white officers' club. . . . Selway has got them in arrest." Hunter told Owens that he had received permission from the air staff to establish separate clubs. Owens replied, "They can't claim discrimination on that, one officers' club is student and the other is permanent."[80] Most of the phone conversation between the two officers, however, referred to the club as white. Their failure to use the word "supervisors" was more than a question of semantics.[81]

The following two days black officers again entered the club and were also arrested. On 7 April the judge advocate advised Selway to release all of the arrested officers, with the exception of the three who had forced their way into the club. Selway complied but closed the club to prevent further disorders. On 9 April Selway issued a new regulation designating particular facilities for each group, without citing race. All officers in the 477th were listed as trainees, except those who were specifically designated as "Command or Supervisory or Instructor" personnel. The regulation also stated that all members of the two housekeeping squadrons—"E" and "C" specifically—were also trainees. There were few officers in these units and only two other black officers on the post: a physician (flight surgeon) and a chaplain. Had nontrainee black officers been allowed membership in the "supervisors" club, such an action might have taken the wind out of the mutinous sail. The First Air Force inspector general reported: "There is a group of approximately 20 Negro officers at Freeman Field who are not assigned either to the 477th Bombardment Group or the CCTS [Combat Crew Training Squadron] . . . and hence are not trainees *per se*. . . . This is important because of the allocation of club facilities as between trainees and base personnel." The inspector noted that the blacks labeled Selway's justification for segregation a subterfuge.[82]

Appended to the main body of Selway's 9 April regulation was a statement that read: "I certify that I have read and fully understand the above order." On that and the following day, at Hunter's insistence, this regulation was read and explained to all Freeman Field personnel. All whites and most blacks signed, but "practically all officers of the CCTS . . . refused." Selway commanded them to sign, but more than 100 refused to do so. A day later, they were read the 64th Article of War, the willful disobedience article, and were given another opportunity to sign. But 101 black officers refused and were arrested. On 13 April, they were sent to Godman under arrest. Selway again opened the white club, only to learn from informants that "approximately 100% of the Negro officer personnel" were about to "present themselves en masse at the club." He immediately closed the club. Throughout the night roving patrols of black officers passed by the club to see if it was open. Selway came upon groups of up to 50 blacks as he toured the base, and while he found them "entirely orderly in their conduct," they were also "surly and uncommunicative."[83]

Throughout these days, Hunter was in daily contact with Pentagon officials. Maj. Gen. Laurence S. Kuter, assistant chief of air staff, expressed sympathy for Hunter's situation and suggested that the First Air Force commander apply his supervisor/trainee separation to his entire First Air Force. This Hunter refused to do. Still, Kuter found Hunter's separation "legal and completely supportable."[84]

General Hunter's unwillingness to apply his regulation to all bases under his command made clear his desire to segregate by race rather than by function. Yet inspector general correspondence to the secretary of war showed that functional separation was stubbornly maintained as Hunter's only goal. The inspector claimed that Hunter and "Selway had deemed it desirable to provide separate club facilities for officers belonging to units of the permanent garrison and officers of units undergoing training at the station."[85] This same inspector agreed with Hunter when he labeled black intransigence a "conspiracy to revolt."[86]

The blacks, however, were not without support. On 11 April, Truman Gibson and the McCloy Committee sought information on the Freeman problem.[87] Also on the same day, the NAACP sent a telegram to President Roosevelt to complain that the Freeman Field situation was having a negative effect "upon civilian and soldier morale among Negro Americans." The NAACP was especially critical of the wholesale arrests.[88]

It was against this background that Hunter called upon the AAF judge advocate, Brig. Gen. L. H. Hedrick, for advice. General Hunter now based his defense on War Department Pamphlet 20-6, which seemed to authorize commanders to segregate. This pamphlet stated that racial segregation was favored by a majority of white soldiers and that this "mass sentiment cannot be ignored." It also held that local commanders had the option to determine if there need be "some separation in the use of camp facilities . . . with the assumption that local conditions [would] be taken into account." Hedrick assured Hunter that the defense of the arrested blacks, based upon Army Regulation 210-10, was not a good defense. Hunter replied that he had "orders from a three star general in the Army Air Forces" to segregate but that he now desired a legal ruling to substantiate his actions. Hedrick then responded, "So far as my opinion goes, you've got it right now, man, I think you're absolutely correct, and I think you were told it was correct." Hunter reminded the chief lawyer of the AAF that he had been assured similarly the previous year and that the end result had been a reprimand for his people.[89] Hedrick thereupon sent Hunter a written opinion which stated:

> Paragraph 19, AR [Army Regulation] 210-10, 20 December 1940, is not interpreted as a requirement that all officers on a base be permitted the use of all clubs. It is the view of this officer that this regulation was designed to insure every officer the right to membership in an officers' club; but does not prohibit a reasonable division of club facilities where circumstances make such division necessary or desirable from a practical, disciplinary, or morale standpoint. It should also be noted that this paragraph imposes a restriction upon post commanders restricting the use of public buildings . . . but does not extend a right to the individual officers . . . BY COMMAND OF GENERAL ARNOLD.[90]

On 17 April, the Chicago Urban League requested Congressman William A. Rowan (Dem., Ill.) to investigate the problems at Freeman Field. The league called his attention to the unit promotion policy which denied all blacks command responsibility while ensuring in some cases that noncombat veteran whites were promoted to command positions over combat veteran blacks.[91] Two days later, Walter White, executive secretary of the NAACP, sent a lengthy detailed letter to Stimson, summarizing the history of the 477th and calling the secretary's attention to the fact that Selway had even designated a black doctor as a trainee.[92]

Pressure upon Congress and from organizations such as the NAACP must have had an effect. On 20 April, General Owens called Hunter to tell him that General Marshall had approved a plan to release the Freeman officers and to drop all charges against them. Hunter, however, cut Owens off in midsentence: "Are those orders to me? They . . . can't issue orders like that, they haven't the authority." Owens agreed: "I know they can't." He also told Hunter that the officers in question were to receive no more penalty than an "administrative reprimand . . . instead of a trial." Hunter replied: "They can't do that. . . . I cannot command under those circumstances. . . . I have court-martial jurisdiction, and they cannot tell me whom I can try and whom I can't. . . . They're backing water." Owens agreed to that too.[93] Marshall not only had ordered the release of the nonsigners but also had decided to try only the three officers who had been arrested for using force to enter the club.[94]

General Owens, in a later conversation with Hunter's chief of staff, Brig. Gen. Edward E. Glenn, expressed his view of air staff support for Hunter. He said that General Arnold had told him to report to Hunter that "we are perfectly pleased and happy and satisfied with his actions." Owens continued: "[The] Chief here feels that his action in the past was perfectly alright [*sic*] legitimate, satisfied with it, and if another event were to come up, he hopes he will handle it in the same manner." Glenn, however, could not accept all of these statements. If Arnold was pleased with Hunter and satisfied with his actions, why had Hunter lost court-martial authority? Owens told Glenn that until the McCloy Committee completed its investigation, Arnold's hands were tied. Glenn asked if McCloy was black, and Owens answered that McCloy was not; but Owens added, "He has one on his staff."[95]

The McCloy Committee Recommendations

As noted earlier, McCloy's Special Troop Policies Committee was set up in August 1942 to serve as a "clearing house for staff ideas on the employment of Negro troops" and partly as a consultation board for civilian ideas on black troops. Assistant Secretary of War McCloy was chairman, and Brig. Gen. B. O. Davis, Sr., was a committee member. William Hastie's successor, Truman Gibson, was also a member of the group.[96] There were, therefore, two blacks on this committee. Also on the committee was Brig. Gen. Idwal Edwards, who later was the prime advocate for air force integration.

The McCloy Committee became deeply involved in the Freeman mutiny. On 5 May 1945, it received a summary sheet that outlined the position of the air corps regarding the situation there. This summary abandoned the pretense of separate facilities for trainees and supervisors and linked Hunter's defense to War Department Pamphlet 20-6, which, the summary alleged, permitted commanders to racially segregate facilities: "Negro officers at Freeman Field . . . have questioned the right of a post commander to establish separate officers' clubs or mess facilities which operate to deny them the full use of such facilities. Freeman Field had separate and essentially equal club and mess facilities and the Commander issued orders which in effect restricted Negro officers from using the facilities assigned to white officers."[97] The summary noted that the blacks argued that segregation was in violation of Army Regulation 210-10, but it pointed out that War Department Pamphlet 20-6 seemed to establish other guidelines, and "the Inspector General . . . recommends that the provisions of paragraph 19, AR 210-10 be modified to incorporate the . . . instructions in War Department Pamphlet 20-6." The summary quoted other major element commanders, all of whom supported racial segregation.[98]

Truman Gibson condemned the summary as well as the report of the inspector general. He declared that Hunter's and Selway's policies were clearly racial, and he ridiculed other practical considerations, such as size of clubs, status of personnel, and the desire to maintain "separate social facilities particularly when the sexes were concerned." Gibson used the inspector's own lengthy testimony to label the summary report and the actions at Freeman a "fabric of deception and subterfuge." He was especially disturbed with the inspector.[99] The committee's reaction was in line with Gibson's findings.

On 18 May, the committee published its report. Selway, it held, had acted within his administrative police powers in arresting the blacks, but his other actions were in conflict with army regulations. McCloy's staff recommended a change in War Department Pamphlet 20-6 to remove any ambiguities concerning segregation, adding to it the specific ban on segregated clubs in Army Regulation 210-10.[100] Later that month, McCloy sent a memorandum to Stimson, disputing all claims of the inspector, Selway, and Hunter and declaring that Selway's actions were "not in accord with existing Army regulations." McCloy also recommended that the inspector's report be returned "with the request that the non-concurrence with Army regulations and War department policies be brought to the attention of the Commanding General, Army Air Forces, for appropriate action."[101]

The air corps disliked these decisions. General Owens, in a letter to McCloy, argued that segregated officers' clubs should be maintained. "It is believed that the Army should follow the usages and customs of the country . . . it has not been the custom for whites and Negros [*sic*] to intermingle socially in homes or clubs."[102]

General Giles wrote a similar letter, recommending that "separate and similar, but not reciprocal club facilities, be made available to white and Negro officers." He added: "It is believed that the greatest over-all harmony between the white and Negro races will be maintained within the Army if the Army follows as closely as practicable the usages and social customs which prevail in this country with respect to recreational facilities. . . . Civilian social clubs of a similar nature are not customarily operated on the basis of social intercourse between whites and Negroes."[103] No longer was there an argument for maintaining separate clubs for trainees and supervisors; now Hunter's defense was simply the need to segregate socially the races, which had been the case all along. But McCloy was unimpressed with these arguments. Separate but equal officers' clubs would be a step back from the position taken by the War Department in the Selfridge Army Air Field case, McCloy argued, and "a reversal of this position would make the position taken in the Selfridge case untenable." He could not believe that the AAF should return to a "policy of separate but equal facilities for white and Negro personnel."[104] Following the McCloy decisions, only the trial of the Freeman Field three awaited resolution.

The defendants were represented by Theodore M. Berry, president of the Cincinnati branch of the NAACP.[105] All were tried for violation of the 64th Article of War, which carried a maximum penalty of death.[106] Although the original intent of the air corps was to try all blacks who had attempted to enter the club and who had refused to sign the club regulation, only Lts. Roger C. Terry, Marsden A. Thompson, and Shirley R. Clinton were brought to trial.[107] The government's case collapsed quickly because Selway would not admit that his order contained any provision which barred blacks from the club. Two defense witnesses testified that the club officer, Major White, said that "colored officers were not allowed to enter the club whether they were base personnel or not." Terry testified that he was not a trainee but an officer in the 18th Air Base Unit and entitled to use the club.[108]

In the end, Thompson and Clinton were found innocent, primarily because they also were base officers. The court found that Selway's orders had violated Army Regulation 210-10, which had been introduced as evidence over the objections of the prosecution.[109] Terry, however, was found guilty of shoving a provost marshal and was fined $150. His was the only conviction. Hunter had to endorse the punishment. He wrote, "The sentence, although grossly inadequate, is approved and will be duly executed."[110] And this final statement closed the file on the Freeman mutiny.

In late May 1945 General Arnold replaced all white officers in the 477th with blacks, commanded by Col. Benjamin Davis, Jr.[111] The change in command was headlined and covered in depth by major black newspapers.[112] Plans, furthermore, were drawn up in May to send the 477th to the Pacific.[113] Gen. Douglas

MacArthur, commander in chief, army forces in the Pacific, was willing to accept the blacks, but his air forces commander, Gen. George C. Kenney, was not. In spite of Kenney's objection, Lt. Gen. Ira C. Eaker continued to prepare the 477th for combat. He had great faith in Colonel Davis's ability to raise the group to combat status.[114] Kenney objected, stating his belief "that it would be a serious mistake to send Negro air combat units to this theater. In the end we would be subject to much criticism by having them operate under necessary restrictions than to have them remain in the U.S."[115] He had intended to segregate the 477th, and he therefore anticipated criticism.

To hasten the 477th's preparation for combat, two of its four bomb squadrons were disbanded to improve the trained manpower pool. In addition two experienced fighter squadrons were attached to the group, thus creating the 477th Composite Group.[116] A First Air Force inspection team reported that morale was very high and the unit would be ready to go overseas on schedule.[117] Termination of war in August 1945, however, prevented the 477th from engaging the Japanese in combat. At war's end, the air corps decided to leave the 477th at Godman Field.

Discrimination did not diminish with the arrival of Colonel Davis or with the coming of peace. Davis requested housing quarters at Fort Knox for some of his officer personnel because of crowding at Godman. He knew that Selway had previously been granted the same courtesy for his white officers. But the post commander at Fort Knox called First Air Force headquarters to complain: "I don't know whether you are familiar with Fort Knox or not, but this is an old cavalry post, we have four General Officers living here . . . by God, they just don't want a bunch of coons moving in next door to them." He also said that he had had a frank, confidential talk with General Eaker, who could not understand why the AAF were "entitled to any quarters at your post."[118] Thus, black airmen would continue to encounter racial problems into the postwar years.

2 Marking Time

ir force blacks benefited little from official policies between 1945 and 1949. The 477th served first at Godman Field and later at Lockbourne Army Air Field near Columbus, Ohio, but it was chronically undermanned and therefore not too efficient. Political realities required the air force to retain the group and would not permit its dissolution despite its condition. Whatever else might be said about the 477th, however, it did provide a measure of prestige and security to several hundred officers and a large number of enlisted men. Some of these men, especially the officers, had to think twice before leaving the shelter of an all-black unit.

Although the 477th and its successor, the 332d, had not participated in a race riot in the postwar era (their lot was a comparatively happy one), other black units became mutinous. Continuing a trend that began during World War II, several black AAF organizations resorted to violence and captured the attention of the AAF leadership. The largest of these riots occurred at MacDill Army Air Field near Tampa, Florida, in late 1946. In damage done and numbers participating, it was probably the largest riot the air force ever experienced, except for a riot at Travis AFB, California, a quarter of a century later. The MacDill riot led to little more than palliatives being offered the men to correct the immediate situation. These included efforts to improve their facilities, ease crowded conditions on base, and limited punishment of the troublemakers.

The Travis riot, on the other hand, led to a complete restructuring of the air force race relations program, the difference being the temper of the times. In 1946, AAF officials blamed Communist agitation for the unrest and made only cosmetic changes at MacDill, leaving most of the real grievances untouched. In 1971, however, the air force was more open to meaningful change. Most of its officials had been educated to the rhythm and consequences of black protest.

There was a brief flowering of social awareness in the immediate postwar era when a board of four generals, chaired by Lt. Gen. Alvan C. Gillem, recommended limited racial integration immediately and a conscious longer-range program aimed at making full use of America's blacks. The board's recommendations, however, were essentially ignored. Nevertheless, the fact that the board recommended steps to integrate the service demonstrates that not all of the military leaders were racially insensitive.

The Army Studies the Postwar Role of Black Troops

In fact, there had been social growth in the army. Recalling the 1925 Army War College study which lamented the limited usefulness of the black American, with his smaller cranium, lighter brain, and cowardly and immoral character, one might find refreshing a 1945 study of the subject, titled "Participation of Negro Troops in the Post-War Military Establishment."[1] This investigation was truly monumental compared with the earlier efforts. It was the first massive attempt to answer the question of how to employ blacks properly in the army. Unlike previous studies of the subject, the army compiled empirical data and sought facts, not opinion. Of course, it discovered biased opinions, but it also gained clear insights. This army attempt to measure qualitatively the value of blacks in the military reflected the impact of social environmentalists upon the American mind. That is to say, black potential was seen as handicapped by a deprived past.

The study had its genesis with the McCloy Committee, as did many efforts that affected army blacks. In September 1944 McCloy sent a memorandum to the other members of his Special Troop Policies Committee. He wrote: "The War Department together with other government agencies has begun the study and preparation of plans for the post-war period." He added that "experience gained during the current war" showed that the "Army was unprepared to deal with the large number of Negroes who entered the service," despite the study of the problem during the interwar period by the "General Staff, Army War College and other military agencies." Whatever policy had been developed had led to racial irritation. Racial problems, McCloy said, were caused by "inadequate preparation. . . . This war has seen a greater proportionate participation of minority racial groups in the Army than at any time in our history. This participation can be expected to continue in the future." He directed the committee to work out a "definite, workable policy" before the final plans for the postwar military establishment had become crystallized. He called upon the War Department General Staff to review its black policies and to make recommendations "based upon a study which will include all our experiences during the present war, both in this country and abroad." The study should begin immediately, so that the War Department would be in a "position to effect any necessary changes in policy which may result from a study either through the proposal of proper legislation or other means." McCloy probably anticipated major changes, as is evidenced by his reference to legislation.[2]

Eight months later, the army began to collect data on this subject. All-black units and organizations with blacks in them were asked to compile a "historic report on actual experiences in training with particular reference to degree of proficiency attained and length of training time required." Above all, an account of black performance was desired. The War Department needed information on "typical irritations or disorders arising from racial conflicts." The statement was to "cover irritations and disorders within the Army itself and between Negro elements or individuals and civilians. . . . This report should include a careful appraisal of cause and effect." The War Department also desired specific recommendations on future training and employment. The statement was to be completed by 1 October 1945, and reporters were asked to be objective. "It should be borne in mind by all concerned in conducting the studies . . . that the objective sought is the factual determination of the most effective utilization of Negro troops in the post-war military establishment. A positive approach is required for the accomplishment of this objective. It is desired that studies requested herein be conducted in such a manner as not to disturb existing arrangements for the training and utilization of Negro personnel. All communications on the subject will be classified secret."[3]

Most of the studies found blacks useful as laborers and left little doubt that they were to continue as laborers in the postwar period. In particular, black cooking skills were frequently praised: "They are best qualified as mess personnel. This statement is confirmed by the fact that the colored mess is the best on this field—both from the standpoint of the preparation of food and sanitation—and is probably at least equal to any in the command." Blacks, however, were not seen as useful in occupational areas requiring greater skills because of their "low educational level." This was in addition to the fact that as civilians, they were rarely employed in occupations which "required initiative or a sense of responsibility." Because they had been denied opportunities both as civilians and as military men, it was concluded that blacks did not possess a "disciplined, alert mind." Time and again, however, those interviewed in the I Troop Carrier Command found that blacks did as well as whites in jobs for which they were qualified, that is, for which they had the aptitude and training.[4]

A Second Air Force report stated that white and black duty soldiers, truck drivers, bakers and cooks were equally proficient but that blacks did not perform as well in administrative jobs.[5] An attachment to the report noted that the "educational and civilian background of the average Negro soldier is inferior to the white soldier," and it complained that blacks' difficulties were caused by environmental factors in their civilian background.[6] Another attachment pointed out that "if Negro personnel are compared with white personnel who have the same education and AGCT test score, there is no noticeable difference" within the occupational specialty.[7]

Third Air Force found that there were "no jobs for which it can categorically be stated . . . that the race is not qualified. It is felt that with Negro personnel of equal intelligence as white personnel in the army . . . Negro individuals and units could be equally proficient as their white counterparts." It also found, on the other hand, that the majority of blacks had very low aptitudes, which lowered the overall proficiency of black units. Racial irritations further undermined black unit morale, resulting in even lower individual performance. Blacks suffered from "poor off-base living conditions, recreational facilities and transportation," all of which had an "adverse effect upon the efficiency of the more intelligent Negro personnel."[8]

Many unit historians, in preparing these studies, cited prejudice as a main cause for low morale and therefore poor performance. Historians at Smoky Hill Army Air Field, Kansas, believed that black proficiency within any given specialty was "equal and in a good many cases higher" than white proficiency and that no jobs were out of reach if blacks were given an opportunity. They again reported that race prejudice caused blacks to lose initiative.[9] Concern for black morale prompted a historian at Camp Pinedale, California, to suggest that blacks should never be a "small minority on any base" and that they would be most efficient if stationed near black communities.[10]

Despite the recognition of environment as a factor in racial questions and a healthy concern for minority morale, a new millennium had not dawned. The willingness of most reporters to acknowledge environment as a factor in explaining poor black performance was firmly positive, but few commentators, if any, deleted modifiers when describing inferior black performance. The fact that blacks did not perform as a group as well as whites was indisputable. The causes might have been significant to sociologists, but the army did not seek to reform society, only to use effectively society's product. Second Air Force reported that of the 6,987 blacks in the command, 86.6 percent were in AGCT classes IV and V, in contrast to only 30 percent of the whites. Blacks had qualified for 83 different job classifications; however, 91 percent of them were assigned to 12 job categories and more than 75 percent of that group to only 5.[11]

All of the above tasks were labeled unskilled or semiskilled specialties. Blacks additionally required more time to train than whites and had to be more closely supervised. Blacks were largely unsuccessful as clerks, airplane and engine mechanics, and radio mechanics and in other skilled jobs. (Yet, all of these skilled specialties had been performed by blacks at Tuskegee, Godman, and at the overseas bases housing the 332d.) Even if the authors admitted that environment made blacks less useful and acknowledged that race prejudice was holding the blacks back, what, then, could the army do with people who were qualified mainly as laborers and lacked "initiative and judgment"? The same authors who noted that environmental factors retarded blacks also stressed that blacks lacked the "necessary intelligence to absorb technical training."[12] Higher headquarters might indeed be in a quandary over the garbled signals it was receiving.

Another report open to subjective analysis was issued by the I Troop Carrier Command. The compiler blamed the inadequate educational background possessed by blacks for their lack of military progress, but he also cited their low intelligence level. He reported that of 1,782 blacks in that command, 740 were duty soldiers (laborers), 180 cooks, and 531 drivers. Further, 1,651 of the 1,782 were categorized in unskilled or semiskilled specialities, that is, 41.5 percent of the blacks were duty soldiers in contrast to only 5 percent of the whites, and 30.19 percent of the blacks were drivers while less than 2 percent of the whites were so employed. Five unskilled and semiskilled specialties employed 85.4 percent of the blacks and only 14.7 percent of the whites.[13]

The report contained not only ambiguities, such as confusion over the meaning of aptitude and intelligence, but also contradictions between the field unit reports and the summary statements, which further distorted the message. For example, the I Troop Carrier Command report condemned blacks for their lack of initiative in failing to achieve a superior performance on the airplane washrack at Bergstrom Army Air Field, Texas. Blacks had been given an opportunity, but they displayed an incapacity to learn the job, and many accidents occurred. The base historian commented negatively about their low intelligence, ascribing to it part of their failure.[14] The report from Bergstrom Army Air Field to I Troop Carrier Command, however, revealed other causes for the apparent lack of success. The lieutenant who supervised the wash crews knew that the blacks were characterized as lacking responsibility and displaying a "total indifference to the job." He also knew washing airplanes was the "dirtiest and meanest job on the base." Cleaning solvents irritated the skin, "particularly the ears, eyes, and feet. The men have wet feet from the time they start work until they finish. Attempts were made through proper channels to secure rubber boots for the men, but these attempts were unsuccessful."[15] What was then interpreted by headquarters as malingering was altogether explicable in the field.

Very rarely were blacks introduced to specialties that adhered more closely to the AAF's mission; yet, when blacks had a real mission, they met the challenge. For example, black airmen were trained in the air cargo and resupply specialty. At first, enough blacks of sufficiently high aptitude could not be found to fill the ranks, and entry standards were lowered. Resupply managers, however, found the results encouraging. They reported, "Considering the relatively low level of AGCT scores and educational achievements of the Negro personnel, minor miracles have been achieved in both training and actual operations in the combat zone." Troop morale was recorded as high, and the accident rate was surprisingly low. The historian found blacks could absorb technical training and that, while whites might learn the material faster than blacks, they also did not stand up as well as the latter "under duress. . . . The Negro has been capable of absorbing complex technical training." Training standards were the same for both races, and graduation requirements were not eased to accommodate the blacks. "Considered as a *group,* divorced from all social and economic considerations, Negro personnel do as well on the whole as comparable white groups."[16]

Most of the AAF leadership, however, ignored such evidence. They looked instead at the gross figures, at the low aptitude which they consistently confused with intelligence, at the longer training time required, and at the fact that most of the blacks were assigned to unskilled specialties. Thus, the leadership concluded that blacks were not worth the employment effort despite the sociological factors. Maj. Gen. Samuel E. Anderson, chief of staff, Continental Air Forces, summarized the theme of the reports cited above and advised General Arnold:

> It is comparatively uneconomical to train colored units and individuals for combat assignments requiring a very high degree of specialization. The length of time required for training the 332d Fighter Group and the 477th Bombardment Group (M)—and the problems that attended that training—clearly illustrate this basic fact. Accordingly, with the anticipated increasing complexity of modern aircraft, and the adjuncts thereto, the training of colored fighting units is not justified. . . .
>
> If it is anticipated that large numbers of Negroes will be called upon in another time of war emergency for non-combat military duties, there should be available a carefully selected, well-trained cadre of Negro soldiers upon which to build a rapid expansion of Negro personnel. . . .
>
> Negro personnel, qualified for military occupational specialties which require a high degree of skill or technical training should be selected by means of a rigorous screening process and given thorough schooling in those specialties. . . .
>
> Negro personnel to be utilized in the intermediate groups of relatively skilled assignments should be carefully selected and sent to special schools to remedy inadequacies in their civilian background, as well as to train them in their military occupational specialties.
>
> Under existing conditions the great bulk of Negro personnel should be utilized in relatively unskilled assignments for which they should receive thorough training, either in the job or in schools.[17]

The First Air Force Report
Beyond the ambivalences, ambiguities, contradictions, and a cold-eyed manner of interpreting data, some straightforward prejudice emerged. The most biased state-

ment was issued by First Air Force, the parent organization of the mutinous 477th. The report was endorsed by General Hunter. He commented that the study had been "carefully prepared by those who have actually had the most intimate connection with the training of Negro air organizations and it is believed that it is an honest and trustworthy document."[18] The men Hunter assigned to study the black problem were Colonel Selway and his staff.[19] In his letter to Selway, Hunter blamed some of the racial problems on "organizations for the advancement of the colored race" and the "Negro press." These groups, he said, agitated "in an attempt to gain social positions in the Army" which blacks did not have in "civilian life and which is contrary to the customs and social usages of the country as a whole." Hunter complained that War Department policies made it "impossible to maintain the same discipline expected and demanded of white troops." Hunter saw reverse discrimination. He declared that the "morale of colored personnel has received considerable consideration but the morale of white personnel has received little, if any." He wrote that the morale of the great bulk of the personnel must receive "serious consideration even at the expense of a minority group." Segregation, he believed, furthermore, had to be maintained to prevent "forced intermingling of whites and colored on a basis of social equality."[20]

The First Air Force report is an interesting document. Nowhere within the report, unlike most others in this series, were the authors identified by name or position. Reviewers throughout the chain of command were not informed that these men had lost command of the group because they had helped to provoke a mutiny. Selway began his account by describing the blacks in the unit as the "cream of their race." Hence a "lack of intelligence or education cannot be considered as a factor responsible for lack of qualification or failure in performance." Blacks were as intelligent and as well educated as men in comparable white units, he alleged, and therefore they should have completed "training within the same period of time as white units undergoing the same training." But according to Selway, such was not the case. He wrote, "In reality, with highly selected white officers and enlisted men for Command, Supervision, Instruction and Inspection, it will normally take from two to three times as long to train Negro enlisted men and officers to do a passable job, as it would take for white enlisted men and officers with an equivalent educational background." This argument was specious. The fact was that the 477th, the unit with which Selway had the most command experience, had spent its first year awaiting the assignment of navigators. Despite this fact, Selway condemned the unit for not becoming combat-ready in the three months it normally took a B-25 group to achieve combat status. The reasons Selway gave for the delay were that blacks lacked initiative, had looked to the white race for generations for guidance, and could not do even routine tasks without supervision.[21]

Selway believed that blacks lacked "desire to go to combat." As evidence, he cited a May 1945 survey of the group which revealed: "Over 90 percent of all enlisted men indicated a desire to be relieved from the Army without delay. Approximately 79 percent of all colored officers in this organization indicated the same desire." This situation was not surprising, considering the fact that Selway was still in command, with many black officers under arrest and with morale low. Selway complained about the low morale, lack of discipline, and high venereal disease rate among the blacks, as well as about the large numbers of black airmen absent without leave. All these factors, Selway believed, indicated an "inherent" and "instinctive" lack of pride or sense of duty among them.[22]

Time and again Selway criticized his troops. He charged: "A great number of Negro soldiers are either willful malingerers or chronic neurotics. . . . Negro personnel lack the intellectual curiosity which is the driving force necessary to obtain mastery of a problem. . . . Negroes as a class are not ready to assume positions of responsibility and leadership."[23] He therefore recommended:

That there be no Negro flying units in the Post War Army Air Forces, because
a. Proficiency attained is barely satisfactory.
b. Training time is three times as long as for a white unit.
c. Performance within the United States is satisfactory only under white command and supervision due to the lack of leadership and reliability of Negro personnel.[24]

Selway suggested other uses for blacks in the new era. He stated, "There should be a small detachment of Negro enlisted men on stations (where required), to perform base duties normal to the individual's civilian occupation." "These detachments," he believed, "[should] be commanded and staffed by white officers only."[25] Selway's recommendation, however, ignored the combat record of the 332d and the outstanding safety record of the 477th, as well as the latter's practice bombing skill. He also ignored the manning problems that had plagued the unit. Indeed, it was piecemeal manning, not black incapacity, that in fact ruined the 477th.[26]

Summary Report for General Arnold

The task of evaluating and digesting Selway's report and all of the other reports mentioned above was assigned to Lt. Col. Louis Nippert, a Headquarters AAF staff officer assigned to the Postwar Planning Branch. On 17 September 1945, after studying Selway's report, along with all other studies and data received from overseas units, he prepared a summary of the ambiguous and contradictory data for General Arnold. Nippert wrote that enlisted blacks had been generally accepted for specialist training on the same basis as white troops except that black "aviation cadets . . . were accepted with a lower stanine (aptitude) score in order to secure sufficient candidates to meet Negro pilot requirements." He noted that training time was the same for black as for white pilots and that the "proficiency attained compared to whites" but that the "elimination rate and accident rate was higher for Negroes than for whites."[27] Admitting comparable proficiency levels between Tuskegee graduates and others, Nippert drew comparisons between black flying units and similar white organizations. He reported, "The training time for Negro units was considerably longer than for white units."[28] He said that black airmen "performed creditably," that blacks in technical schools with AGCT scores similar to those of whites in the same schools had the same training time, and that their proficiency was equal.[29]

In a lengthy discussion of the data, Nippert judged that aptitude scores had been lowered beyond what was "justifiable in order to obtain any number of Negro pilot trainees. In some instances it was necessary to accept candidates with stanine (aptitude) scores as low as '2' in order to meet the pilot requirements." Even though the AAF had accepted blacks in this low category, the service still fell short of the desired number. Nippert concluded: "As an individual, compared with white pilots of the same stanine, the Negro attained the same degree of proficiency within the training time. . . . Given proper selection of personnel and training, there is no evidence that the Negro cannot do a satisfactory specialized job whether administrative or technical." Nippert found when comparing training time for whites and blacks—plotted against AGCT scores—that blacks did as well as whites at the same AGCT level.[30]

Nippert, however, probably because of the contradictory and largely negative data, could not avoid generalizations. He wrote that black officers were

> below average in common sense, practical imagination, resourcefulness, aggressive-
> ness, sense of responsibility, and in their ability to make decisions. They are prone to
> accept lower standards and to make allowances for misbehavior. . . . Enlisted men
> were not as satisfactory as whites. . . . They were not dependable; they were careless
> about equipment; they were below average and not industrious; they were race con-
> scious and considered 'discrimination' as the reason for routine orders and assign-
> ment of duties. The feeling of being discriminated against is considered . . . the great
> shortcoming of Negro soldiers.[31]

This last point received much attention in Nippert's report. Northern blacks, he noted, were unwilling to "accept restraints imposed upon" them by southern civilian communities. Blacks reacted negatively to the "social segregation which such restraints" implied. The majority of the complaints concerning segregation came from northern blacks or were "inspired by Negroes from northern cities." Friction occurred because blacks insisted on a "strict interpretation of paragraph 19 of AR 210-10 relating to the common use of officers' clubs by both white and Negro officers." Problems arose as well because blacks believed that the "exercise of command function is not an exclusive prerogative of the white officer and that equal opportunity for both command and promotion should be vested in the Negro officer of demonstrated qualifications."[32]

Nippert, however, was not entirely sympathetic to the black plight. He believed that many complaints had proven to be of an "inconspicuous nature, submitted either through ignorance or pique, and in many cases doubtlessly fomented by professional agitators either within the military ranks or members of some civilian organizations dedicated to keeping alive the racial issue. This is attested by the fact that many of these complaints are supported by newspaper clippings and by the similarity which complaints from widely separated sources sometimes bear to each other." Black complaints were usually submitted in "complete disregard of prescribed military correspondence channels." These were "often inspired by outside sources." The "greatest single source of complaints from both Negro enlisted and Negro officer personnel has to do with alleged segregation . . . usually related to War Department theaters, post exchanges, service clubs, officers' messes and officers' clubs." Nippert acknowledged that the War Department no longer designated such facilities and activities on a racial basis, but the department did permit such facilities to be designated for specific units. This had led to "sharp clashes . . . either through the failure of Negro personnel to understand the differentiation between unit designation and racial designation, or by a willful desire to ignore the designation on the pretext that it merely serves the purpose of racial discrimination."[33]

Nippert, however, was mistaken about this. The actual language of the army letter of 8 July 1944 which desegregated facilities clearly stated: "No exchange will be designated for the exclusive use of any particular race. Where . . . branch exchanges are established, personnel will not be restricted to the use of their area or unit exchanges, but will be permitted to use any other exchange on the post or station." The same applied to recreational facilities.[34] Nippert showed little sympathy for blacks who desired to test their newly won rights.

He concluded his report with further recommendations culled from the massive data he had accumulated. He accurately recorded the majority sentiment:

1. Negro personnel be trained on the same basis and standards as whites.
2. Qualified Negro personnel be obtained for pilot training and for technical specialties by careful screening and selection.
3. Negroes be utilized in positions consistent with their qualifications in the following manner:
   a. In separate combat flying units not to exceed the size of a group.
   b. In separate service units not to exceed the size of a group in support of the flying units.

    c. In other separate established . . . units, not to exceed the size of a battalion, in which Negroes performed most satisfactorily in World War II and in such other units as their capabilities warrant.

    d. In base units in jobs requiring the maximum of their capabilities.

    e. In command of Negro units to the maximum extent possible.

    f. In overseas assignments on equal basis with whites.

    g. In ZI [Zone of the Interior] assignments in locations favorable to their welfare.

    h. In disciplinary matters there should be no favoritism or discrimination.

    i. Officer[s] and NCO's [noncommissioned officers] assigned to Negro units should be carefully selected and trained.

4. Segregation.

    a. Negroes should be segregated into administrative units.

    b. Segregation for recreation, messing and social activities be established in accordance with the customs prevailing within the surrounding civilian communities.

5. Number.

The Army Air Forces should receive only the proportionate share of Negroes in the Army as a whole based on the relative size of the three major forces and the number of Negroes in the Army Air Forces should not exceed 10 percent of the total personnel assigned to the Army Air Forces.[35]

Nippert's recommendation that the AAF maintain segregation was in accord with the prevalent opinion contained in the reports. Segregation was clearly favored by all who submitted reports on the use of blacks in the postwar military, except for Colonel Parrish, the Tuskegee Army Air Field commander.[36] In his report, Parrish stressed that Tuskegee graduates met AAF standards and that all airfield mechanical work was performed by "Negro mechanics with no assistance or supervision from white mechanics." All administrative work, Parrish said, was performed by black enlisted men because there were no white enlisted men at Tuskegee. Colonel Parrish further stated:

> It is a discouraging fact that Officers of the Army Air Forces whose scientific achievements are unsurpassed, and whose scientific skill is unquestioned in mechanical matters and in many personnel matters, should generally approach the problem of races and minorities with the most unscientific, dogmatic and arbitrary attitudes. . . . Whether we like or dislike Negroes and whether they like or dislike us, under the Constitution of the United States, which we are all sworn to uphold, they are citizens of the United States having the same rights and privileges of other citizens and entitled to the same applications and protection of the laws.[37]

Parrish despised the practice of segregation and considered the existence of Tuskegee an AAF punitive measure. He further believed that segregation was self-defeating and that the army could never convince blacks, while they were being shunted off into a corner, that the standards applied were the same for them as for whites. Parrish wrote: "Incompetent Negroes are pleased by mass treatment and assignment since they do not then have to compete and are not blamed for individual failure but only for being a helpless part of a mediocre group." He argued that inept whites were also aided by segregation and commented: "An incompetent white commander or supervisor, while of course protesting against the assignment, can always try to cover up any deficiencies in leadership or ability by unscientific theorizing about 'Negro characteristics' ad infinitum. Unfortunately he can also easily point out the multitude of special problems in everything from administration to public relations that are daily dumped upon him and actually justify almost any failure." Parrish recommended the "employment and treatment of Negroes as individuals which the war requires and which military efficiency demands." He plainly disputed the idea that permitting blacks into officers' clubs would result in disorder and riot. He concluded with a plea for racial integration:

> Either the constitution and the law must be changed or we must make some open concession, some positive step toward adjustment rather than defensive, bewildered evasion, at least where the officers are concerned. Negro officers should either be assigned according to qualifications or dismissed. They cannot forever be isolated so that they will always be non-existent at meal time or at night. This has nothing to do with social problems or marriage, but only with a place to eat and sleep, and occasionally relax. The more rapidly officers in the air corps learn to accept these practical matters, as many of us have learned already, the better the position of everyone concerned. The answer is wider distribution, rather than greater concentration of Negro units, officers, and trainees.[38]

Parrish's report may not have influenced Nippert's summary, but the former did have an opportunity to express personally his views before the Gillem Board, which convened in the summer of 1945. Nippert's report was also submitted to the board, and he appeared before it. This board of four generals[39] was asked by the secretary of war to prepare "a policy for the use of the authorized Negro manpower potential during the postwar period including the complete development of the means required to derive the maximum efficiency from the full authorized manpower of the nation in the event of war."[40]

The Gillem Board Recommendations
The Gillem Board examined much material and interviewed an impressive number of people, all of whom had extensive dealings with blacks and many of whom were black leaders determined to achieve integration within their lifetime. Considering the conflicting evidence the board studied and the fact that the uniformed

witnesses and military data were overwhelmingly against even limited integration, one can only conclude that the Gillem Board probably set out to modify drastically the army's racial policy. The board's evidence may or may not have supported its conclusions, but its recommendations were far in advance of the national or military temper of the times, and ultimately its program was never adopted. Its counsel stood in sharp contrast to the conclusions of earlier panels. The black press applauded the board's position,[41] but the army did not get in step.

It is not difficult to understand why the black press favorably received the report. The Gillem Board's memorandum to the chief of staff called for peacetime utilization of blacks in proportion to their representation in America's population, an approach not accepted in the interwar period. It also recommended using blacks on a "broader professional scale than has obtained heretofore." Combat and service units were to be organized "from the Negro manpower available in the postwar Army to meet the requirements of training and expansion and in addition qualified individuals [were to] be utilized in appropriate special and overhead units." The board also suggested that "all officers be accorded the same rights, privileges and opportunities for advancement."[42] It recommended that "experimental groupings of Negro units with white units be continued in the post war Army."[43] The board further suggested that blacks be stationed in areas where "community attitudes are most favorable and in such strength as will not constitute an undue burden to the local civilian population." It also proposed that at mixed posts, War Department policies "regarding use of recreational facilities and membership in officer' clubs, messes or similar social organizations be continued and made applicable to the post war Army."[44] Recognizing that these suggestions heralded a change, the board called for the "indoctrination of all ranks throughout the Service as to the necessity for an unreserved acceptance of the policy."[45]

The Gillem Board advised the chief of staff that it was time for a reworking of black policy. "The principle of economy of forces indicates," it said, "that every effort must be expended to utilize efficiently every qualified available individual in a position in the military structure for which he is best suited. . . . We must strive for improvement in the quality of the whole." Blacks were termed "no small part of the manpower reservoir." The black, it said, was ready and eager to accept "full responsibility as a citizen" and "should be given every opportunity and aid to prepare himself for effective service in company with every other citizen who is called."[46]

Perhaps more important than black eagerness to serve was the change observed by the Gillem Board in white attitudes toward blacks: "During the last few years, many of the concepts pertaining to the Negro have shown changing trends. They are pointing toward a more complete acceptance of the Negro in all the diversified fields of endeavor." Their acceptability was important "from a military viewpoint. . . . Many Negroes who, before the war, were laborers, are now craftsmen, capable in many instances of competing with the white man on an equal basis." The Gillem Board cited the recent increase in educational opportunities for blacks, especially in the North and West, where colleges and universities admitted them "solely on the basis of individual merit and ability." The board provided the chief of staff with charts and statistics which showed a vast improvement in black education between the wars. The board recommended that the change be introduced rapidly, stating its "considered opinion . . . that a progressive policy for greater utilization of the Negro manpower be formulated and implemented now. . . . The Nation should not fail to use the assets developed through a closer relationship of the races during the years of the war." The board clearly called for a program that "*must* eliminate, at the earliest practicable moment, any special consideration based on race."[47] It said further:

> Courageous leadership in implementing the program is imperative. All ranks must be imbued with the necessity for a straightforward, unequivocating attitude towards the maintenance and [preservation] of a forward thinking policy.
>
> Vacillation or weak implementation of a strong policy will adversely affect the Army. The policy which is advocated is consistent with the democratic ideals upon which the nation and its representative Army are based.[48]

The Gillem Board also recognized that more than courage was required to implement this change. It recommended setting up a "War Department General Staff Group . . . who can devote their entire time to problems involving minority racial elements in the military establishment . . . . Creation for the same purpose of a similar group in the staff of each major command is necessary."[49] Had the armed services accepted these proposals in 1945, much grief might have been avoided in the postwar period. It was not until the mid-1960s, long after the work of the Gillem Board had been forgotten, that such staff organizations were established at the headquarters level, and these did not become effective in smaller units until the 1970s.

In making these recommendations, the Gillem Board had before it the combat record and failure of the 92d Division in Italy, a large unit with approximately 20,000 men. Their poor showing did not particularly concern the board; the latter simply ascribed the collapse to poor leadership. It stated, "The failures of Negro units have in almost every case been attributed to the lack of leadership qualities of junior officers and non-commissioned officers."[50] Of crucial importance to the board was the comparative success of several thousand blacks who fought side by side with whites in the last months of World War II.[51] The white commander of the 92d Division testified that blacks could not "be made into good infantry soldiers or even satisfactory ones."[52] Yet, the Gillem Board demonstrated a positive inclination to favor examples of black courage and effectiveness. The experimental grouping of blacks and whites in late World War II in Europe was probably a pivotal factor in the board's considerations.

In December 1944 Gen. Dwight D. Eisenhower faced a severe shortage of riflemen in Europe during the Battle of the Bulge. Lt. Gen. John C. H. Lee proposed to give men trained in service specialties the opportunity to fight, blacks included. Men above the rank of private first class had to take reductions to that rank to enter combat. By February 1945 some 4,562 blacks had volunteered, and many of these accepted reductions in rank. Approximately one-half of them fought alongside whites in the closing days of the war. Although the black volunteers had higher AGCT scores than the mass of blacks, their scores were lower than those of the white volunteers and other whites in the units. The black volunteers had fewer disciplinary problems than their white colleagues while training for combat. They subsequently were formed into segregated platoons within white companies, but they took their meals and whatever battlefield comfort they could find with white soldiers. The first black platoon was combat-ready on 1 March 1945 and, according to all accounts, fought well. The men were eager to engage the enemy, paid strict attention to duty, were aggressive, and won the admiration of whites about them. When other black platoons suffered combat casualties, blacks then fought as squads within white platoons and eventually as individuals. There were no reported racial incidents, turmoil, or animosities.[53]

Also important to the Gillem Board in its evaluation of black performance was a report titled "Opinions about Negro Infantry Platoons in White Companies of Seven Divisions," compiled by the Information and Education Division.[54] It revealed that whites who fought alongside blacks were much less eager to maintain segregation than those who did not have integrated experiences. Only 250 responded to the survey, yet the report carried enormous weight with the Gillem Board. Most of the respondents (64 percent) said they had been relatively unfavorable toward blacks joining their company prior to serving with blacks in combat. None said they had become less favorable after the experience, and 77 percent said they were more favorable to the idea of blacks serving with them. The remainder indicated no change in their attitude. All whites were asked how well blacks performed in combat; more than 80 percent responded that blacks performed very well, and none complained that blacks performed poorly. When asked how blacks compared with whites as fighters, only 5 percent of the officers and 4 percent of the enlisted men answered "not as well," and 69 percent of the officers and 83 percent of the enlisted men said they fought just as well. The remainder thought blacks fought better than whites or offered no opinion. Most of the interviewees believed that in the future, blacks and whites could serve together in the same company but that they should be placed in separate platoons.[55]

Similar questions were addressed to white combat veterans in the European Theater who had not experienced platoon integration. These men were told that some
army divisions in their theater contained black and white platoons and were asked
how they would react if their unit "were set up something like that." More than
60 percent stated that they "would dislike it very much." The researchers found
that the geographical origin of a white soldier's home had a negligible effect upon
his response. Northern whites were almost as much opposed to platoon integration as southern whites.[56]

The implications of the survey were clear. White opposition to integration de-
creased once men had been integrated. The solution to manpower problems might
be simple: white opposition will disappear once mixing is a fact, and this is what
the Gillem Board attempted to accomplish. The army, however, was apparently
unimpressed with the experiment conducted in the European Theater and never
adopted the board's program. It should be stressed that the board appeared to know
what it wished to prove and selectively highlighted the evidence to do this. The
choice of people to be interviewed also seems to support this conclusion.

Not everyone interviewed by the Gillem Board was friendly to the black cause,
but most were; and it would have been difficult to select 52 officials at random
within or outside of the ranks of the army and to find as many in favor of integration. Some whites were hostile, but many were not. Indeed, one black opposed
integration, but he probably did this more out of fear of a white reaction than from
a genuine opposition to integration. William H. Hastie also testified before the
board. The former civilian aide and Truman Gibson's predecessor, Hastie had, as
noted above, resigned his position in protest over segregation and condemned its
inefficiency. He told the board that the armed forces created artificial units simply
to absorb black inductees. He said there had been a "tendency to magnify the difficulties which integration might raise," and he advised the board not to be concerned with civilian attitudes because these need not "prevail over Army policy."
Army integration, he said, would be "less difficult than in the civilian community
because of military training and discipline." Hastie also called for integration at
the higher unit levels of individuals without regard to race and urged that the mixing take place immediately.[57] His successor, however, took a different course. Gibson held that complete integration would not work but recommended that "selected Negro individuals should be treated as individuals rather than Negroes." He
advocated a flexible policy calling for the maintenance of separate black platoons,
companies, and battalions within larger white organizations. He suggested that
white officers should be assigned to black units to gain experience in command of
blacks. He called for the peacetime training of sufficient numbers of black officers
and enlisted men to provide cadres in an emergency. Finally, he sought the establishment of special training units to raise the educational level of black soldiers.[58]

More militant was Brig. Gen. B. O. Davis, Sr., who twice testified before the board. He argued that blacks had been misassigned because of segregation, and he pointed to their success in integrated companies in the European Theater as proof of the success of integration. He openly criticized the policy that was more concerned about mixed eating and billeting than military effectiveness. He warned the board of the dichotomy between American ideals and practices and how negatively this must impress "foreign people such as the French, Russians and Brazilians." He called for integration and suggested that whites might be prepared to accept it through an education program.[59]

His son, commander of the 477th Composite Group, also advocated integration but called for a gradual approach out of fear of white reaction. For the younger Davis, it was a question of leadership. If unit commanders were carefully chosen, and if they were convinced that the War Department truly sought to end discriminatory practices, prejudice would end. He recalled for the board the "silent" treatment he had experienced at West Point after an upperclassman ordered his classmates not to speak to him. The war had not eliminated this bias, he said, since the "attitude that there is no place for the Negro officer still exists in the Army."[60]

In addition to black military men and representatives from the War Department, distinguished civilian black leaders testified. Frederick Patterson, president of Tuskegee, called for black employment based solely on ability. Charles Houston of the NAACP Legal Defense Fund informed the board of the increasingly important role blacks were playing in American society. And Walter White, executive secretary of the NAACP, demanded the end of segregation because it was inefficient and provoked racial friction.[61]

White civilian and military witnesses partial to the black cause also appeared before the board. Colonel Parrish stated that army policy had created resentment and precipitated the formation of groups of agitators. He asked the board to avoid the use of the controversial term "integration" and to try simply to speak of "assignment by qualification." Blacks wanted only "equality of opportunity and individual treatment," and Parrish favored that too.[62] Lt. Col. Charles Dollard of the Army Information and Education Division also testified. Formerly a social scientist with the Carnegie Foundation, he had participated in the Gunnar Myrdal study on American blacks, which produced the landmark volume *American Dilemma*. Dollard, then a member of the American Council for Race Relations, called for integration starting from the bottom. The army, he claimed, lagged behind the civilian population in race relations, and he called for the individual integration of the American black.[63] Two professional historians, both working with the army, were called upon to testify. Walter L. Wright testified that the service was not abiding by the principles of democracy. Blacks wanted total integration, he argued, yet that seemed infeasible. Integration of squads and platoons seemed more likely to work at that time. He suggested integration in active units, in which the men would not have "too much time to sit around and quarrel."[64] Bell I. Wiley was less positive. He opposed the creation of black infantry officers but did recommend the assignment of black officers to other army branches, such as the artillery, engineers, and service elements. He also recommended the retention of separate officers' clubs.[65]

The other white witnesses ranged from those who wished to maintain the status quo to those who were openly hostile to integration. The former tried to balance evidence at hand. Basing their conclusions on the overall record, they called for a most gradual change in racial policy. Gen. Carl Spaatz, who succeeded General Arnold as AAF commander, argued that the most carefully selected black crewmen and pilots could not form an outfit of better than average efficiency. He expressed doubts that the individual black "could stand the pace if integrated into white crews." He acknowledged that some blacks had command ability, but he did not want them in command of white officers. He suggested they might be employed as technical specialists on white installations so long as there were enough of them to permit their own mess and barracks. If the AAF was to be integrated, he suggested it should start in service units and at carefully selected installations. He favored segregated training installations for pilots, but integrated ones might even be tried at this level, providing the greatest care was taken in selecting the training site. He was not worried about integration in the advanced service schools because of the careful selection of the students—white and black.[66]

Less positive was the testimony of General Eaker, deputy commanding general and chief of air staff. Individual integration of blacks would be unwise, he said, because blacks and whites do not do "their best work when so integrated." Eaker suggested that if the army were racially integrated, it might have difficulties in recruiting white volunteers. The War Department, he warned, "should not conduct social experiments." Although he doubted that any black officer would be commissioned on merit if competing with white candidates, he did find Col. Benjamin Davis, Jr., to be outstanding. In fact, he credited Davis for the success of the black flying units. It was Eaker's view that while blacks could be promoted to any rank required by the size of black units and the best might be placed in staff jobs, they should not be placed in command of white troops. He said that blacks should not attend white flying schools because they required more training time than whites and "would not graduate in a school run by white standards."[67]

Brig. Gen. Dean C. Strother was more negative. He claimed that the 332d was never decorated because it was not good enough and that it was inferior to all white groups in the theater. Nearly all credit for the unit's limited success he credited to Davis. Whenever Colonel Davis was absent, the unit deteriorated. Except for Davis, the officers lacked leadership, initiative, aggressiveness, and dependability.[68]

Brig. Gen. Edwin W. Chamberlain stated that some of the AAF units were worthless. Blacks, he advised, lacked the intelligence to do well. In his view, integration should not even be attempted until five or ten years after it was proved that company integration had worked. In any case, the army was ahead of the public in racial matters.[69] George L. Weber, a regimental commander in the 92d Division, said that the "poorest white officer was more dependable than any Negro officer." He favored southern white officers for black units because they had no tendency to be "lenient or fraternize with the troops." He warned against formation of division-size black units.[70]

The expert testimony of white combat commanders was entirely negative. Yet it was balanced and, in the view of the board, outweighed by the testimony of noncombat commanders, social scientists, and professional black advocates. Military men who would consider the evidence of Walter White, executive secretary of the NAACP, and William Hastie more significant than that of Generals Carl Spaatz, Ira Eaker, and Edwin Almond were rare.

Although Gillem's military contemporaries and superiors balked at integrating on a limited or on any other basis, the reform was recommended by the Gillem Board. Contained in the Gillem Board Papers collection is the original of a highly bigoted letter from a senior general, with the salutation and complimentary close removed. The document is dated 25 June 1945. The sender asks if his correspondent had been requested to provide information to the study "Participation of Negro Troops in the Post-War Military Establishment." The letter further reads:

> It is an elaborate questionnaire on the performance of Negro troops in the war. To my horror, my own section without my knowledge, set up a board of senior colonels to get the answers. So the questionnaire, which is stupid, and the method of getting it accomplished here, which is more so, will get for the War Department the greatest mass of opinion, superstition, and legend it will receive on any subject.
>
> Having thus expressed myself, there is fortunately a brighter side. General Almond, commanding the 92d Division, has meticulously preserved every scrap of paper in the Division which he will turn in to the AG [adjutant general] when he is relieved or the Division is inactivated. Dwight tells me that there are some good unit histories of Negro service units, thanks to a good historian in our Base Section. The Inspector General's report of the near break thru of the 92d's position on Christmas day was delivered directly to General Joseph T. McNarney. . . .
>
> In general, opinion all over the theater is that Negro troops are no good whether air (the colored fighter squadrons are famous primarily for strafing our own troops), ground (the 92d always had another full division spotted in reserve behind it), or service (you can have all my Negro units without replacing them). I've talked to several small unit commanders who are extremely bitter about their experience and convinced that Negro troops are simply not worth the effort. I thought the commanders good men and am convinced they tried hard.[71]

One can conclude that the board knew the origin of the letter and that it was authentic because it was preserved. The names probably were removed to protect the sender and the recipient from any possible future embarrassment. Against such deep-seated feelings, the Gillem Board recommended an evolutionary program to bring about racial integration!

Once the board's findings were complete, its recommendations were circulated, and ranking military men as well as civilian officials in the War Department were asked to comment. Army Lt. Gen. J. E. Hull suggested that all black enlisted men be assigned to all-black units and that no black officer be given command of white troops.[72] Air Force Maj. Gen. Idwal Edwards agreed in general with the board's recommendations but warned of the "ineptitude and limited capacity of the Negro soldier."[73] Army Maj. Gen. Daniel Noce was most critical of the nonsegregation features of the board's report. He wrote:

> For the present and the foreseeable future, social intermingling of Negroes and whites is not feasible. It is forbidden by law in some parts of the country and is not practiced by the great majority of the people in the remainder of the country. . . . To require citizens, while in the Army, to conform to a pattern of social behavior different from that they would otherwise follow would be detrimental to the morale of white soldiers and would tend to defeat the effort to increase the opportunities and effectiveness of Negro soldiers. It would be a mistake for the Army to attempt to lead the nation in such a reform as social intermingling of the races.[74]

General Eaker, responding for General Spaatz, also criticized the report: "We should not organize certain types of units for the sole purpose of advancing the prestige of one race, especially when it is necessary to utilize these units up to strength. As the report points out, the formation of Negro combat groups was the result of political pressure from a highly organized minority. In order to fill quotas for Negro pilot training, students were accepted with stanine ratings as low as two (2), whereas the requirements for white students was seven (7)." Eaker also criticized the concept of experimental white and black groupings, as in Europe during the closing days of the war, because the AAF units were not suited for that type of experiment. He stated further:

> The Board recommends that Negro units be stationed initially in localities where community attitudes are most favorable. The AAF agrees that this is the best policy, but we find it is extremely difficult to put into effect. We have endeavored for more than two years to find some suitable base for the permanent assignment of our one Negro tactical group. Whenever a base was tentatively selected for the unit, the civic officials vehemently protested even though a large proportion of the population was Negro, Syracuse, N.Y.; Columbus, Ohio; and Windsor Locks, Connecticut being

cases in point. Some communities even threatened local voluntary bans against selling merchandise to personnel of the unit in case we overrode their objections. . . .

The Army Air Forces believes that the difficulties of the colored problem will be with us as long as any extensive race prejudice exists in the United States. The real solution to the problem lies in the overall education on this subject and will undoubtedly take generations to accomplish. In the meantime, it is believed that the War Department should use great care to march in the van of popular opinion, but that it should never be ahead of popular opinion on this subject; otherwise it will put itself in a position of stimulating racial disorders rather than overcoming them.[75]

The civilian component in the War Department was not as negative. Gibson wrote to Secretary of War Patterson that the board had acted in a responsible manner to make the best use of the nation's manpower potential. Gibson recognized that the ultimate aim of the board was "a completely integrated Army." He favored the gradual approach the board had recommended and urged that "the report of the Gillem Board be accepted." He called, furthermore, for an explicit statement that the present policies "*requiring* segregation are no longer binding," and he asked for a clearcut pronouncement that the "*eventual* goal is the elimination of segregation."[76] Gibson feared that the language of the report was too ambiguous. His supervisor, John J. McCloy, who had no particular objections, described the Gillem Board report as a fine achievement.[77] As in testimony before the board, uniformed participants were negative and civilian witnesses positive. In 1946 the Gillem Board report was published almost without any modifications and was identified as War Department Circular 124, 1946. The circular would have established a new, forward-looking racial policy if it had been enforced.

Army officials, however, believed the recommendations too advanced and the proposed changes too rapid and therefore ignored the report's major suggestions. In fact, the recommendations were premature. American society remained segregated, and the army thought the majority still had to be convinced that integration was the best way. The Gillem Board understood this and urged adoption of an intensive education program to convince army personnel, from top to bottom, of the wisdom of its evolutionary integration policy. The result was *Army Talk 170*, a pamphlet on black soldiers. War Department Circular 76, 1947, required that "commanders of all echelons . . . insure indoctrination of all personnel, including officers, under their command by establishing a course of instruction based on War Department Circular 124, 1946 and *Army Talk 170*." The circular established that instruction would be completed within seven training days and in a period of not less than three and one-half hours.[78]

The pamphlet contained three sections. Part one discussed black manpower in the army; part two described the successful integration of blacks in combat units in Europe; and part three called for harmonious race relations because the military mission demanded it. Each section contained detailed notes for discussion leaders. Instructors were advised that the mention of race was "likely to touch off sparks from individuals who have deep seated beliefs, convictions, or prejudices." Leaders were told to advertise the Gillem Board's overall objective: "increasing effectiveness of the Army."[79]

The purpose of the first part of the discussion was to describe how the army proposed to resolve its special manpower problem. It stressed that the general run of black soldiers had less education, civilian training, and experience in highly mechanical fields than whites and that blacks scored lower on the AGCT. But it also noted that there were blacks with very high scores and others who were well educated. Also, segregation had not resulted in the most effective use of black manpower and had been accepted by the army merely to prevent friction. Discussion leaders were to tell participants that the Gillem Board recommended the abolition of large all-black units and the employment of blacks with special skills as individuals in overhead and other special units.[80] The pamphlet cautioned that the army was not an agent of social reform; therefore, it would do nothing to alter the existing racial community pattern around posts. Such matters were the concern of the civilian community. Within its own ranks, however, the official position of the army was "that basic equality of opportunity to all soldiers, irrespective of race, is essential to highest military effectiveness." Racial discrimination was termed fatal to military efficiency. *Army Talk 170* further stated that recreation facilities, while they might be designated for specific units, must not be closed to members of any race. "In the interest of the maximum use of authorized manpower," the pamphlet stated, "the Army's ultimate aim is to be able to use and assign all personnel in the event of another major war, without regard to race."[81] Thus the army went on record as striving for eventual integration.

The second section, "Negro Platoons in Composite Rifle Companies—World War II Style," recounted the experimental integration in Europe at the end of the war. Discussion leaders were told, "The success of this type of integrated organization was a major factor in the War Department's decision to increase, broaden, and to some extent integrate the peacetime use of Negro manpower." In the process of praising black performance, the authors of this section gave attention to the polls which revealed that men who had served with blacks were much more receptive toward integration than those who had not.[82]

Part three of *Army Talk 170* examined racial problems on the world stage. Whites were a worldwide minority, and many "of the non-white people in Asia, Africa, and Latin America are looking to America as the leading democracy, for a picture of how democracy works or can be made to work, and they are paying close attention to the way in which our minority problems are solved." The pamphlet stressed that "playing on minority differences was a device used by Hitler and Mussolini, and we do not wish to use the Axis method on ourselves." This segment of the pamphlet spoke also of the psychology and sociology of prejudice and asked the discussion leaders to discuss prejudice with their groups. The pamphlet ended with the Gillem Board's emphasis upon military efficiency: "The Army does not propose to change your prejudices. What you think or do is a concern of the Army only so far as it affects Army effectiveness. *Think whatever you want personally, but don't throw a monkey-wrench into the machine.*"[83]

Despite a well-thought-out program of indoctrination and the obvious sincerity of the Gillem Board, its policy was aborted. A classified report prepared in 1949 by President Harry S Truman's Fahy Committee noted that none of the Gillem Board's major or minor recommendations were carried out. The committee accused the army and the air force of obstructionism. Well-qualified blacks were to be integrated into overhead units, but the army attempted to evade this provision. Some commands had no blacks in overhead units, and others assigned blacks to their overhead units only as cooks, duty soldiers, and truck drivers. "In the overhead of the . . . third Army . . . there were 29 finance clerks, and no Negroes, 37 white motion picture projectionists and no Negroes, 478 white writers and no Negroes. Throughout all commands the use of Negroes in overhead in signal, ordnance, transportation, medical and finance military occupational specialties (MOS) was minimal." Some commands, the Fahy Committee charged, "flatly refused" to use blacks in overhead positions, notwithstanding the directive nature of War Department Circular 124. More than half of the army schools, furthermore, were officially closed to blacks, on the grounds that there were no positions open to them to employ techniques learned in these schools. According to the committee: "The files of the historical records section reveal no consistent enthusiasm for, and very often active opposition to, any positive measures for implementing the policies of the Gillem Board." The committee blamed the failure to implement the recommendations on the army's refusal to establish a special staff group within the army staff to monitor this program.[84]

To observers today, it would appear that the Gillem Board's recommendations were timid and their nonimplementation inconsequential. In the context of the 1940s, however, the Gillem Board understood its suggestions to be anything but timid and must have been disappointed when the army failed to carry out its program. A special concern of the board was the role segregation played in creating racial friction. In nearly every instance, it held that racial problems arose because of the "Negro's real or fancied feeling that he is being discriminated against and must take positive action, which in some cases results in riots." The board placed the blame for race riots squarely upon commanders. It stated:

If transportation to and from the post is inadequate, he [the commander] must try to foresee all friction and bad feeling due to overcrowding or lack of transportation by conferring with officials of transportation lines or arranging for Army transportation. If restaurants and stores in adjacent communities do not accommodate Negro trade, a talk with the secretary of the Chamber of Commerce is indicated. . . . They must demonstrate a real desire to understand and care for the troops under their command regardless of race or color. They must, by their attitude and actions, gain the confidence of the men under them. . . . Commanding officers who fail to carry out promptly the letter and spirit of approved policies should be relieved.[85]

Race Violence

The board's regard for proper command actions to prevent riots was historically valid. There had been race riots, some resulting in death, in the armed services during and after World War II. The Gillem Board understood the relationship between discrimination and riot, and it appears that this may have been a factor in promulgating the new policy.

Historian Ulysses Lee, in *The Employment of Negro Troops,* describes the World War II riots the army suffered. Racial friction, he wrote, was a "continuous cause for concern within the War Department and in the Army's higher commands." The summer of 1943 was the high point of violence, although riots had occurred in all of the war years. "Serious disorders"—those resulting in death or serious injury—occurred in 1943 at Camp Van Dorn, Mississippi; Camp Stewart, Georgia; Fort Bliss, Texas; Camp Philips, Kansas; Camp Breckinridge, Kentucky; Camp Shenago, Pennsylvania; and elsewhere.[86]

Very early in the war, counterintelligence officials worried that the Japanese were propagandizing blacks to sabotage the U.S. war effort. For example, agents were concerned about the "Ethiopian Pacific Movement," which was said to have counseled blacks to start a "whispering campaign; when they tell you to remember Pearl Harbor, you reply 'Remember Africa.'" The movement supposedly advised blacks to evade the draft and help organize front organizations for propagandizing blacks. The Ethiopian Pacific Movement, as well as two other groups—Emanuel Gospel Mission and the Afro-Asiatic League—were alleged to have circulated pamphlets printed by the Japanese government.[87]

There was an official proclivity to view black agitation as proof of enemy propaganda or even sedition. Six consecutive editions of the AAF magazine, *Intelligencer,* in 1944 warned of increasing black militancy. Blacks were demonstrably happy over the War Department decisions in 1944 to desegregate recreational facilities, but the white press in the South was virulent in its opposition to relaxation of segregation. The *Intelligencer* remarked, "*The Daily Worker* joined the Negroes in recounting successes." The magazine noted that the use of "nigger" was becoming more objectionable to blacks and the term was reportedly provoking racial incidents. The *Intelligencer* also cited 68 racial outbursts within the Fourth Service Command over the question of local transportation. Increasingly, the magazine reported, blacks were violating "'Jim Crow' seating laws." According to the *Intelligencer,* at Camp Sutton, North Carolina, "Negro troops have a plan to take over the camp and the nearby town of Monroe. Weapons have been stolen from the Ordnance warehouse. Numerous incidents have been caused by Negro soldiers from the camp, such as: insubordination to white officers and MPs [military policemen], stoning vehicles occupied by white personnel, overturning of white taxicabs, and storming a post theater." The magazine reported a riot at Fort Francis E. Warren in Wyoming which involved "mob action on the part of 8,000 colored soldiers." It also identified a secret "Racial Club" organized in Greenville, S.C., with about 150 members, and expressed the belief that the club was "part of a national organization . . . connected with the NAACP. . . . Object of the club is to secure 'equal rights' and protect members from discrimination." The magazine cited another incident in which 16 black pilots en route from Walterboro Army Air Field stopped in a "white only" cafe in Fairfax, South Carolina. When refused service, they told the "white proprietress to 'go to hell' and drew their revolvers. They left the cafe with shouts of 'Heil Hitler' and went to the railroad station." A black member of the Women's Army Corps (WAC) who was refused service in Evansville, Indiana, had to be dragged away by the police. Over a period of months the *Intelligencer* recorded similar incidents.[88]

In addition to the altercations at Selfridge Army Air Field and Freeman Field, both previously discussed, there were numerous other incidents at air bases in the United States and abroad. Some of these involved the stealing of weapons and race violence. At Herbert Smart Airport in Macon, Georgia, an entire aviation squadron on 11 November 1944 simply refused to obey orders to proceed with the day's training. The blacks were called into the base theater for a meeting, but the base commander lost control of the situation. Blacks also protested vigorously at Amarillo Army Air Field, Texas, in late 1944 when they were not allowed to use the facilities of the service club. The AAF alleged that club employees, who refused to wait on black personnel, stated that their presence "would prevent the local white girls from entering the club."[89]

The MacDill Riot

Despite the Gillem Board's admonition to remove racial irritants, the military post pattern remained the same following the war, provoking a major riot at MacDill Army Air Field in Florida in October 1946. The blacks apparently were unhappy many months before the riot and had written about the situation at MacDill in a letter to the *Chicago Defender* in April 1946. They complained that black servicemen awaiting their discharge were assigned menial duties at a civilian airfield while whites awaiting discharge were not so detailed. Whites apparently were allowed to leave the area for home once discharged, but blacks continued to work as laborers for the civilian airfield until the day their enlistment ended. There were, in addition, many complaints about segregation on the post and the fact that the blacks did not get a fair division of recreation funds for dances.[90]

Tension became acute, and a riot erupted on 27 October 1946 at the black non-commissioned officers (NCO) club. It began with a fist fight during a dance, and someone called the officer of the day (OD) to quell the disturbance. A half hour later, the OD received a second report that a "disturbance of greater intensity was occurring at the club." Numerous black privates trying to crash the NCO dance apparently provoked the trouble. These angry men "worked themselves up to mob violence and began throwing beer bottles and rocks through the NCO Club windows." When the OD again arrived at the club, the "disturbance [had] reached riot proportion." A "mob of approximately 150 colored soldiers . . . began yelling, brandishing clubs, and throwing beer bottles." The situation became more tense with the arrival of the military police, who attempted to disperse the crowd of blacks. The mob threatened to charge the military police, who then fired a volley of shots, forcing the black soldiers to retreat into the NCO club. During the shooting one military policeman was "lacerated on the temple, and a colored soldier sustained a bullet wound." Soon the "mob dissipated at the NCO club," and another "gathered at nearby Dispensary B where Pfc. James Treadwell . . . , spokesman, expressed his displeasure in no uncertain terms to Lt. Col. Russel G. May, Commandant of Colored Troops, of the shooting fray at the NCO Club, and threatened him bodily if the matter was not adjusted."[91]

While May discussed the riot with Treadwell, two other men, Joseph and Richard Plesent, went to a barracks "with the expressed purpose of inciting its occupants to arm themselves with clubs and fall out." Soon a "mob . . . converged on MacDill Avenue Gate" where it "overcame and disarmed an MP, smashed windows, tossed furniture into the street, dismantled the telephone and barricaded the gate entrance. . . . The two mobs, approximately 300 colored soldiers, many of whom were armed with rocks, bottles, clubs and bed posts, formed one mob gathering at MacDill Gate where they kept yelling and shouting profanely, absolutely refusing to disperse upon orders from their commanding officer."[92]

The rioters then attempted to invade the civilian housing project near the MacDill gate. This was a white-only government project called Gadsden Homes. Some whites reported that they had overheard blacks shouting that they were going to get "some of that 'white stuff,'" and 15 or 20 of the blacks left the gate. They were met by an armed white sergeant, who singled out one of the rioters and threatened to shoot if the soldiers did not back off. The black soldiers returned to the gate and began to agitate for guns. The county deputy sheriff arrived shortly thereafter with nine carloads of heavily armed men, which further excited the blacks. It was not until 2:30 A.M. the next morning that the crowd dispersed.[93]

Earlier, Colonel May, surrounded near the barracks, had vainly tried to get the men to calm down. There were rumors that men and women at the club had been shot, and shouts of "no more Jim Crow laws" punctuated May's pleas. When he tried to get the men into their barracks, Treadwell shouted, "No, don't go back, don't listen to that white son of a bitch." May then tried to get the men into a mess hall for coffee, and Treadwell shouted: "Don't go to the mess hall. He'll surround it with MPs and shoot us down like dogs." Treadwell told May, "I hate the United States from East to West and North to South and every bastard in it."[94]

The outburst led to an investigation into its causes. But examination of the racial situation provided the chief of staff of Strategic Air Command (SAC) with much more information than merely the causes for the MacDill riot. In the previous 90 days there had been 22 mass disturbances in the military, all attributed to "Communist propaganda with the definite objective of infiltrating the armed forces, which has manifested itself by inciting the Negro soldier to demand preference rather than equality." Some military men believed that the Communists were also exploiting to the fullest an exaggerated idea of the black contribution to the "successful completion of the war."[95]

Presumably to uncover Communist agitation, a counterintelligence special agent was assigned to the black unit. The agent, a "Mr. Walter L. Harris (colored)," was in the unit between 2 and 22 November and reported in writing upon completion of his investigation. He discovered that the riot was spontaneous and found no evidence of Communist agitation. He cited, rather, decided bitterness toward MacDill because of a "lack of proper on-duty and off-duty activities." There were few or "no technical jobs available to the colored soldiers and very little encouragement given them to attend technical schools." They believed there was no "future for them at MacDill Field or in the Army." Because they were not assigned responsible jobs, they "lost interest" and began to "drift," to engage in "goldbricking," and to try for a discharge as mental incompetents. Harris, who believed he had been completely successful in winning the acceptance of the blacks, said that these problems—when coupled with the question of unsuitable recreational facilities—weighed heavily on the men and led to their "demoralization . . . breeding dissension and [the] subsequent display of emotions."[96]

Despite the report of the counterintelligence agent, the MacDill file continued to blame the unrest on Communist agitation. An undated and unsigned intelligence estimate labeled "Communist Party Programs as Related to Its Activities against the Armed Forces" stated, "Communist dominated papers are efficiently carrying out propaganda aims of the Communist Party." In preparation for the final clash with capitalism, according to this report, the party and its organs would attempt to undermine the army by agitating blacks over segregation. This particular estimate cited the *Pittsburgh Courier* as a leading offender.[97]

Whatever the causes for the riot, the facts of the destruction were there, and trials were held. The riot leaders, having in the meantime confessed, were brought to trial at MacDill. The press was admitted to the open proceedings, and some black officers were appointed members of the court. Of the 11 men tried, 9 were convicted. Of these, some received heavy sentences. Treadwell was sentenced to 1 to 20 years at hard labor, forfeiture of pay and allowances, and a dishonorable discharge. Others were given from 1 to 25 years at hard labor. The *New York Amsterdam News* complained that the men were tried in the "utmost secrecy" and were being "railroaded to prison." The black press further claimed that southerners on the court were determined to punish the blacks and that the two black officers on the court were frightened. But the trial was public; the men had confessed; and there were numerous witnesses to the events.[98]

The riot led to an inspector general's visit to the airfield. The SAC inspector discounted Communist influence, but he also made no recommendation for improvement of the living conditions of the blacks. His main concern was to prevent future riots, and he criticized the fact that MacDill had no riot plan. He noted that blacks believed they had won a moral victory and also that they could have taken over the whole base if they had not been discouraged from doing so. He wrote: "Force properly used, such as tear gas and fire hoses, backed up by arms may prevent the loss of a number of lives [because] colored men respect armed might and guns." He advocated strict discipline because at MacDill it had "not been severe enough." He wrote that southern customs created problems and that northern blacks "with low mentality resent the customs of the South." All of his recommendations called for better riot control and the rapid discharge of black dissenters. He made no recommendation to increase recreational facilities for blacks or to delve into the deeper causes of the riot, only that the situation should not be permitted to get out of hand again.[99]

MacDill was not the only air base to experience a riot. In January 1947 officials at Fort Worth Army Air Field, Texas, encountered similar difficulties with black enlisted men. Here, blacks challenged white prejudice more directly. The *Pittsburgh Courier* had reported two months earlier that Fort Worth Army Air Field blacks resented white prejudice. Approximately 1,000 mistreated and segregated black soldiers signed an open letter in which they declared that their life was "unbearable, un-american, prejudiced, discriminative, and segregative [*sic*]." They stated further:

> It was believed by large numbers of us that after we had served our country during the past emergency, faithfully and loyally, both here in the states and on foreign soil

. . . that the infectious diseases of hate, segregation and discrimination would vanish. . . . In the Army, inseeded with these evils, the tension is growing worse. . . .

It is our opinion that approximately 98 percent of colored soldiers on this station are used as nothing less than common labor which does not involve training of any nature.

For example, a man does not have to be trained to be a kitchen police, a janitor, or a street or area cleaner. . . .

Yes, join the regular Army, travel, education, good pay, benefits under the GI Bill of Rights and many other so-called advantages. . . . This is what the Army launched as a campaign to enlist men in the Army, but what's on paper is not practiced here. We have joined the Army Air Forces and what can we say we've received: Unjustified treatment as soldiers and as men, rotten food and not enough of that, unsanitary quarters and mess halls, the uncongenial attitude of white civilians both on the base and in the town of Fort Worth, Tex., together with the unsoldierly treatment by certain officers in this squadron.

The letter also complained of an inadequate dayroom, service club, and post exchange, as well as a one-chair barbershop installed for 1,000 blacks. The final complaint was that a medical officer had used the term "nigger" in a medical lecture.[100]

In essence, the complaints were much like those identified by the undercover agent at MacDill, and similar, but less violent, results were attained. On 6 January 1947, a black private, who entered the service club and bought cigarettes, was accosted on his way out by a white corporal. The corporal shoved him against the wall and called him a "black-son-of-a bitch," whereupon the black invited the white outside. The white corporal, noting that some blacks were waiting for the private, called for help. Soon 10 to 12 blacks gathered, and the whites who had left the club rushed back in and locked the door. Then approximately 50 to 60 blacks arrived and threw stones at the club. General fighting erupted, which was stopped upon the arrival of the military police.

In a pretrial investigation, the white corporal admitted that he had told the black private that he had no right to use the service club (the corporal later admitted that he knew the statement was incorrect). The other whites who came to the corporal's aid also knew that blacks were entitled to use the club but pitched in to see that "colored were kept out of the club." Two men, one black and one white, were court-martialed.[101]

A counterintelligence agent also was sent to Fort Worth. He found no evidence of Communist agitation, but Col. J. K. Fogle of SAC headquarters commented on this point. He wrote that the agent found that "no *direct* Communist agitation is taking place. Therefore the recent uprisings can be attributed to the general breakdown of military discipline that occurred upon the cessation of hostilities in 1945. The Negro soldier has been slower to react to the return to normal discipline than the white soldier and requires unusually fair but firm and interested direction. It is known that the breakdown of military discipline in 1945 was planned and agitated by the Communist Party—and, of course, the Negro was a most receptive prospect."[102]

The MacDill archive file contains other reports of racial trouble. Violence broke out in a black mess hall at Roswell Army Air Field, New Mexico, in early December 1946; and again a counterintelligence agent was called to investigate. Also in the same month, on a bus en route from Fort Worth to the airfield, a white soldier asked a black to move to the rear of the bus and demanded his seat. The black refused, and the white tried to use force. At this point the blacks in the back of the bus "started opening knives, whereupon the white soldier forgot the issue." The report concluded with the comment that "Joe Green, white CP [Communist Party] organizer, is believed to be in Fort Worth area on a temporary visit. Information is fairly reliable."[103]

Not everybody assumed that unrest in black units was a product of Communist influence. Some introspective individuals attempted to find a solution. For example, SAC's Fifteenth Air Force studied the problems of black troops following the MacDill riot. The 15th Air Force historian acknowledged that War Department Circular 124 (based on the Gillem Board recommendations) called for greater utilization of blacks, but he stated that the "practical application of this policy was fraught with vexing problems." The historian cited resistance from commanders who frustrated implementation. In response to a "question on upgrading colored personnel, one base commander replied: 'Upgrading! I'll upgrade them!'" Whereupon, during the next 30 minutes the commander denounced the blacks, denigrated their worth and intelligence, and recommended their repression.[104]

Most of the responses the historian received were similarly unfavorable. As a solution to the problem, he recommended a "colorblind" attitude. Moreover, he found that the Gillem Board recommendations were not detailed enough to offer guidance or to counter the long-standing customs of discrimination. SAC officials thought enough of the problem to place the question of the utilization of black personnel on its February 1947 Commanders Conference agenda. Such matters as distribution, utilization, enlistment, and reenlistment were discussed. Although 18 percent of SAC was black, most of the men were stationed at only two locations: MacDill (Florida) and Salina (Kansas). More than a third of the personnel at MacDill were black (1,966 men), and overcrowding had still not been alleviated there. The commanders found that utilization of blacks was not what it should be. They suggested that it would improve only after intensive education of white personnel and better use of "race relations and democratic principles."[105]

In April 1947 *Army Talk 170* was distributed to SAC bases, but the Fifteenth Air Force historian found the results questionable. He wrote, "What value, if any, resulted from the foregoing studies or talks on the policies for utilization of Negro personnel in the Fifteenth Air Force cannot be determined." He noted that blacks continued to be assigned to base units (housekeeping organizations), engineer aviation battalions (ditch-digging units), and aviation squadrons (also housekeeping units). All these units were segregated. However, Fifteenth Air Force headquarters asserted that assigning blacks lowly tasks was not discrimination because whites also performed these jobs.[106]

When SAC proposed that the Fifteenth Air Force accept the assignment of additional blacks, it declined on the ground that "adverse local conditions in the immediate vicinity" of its bases coupled with political influence negated such a move. The SAC historian lamented, "It can be said that at year's end, 1947, the utilization of Negro personnel still posed difficult problems and a successful formula for their utilization was still being sought."[107]

Air Force Blacks in the Postwar Period

Indeed, a solution to the problem of black utilization was not found until the advent of integration. Meanwhile, blacks continued to suffer the abuses of a system that denied them opportunity. The AAF also suffered from a policy that caused low morale and underutilization of a significant percentage of the force and created social ferment. The military was not totally insensitive to the needs of blacks; but military sensitivity was too shallow to overcome long-held biases.

After Germany surrendered, the army decided to assign homecoming blacks to areas of the country where they might be welcome. The assistant chief of staff attached a map to a letter of instruction designating zones of assignment. The Deep South was identified as an area where "conditions were not likely to be suitable." A band across the border states through West Texas was designated a favorable zone. The North was divided into two zones, "favorable" or "may be improved." The letter advised those responsible for relocating black units that the assignment of black troops was of importance in the interests of avoiding racial situations. If at all possible, measures were to be instituted in conformity with the military exigencies to select stations in zones in which the racial climate was favorable.[108] The overcrowded MacDill Army Air Field, however, was listed in the suitable zone.

Ambivalence best describes the official attitude toward blacks in the immediate postwar period. America did not suffer a postwar economic recession; war-torn Europe had to be rebuilt, and well-paying jobs in industry became plentiful for whites. In the meantime, the army (including its air forces) found itself short of personnel.[109] AAF headquarters decided to permit blacks to exceed the World War II and Gillem Board quota of 10 percent. It maintained, "Due to the present critical need for manpower in the Army, it is necessary that voluntary enlistment of Negroes be continued and that this personnel be effectively utilized." By 1 July

1946, it was anticipated that the army would be approximately 15 percent black, and nothing should be done to limit them to the 10 percent quota.[110]

The AAF announced a policy that there would be "equal training and assignment opportunity for all military personnel." Assignments were to be based on the skills and abilities, mental and physical, "of individuals to meet, or to be trained to meet, these requirements." The AAF insisted that "commanders take affirmative action to insure that equity in training and assignment opportunity is provided all personnel."[111]

Implementation of this policy, however, was not based on ability, mental and physical, but on race. Personnel regulations listing assignment specialties available to enlistees and reenlistees continued to identify jobs by race, to the substantial advantage of the whites. Blacks, furthermore, were not assigned to certain geographical locations.[112] These restrictions, while not new, continued to antagonize blacks and their civilian spokesmen. In denouncing this policy, the *Pittsburgh Courier* declared, "Proof that the U.S. Army is the same biased arm of pre-World War II days was in indisputable evidence." Its readers were told that "colored soldiers, without exception, were still being relegated to labor units in the European-Mediterranean theaters where the fine assignments and opportunities, with ratings, were listed for white men only." The newspaper cited assignments in the regulations that were limited to white enlisted men.[113]

Yet, when the War Department was queried by President Truman's Committee on Civil Rights about the status of blacks in the army, the secretary of war answered that blacks were no longer restricted as they had been in the past, and he added: "War Department policy has been and continues to be to train all individuals and units to such a degree of efficiency that they can effectively perform their mission, in war and in peace. Training policies do not differentiate between races or troops; opportunities, requirements, and standards are the same for all."[114]

The fact remained that blacks posed a major problem. The AAF, following the massive demobilization, found a need for blacks because white men were not enlisting in sufficient numbers to perform the defense mission. Generally myopic about how policies affected blacks, the service did not agree that the solution to the problem was integration. Tactical Air Command (TAC) complained that it had "too many *colored* personnel," yet the AAF accepted all blacks it could because of its manpower needs. By limiting blacks to a few specialities and by not permitting them to be used in aviation specialities at sites apart from Lockbourne Army Air Field, home of the 477th Composite Group, TAC indeed had a problem. By the end of 1946 approximately 5,000 of the 18,000 enlisted men in the command were blacks. TAC recognized that blacks were joining en masse because the "military offered a refuge from social and economic pressures," but the command had more blacks than it could employ. Even though the AAF suspended black enlistment in mid-1946—because of the extraordinary rise in enlistments—TAC still had more than it could absorb. The command acknowledged its inability to use, elsewhere, excess specialists assigned to Lockbourne because segregation precluded their relocation. Like the AAF at large, TAC was in a difficult situation. All units needed skilled men, but trained blacks could not be employed to the extent of their abilities or wherever needed.[115] Segregation, therefore, proved burdensome for all.

TAC could not resolve its black problem because the military was unable to solve its racial dilemma. In 1948 TAC complained of excessive assignment of blacks, citing a higher percentage than other commands in the air force. Repeatedly, the command tried to reduce the number to 10 percent, but without success.[116] Although TAC was troubled by the question, integration was never proposed as a solution. Lockbourne had a "chronic shortage of both rated and non-rated Negro officers, an overage of submarginal enlisted men, and [frequently suffered] losses of skilled airmen to overseas shipment." At Lockbourne, "Negro personnel could be employed as individuals in any unit [in] which their Military Occupational Specialties could be utilized," while on other bases blacks could be used only "on a unit basis." Consistent with this policy, wing commanders, with few exceptions, chose to assign their black troops to one squadron—the General Service Squadron (Squadron F)—and "such personnel as were assigned over and above that squadron's authorized strength were considered surplus to the needs of the station, as well as surplus to the needs of the Command." In many instances, highly trained and skilled technicians performed duties as janitors without regard to their capabilities or potentialities, which was an "unjustifiable waste of training and skill."[117] Recognizing this, TAC might have condemned segregation but did not. TAC continued to complain about policy limitations without suggesting remedies other than to recommend a reduction of the number of blacks.

In March 1948 TAC issued a staff study titled "Utilization of Negro Manpower," in which it called for a change in the air force recruitment policy to prevent reenlistment of submarginal individuals. To absorb excess blacks, it suggested creating an additional squadron designated for blacks, a Squadron E (transportation). It further recommended better selection criteria for choosing white officers to command black units. The study also suggested that "skilled Negro personnel be either reassigned as individuals to Lockbourne Air Force Base or declared surplus to the Command." It also wanted all Squadron F units within the wing organization to be designated an all-black unit throughout TAC.[118] All of these proposals involved segregation, none suggested ending it, and none were carried out.[119]

Lockbourne suffered because 35 percent of its men were in AGCT categories IV and V. These men were untrainable for some of the critical specialities required by the unit. Yet, the air base had a sufficient number of skilled airmen in certain specialties, who could be drawn upon and reassigned to overseas bases. To keep Lockbourne manned and operational, however, TAC had to raid other bases within the command for skilled blacks. Officer manning in particular became critical. The TAC historian wrote, "Certain color differences made it impossible to assign officers to the Group except those who were recruited and trained for that Group." This meant that whites could not be assigned because the 332d was commanded by a black. There were also too few blacks attending pilot training to meet the projected needs of the group. Since black aviators could fly only with that unit, they could not achieve a rank commensurate with their experience and skill, and everyone remained frozen in grade. Gen. Elwood R. Quesada, TAC commander, wanted to replace Colonel Davis and his staff with whites because Davis was well overdue attendance at war college, but the Pentagon refused to sanction the move.[120] SAC also agonized over the employment of blacks and tried to assign black personnel to all of its bases, but local community prejudice and pressures hindered ease of movement. Housing and demographic statistics indicated that Spokane AFB, Washington, and Castle AFB, California, might accept blacks. But before taking direct action, SAC surveyed the local communities for "housing available, Negro population in the city and nearby area, and feelings expressed by local authorities." Both Castle and Spokane had close at hand a small black population, but public sentiment in the adjacent communities was clearly against assignment of black troops. SAC headquarters, therefore, recommended that blacks not be assigned to either base.[121]

SAC also looked at Selfridge AFB, Michigan, north of Detroit. But the city attorney for the nearest town, Mount Clemens, reported: "The housing situation is very bad, as there has been little building since the War, and our population has increased. From a quick survey, it would appear that there is no housing available for the families of colored troops as the colored people in Mount Clemens are already crowded in to the few areas open to them."[122]

Blacks in SAC, furthermore, were not well utilized. The SAC history notes, "Most personnel used were with Aviation Engineer troops on temporary duty at installations for construction purposes" There was little hope in such units for promotion. The historian suggested that blacks could be better used if they could be moved to bases that had none assigned. But there was reluctance within the civilian communities and on the part of prospective base commanders to accept them.[123]

Only at Godman Field and later at Lockbourne Army Air Field were blacks fully utilized. Positions in flying, maintenance, and the inner administrative workings of the group and wing were all manned solely by blacks. Colonel Davis was highly regarded, and TAC was reluctant to replace him with anyone but a white. Blacks were also employed at Tuskegee Army Air Field until it ceased operations in the spring of 1946. After the cessation of hostilities, it was not a truly active base. Still,

Tuskegee ended its career under a white commander and with whites holding nearly all leadership positions, although toward the end some blacks had worked their way into a few leadership and management positions.

The white citizens of Alabama remained ambivalent toward Tuskegee. The base historian recorded that the local "white people are willing, and the writer emphasizes willing, that the station remain in its present location provided it is always under the command of a white officer and had white officers in positions of control." He wrote that if the white leadership was withdrawn, "the local white citizens would like to have the station closed immediately. There are white merchants in Tuskegee, however, who realize that the field is a great source of revenue, but even these would prefer that the colored personnel send their money to town and not come with it."[124]

Naturally, after the war, the school slowly wound down, producing fewer pilots each quarter, and the staff dropped commensurately. In September 1945 20 pilots earned wings, and a month later only 9 graduated. After Japan surrendered in August, students were allowed to resign from the program and the air corps in practically any phase of training.[125] As the faculty diminished in size, the number of blacks on the faculty and staff increased slightly, but it never reached a significant fraction of the total.[126] When Class 46A graduated from Tuskegee in March 1946, it was the only group of students to graduate from an AAF flying school that month.[127] The following 15 April, Tuskegee was transferred to TAC from the Flying Training Command, thus terminating its existence as a flying school. After the last blacks won their wings at Tuskegee, black aviators began to train with whites without fanfare and nearly without comment at Randolph Army Air Field, Texas. Because there were so few of them, or in spite of that fact, segregation was not practiced at Randolph.[128] The issue which had prompted William Hastie to resign was quietly resolved.

But Tuskegee did not end its existence without controversy. The president of Tuskegee, Frederick D. Patterson, tried to keep the airfield open as a permanent base for all blacks flying in the postwar era. He wanted to retain the flying school and the tactical units in the Alabama community. Soon after recommending this to General Marshall, Patterson withdrew the suggestion, probably because of pressure from within the black community. The black press was bitter in its criticism. The *Pittsburgh Courier* viewed with "apprehension" Patterson's urgings to the chief of staff. Most of the newspapers condemned him for his desire to promote segregation at a profit to his institution. The *Norfolk Journal and Guide* scolded the Tuskegee president for not first consulting the pilots themselves, who, the newspaper knew, objected to such a move.[129] The black leadership, as expressed in its leading newspapers and its organizations, fought for integration and nothing less because segregation remained intolerable to blacks.

Ben Davis's Air Force

The 477th, however, remained a segregated unit. At Godman Field the group—consisting of one bomber squadron and one single-engine fighter squadron—continued to exist, if not to prosper. Their first designated mission was not flying but rather was discharging personnel who no longer desired to remain in the service. The group trained men and flew in air shows to maintain proficiency, but it steadily lost personnel through separation and airplanes through age and accidents. By mid-February 1946 the unit was reduced to 16 B-25s and 12 P-47s and to 256 officers and 390 enlisted. Four months earlier, the group had had 243 officers and 949 enlisted men. From the aftermath of the Freeman Field mutiny in 1945 to the dissolution of the black wing at Lockbourne in 1949, Colonel Davis was the commander.[130]

On 13 March 1946 the 477th moved to Lockbourne Army Air Field, Ohio. The unit for some time had wanted to move from Godman to a better location, and the men and government searched for a new site. But as General Eaker noted in a letter to the Gillem Board, the unit was not welcome anywhere. Even in Ohio the editor of the *Columbus Citizen* opposed the unit's move to Lockbourne Field, just south of the city. Objecting to American "servants" doing the fighting for America, he labeled the 477th a bunch of "trouble makers" and wrote that he could prevent the move "if I really wanted to." He maintained, "This is still a white man's country." The relocation, however, was made despite his objections. Davis subsequently noticed a "definite rise in morale of all personnel" as well as an increase in effort. Godman was an old and dilapidated airfield, while Lockbourne was in much better condition.[131] The black flying unit remained at the latter until the air force was integrated.

Once there, the 477th's mission did not change. TAC described it as the "demobilization and recruitment of military personnel" and active training to maintain combat readiness.[132] Accordingly, the unit participated in war games and flew proficiency and tactical missions. The airmen practiced bombing and rocket firings on ranges and performed maintenance chores to keep the unit flying. During 1946, their flying safety record was either comparable to TAC's or even slightly better. Throughout that year the group organized a public relations effort entertaining the citizens of Ohio with air shows, field days, firepower demonstrations, static displays, and other activities to inform the people about their flying mission. The 477th also participated in air shows and other aerial demonstrations elsewhere in the United States.[133]

When Tuskegee closed in mid-1946, black pilots who desired to remain in the AAF were reassigned to Lockbourne. This put great pressure upon the squadron's aircraft. The large number of pilots could not get in the minimal flying hours necessary to maintain their proficiency without the addition of more aircraft or a reduction in the number of pilots. At this time they also faced chronic shortages of maintenance personnel. The pilot flying crunch eased after aviators began to separate at a faster rate than was desired. By the fall of 1946 the fighter squadron had only 22 of its authorized 78 pilots. The unit suffered even greater losses in some of its important enlisted specialties.[134]

The black press monitored the activities of this unique organization, and in fact, much of its total military coverage was devoted to Davis's group. When the bombers and fighters flew to Blyth Army Air Field, California, to participate in an amphibious operation, the *Pittsburgh Courier* reported their flying activities and commented that General Quesada had high praise for the unit's performance.[135] In spite of these achievements, a lower percentage of black officers won regular army commissions than white. The *Pittsburgh Courier* front-paged the complaints of black flyers about this situation and concluded, "No one is on their side." Thus, of the 9,800 officers in the army selected for augmentation, only 31 were blacks.[136] Regular officers have much greater tenure than reservists, and a regular commission was highly prized.

When either of the Davises made public pronouncements, the black press gave their statements extensive coverage. The elder Davis spoke at a church meeting in Columbus in the summer of 1946, and the *Pittsburgh Courier* captioned the article: "Armed Service Bias Is Shame of the Nation." On this occasion, Davis said that segregation was destructive of morale and that there was "no such animal" as separate but equal. He called for integration at once.[137] His son, in a later speech, compared the navy's racial program to the AAF program and found the latter wanting. He had observed navy integration on a cruise and found that morale among blacks was higher in the navy than in the AAF. Integration, he said, had not resulted in racial friction even within the confined quarters of ships.[138] Both father and son had been on record favoring integration, and neither feared issuing public statements to the black press about sensitive matters. The black press also sounded an alarm at any hint that the 477th or its successor, the 332d, would be dissolved.[139] If the unit was to be disbanded, the men would have to be integrated into other units, and no other approach was acceptable.

The 477th ceased to exist in mid-1947 but was immediately replaced by the 332d Group (later the 332d Fighter Wing). On 10 July, the B-25s were deactivated after taking part in combat exercises in central Georgia. Their mission was to drop bombs and strafe simulated enemy targets. After these operations, they were praised by Maj. Gen. Paul L. Williams, commanding general of the Ninth Air Force. Williams later commented that the "record of the parent units composing the 477th is well known to every student of World War II history." He expressed pleasure with their accomplishments in their first year at Lockbourne.[140]

The 332d Group was formally activated on 1 July 1947 and comprised three fighter squadrons: the historic 99th, 100th, and 301st. The group's mission was the "continuous training of officers and enlisted personnel by an actual on-the-job training program that will broaden military experience and permit training in administrative and technical duties which will qualify personnel for their peacetime responsibilities and also train component units and crews in accordance with proficiency standards prescribed by higher echelons." The B-25 pilots were retrained to fly fighters, but 25 officer crew members were removed from flying status on 1 July as a result. These were mainly navigator-bombardiers, who could not be absorbed into white units, even though there might exist a need for them.[141]

In the next six months, during their checkout period, parts of the group took part in war games and maneuvers at Myrtle Beach, South Carolina, at Turner Field, Georgia, and at Fort Knox, Kentucky. For all intents and purposes, this unit flew missions similar to that of any other TAC fighter group. In August the group was redesignated a wing, though it was still chronically undermanned. When the air force became an independent service on 18 September 1947, the group retained its status, and the occasion is hardly mentioned in its history. The 332d had been segregated in the army and remained segregated in the air force. Of the 15,473 black airmen in the air force, more than 10 percent were stationed at Lockbourne, and of the 257 black officers, more than 75 percent were based there.[142] The remainder of the officers were scattered over the world, many as commanders of all-black aviation squadrons.

There were 55 groups in the air force at the end of 1947, and few blacks were pleased with the minuscule size of the black component. Air force plans to expand to 70 groups did not include creation of additional black flying units. The *Baltimore Afro-American* warned its readership: "Wake Up, People! Realize what is happening before it is too late." Congress authorized the air force to expand to 70 groups, and this "has not done us a particle of good." Having only one group was "objectionable because it was segregated" and "represented less than 2% of the Air Force strength although we are supposed to have 10% . . . and did not cover all types of planes and services." The newspaper further lamented that there were only "eight colored flying cadets in training for pilots." Blacks were moving backward, the paper complained, because fighter planes did not require crews and teamwork. The air force was accused of "holding our boys down to fighter planes. . . . They never have a chance to 'check out' in multi-engine planes." Because of the nature of fighter aircraft, there was no possibility to employ the "few colored bombardiers and navigators that were trained in the last war." The article commented upon the lack of promotion potential for blacks and concluded, "If this is democracy, democracy stinks!"[143]

The 332d, however, continued to fly. Throughout 1948 the unit was plagued by manpower shortages and an inability to employ the men in specialties for which they were trained. As of 1 January 1948, 49 of 80 officers and 102 of 338 enlisted men were "utilized out of their Military Occupation Specialty." Six months later, the unit was short 3 medical officers, 1 electronics officer, 28 fighter pilots, and an undisclosed number of enlisted men.[144] The unit could ill afford to be short of so many fighter pilots.

In addition to manpower problems, the familiar social problems plagued these men in the postwar era. Men of the 332d were socially segregated while on maneuvers in the southern states as well as in other places. During war games, they were generally messed and billeted separately and also attended separate clubs.[145] Most of these events escaped the black press. In mid-1948, however, the *Pittsburgh Courier* protested the exclusion of the 332d's officers from the Camp Campbell, Kentucky, officers' club. When the post commander offered to open a separate club, blacks participating in the exercise objected. Although the newspaper reported that Secretary of Defense James Forrestal was studying the issue and that such segregation practices were against regulations, nothing came of the protest.[146]

During its last year the 332d was undermanned, segregated, and largely neglected. From June 1948 to June 1949, however, it suffered several fatal accidents but participated in Operation Combine III (one of the largest war games in the immediate postwar era), successfully passed an operational readiness inspection, won an air force gunnery meet in May 1949, and celebrated Sgt. Mal Whitfield's victory in the 800-meter run in the 1948 Olympics. On 1 June 1949 the wing had 242 of its authorized 260 officers assigned but only 1,381 of its 1,931 authorized airmen. On 30 June 1949 the 332d concluded its history as a black wing.[147]

Why were there chronic manpower problems? An October 1945 memorandum written by Lt. Gen. Hoyt S. Vandenberg, vice chief of air staff, to General Arnold may provide an answer. Vandenberg's recommendations appear to have been generally followed after the war. More important, in 1948 Vandenberg succeeded General Spaatz as chief of staff of the newly created independent air force, and he brought the air force into the integration era. His personal papers lack references to blacks, and few of his associates, subordinates, and superiors have been able to comment about his attitude toward blacks in the air force. Perhaps the only time Vandenberg is on the record on this subject may be found in the October 1945 memorandum written to General Arnold:

> Comparing Negro to white applicants, approximately 17 times more colored applicants must be screened than white to obtain the desired number. . . . Due to the lower average intelligence of the Negro, the elimination rate in the Negro pilot training program from pre-flight throughout advanced was much higher than the white. . . . On a comparative scale, the colored will be grouped in the lower or minimum qualifying scores whereas the white applicant will be spread evenly throughout the range. . . . Minimum qualifying scores had to be lowered for the colored pro-

gram; that is, where the minimum qualifying stanine score for a white pilot was normally 7, Negro qualifying score was lowered to 4 generally, and for short periods had to be disregarded entirely for those individuals who were [physically?] qualified for aircrew training. A considerably higher percentage of colored applicants than white volunteered for elimination because of fear of flying. Upon graduation the average colored graduate was generally about equal to what would be considered a weak average for the white; and in many instances to maintain the colored units, it was necessary to pass borderline cases that would have been eliminated had the applicants been white. . . . The outstanding deficiency in the Negro officer was lack of leadership . . . it was necessary to fill . . . key positions with white personnel. Similarly, upon activation of the one medium bomb group, it was necessary to return Colonel Davis from the Mediterranean theater to assume command. No other Negro officer had developed sufficiently to assume this position.[148]

Vandenberg cited what he considered to be the poor combat record of blacks, noting that the 332d during the war in one 11-month period had "91 air victories compared with 1,024 to the remaining three groups of the Wing; or an average of 8.3 victories per month for the 332d as compared with 24.2 per month for each of the other groups." He further stated:

Notwithstanding the claims that all people are created equal, the vast majority of whites insist on racial segregation. To avoid incidents and to provide for harmony in [the] services, both for whites and colored, segregation is essential if Negroes are to be selected for training. . . .

Due to lower average intelligence, the demonstrated lack of leadership, general poor health, and extremely high elimination rate in training, it is far more expensive to train Negro officer personnel than white. Also statistics indicate that the end product obtained in Negro training is much less efficient than that obtained in white. Particularly in the commissioned bracket, the training of Negro personnel is not economically sound.

Due to the excessive cost of training Negro aircrew and commissioned personnel, as well as the generally poor results obtained from the graduates, further training of Negro personnel cannot be economically justified. Further, no compromise in procurement or training standards should be made in peacetime in order to obtain Negro applicants. If training of colored applicants is to continue, they should be required to meet the same rigid standards in selection and training as whites.[149]

It would be unfair to assume that Vandenberg did not alter his views in the three and one-half years between the appearance of this memorandum and the successful integration of the air force. The memorandum is important, nevertheless. Blacks were commissioned and permitted to fly after the war, but there is no record that they were accepted at lower standards than whites. If the 332d could not be maintained by any other device during the war, how else could it have been manned after the war? It would seem that Vandenberg's recommendation had influence.

When the air force integrated in 1949, blacks made up about 0.6 percent of the officer corps, a lower percentage than during the war years. Whatever Vandenberg's views on segregation in 1949, when he stated them in 1945, they were not different from those of any other high uniformed official with the exception of Colonel Parrish. The record will show, however, that in 1949, when the air force integrated, a plan was ready, and the air force integrated with grace, speed, honesty, and success. Air force integration was aided by presidential politics and mainly by the man Vandenberg selected to be his deputy chief of staff/personnel, Lt. Gen. Idwal Edwards.

egregation had proved to be a decidedly inadequate personnel policy. Segregated units could not rise above the low performance of their members, forcing the military to underemploy those blacks who had the perseverance and intelligence to rise above a deprived past. Although some air force leaders might doubt that blacks could do work equal to whites, virtually all were in agreement that segregation was inefficient. Arguments arose over what to do about the situation. The air force wanted to employ blacks more efficiently, but it did not believe that it could break out of the circle of prejudice it was helping to maintain. The logical answer was desegregation, but the air force and American society were not ready for it.

Desegregation and integration came anyway. Many causes precipitated this result. The air force integrated because its chief of personnel wanted to end manpower waste and its service secretary independently supported the move. Almost as important was President Truman's Executive Order 9981 of 26 July 1948 to the armed services to foster equal opportunity. While the army did not take action on Truman's directive until the Korean War, the president's order was the catalyst to the air force, without which there would not have been as rapid a movement toward air force "unbunching."[1] The air force decision to integrate had been announced prior to the issuance of Truman's executive order, and integration followed the president's action by ten months. In the rest of the services, it was more than two years.

The Air Force Shifts Policy

Although it was not fully recognizable at the time, there had been a fundamental shift in American attitudes after World War II. That the military services were the first elements in American society to integrate and become for all intents and purposes the most completely integrated element in society is attributable to hardheaded military pragmatism and, secondarily, the effects of the normal American political processes. Legitimate pressures were placed upon President Truman to demonstrate his willingness to humanize U.S. race relations.

Before Truman issued his executive order, the air force had studied the impact of segregation upon its own effectiveness. Lt. Gen. Idwal H. Edwards, air force deputy chief of staff for personnel, had initiated the inquiry. As a member of the McCloy Committee during the war, he had long maintained that segregation was a waste of manpower. Soon after air force independence in September 1947, Lt. Col. Jack Marr, a staff officer in Air Force Personnel, was put to work investigating segregation.[2] Edwards did not believe the black flying units of World War II had been effective. Although he recognized individual flying ability, he found the aggregate constituted a poor combat unit.[3] It seemed to him that talent and well-maintained equal standards were the answers. He recognized deficiencies in air force black personnel policy and decided that "corrective action was clearly indicated." Edwards saw waste and inefficiency in employing only blacks within the "limited structure of Negro units and Negro vacancies." He noted that there were some specialties in which there were "more qualified Negroes than there were vacancies; in other specialties there were more vacancies than there were qualified individuals to fill the vacancies." The obvious problem was that the black surplus could not be employed elsewhere because of segregation. Edwards also found that the 10 percent quota further aggravated the problem. The quota system and segregation in particular combined to undermine the 332d at Lockbourne AFB. Edwards pointed out that the unit was "incapable of duplication or expansion, and, therefore, provided no mobilization potential." More seriously, "if the unit were committed to combat, it was virtually certain that qualified replacements could not be provided to maintain it."[4] He obviously referred here to the wartime problems of finding qualified cadets for the 332d and 477th and of the necessity to lower entrance standards to obtain adequate numbers.

Marr's study and Edwards's attitude influenced General Spaatz, the first air force chief of staff, to issue an encouraging statement on integration. In an April 1948 letter to Lemuel E. Graves of the *Pittsburgh Courier,* Spaatz promised that air force blacks would soon be "used on a broader professional scale than has obtained heretofore." The chief also told Graves that blacks would soon compose 10 percent of the air force and would continue to serve in combat units. He stated that all airmen would be guaranteed equal opportunity regardless of race. His summary paragraph is most significant. He wrote: "It is the feeling of this Headquarters that the ultimate Air Force objective must be to eliminate segregation among its personnel by the unrestricted use of Negro personnel in free competition for any duty within

the Air Force for which they may qualify. The limit of attaining this end will, naturally, depend on the degree to which that attainment affects the effective operation
of the Air Force."[5]

The wording in the above paragraph was repeated exactly by Assistant Secretary
of the Air Force Eugene Zuckert when he testified in April 1948 before the National Defense Conference on Negro Affairs, a group of distinguished blacks.
Zuckert told them that the "Air Force accepts no doctrine of racial superiority or
inferiority." Edwards was present when Zuckert read the statement.[6] This air force
position was in sharp contrast to that of Army Secretary Kenneth Royall. He told
the conference that he would maintain segregation because it worked better than
integration but that he would continue to work to improve the lot of blacks within
a segregated environment.[7] Among the blacks present—James C. Evans, Charles
Houston, Mary McCleod Bethune, Sadie T. M. Alexander, Truman Gibson,
Mordecai Johnson, Walter White, Roy Wilkins, and others—there was unanimous
belief that segregation was inconsistent with improving the racial situation. Because of Royall's position, the conference broke up. On the other hand, General
Edwards, who testified after Royall, endorsed desegregation.[8]

Royall was probably disturbed about the air force statement. A few days later he
wrote to Secretary of Defense Forrestal complaining that the "Air Force did not
make it clear that they followed and planned to follow the same course as does the
Army. . . . The demonstrated tendency of one of the services unjustly throwing the
burden on the other is not conducive to the correct spirit of unification and adds
to the already unfortunate situations that have recently arisen."[9] It would appear
that Royall's objections to the air force taking the initiative in race relations was a
major obstacle to the latter promulgating the new policy. Richard Dalfiume identified him as the individual who caused the air force to delay implementing its new
policy for a year because the army was unwilling to be alone in maintaining segregation. Lee Nichols gave the same explanation for the air force delay.[10]

There must, however, be more to the story. Secretary Forrestal was a well-known
advocate of integration and had begun the process when he had been secretary of
the navy.[11] His successor as defense secretary, Louis Johnson, also was in favor of
integration. In addition, it is known that Secretary of the Air Force Stuart Symington wanted to desegregate. Symington, who is given credit for participating in the
formulation of President Truman's Executive Order 9981, was characterized as a
man "who refused to recognize racial distinctions and who used high-powered
business methods to bring racial equality to the Air Force."[12] As early as 1947, Symington was on record that blacks should be able to enter the air force solely on their
merits. Lee Nichols, furthermore, credits Symington for inspiring the Marr report
that challenged segregation.[13] Dalfiume is no less charitable toward Symington.[14]
How, then, does one explain the one-year delay in bringing about integration if

the defense secretary and the air force secretary were in agreement over integration and if the navy had already ended compulsory segregation? Ascribing the air force delay to Royall is inadequate and an oversimplified explanation, although he probably played a major part.[15] Another cause must be found among air force leaders who opposed such a radical policy.

Trying to identify the opponents to integration decades after the event poses problems. Air force integration was one of the great success stories of the civil rights movement. Almost instantly the 332d was dissolved, and the unit's pilots, mechanics, and technicians were dispersed throughout the air force, performing their mission without rancor or disruption. In rapid order also, the black service units disappeared, until there were none three years after the new policy had been initiated. The air force almost completed integration before the army began. Unlike the navy, the air force did not undertake a simply token action (there were no air force black steward corps personnel waiting tables ten years after the inception of integration). Therefore, it is difficult to identify those air force leaders who opposed integration, but it is inconceivable to imagine that Royall's objection deterred the air force from doing what it really wanted to do for a year.

According to Lee Nichols, there was stubborn resistance from many air force officers to the preliminary integration proposals. After the Truman orders were issued, there were alarmed reactions from air force generals who predicted serious disturbances. According to Nichols, General Edwards told Symington that he had "found solid opposition among [air force] officers to integrating Negroes and whites in the same units."[16] Dalfiume wrote that Edwards "faced bitter opposition to a policy of integration from Air Force officers" when he first broached the new program.[17] Nichols added that many air force "officers, particularly southerners, were certain the radical departure from past practices would start a chain reaction of riot, disruption and desertion."[18] Whatever role Secretary Royall played, he had support among highly placed officers in the air force. A selling job of some magnitude had to be done.[19]

Many retired generals interviewed for this book stated that there was no real opposition. But when my tape recorder was turned off, they did admit that various high-ranking officers had indeed opposed integration. Some of these generals—highly placed in the Office of Air Force Personnel and elsewhere—were strongly against integration.[20] Eugene Zuckert, Symington's project officer for integration, maintained that the delay in implementation was caused by the "selling that had to be done in the organization." He recalled the names of several generals who opposed integration, including the influential Gen. George C. Kenney, who flew to Washington to convince Zuckert that "integration, the living integration, barracks integration, dining hall integration was not good for Negroes." It seemed evident to Zuckert that Kenney's objections stemmed from his own prejudices. Zuckert added,

"There was a lot of that around."[21] General Parrish noted that one of the key generals in the Office of Air Force Personnel always referred to blacks negatively.[22]

Gen. Dean C. Strother, chief of air force military personnel and formerly commander of the numbered air force controlling the 332d during the war, also opposed integration. He was unimpressed with the wartime record of the 332d. It was, he said, very deficient when Colonel Davis was not there to lead the group. Even in the 1970s, he continued to believe that integration was a mistake. He recalled his previous experience with the unit. He related in 1974: "I thought we were rushing into it. That was my view at the time and still is. I think they rushed into it too fast; they've almost ruined the services." General Strother maintained that most of the air staff also thought that the air force was rushing into integration. He was certain that the "greater bulk of the people on the Air Staff shared" his view. "Once ordered," Strother said, "we all did it as best we could." He commented that Edwards and Zuckert carried out integration almost by themselves. Zuckert had explained to Strother that integration was a "political thing. . . . It's going to happen sooner or later, so let's do it now." A key to accomplishing it, to Strother, was the Truman executive order. Strother admitted that it would not have been done so fast without the order, and he concluded: "Truman put out a damned flat order and the Air Force ran with it. Being good soldiers we did the best we could with what we had."[23]

Strother remained at the Office of Air Force Personnel until integration was completed, and he is probably representative of the opposition that had to be overcome. Nichols said that Symington had to override these objectors and had to tell the generals to stop their "double talk and act."[24] Symington stated that he had told the air force generals that he expected no one to frustrate integration. "If you don't agree with the policy," Symington had said, "then you ought to resign now. And, we don't want to do it halfway."[25] The record shows that air force integration was carried out with grace and speedily and that Truman's order did in fact change the atmosphere but, obviously, only in the air force.[26] General Edwards noted that Truman's order was instrumental in accomplishing his mission.[27] Symington said that integration was the "right thing to do morally . . . , the right thing to do legally . . . , the right [thing] to do militarily." He also cited another imperative: "The Commander-in-Chief said that this should be done and so we did it."[28]

When Edwards briefed air force senior commanders in April 1949 on the new personnel policy, he cited Truman's order. He told them that the president had ordered integration and had also created a body—the Committee on Equality of Treatment and Opportunity in the Armed Services (the Fahy Committee). Its job was to monitor integration progress within the armed forces. This committee was *authorized and directed to examine the rules, procedures, and practices of the services to determine in what respect such rules, procedures, and practices may be altered or im-*

proved with a view to carrying out the policy of the President."[29] Edwards emphasized the above words from the executive order to make it clear that the air force was being monitored to ensure that it fully implemented the order of its commander in chief. Edwards, it appears, used the fact of Executive Order 9981 as a tool to bring about a policy he strongly desired.

Edwards told the senior commanders that the "Air Force [had] adopted a policy of integration under which Negro officers and airmen may be assigned to any duty in any Air Force unit or activity in accordance with the qualifications of the individual and the needs of the service." This was done out of a need for efficiency, economy, and effective airpower. He said the new policy did not mean the "immediate end of all Negro units in the Air Force. It definitely will mean that Negro personnel will not be restricted to Negro units and will be procured, trained and assigned on the basis of individual merit and ability rather than on basis of Negro quotas to man Negro units." Edwards informed the commanders that the policy had been under review for some time and that the chief of staff was on record against quotas and special consideration based on race. General Vandenberg, he said, was opposed to forcing or retarding a man's military development on the basis of race and believed that such was "debilitating and detrimental to the organization as a whole."[30]

Edwards explained that two initial actions were planned. First, the 332d Wing should be deactivated on or before 30 June 1949. A screening board would be established to check on the qualifications of the men and to reassign them. "The objective," he said, "is to reassign throughout the Air Force, worldwide, the skilled and qualified individuals from Lockbourne." Such personnel would be "assigned to white units, just like any other officer or airmen of similar skills and qualifications." Edwards told his audience that the numbers involved were not large, estimating that only 200 officers and 1,500 airmen would be "sufficiently qualified and proficient for assignment to white units." He told them that such men could be "absorbed without difficulty," if "spread out thinly and evenly."[31]

The screening board led to anxiety among some blacks and angered others. It was obvious that more would be accomplished than just facilitating relocation. There were more than 200 officers and 1,500 airmen at Lockbourne, and apparently Edwards did not anticipate that all of them would pass the screening. Blacks had the same specialty codes as whites, but the former had also to pass a special muster. Edwards said that Colonel Davis knew of the screening board and fully understood "the implications of this policy. . . . He intends to recommend Negroes for assignment to white units only in those cases where the individual is, first, of such temperament, judgment, and common sense that he can get along smoothly as an individual in a white unit, and secondly, that his ability is such as to warrant respect of the personnel of the unit to which he is transferred." The order of priorities is interesting, for it placed the personality factor above specialty qualification. Apparently Edwards did not want blacks who were identified as troublemakers or who were overtly resentful. He said that "unqualified or unusable" blacks would be "discharged under current regulations." Those who were usable would be recommended for assignment to black service units.[32]

One could interpret Edwards's policy, at least initially, as one of evolutionary gradualism. The approach adopted then was to dissolve the 332d, see how it went, and gradually follow this with the breakup of the black service units. All other commands would also conduct screening boards and reassign skilled and qualified individuals to white units. Edwards told the Commanders Conference that the screening boards represented "only the initial implementation of the policy. The matter must be watched closely to assure continued implementation of the policy." He announced the end of the black enlistment quotas and told his audience that blacks would not be subject to quotas for admission to schools. They would, he said, have to meet the "same standards as anyone else, and will be classified, assigned, promoted or eliminated in accordance with standards which will apply equally to all personnel."[33]

Why did General Edwards decide to maintain the all-black service units indefinitely? Perhaps he did not expect that many blacks would be assigned to white units. He stated: "The number of Negroes who will be assigned to white units will probably be about 1 percent of the white strength. This figure is supported by experience in numerous civilian enterprises and by the experience of the Navy in implementation of a very similar policy." Blacks in 1948 constituted about 6 percent of the air force, and if all were integrated, they should have made up the same percentage in the previously white units, unless many were eliminated through screening and others were relegated to service units. Edwards recognized that some blacks were not suited for assignment to white units for various reasons and "that the retention of this type of Negro in a Negro unit is authorized."[34] This probably indicates that at least in the spring of 1949, Edwards expected to go no further than the navy.[35]

In his several references to the navy, he admitted that the "principal point of discussion within Air Staff" involved housing blacks and whites in the same barracks. But he found some solace in the navy's experience. He stated, "In the Navy, and I have checked this by personal observation, implementation of this policy has relieved rather than emphasized the situation." He said blacks were assigned to compartments aboard ship with whites doing the same job and that since "the number of Negroes is small, 1 percent, and the Negro individuals are well qualified for their jobs, they are accepted by their associates on the basis of merit and ability."[36] The only way the navy could have limited integration was to assign most of the blacks to the stewards' corps, which is what happened.

Finally, Edwards advised the commanders that they had an escape valve, if a problem arose. Squadron commanders, he said, were "not prohibited from assigning separate sleeping accommodations within the unit. We do not believe this will be necessary but it may aid in the smooth implementation of the Air Force policy." It was, he said, purely a matter for local determination. (This particular clause, however, was deleted from the final draft of the integrating directives.) Edwards ended his presentation by reiterating to the commanders that desegregation had been approved at the highest levels and that it would work because it had proven itself in the navy. "The Navy has had this system for years and has found it wholly practicable. It is in effect at such southern naval stations as Corpus Christi, Texas; Norfolk, Virginia; Memphis, Tennessee; New Orleans, Louisiana; and the Navy reports 'No trouble.'" He urged commanders to give the new policy their personal attention and to exercise positive command and control to minimize frictions and incidents. He added that unless younger air force commanders were "guided and counselled by the senior commanders in unbiased implementation, we may encounter serious trouble which the Navy has ably avoided." This policy, he concluded, "must have your *personal attention* and *personal control.*"[37] It seems obvious that the planned policy was not as revolutionary as what would take place and that there was no immediate expectation on Edwards's part of complete integration.[38]

The policy that Edwards outlined was elaborated in two air force letters, No. 35-3, dated 11 May 1949, which described air force personnel policies, and a separate classified letter addressed to "Commanding Generals, Major Commands," which required implementation of the first letter. Both letters were rewritten a number of times, but except for deleting a statement of the right of local commanders to segregate blacks in all-black units or living quarters, changes made were minor. The first letter, echoing in tone the president's executive order, stated:

It is the policy of the United States Air Force that there shall be equality of treatment and opportunity in the Air Force without regard to race, color, religion, or national origin.

To insure uniform application of this policy the following supplemental policies are announced.

a. There will be no strength quotas of minority groups in the Air Force troop basis.

b. Some units will continue to be manned with Negro personnel; however, all Negroes will not necessarily be assigned to Negro units. Qualified Negro personnel may be assigned to fill any position vacancy in any Air Force organization . . . without regard to race. . . . Commanding officers are hereby directly charged with the responsibility for implementation of the above policy.[39]

The last sentence is of particular significance, for it is quite explicit. It determined who had to shoulder the responsibility for the success or failure of integration. Commanders were also informed that they had to "insure that all personnel in their command are indoctrinated thoroughly with the necessity for the unreserved acceptance of the provisions of this policy."[40]

In the first draft of the letter, dated 31 December 1948, the following paragraph appeared: "Where personnel of various races are assigned to the same unit, commanding officers are authorized to take whatever reasonable measures they consider in keeping harmony among the personnel to include the provisions of separate sleeping accommodations within the unit, if considered necessary; however, there will be no racial distinctions made in the utilization of government facilities under the jurisdiction of the Air Force."[41] This paragraph remained in all versions, generally undated, until the final draft. In view of General Edwards's comments of 12 April 1949, the contents of the above paragraph must also have been the policy at that point.

The classified implementing letter spelled out what was expected of the major commanders:

Negro personnel may be assigned to any position for which qualified, and may be permitted to attend appropriate service schools which will enhance their qualifications and value to the Air Force based upon the merit and ability of the individuals concerned and without reference to "Negro quotas" or "Negro vacancies. . . ."

The implementation of AF Letter 35-3 can best be accomplished through the careful selection and assignment of skilled and qualified Negro personnel to appropriate duties in Air Force units. . . . It has been proven . . . that well-qualified individuals can be absorbed into white organizations without insurmountable social or morale problems arising as a result of such assignment.

The letter then described the plan to break up the wing at Lockbourne and reassign the men to other units according to their specialties. This precluded unit commanders from employing black airplane mechanics as janitors. Men at bases other than Lockbourne who already worked with white units were to be permanently transferred to those units and live with the assigned personnel. Others employed in all-black units but possessing abilities to work in white units also were to be transferred. Black airmen with qualifying aptitudes were to be sent to school. The one concession to segregation was that blacks who desired to remain in all-black organizations could do so voluntarily. No time limits were placed upon the life of these units. Truman's Executive Order 9981 was appended to this letter, and commanders were instructed to put these policies into effect without delay but doing so "gradually, smoothly, and without friction or incident." Prompt and appropriate disciplinary action was to be taken where necessary to prevent friction or incidents.[42]

In the early drafts of this letter, Colonel Marr added a paragraph (later deleted) explaining how well integration had worked in the navy and how perhaps problems could be avoided in the air force. He urged:

> Care should be taken to insure that a reasonably small number of Negro personnel is assigned to any individual white organization; in no case will the Negro enlisted strength of the organization exceed 10 percent of the total enlisted strength of the organization without approval of this headquarters. This limitation will not apply to student populations, processing stations or similar activities, and of course does not pertain to organizations manned entirely by Negro personnel. . . . Negro individuals who are considered by the appropriate commander as being best suited for assignment to a Negro unit will remain in their present assignment unless eligible for separation from the service under current directives.[43]

It is easy to see that the last sentence as well as the entire paragraph could well vitiate the policy if left in the hands of unsympathetic unit commanders. These two provisions coupled with barracks segregation might have undermined integration, and it was important that they be deleted. The President's Committee on Equality of Treatment (the Fahy Committee) deleted much of the paragraph and the provision allowing commanders to designate blacks for all-black units.[44] The committee did not, however, delete the statement regarding barracks segregation, but Assistant Secretary of the Air Force Eugene Zuckert did. "I wouldn't want to give the commanders that kind of sweeping power," he said. "I would be afraid of how it might be exercised."[45]

Clearly, political pressure played almost no part in Edwards's decision or in the form of implementation. Army historian Morris MacGregor, who extensively investigated the question of armed forces integration, concluded that integration was not forced and that integration came after each service proved "conclusively to itself that segregation was an inefficient way for the armed forces . . . to use its manpower." Although he considered the civil rights movement a factor, MacGregor believes pragmatism was the key.[46]

The military was aware of the activities of black pressure groups and read black newspapers in order to understand their views of military affairs. A 15 April 1948 memorandum to the air force director of military personnel indicates that his office was aware it was being monitored by black pressure groups. The air force did not plan to use surplus black navigator/bombardiers after the war, yet these men continued to draw flight pay although they did not fly. According to the memorandum, five officers at Lockbourne were not assigned to bomber or transport crews because all these units were white. The dilemma was clear: to continue "these Negro officers on flying status and risk criticism which alleges unjustifiable use of pay, or . . . to remove these Negro officers from flying status and risk criticism which alleges racial discrimination." The authors recommended that the five officers remain on flying status, rather than risk criticism of the air force from black organizations. They feared that charges would follow and be more damaging to the air force than criticism arising from a liberal interpretation of the justification of retaining these officers on flying status.[47]

Although notions of efficiency mainly motivated air force officials, this is not to say that political pressures had no influence. Politics played a significant role in President Truman's decision to issue Executive Order 9981 and to move the recalcitrant members of the air force hierarchy. When Truman decided to run for a second term in his own right in 1948, he needed all the voter support he could find, including the black vote.

Political Pressure and the Election of 1948

Truman's order had a long period of gestation, going back to the publication of *To Secure These Rights* in the fall of 1947 by the President's Committee on Civil Rights.[48] Established the previous January, this group strongly recommended armed forces integration. In his earlier campaigns for public office, Truman had actively sought black votes from his Missouri constituency. Later, as a senator from a border state, he compiled an adequate record on civil rights, although he was "no zealot" on the subject.[49] As president, Truman inherited the unresolved "civil rights conflict" of the Roosevelt administration but not "the good will and affection" most blacks had for his predecessor. Roosevelt, who rarely supported or endorsed civil rights legislation, had been unwilling to attack the many forms of discrimination existing in the United States. In particular, he had not wanted to antagonize southern Democrats, whose votes he needed to implement his economic programs. Nevertheless, blacks still considered Roosevelt a friend.[50]

The question of Truman's motivation has sparked a debate among historians. Professor William C. Berman holds that Truman responded to the issue of civil rights in a way that maximized "political benefits for him and his party." Throughout, writes Berman, Truman was politically wary and canny and always ambivalent because he opposed social equality. Berman acknowledged Truman's rhetoric, but he said this was not "synonymous with active support" for legislative action. Berman agrees that Executive Order 9981 was Truman's greatest civil rights achievement and a racial breakthrough but attributed its adoption to pressure from A. Philip Randolph, Walter White, and others and to the overwhelming desire to win black votes in 1948. According to Berman: "Negro votes . . . not simple humanitarianism—though there may have been some of that—produced whatever token gains Negroes were to make in the years Truman inhabited the White House."[51]

Similarly, Professor Barton J. Bernstein maintained that Truman's civil rights legacy was ambiguous. He claimed that the president was "surely not sympathetic to demands for bold social reform; he was not deeply troubled by the plight of American Negroes, and he did not oppose racial segregation." Only "slowly and falteringly" did Truman move beyond "the racial prejudice of his section." Bernstein found that Truman's rhetoric was important, if not decisive, and that as he recognized the need for black votes, he became more active. Bernstein found Truman a reluctant liberal in civil rights, even when judged by the standards of the 1940s.[52]

Whether Truman responded to political realities and necessities or was motivated by hatred of injustice is not a major issue. In fact, if Truman had no sympathy for the problems of blacks—although it can be demonstrated that he had some—the results of military integration might have even greater significance. If this action, "the most stunning achievement of the Truman era in the field of civil rights," was not the result of his sensitivities, it must have been the product of ballot-box pressure, and that may say more for the legitimacy of American democracy than the president's motivations.

Prior to the 1948 election, Truman issued several statements about human rights that deeply antagonized the South,[53] but more important, he created the President's Committee on Civil Rights. Even Berman and Bernstein admit that Truman had been struck by the violence that confronted blacks returning from World War II. He responded to the blandishments of his civil rights adviser, David Niles, by appointing a committee to inquire into the problem and recommend a program of corrective action.[54] Truman was particularly upset over the blinding of Isaac Woodyard in South Carolina by a local police chief.[55] He appointed the President's Committee on Civil Rights on 5 December 1946 and instructed it to "inquire into and . . . determine whether and in what respect current law enforcement measures and the authority and means possessed by Federal, State, and local governments may be strengthened and improved to safeguard the civil rights of the people."[56]

The committee, composed of distinguished and successful Americans, was interracial in composition and represented men and women of the three major religious faiths. It decided to focus attention "on the bad side of the record—on what might be called the civil rights frontier." The committee did not comment on what the United States had accomplished, only on how far this country had to travel to live up to the promise of its own Constitution.[57]

Although the committee studied all forms of discrimination and made recommendations designed to guarantee voting rights and other civil liberties, the longest single subchapter in their report, *To Secure These Rights,* was devoted to discrimination in the military. "Prejudice in any area," the committee wrote, "is an ugly, undemocratic phenomenon; in the armed services, where all men run the risk of death, it is particularly repugnant."[58] The committee praised the progress the military had made since the war but noted, "There is great need for further remedial

action." It specifically criticized the small size of the black component in the navy
and coast guard, the fact that the marines limited blacks to stewards' duties, the
army quota and tiny cadre of black officers, and the minuscule ratio of black officers to enlisted men when compared with the white ratio. It also criticized the con-
centration of blacks in the lower enlisted ranks and complained that entrance requirements to the military academies were undoubtedly based on race because too
few young black men were enrolled at the academies. Finally, it commented about
the poor treatment black soldiers received from civilian communities.[59] The committee praised the limited combat integration that had occurred late in the European war, noting that it served to prove that segregation was not the sine qua non
of military efficiency and that integration could work. The committee cited a poll
taken by the Research Branch which showed that whites in an integrated environment did not remain adamant segregationists.[60] The committee, therefore, recommended military integration.

In doing this, the members were probably influenced by a staff memorandum
that looked beyond simple military efficiency as a rationale for integration. The
staff memorandum states:

> The importance of the armed forces in the struggle of minority groups for full
> achievement of their civil rights is too obvious to require labored discussion. The
> armed forces are one of our major status symbols; the fact that members of minority
> groups successfully bear arms in defense of our country, alongside other citizens,
> serves as a major basis for their claim to equality elsewhere. For the minority groups
> themselves discrimination in the armed forces seems more immoral and painful than
> elsewhere. The notion that not even in the defense of their country (which discrimi-
> nates against them in many ways) can they fight, be wounded, or even killed on an
> equal basis with others is infuriating. Perhaps most important of all is the role of the
> armed forces as an educator. Military service is the one place in the society where the
> mind of the adult citizen is completely at the disposal of his government. The use of
> armies to change public attitude is an ancient and well-established tradition. In the
> recent war Great Britain and the Soviet Union, as well as the Axis powers, success-
> fully used the time during which their men were in service to "educate" them on a
> broad range of social and political problems. . . . Finally, the armed forces can pro-
> vide an opportunity for Americans to learn to respect one another as the result of co-
> operative effort in the face of serious danger.

The document treated the subject of discrimination and segregation historically
and included statistics to prove that blacks were the subject of discrimination in
the military.[61]

Among the committee's recommendations on voting rights, employment opportunities, schooling, and segregation in general were several suggestions on the

military. The committee called for congressional "legislation, followed by appropriate administrative action, to end immediately all discrimination and segregation based on race, color, creed, or national origin in the organization and activities of all branches of the Armed Services."[62] It believed that segregation was an injustice and weakened national defense.[63] The committee was quite specific in its requirements for a law, trying to avoid the difficulties that had arisen in the past when language had been vague. It recommended: "Legislation and regulations should expressly ban discrimination and segregation in the recruitment, assignment, and training of all personnel in all types of military duty. Mess halls, quarters, recreational facilities and post exchanges should be nonsegregated. Commissions and promotions should be awarded on considerations of merit only. Selection of students for the Military, Naval and Coast Guard academies and all other service schools should be governed by standards from which considerations of race, color, creed or national origin are conspicuously absent."[64]

The committee's second recommendation was more radical. It suggested using the military to change the customs and mores of the country, especially in those geographic areas where segregation was a legal practice. It proposed "the enactment by Congress of legislation providing that no member of the armed forces shall be subject to discrimination of any kind by any public authority or places of public accommodation, recreation, transportation, or other service or business. . . . The government has an obligation to protect the dignity of the uniform of its armed services. The esteem of the government itself is impaired when affronts to its armed forces are tolerated. The government also has a responsibility for the well-being of those who surrender some of the privileges of citizenship to serve in the defense establishment."[65]

If the federal government also moved to force hotels, restaurants, theaters, and bus stations to desegregate for servicemen and women, presumably it would be a short step to total desegregation. This tactic was in the minds of some committee members. Their first goal, then, was to protect servicemen from indignities, and their second was to use the military to change customs that the committee found repugnant.[66]

On 29 October 1947 Truman met with the committee and received its report. He told the group that he hoped it would be as broad a statement as the "Declaration of Independence" and provide "an American charter of human freedom in our time."[67] One member reported that the president thanked the committee with "sincerity, warmth, and a genuine sense of gratitude."[68]

Several months after release of the report, the president, on 2 February 1948, sent a special message to Congress dealing with the subject. He declared that there was a "serious gap between our ideals and some of our practices," which "must be closed." He urged Congress to enact legislation establishing a permanent Commission on Civil Rights, a Joint Congressional Committee on Civil Rights, and a civil rights division in the Department of Justice. The president also requested the passage of new laws to strengthen existing civil rights statutes, provide federal protection against lynching, and protect the right to vote. He informed Congress that he was instructing the secretary of defense to eliminate the "remaining instances of discrimination in the armed services" as rapidly as possible.[69]

Meanwhile, black leaders became more vocal in their demands for presidential action. In October 1947 Grant Reynolds and A. Philip Randolph organized a new "Committee against Jim Crow in Military Service and Training." This organization lobbied against continuing segregation in the military, with the goal of ending discrimination via an amendment to military draft legislation then before Congress, which would require integration of the armed forces. Members of Congress in 1947 and 1948 had been unsuccessful in amending the draft bill. In April 1948 Randolph met with Truman to solicit his support for the draft amendment. Randolph later reported his meeting to members of the Senate Armed Services Committee, informing the senators of the subject of his discussion with Truman. He said he told the president that blacks were in "no mood to shoulder a gun" while "denied democracy" in the United States. If Congress passed a bill without assurance of equality, Randolph said he was prepared to call on blacks to resort to mass civil disobedience and to refuse to register for the draft. Sen. Wayne Morse (Rep., Oreg.), upset by these statements, termed them potentially misguided and treasonable.[70]

The black press, monitoring the draft controversy, urged adoption of a new draft bill designed to break down bias[71] but was less militant than Reynolds and Randolph. The *Pittsburgh Courier* reported a lack of unanimity among blacks regarding Randolph's statements. Truman Gibson and Reynolds engaged in a heated discussion before the Senate Armed Services Committee. Reynolds accused Gibson of being a "Negro Judas Iscariot" who had gained "financial advantage" at the expense of "his people." Congressman Adam Clayton Powell, Jr. (Dem., N.Y.), told the Senate committee that he and the "vast majority of the fifteen million Negroes in America" supported Randolph and Reynolds. "Negroes," he exclaimed, "are sick and tired of the hypocritical pretense at democracy now being evidenced by Congress." He declared that Gibson did "not even represent the minority opinion" among blacks and called him a "rubber stamp Uncle Tom." He also called segregationists "traitors" and concluded that there were not "enough jails to hold the Negro people who will refuse to bear arms in a jim-crow Army."[72]

While the *Pittsburgh Courier* inflamed opinion on page one, it sought to cool things down on the editorial page. The newspaper described Randolph and Reynolds as extremists. It said that blacks were "unquestionably bitter about the useless and unnecessary jim-crow policy which the armed services persist in perpetuating . . . but there is little indication at this time that there is any appreciable support for a policy of civil disobedience in order to defeat it." The newspaper told its readers, "Alone among the various elements constituting the American Nation the Negro has never produced any traitors and we do not believe he ever will." It stated, furthermore, that it would be a "catastrophe" if the nation's white population ever thought that blacks would "hamper national defense in any way." The *Courier* emphasized that it had always opposed military segregation, but that "if the majority of the American people are not at this time prepared to drop the color bar in the armed services, Negroes must and should bow to the popular will as they would expect any other minority of the population to bow to the will in any other case." It reasoned that in a "democracy it is necessary to take the bitter with the sweet. We should battle this issue to the point of decision, and then, if defeated, gracefully accept the decision and cooperate in its implementation. BUT WE SHOULD NEVER ABANDON OUR FIGHT AGAINST DISCRIMINATION."[73]

A hasty poll conducted by *Newsweek* magazine indicated that only 14 percent of the blacks polled would refuse to register were segregation to continue, while 71 percent were inclined to favor Randolph's proposal. *Newsweek* found no unanimity of opinion among black organizations about Randolph's program.[74] The draft bill was signed on 24 June 1948 without a provision ending segregation, and a month later Truman issued his military executive order. When Executive Order 9981 was promulgated, Randolph and Reynolds dissolved their organization.

The Randolph-Reynolds pressure may have been instrumental in Truman's decision to issue his executive order. Other political advisers, however, probably had a more significant role. In a 43-page confidential memorandum written in late 1947, Clark Clifford, special counsel to the president, outlined a strategy to win the election in 1948. Three pages in this report dealt with the necessity of winning the black vote. Clifford argued that since 1932 the majority of blacks had voted Democratic and that in 1948 the black vote could be pivotal. He noted that Truman's likely Republican opponent, Thomas E. Dewey, was assiduously cultivating the black vote because he considered it a foundation for his victory. Clifford warned the president that blacks might swing back to the Republicans if something positive was not done to retain them. He noted that blacks—under the tutelage of Walter White and other intelligent, educated, and sophisticated leaders—had become cynical, hard-boiled traders. Blacks believed that the "rising dominance of the southern conservatives in the Democratic councils of the Congress and of the party made it only too clear that . . . [they could go] . . . no further by supporting the present administration." Clifford suggested that Truman emphasize the great improvement in the economic lot of blacks during 16 years of Democratic hegemony. However, he advised that such demonstrations were wearing a bit thin. Clifford warned that without "new and real efforts (as distinguished from mere political gestures

. . .),'" the blacks might vote Republican. He noted that blacks held the balance of power in Illinois, New York, and Ohio, and he feared their defection.[75]

The president's counselor followed his gloomy predictions with several recommendations. Republicans, Clifford wrote, would spare no effort wooing black votes. He forecast that in the next session of Congress the Republicans would offer an FEPC bill, an anti–poll tax law, and an anti-lynching proposal, accompanied by a flourish of oratory on civil rights. The president, Clifford noted, would make a "grave error" if he permitted the "Republicans to get away with this." He urged Truman to go as far as possible in recommending measures to protect the rights of minority groups. This course of action, Clifford advised, was sound strategy and might "cause difficulty with our southern friends but that is the lesser of two evils."[76]

A direct recommendation to integrate the services to avoid the loss of black votes came from William L. Batt, a Democratic Party researcher. He had agonized over the potential loss of black votes in New York and elsewhere because of the third-party candidacy of Henry A. Wallace, former vice president under President Roosevelt. Truman's advisers feared that from 20 to 30 percent of the blacks might vote for Wallace, and some leaders in New York said that 75 percent of the blacks in their districts would do so. Batt claimed that the black vote was within Truman's power to salvage. He cited steps suggested to him in discussions with Truman's adviser Phileo Nash and young black leaders. He recommended that the president issue two executive orders, one to create an FEPC for the executive branch of government and one to end discrimination in the armed services. Batt did not disregard a southern revolt and suggested this possibility be examined.[77]

The Republican platform increased pressure on Truman to do something more than talk about civil rights. The platform was forward-looking and expressed opposition to continued segregation in the armed forces. Truman, wary of losing southern support, wanted the Democrats to repeat the innocuously vague civil rights proposition adopted in the 1944 platform. This plank, he believed, would not antagonize southerners. It proved, however, much too weak for Hubert Humphrey and other liberals as well as blacks. Humphrey and his supporters urged Truman to accept the recommendations contained in *To Secure These Rights*. The president was able to control the platform committee sufficiently to retain the weak statement, but Humphrey and other Democrats forced the issue to the floor of the convention and won acceptance for the minority—more liberal—plank, thus precipitating the Dixie revolt and walkout,[78] whereupon the segregationists organized a States' Rights ticket headed by Gov. J. Strom Thurmond of South Carolina. Whatever chance Truman might have had of holding the support of southern segregationists was lost on 26 July when he issued Executive Orders 9980 and 9981 following the Democratic convention.[79]

Truman's Executive Order 9980 dealt with equality of treatment in the civil service, and Executive Order 9981 dealt with equal treatment within the armed services. The latter was an innocuously worded instrument. It stated:

> It is essential that there be maintained in the Armed Services of the United States the
> highest standards of democracy, with equality of treatment and opportunity for all
> those who serve. . . . It is hereby declared to be the policy of the President that there
> shall be equality of treatment and opportunity for all persons in the Armed Services
> without regard to race. . . . There shall be created in the national Military Establish-
> ment an advisory committee to be known as the President's Committee on Equality
> of Treatment and Opportunity in the Armed Services . . . the committee is autho-
> rized . . . to examine into the rules, procedures, and practices of the Armed Services
> . . . to determine in what respect such rules, procedures and practices may be altered
> or improved with a view to carrying out the policy of this order.

No reference was made to segregation; the order was similar to previous statements
on equality of opportunity, which had resulted in no positive gains. In fact, for several years thereafter the segregated army maintained that it was in full compliance
with Truman's executive order. Truman clarified his intent when asked by a reporter
on 29 July if "equality of treatment and opportunity" meant an *eventual* end to segregation. Truman answered, characteristically in one word, "Yes."[80] On 3 August,
Sen. J. Howard McGrath (Dem., R.I.) received from Truman further clarification
of the language in the order, and McGrath publicly stated that it was the president's unquestionable intent to eliminate segregation in the services.[81] Shortly
thereafter, on 17 August 1948, Clifford recommended that Truman speak out more
fully on civil rights. Clifford urged the president to refer to his votes in the Senate
in support of the wartime Fair Employment Practices Committee (FEPC) and his
executive orders to end discrimination in the government and in the military.
Clifford stressed that the president's record "proves that he acts as well as talks Civil
Rights."[82]

Undoubtedly Truman's words and deeds had an effect, and the black vote became indispensable to his victory over the other candidates. His posture also influenced the tone of the editorial policy in the major black newspapers in 1948. As
in 1944, the black press—except for the *Chicago Defender*—endorsed Dewey. In
1948, however, anti-Truman comment was less vociferous and more muted compared with that of the 1944 elections.

During the wartime election, the black press had urged blacks to vote for Governor Dewey of New York. On 28 October 1944 the *Baltimore Afro-American* headline in one of its last issues prior to the election declared in red capitals: "Citizenship for All." In smaller but prominent black type, it reported: "Dewey Pledges
Full Citizenship for All and National Program to Combat Bias." The paper cited

Dewey's statements in which he promised that his "administration will have but one prejudice: it will be prejudiced against injustice." The editorial column exclaimed redundantly that "The AFRO is for Dewey."[83] On the same date, the *Pittsburgh Courier* editorial cartoon on page 1 showed a black voting for Roosevelt, the caption stating, "Every vote for Mr. Roosevelt is a vote for Rankin-Connally-Cox-Bilbo-Eastland and all that the southern politicians represent, segregation-lynching-poll tax."[84] The front-page *Courier* editorial listed the key positions held by southerners in the House and Senate. The editorial cartoon stated: "We must make prejudice unprofitable" and "Dewey pledges to correct conditions of inequality."[85]

In 1944 the *Courier* and other black papers had campaigned as much against Roosevelt's selection of Truman as against Roosevelt. One headline read: "South has little to fear from Truman of Missouri." The article, written by Morris Milgram, claimed that Truman did not believe the FEPC would pass Congress and that he was against social equality. The paper quoted him as saying, "There will never be social equality!" Milgram asked Truman if blacks were served in public accommodations in Independence, Missouri. According to Milgram, Truman replied, "No, they're not, and they never will be." Truman also was quoted as saying that he had never entertained blacks in his home and never would. Elsewhere in the *Pittsburgh Courier,* the writer described Truman as a friend of "Filibuster tycoon" Senator Connally and charged that the Democrats had sacrificed Henry Wallace to please prejudiced southern politicians, replacing Wallace with Truman. Milgram stated further, "Negroes who vote for the re-election of President Roosevelt this fall, should also PRAY AS THEY VOTE . . . PRAY THAT MR. ROOSEVELT CONTINUES IN GOOD HEALTH."[86]

In the *Courier*'s final edition before the election, the newspaper reprinted a *Baltimore Afro-American* editorial which was also reprinted in at least four other major black newspapers. This editorial was highly critical of Truman and claimed he was linked to the Ku Klux Klan. The writer also criticized President Roosevelt for permitting segregation in the military and assured readers that "Governor Dewey will not tolerate" such a policy.[87] On the front page of the 28 October 1944 edition preceding the election, the *Courier* printed a story about Truman and the Klan under the headline: "Eyewitnesses Swear Truman was member of Ku Klux Klan." The paper told its readers that the black press, with 71 percent of the black circulation, supported Dewey.[88]

In 1948 the ratio did not differ, but the black attitude toward Truman was different. The black press had chronicled President Truman's speeches and statements on civil rights and followed carefully the progress of the President's Committee on Civil Rights and hailed its report when published. In the summer of 1947, furthermore, Truman became the first president to address the convention of the NAACP. The *Pittsburgh Courier* quoted extensively from his speech at the Lincoln

Memorial, which was carried on a nationwide radio broadcast. Large headlines informed readers, "Truman Raps Prejudice."[89] The President's Committee on Civil Rights report was hailed by the *Courier.* The entire report with commentary was published in several issues of the newspaper, which stated that it had blasted the "Nation's Civil Liberties Hypocrisy." Photographs of the president were prominently displayed, with the paper stressing that Truman had received the report favorably.[90] Later, when the president sent his civil rights message to Congress, the same paper praised him in an editorial feature, "The Courier Salutes." It applauded his courage and said that his message might go down in "history with the emancipation proclamation."[91] He was praised for resisting southern pressure after the message was delivered. Headlines read: "Pres. Truman Defies South," "Will Not Retract Statement," and "Ignores Threats of Revolt in Dixie."[92] These articles made it very difficult for the *Pittsburgh Courier* or any other black newspaper to remain militant in support of Dewey in 1948.

Following publication of Executive Order 9981, the *Courier* carried a banner headline on its front page: "President Truman Takes Steps to Abolish Jim Crow in the Armed Services." The newspaper did take note in the next few issues that Truman's language was perhaps temperate, but there was no disguising its pleasure over the start he had made.[93] As the election drew near, the *Pittsburgh Courier* and most of the black press again threw their support to Dewey, but without the anti-Truman rancor evident in 1944. On 25 September the *Courier* announced for Dewey, but in an accompanying editorial the publisher noted that blacks were "indeed, fortunate in having all of the three major candidates for President favorably disposed to the advancement and protection" of their rights. The editorial supported Dewey because he was not shackled by the "Bilbos" of the South, but it commented favorably on Truman's record.[94] Later, the paper maintained that Dewey's deeds as governor of New York were more significant than Truman's words. It also predicted a runaway Republican victory.[95] It appears that the anticipated Dewey victory might have been a factor in holding the *Courier* in the ranks of the Republicans. Truman's words were more favorable than those of any other president since Lincoln, but the paper may have been unwilling to lose favor with an anticipated Dewey presidency.

As became evident, most 1948 prognosticators including the *Pittsburgh Courier* bet on the wrong horse. They were misled by the strength and choice of the black voter. Clark Clifford and the black press knew that the black vote was the key to an election victory, and Truman's speeches and actions apparently won it for him. The *Pittsburgh Courier* had followed the population shift of blacks from the South to the North and had predicted that the black vote would hold the whip hand in 1948. The newspaper discovered that blacks were the balance of power in 12 northern states, constituting 228 electoral votes, while 11 southern states which denied most blacks the right to vote controlled only 127 electoral votes. The newspaper stated: "If the Negro is going to gain his civil rights in America, this is the year. It's now or never, for he can drive a hard bargain with his strength in those fifteen states which can elect the next president without any help from the rest of the Union. This is the Negro's big chance."[96] When Truman won, the *Pittsburgh Courier* credited the black vote for the margin of victory.

The first edition following the election claimed that blacks in Illinois, California, and Ohio "put Truman in the win column." It also asserted that black votes in the South for Truman outnumbered those cast by whites for the Dixiecrat candidates.[97] Later, in a more detailed article, the paper stated that 69 percent of the blacks voted for the incumbent. It reported that Mound Bayou, Mississippi, voted two-to-one for the president, the first time a Democrat had ever carried that community. The *Pittsburgh Courier* also showed that Truman carried Harlem, New York, by a wider margin in 1948 than had Roosevelt in 1944, despite the Wallace candidacy and Dewey's popularity in his own state. In fact, Truman emerged more popular among blacks nationally than Roosevelt.[98] In the key states of Illinois, Ohio, and California, his plurality in black wards was so great as to overcome large deficits in white wards. Dewey did not win a plurality of blacks in a single state.[99] The *Pittsburgh Courier,* in a rare move, published several letters to the editor criticizing the paper's editorial policy during the presidential campaign. One accused the *Courier* of taking money from the Republicans: "You were not very clever in concealing what now appears to be a fact. Your tune changed too abruptly, and that was after the Republican machinery was well organized, and money collected with which newspaper support was bought." The heart of the author's indictment came at the end of his letter. "In my opinion," he said, "Mr. Truman is the first president since Lincoln's time to go to bat to try to improve the general status of Negroes in this country." Other correspondents claimed the newspaper had accepted bribes, and others denounced its editorial support of Dewey as a "doublecross of Negro principle." One letter called the *Pittsburgh Courier* less meaningful than a "rotten apple." Not a single letter supported the newspaper in its editorial advocacy of Dewey.[100]

Perhaps because of Truman's newly discovered constituency, or in spite of it, the president set out after his election to implement Executive Order 9981. He had provided a mechanism for implementation in his original order which created a Committee on Equality of Treatment and Opportunity in the Armed Services, popularly known after its chairman, Charles Fahy, as the Fahy Committee. Historians who have studied the Truman administration have praised the actions of the Fahy Committee. Even the most cynical commentators believe that the "importance of the Fahy Committee cannot be overrated. . . . The presence of the committee . . . institutionalized Presidential interest in improving the status of Negro personnel within the Pentagon. Its presence . . . served as a base for collecting quantitative data on Negro service . . . and finding and checking resistance to the Presidential order."[101] Other historians, more sympathetic toward Truman, hold that military racial improvements could not have been accomplished had not Truman "appointed and unwaveringly supported" his Fahy Committee.[102]

Although the committee was established in October 1948, it did not meet until the following January.[103] On 12 January, Truman conferred with the four service secretaries and the members of the Fahy Committee. He informed them that he was not interested in better treatment or fair treatment but in "equal treatment in the Government Service for everybody, regardless of his race or creed or color." He wanted the spirit as well as the letter of his order carried out. Secretary of Defense Forrestal told Truman that the air force had a very progressive plan. Secretary Symington added that the plan would "completely eliminate segregation in the Air Force." He stated: "We have a fine group of colored boys. Our plan is to take those boys, break up that fine group, and put them with other units themselves and go right down the line all through those subdivisions one hundred percent." Truman said, "That's all right." The president also stated emphatically that what he had ordered was not a publicity stunt and that he wanted concrete results.[104]

About the time of the first committee meeting with the president, John H. Sengstacke, publisher of the *Chicago Defender* and a member of the committee, sent a memorandum to his associates on the Fahy Committee titled "An Outline Discussion of the President's Executive Order 9981." He wrote that democracy implied that all people participated in decision making and that all benefits were distributed to all people. It also meant that men were ruled by law and not by other men. Sengstacke stressed that Truman's order also meant a military colorblind to such factors as an individual's religion or national origin. The Fahy Committee must do more, he wrote, than simply investigate discrimination. It had a mandate to "eliminate discrimination in the armed forces." Sengstacke recommended positive action to eliminate discrimination and to discard segregation. He admonished his colleagues to beware of those who would say that equality of opportunity could be achieved within a framework of segregation. Such a person was a "foe to the full emancipation of the Negro people." The president's order, he said, required the elimination of segregation, and the committee should design a major program to carry out that mission.[105]

On 13 January the air force presented to the Fahy Committee its proposal as outlined in the draft copies of Air Force Letter (AFL) 35-3 and the implementing classified letter. The committee was pleased with this action but recommended deletion of a provision whereby local commanders would determine which blacks were to be assigned to all-black units and elimination of the 10 percent quota. Once the air force had removed these provisions, the committee decided to stand back and let the air force conduct its own program. The committee was not disappointed.[106] Fahy advised the president that implementation began on 11 May 1949 and that the committee awaited further results before making additional recommendations to the air force. Fahy wrote, "Meanwhile it [the committee] is watching with interest: (1) the variety and success of assignments for the flying personnel of Lockbourne; (2) the extent of reassignment of Negroes in Air Force Commands to white units; (3) the number of Negro units which are kept in being; (4) the extent of new enlistments of Negroes for flight positions; (5) the extent of Negro enlistments for skilled ground positions in the Air Force."[107] The Fahy Committee, in other words, was determined to ensure that the air force was honest in its policy. Within six months, this service created 1,301 integrated units, leaving only 59 predominantly black units. This is to be contrasted with the 106 all-black units and 167 integrated units that existed on 1 June 1949.[108] The Fahy Committee, after its initial recommendations, made no other substantive proposals to the air force because there was no need to do so.

In reality, the Fahy Committee had little direct effect on the air force other than to require that the service delete the two provisions which in ungenerous hands might have rendered the program a token gesture. In a sense, what the committee accomplished was critical, but its involvement with the air force was minimal when compared with its relations with the other services.[109] Suffice it to say, the army tied the committee in semantic knots, claiming even after the committee had disbanded that segregation and Truman's order were harmonious! The army did not attempt to integrate until more than a year after the Fahy Committee terminated its advisory role. The navy continued a policy of tokenism into the 1960s.[110]

One final point needs emphasis. Air force integration placed pressure upon the other services to do the same. Thomas Reid, chairman of the Personnel Policy Board (created by Forrestal to formulate a general policy for the three armed forces so that they could end segregation before the Fahy Committee dictated a policy), said that Symington and Zuckert made his job easier because they accomplished integration. The air force then became the model for workability for the other services. Reid told the army and the navy that if they copied the air force, they would carry out the orders of the president and the objectives of the Fahy Committee.[111] In committee hearings, air force representatives repeatedly testified that their service was against segregation, believing that their program would be good for America as well as for the air force.[112]

Air Force Integration

Before the air force proceeded to integrate the service, it uncovered doubts among black airmen. The *Air Force Times* and the *Army Navy Journal* reported that some blacks were apprehensive about integration. The two military journals treated the subject differently. The *Air Force Times* reported the concerns of black airmen in a generally positive account;[113] the *Journal* interpreted these fears as casting doubt about the entire integration scheme. The U.S. Army, the *Journal* claimed, questioned the racial integration program, arguing that it was unnecessary because blacks had equal opportunity. The *Journal* also highlighted Gen. Omar Bradley's seemingly negative remarks about integration and concluded that "most officers and enlisted men believed that the abolition of separate white and colored units would harm rather than help" equal opportunity. It quoted a black NCO who claimed he had equality and doubted he would get it in a white unit. The *Journal* advocated "equality of treatment and opportunity but no mixing of the races."[114]

It would appear paradoxical that on the eve of integration some blacks sought to resist integration, but such was the case. In February 1949, two black officers from Lockbourne visited the NAACP national headquarters to express their fears about pitfalls and loopholes in the air force plan to integrate. They suggested that the air force plan might in fact be a blind to eliminate the effective force of blacks in the air force. They did not want to be caught mesmerized, watching the "holiday sized integration flag," while racists eased them out of prestigious well-paid positions. The officers represented other black airmen and proposed an alternative plan "to counteract any idea the Air Force may have for completely eliminating (or nearly so) the Negro from the active participation in the . . . United States Air Force." They attached to their plan a memorandum titled "Does Integration and 'Negro Screening Board' Mean Progressive Elimination of Air Force Negro Personnel?"[115]

In response, NAACP Special Counsel Robert L. Carter visited Lockbourne and, after completing his investigation, advised his headquarters that the fears expressed were those of a majority of the base personnel. He related that this visit was kept secret from Colonel Davis at the insistence of the protesters.[116] Carter said further that the framers of the protest believed that the air force proposal was a plot to "ultimately eliminate the Negroes from the Air Force." They claimed that assigning blacks to all the major air commands was a fraud. They argued they would have to be gullible to believe that officers from their wing would be assigned positions of comparable responsibility in integrated units, and they in fact sneered at such a prospect. They scoffed at the view that flyers might be assigned as staff officers. They feared an individual officer would become "third assistant to another major to be buried to make sure he causes no trouble." They were also concerned for those who with only fighter experience might be transferred to bomber outfits. They predicted, "At the end of five . . . years, there will be only forty or fifty Negro officers in the Air Force." They especially feared decisions of screening boards. For example, the protesters wrote:

Now take an ordinary captain assigned to the 301st Fighter Squadron, 332d Fighter Group, who must first get by a "screening board" which is some additional machinery he must get by because he is a Negro officer, in spite of the fact that he was graduated from a Flying School staffed and operated by Regular Air Force Personnel (White), sent to Italy . . . flew fifty . . . missions, returned to the states . . . and has been flying by Air Force standards since, acquired 1500 to 2000 hours. This captain now must be rechecked after five to six years in the Air Force, and to determine whether he is "temperamentally unsuited." That's a rather indefinite term to say the least. . . . Do you envision this captain taking over leadership of a flight . . . ? We have no allusions [sic] . . . we understand what the results will be.[117]

The air force, they lamented, had deliberately held back their promotions, resulting in a great loss of income, and now was preparing to take their jobs from them as well. Even if they were permitted to hang on, experienced black officers and NCOs would never be given positions of responsibility over whites. They recommended, therefore, that the 332d and Lockbourne be retained; as vacancies arose, these should be slowly filled by whites. They also advocated elimination of screening boards, fearing these would turn into a "machine which tends to hold cliques and gives way to eliminating qualified officer and enlisted personnel not because of not being able to qualify, but because of personality conflicts and party politics which has [sic] been the evil in the organization."[118]

Various interpretations might be made of the memorandum sent to the NAACP, but underlying the protest was the idea that the men preferred segregation at Lockbourne to what they considered to be less than vague promises of equal opportunity in an integrated air force. Their proposal would have crippled integration, for even if their ideas had been feasible, they could not apply to other all-black units; the men in the latter units were even more vulnerable than the Lockbourne aviators and support personnel. The NAACP did not share the fears of the Lockbourne group and took no stand against the air force plan. The national organization carefully monitored the activities of the air force. In October 1949, Roy Wilkins sent an office memorandum to all NAACP branch offices stating that the "Air Force has a non-segregation policy and is working it out in practice much faster than the Navy—ask any Negro in the Air Force."[119]

On 11 May 1949 Colonel Davis was called to the Pentagon for a full briefing on the implementation of AFL 35-3, and two days later General Strother briefed Davis's key subordinates. On 14 and 15 May teams of evaluators—screeners—arrived at Lockbourne to review the qualifications of its personnel. Davis decided that he would be the president of the Personnel Redistribution Board. On 17 May aptitude testing and interviewing began.[120] Officially, the screeners evaluated black personnel to determine which officers and airmen were qualified for immediate and general reassignment in their specialties, which men required or desired additional training, and which personnel were to be retained in the duty they performed at the time of the screening.[121]

At the same time other factors came into play. General Edwards informed the Fahy Committee—in response to a question about screening boards by Lester Granger of the National Urban League—that members of either race who were "so inflexible that they could not accommodate themselves to this system in the services" were to be discharged or separated. Granger also inquired about those blacks who were not ready for a free association with whites, and he asked if "adaptability in an interracial situation would be the qualifying factor." Edwards answered, "This is our intent."[122] In any case the screening boards were not as deadly as some had feared.

All officers in the 332d were screened within a week by Davis and board members representing the Continental Air Command, the Air Training Command (ATC), and Headquarters, U.S. Air Force (USAF). Of the black officers screened, 24 were recommended for schools, 158 for reassignment in their specialties, and 10 for separation. Among the enlisted men, 145 were recommended for schools, 811 were retained in their specialties, 3 were assigned instructor duty, and 40 were to be separated. One-fifth of the officers and enlisted men were sent to the Far East and very few to Europe; the remainder were scattered throughout the United States.[123]

The same policy was adopted by all air force commands. The *Air Force Times* informed its readers about the screening at Chanute AFB, Illinois, where 214 black airmen were tested and interviewed by a five-man team from the ATC. The newspaper reported that the board, broad in scope, was "empowered to hear cases of Negro personnel and to make decisions concerning retention or discharge from the service of those thought to have a lack of interest, lack of initiative, or lack of ability to absorb further training or benefit to the Air Force."[124]

When Lockbourne completed its evaluation, it recommended that 23 percent of its men be discharged, a percentage slightly higher than the air force average. A report prepared on the first eight screened air installations—and the evaluations of approximately 2,000 of the nearly 26,000 blacks in the air force—demonstrates that 1.35 percent were programmed for instructor duty, 19.6 percent were sent to technical school, 59.20 percent were retained in their current specialties, and 19.84 percent were scheduled for discharge. The report also shows that there were 368 black officers in the air force, making up 0.6 percent of the officer force, and 25,523 enlisted blacks or 7.2 percent of the enlisted force.

By the end of 1949 there were still 7,402 blacks in all-black units, but 11,456 were in mixed units and 7,033 in "pipeline," that is, to be assigned to integrated training units. Of the 1,356 officers in flight training (these were inputs from the Reserve Officer Training Corps [ROTC] or the academies), only 11 (0.8 percent) were black, and the figure of only 22 of 2,085 (about 1 percent) for aviation cadets was as depressingly low. Approximately 11.6 percent of those in basic training were black, perhaps indicating an increased incentive to join an integrated force; and 6 percent of those in technical school were black, participating in 61 percent of the technical training courses offered by the air force at the end of 1949.[125]

The black press closely monitored the evaluations and reported weekly on personnel actions at a number of bases, but especially those at Lockbourne. The *Pittsburgh Courier,* skeptical about the integration of Lockbourne, did not give the integration story major prominence. Written by Lem Graves, Jr., and captioned "Integration at Last?," its article argued that the air force had to reduce the number of groups and decided to economize by liquidating the 332d. It wanted to know the meaning of some of the moves. What did it mean when the air force said, "Some units will continue to be manned by Negro personnel"? Graves wrote, "Only about 4,000 of the Air Force's 20,000 Negroes are to be integrated at present and this has given rise to some cynical comments." He also noted that regulation did not require an end to "jim-crow recreational, mess, barracks, and other facilities on posts." He did acknowledge that the air force had promised to integrate these facilities quickly.[126] In sharp contrast, an entire page in a later edition was devoted to the graduation of the first black from the naval academy.[127]

As weeks passed, however, the *Pittsburgh Courier* changed its opinion of the air force, apparently realizing that blacks were getting a fair deal and that other air bases in addition to Lockbourne were being integrated as well. The *Courier* listed the assignments of the men and called the job complete on 22 October 1949 with decidedly premature headlines: "The Job Is Done!" and "Air Force Completes Integration."[128]

In an interesting sidelight on the closing of Lockbourne, Ohio reporters at a press conference were overwhelmingly concerned with the economic impact of the breakup of the 332d and asked few questions about desegregation. It will be recalled that the 332d had not been warmly received when it had arrived in the state. Reporters from the *Columbus Citizen, Columbus Dispatch,* and *Cleveland Call Post* were briefed by Davis on the reasons for integration and the need of screening boards, and he asked for questions. Only after many questions about the future of Lockbourne did the reporters focus on racial integration.[129] The fact of integration, perhaps, was little more than a routine story for these men. It turned out to be a routine personnel action for the air force.

The implementation of integration proceeded well because General Edwards made it clear in a speech of April 1949 and in subsequent implementing instructions that it was the commander's responsibility to make integration work smoothly and that failure to implement would be interpreted as failure in command. Maj. Gen. Laurence S. Kuter, commander of the Military Air Transport Service, told his field commanders: "Selected and qualified Negro officers and men will be assigned to duty throughout the Air Force without regard to race. Direct attention to this changed condition is required throughout the Command. Judgment, leadership, and ingenuity are demanded. Commanders who cannot cope with the integration of Negroes into formerly white units or activities will have no place in the Air Force structure."[130]

Edwards addressed personal and unofficial correspondence to all major air commanders, asking for their cooperation and for private comments on the racial situation. He had the "utmost confidence that our major commanders will implement these policies with a minimum of friction." He cautioned, however, that the whole country would be watching and warned that the policy was directed by the president as well as the secretaries of defense and air force. The last, he said, was "personally interested in its smooth implementation." Edwards informed the commanders why he was doing this unofficially: "I am reluctant to direct the submission of this information through normal official correspondence for the obvious reason that it would only serve to highlight the problem, and by implication, indicate that we anticipated trouble in the implementation of this policy."[131] He wanted reports in detail on any racial incidents or difficulties, as well as actions taken. He also wanted to know of troop and community reactions to the policy and which parts of it failed, if any.

Only a few of the replies to Edwards have survived, because they were sent through personal channels. A letter from Maj. Gen. Curtis E. LeMay, commander of SAC, spoke of smooth progress. Referring to Edwards's letter of 29 July, LeMay told him that he had contacted his unit commanders through personal correspondence. LeMay said that they were "making a serious effort to achieve its success." In LeMay's opinion, the policy was workable, but it required a maximum in flexibility to carry it out. He admittedly worried about social integration in southern communities and advised that there could be common use of recreational facilities but that social events would have to be scheduled separately. He promised to keep Edwards informed.[132]

LeMay also briefed his commanders on the necessity of exercising personal leadership. He told them that on certain stations, barracks integration would be gradual, extended initially to no more than 25 percent of those eligible. LeMay also informed his unit commanders that there had been unrest at Davis Monthan AFB, Arizona, because nearby Williams AFB had integrated socially, while Davis Monthan AFB had not. He further reported that some whites stated they would not reenlist because they could not live with blacks. Finally, he mentioned a group of blacks who were apprehensive because they were about to be transferred from California to Louisiana.[133]

When SAC's Eighth Air Force failed to act on barracks integration by October 1949, LeMay wrote its commander, Maj. Gen. Roger M. Ramey, to bring him in line::

> In your recent report on the success of integration of Negro troops in your command you stated that your units are still housing Negro troops in the Base Service Squadron rather than with the organization to which they have been assigned. . . . The requirement to billet and mess Negro troops with the white units which they are assigned is a basic concept of Air Force Letter 35-3 and will be included in a regulation to be published by this headquarters. The Air Force policy on integration of Negro troops is explicit and is expected to reach general accomplishment by the end of the calendar year. Therefore, if your commanders are to have the maximum time available to smoothly effect this required integration, it would be advisable to move to the next step—that of housing and messing.[134]

Such command interest ensured the rapid accomplishment of the mission, and the Fahy Committee was pleased at the manner as well as the celerity of air force integration. In late 1949 and early 1950 the executive secretary of the committee, E. W. Kenworthy, traveled with Jack Marr to inspect seven air force bases: Maxwell AFB, Alabama; Keesler AFB, Mississippi; Lackland AFB, Texas; Davis Monthan AFB, Arizona; Williams AFB, Arizona; Bolling AFB, Washington, D.C.; and Scott AFB, Illinois. In their travels, they discovered only one all-black service unit, at Maxwell AFB. Kenworthy reported that statistically about two-thirds of the air force blacks worked and lived in integrated conditions, with the remainder in service units. "Wherever I went," he wrote, "I saw Negro mechanics servicing and repairing planes in hangers and on the line. There were Negroes in radio repair. There were Negro instructors in classes. I saw Negroes in personnel work and in Air Police. There were Negro jet pilots." He admitted he did not see the entire range of air force jobs, but he did see a fairly broad sample, and wherever he went he observed "Negroes working with whites." He noted that air force policy statements had been limited to military utilization, leaving recreation and social life to the individual commanders. In the latter case, he found no fixed pattern.[135]

Thus, at some bases he found that swimming pools and clubs as well as dances were completely integrated, while at others there was "tacit, though incomplete and unenforced segregation in service clubs and pools," and separate dances for white and black enlisted personnel. Everywhere he saw integrated officer and NCO clubs, and "colored officers and NCOs made use of these clubs."[136] He saw less social integration at swimming pools. He wrote, "Negroes are no longer prohibited from using any pool, though the local custom varies." At bases which had two pools, apparently blacks preferred to use their own even when not required to do so. At other bases there was completely free use by both races. The same could be noted at club dances. Some were thoroughly mixed; others were not as well integrated. But "movies and athletic contests were everywhere unsegregated," and blacks were active on most service teams. He did find some air base commanders refusing to schedule southern athletic teams that would not play mixed military teams.[137]

Kenworthy spoke to many blacks and whites about integration and found many of the former were nervous about their continued prospects but were "agreeably surprised at [integration's] success." He found one black officer who believed that he would have had more retainability had he remained in the segregated 332d, but Kenworthy regarded him as an exception and stated: "I had the feeling that the Negroes were extremely anxious lest some untoward incidents should jeopardize the program, and they seemed determined this should not happen. Consequently they appeared to be acting with great circumspection, and while they were striving hard to take advantage of new opportunities in jobs and school, they were letting social relationships develop casually and naturally."[138]

Kenworthy noted that the southern press was critical of air force policy but that the bases in the South did not permit this to affect their on-base programs. He illustrated this by showing the complete working and school integration at Keesler AFB, Mississippi. He also commented on some voluntary social segregation. The base commander went a step further and forbade the scheduling of athletic events with local teams that would not play against blacks. Kenworthy did note that off-base social facilities available for blacks were deplorable. He visited "taverns, pool rooms, restaurants, and whorehouses" and found them appallingly filthy and degraded. He knew that the higher venereal disease rate for blacks had to be ascribed to these substandard conditions. He also knew that it was not his responsibility to investigate this but thought the President's Committee on Religion and Welfare in the Armed Forces might wish to do so.[139] Most blacks remained on base, where treatment was equal and more wholesome, but Kenworthy remained distressed at the fact that "men who have superior abilities required to take advanced technical training and are a credit to the armed services of their country should be forced to seek recreation in such spots."[140]

At Lackland AFB, Texas, Kenworthy noted that black counselors advised both blacks and whites and that basic training at this base was totally integrated. He found blacks attending most schools at Lackland and noticed no social segregation among officers but some among NCOs.[141] The situation at Maxwell AFB, Alabama, however, was not as satisfactory. Only a small number of blacks were assigned to white units. Most black airmen had duty assignments to the 3817th base service squadron. This squadron was manned by 269 blacks, and although they worked with whites on a duty interspersal basis, they were housed in separate barracks and fed in their own mess. Kenworthy found the separate facilities pleasant and no different from the white facilities and considered the food "plentiful" and well prepared." He reported that the men had voted to remain separate, except for 14 who were immediately transferred to the barracks of the employing units. The handful who had transferred said that they were well treated in the former white units. The 3817th had its own service clubs, swimming pool, and movie theater. Conditions, however, were not hopelessly rigid even at Maxwell. An incident was reported in which three blacks attempted to attend a base service club dance and the local civilian chaperone demanded that they be sent away. An officer on the scene refused to dismiss the blacks, but a local newspaper complained about the disturbance. A similar conflict occurred at the base swimming pool, but there again the blacks were made welcome. Within the 3817th's complement of men, only 58 were involved in actual base service activities, and 211 were assigned to 29 separate organizations, including the Air University Library, Base Operations, and Wing Headquarters.[142]

Despite his negative experience at Maxwell AFB, Kenworthy was very pleased with the success of the new integration policy and credited two factors for its favorable outcome—command leadership and the willingness of the men to accept integration. He found that the officers had been initially apprehensive about the new policy but discovered their "fears to have been completely groundless." These men were "amazed at the ease with which the new policy had been effected and the absence of trouble." Even southern officers who disliked racial integration and expressed a desire to return to segregation had admitted the new policy worked well and without friction. Most officers told Kenworthy that the new policy meant increased military efficiency and an end to chronic charges of discrimination. These men found that placing blacks and whites together in a competitive environment with rigid standards of equality improved race relations. Kenworthy concluded:

> The new racial policy of the Air Force supplies its own moral and military justification. Nevertheless, it is in my opinion after visiting seven bases, that the success of this reform can be attributed in large measure to the quality and resolution of command.
>
> The Air Force issued its policy and let it be known that ungrudging compliance with the spirit as well as the letter was expected. Thereafter it left implementation to local commanders.
>
> Individual commanders used their own judgment in putting the policy into effect. Some commanders carefully briefed their staff officers, who in turn briefed squadron commanders, and so on . . . . Other commanders treated the new policy as merely a routine administrative procedure, and simply issued orders to their staff. . . . [The] difference in method had little effect on results, so long as there was determination to carry out the order. To this resolution of command can be attributed, I

think, the ease with which this policy has been effected. Unquestionably, however, the almost total absence of opposition that had been anticipated in the enlisted men is a contributing factor in the success of the policy. The men apparently were more ready for equality of treatment and opportunity than the officer corps had realized.[143]

Changing Military Attitudes

Anticipated hostility by white enlisted men had long been a reason for not integrating. Throughout the years the military had actually polled whites to obtain their attitude toward integration. The results of the polls generally indicated that whites opposed it, although a poll taken after the limited integration of 1945 and another during the Korean War showed that whites who had served with blacks had no great antipathy toward integration.[144] The army, still attempting to stave off integration, polled its enlisted men during May and June 1949 and found that 32 percent "definitely opposed" any kind of limited or total integration, while only 39 percent were "not definitely opposed to integration." The service found also that more than 60 percent were "definitely opposed to *complete* integration." The expected majority (73 percent) of southerners expressed negative views, but 50 percent of the northerners had similar attitudes. The results were clear.[145] There took place, however, subtle changes in attitudes within the air force, of which the Pentagon was not always aware.

Only those familiar with studies that emanated from the senior and intermediate air force and service schools during this postwar period would have noted the change. The studies indicated a reversal away from racism and the extreme prejudice evident a decade earlier and a willingness to experiment. The student recommendations were not radical, but their attitude was fundamentally different. No longer did they stress black congenital inferiority, but rather they blamed whites for retarding black development. With such thinking, a change in policy was possible. The reports of the late 1940s were in advance of air force practice and even official policy. Most historians believe the post–World War II years to be a racial turning point, and the Air War College, the Air Command and Staff College, and the Industrial College of the Armed Forces (ICAF) studies bear out that assumption. What they reveal is tentative, hesitant, ambivalent, and ambiguous, but for all that, when measured against the reports of the previous decade, these postwar studies were positive.

The clearest example, of course, and one that is hardly ambiguous is Noel Parrish's thesis, which he wrote while attending the Air Command and Staff College in the spring of 1947. He was the first to discuss this subject after the war and clearly supported integration. He found that segregation damaged international relations, that the navy had proven integration could work, that industry had demonstrated its success, and that efficiency and justice demanded it. He wrote:

Compulsory segregation in the armed forces is an evasion of two simple facts. The facts are: Thirteen million Americans are classified by custom as Negroes; law and necessity confer upon these Negro Americans the rights and responsibilities of American citizenship. Decency and justice may be ignored, as they often are, but the facts remain. . . .

There is no more obvious illustration of the rights and the responsibilities of citizenship than service in the Armed Forces. Any limitation on a man's equal right in the service of the nation tends to destroy the equality of his responsibilities. . . .

Segregation is the refusal to apply the American system to Negro individuals.[146]

Parrish's statement was the clearest call, but not the only one. Lt. Col. Solomon Cutcher, in his Air Command and Staff College thesis, declared that beliefs in racial superiority were bigoted hypotheses maintained by those who had an interest in perpetuating racism because they benefited from it. The armed forces of the United States, he wrote, "cannot afford to subscribe to any doctrine based upon a premise of permanent racial superiority anymore than they can afford to wage war with antiquated weapons." Cutcher claimed that the limiting factors affecting blacks in 1948 were "scientifically proven to be products of environment and not characteristic of race." He blamed racial friction within the service on whites who had entered the military with racist beliefs. It was his view that it was the mission of the military to reeducate bigots in order to create a more efficient force.[147]

In the interim between the issuance of Truman's executive order and the air force's announcement of integration, there appeared cautious essays in support of integration. Lt. Col. John B. Gaffney, an Air Command and Staff College student, called for the "gradual and eventual elimination of racial segregation" because such a policy would lead to a more "effective utilization of all personnel" and because it would be economical. He recommended indoctrination of all personnel to make such a program work.[148] Another officer at the school, Maj. Hugh D. Young, stated that the air force was unprepared for large-scale use of blacks and should prepare itself. He wrote, "Certainly as a nation we have expended valuable energies in perpetuating the wasteful and sterile luxury of bi-racial [sic] institutions, we have actually wasted the human resources of Negro Americans by submitting them to [the] relentless system of frustration and rejection." He noted that American whites were no less bigoted within the military than outside it, and he warned against inflexible race mixing. Indiscriminate mixing might lower morale, even of the blacks who might be stationed with prejudiced whites. Pressure politics, he warned, must not force the air force to adopt a morale-lowering, inefficient policy, and all changes should be made in the direction of a more efficient air force.[149]

In 1948 a major study, "Training and Utilization of Manpower," was prepared at the ICAF in Washington, D.C., for use in an "Economic Mobilization" course. It was written by a study committee consisting of 22 officers from the air force, army, and navy. The committee's overall goal was to examine critically the problems of wartime manpower utilization, to evaluate the "effectiveness of the methods and techniques used to meet these problems in World War II," and to propose future procedures. Almost one-half of their final report was devoted to an examination of "The Negro."[150]

According to the study committee, there were no racial characteristics that distinguished men, and such differences as were noted were cultural. The group maintained that the "feeling that the Negro is an inferior product of humanity and unfit to associate with the white population is a prejudice born in the era of slavery. It was stimulated in the South by the experiences of the Reconstruction Period and is nourished even today."[151] The committee pointed out the myriad of ways blacks had been discriminated against in housing, schooling, and in employment but did not suggest that the services could cope with the problem of national prejudice and its by-products. This body advocated federal assistance to upgrade the educational level of the blacks and insisted that the South make educational opportunities truly equal. The study noted the wide financial differentials between white and black schools to be disheartening for the latter.[152] The committee discovered that blacks were less healthy than whites and attributed this to discrimination in health care. In all, the study group argued that racism denied to the United States healthy, educated, and cultured blacks; and thus the military was deprived of the full benefit of the black segment of the population.[153]

The committee advocated a separate but truly equal distribution of facilities to bring the blacks up to white levels and to make the former more acceptable in a socially integrated society.[154] The study group was aware of the manpower drain of the last war and believed the United States could not fight another, which the study estimated would require a labor force of 70 million men, with 10 percent of the population in prejudiced deprivation.[155] This argument led to a dilemma. The ICAF committee knew that deprived blacks did not have the required skills. To train them, it was necessary for employers to hire them and for white workers to be willing to work with them. The committee thought that time could solve the problem in peacetime but that war might create tensions. The writers were particularly fearful that men like A. Philip Randolph and other black leaders might seize the initiative in another war to force changes that might adversely affect the white population. They were appalled by Randolph's suggestions that blacks evade a segregated draft. Clearly something had to be done, but the committee did not know what could be done. Blacks needed greater economic opportunities, but the study maintained management and labor should not be forced to accept them.[156]

The military, argued the study group, was in similar straits. Only as society changed could the military employ more blacks.[157] The ICAF students agreed that a division into white and black units was not the answer and that placing blacks in service units was unfair to the nation. For the students of this problem, the solution was to develop leadership, provide extensive training, and employ blacks "with or near white troops in order that their conception of standards may be raised and the white soldiers may be used as "pace-setters."[158]

In the end, the ICAF committee members recommended nothing more than additional study of the problem, but their hostility toward racism and their recognition of its damage to blacks meant that they were on the brink of change. The group wrote:

> Although without logical, anthropological or sociological foundation the suspicions, distrusts, beliefs and attitudes that both Negro and white races have for each other must be considered. While regulations, laws and orders can force the indiscriminate mixing of the races in a military organization, it does not assure per se that such an organization will be effective. . . . Compliance will be with the letter of the law rather than with the spirit behind it. . . . Forced associations can result in discord, distrust, discontent, and racial cliques which are weak foundations on which to build a combat organization.[159]

The committee argued that the services were well ahead of society, and it simply recommended another committee be formed. It proposed:

> The Secretary of Defense [should] prepare a report for submission to the Chairman of the National Security Resources Board outlining the need for raising the general health and educational levels of the American Negro in order that his maximum utilization in time of national emergency be realized.
> The Armed Forces [must] not be influenced by the political pressure of Negro leadership which has a goal secondary to, and which may be detrimental to national security.
> The present policies of each of the three services [should] be subject to such modification as may be practicable based on the rising public acceptance of the Negro.[160]

Echoing the findings of the group, an air force colonel, Lester L. Kunish, also recognized the wastefulness of the current system and worried about forced integration. He advocated a more complete utilization within a segregated framework but added that as society integrated, so should the military. He wrote: "The Air Force must recognize that eventually the Negro will earn complete parity with the white, and it should prepare him for his greater future role in the military by continuously developing methods of employing him in a way that will not provoke or aggravate racial friction but will integrate him completely and effectively." Still, he saw the future in terms of segregation. "Segregation," he said, "must still be maintained for the good of the Air Force, but gradual studied progress toward complete integration should be made as rapidly as possible."[161]

Other students of the question became more vehement about the effects of racism but were unable to overcome the psychological barrier of recommending something the services were not doing. Maj. John J. Pesch wrote in his Air Command and Staff College thesis: "Racial antagonisms are not the result of inexorable nature nor of inherited instincts, but of deliberate education and cultivation. The qualities which we most dislike in Negroes are precisely those which have been so acquired and are therefore capable of being modified by a different environment." He added, "Treatment of the Negro is the greatest barrier to America's leadership." Since he found blacks educationally inferior to whites, however, he disqualified race mixing. Once blacks had achieved equality of education, he argued, integration could proceed. Although he admitted biological equality, he expected such a solution as integration to "consume decades of time."[162]

Prior to the air force decision to integrate, several studies recommended abandonment of segregation. Maj. James D. Catington, an Air Command and Staff College student, wrote that segregation and discrimination were "erroneous in nature and without foundation in fact." Segregation, he stated, furthermore violated basic human rights and "both the spirit and letter of the Constitution." He advocated an educational program that would make the new air force policy well-known and acceptable to all. He recommended "the complete and active abolishment of the policy of segregation of Negro troops." He suggested that an "adequate and thorough indoctrination of the rank and file of the Armed Forces be undertaken to apprise members of the military establishment of the nature of the non-segregation policy in order to secure an unreserved acceptance by both Negroes and whites alike."[163]

Once the integration policy was promulgated, various authors eagerly supported the program. Lt. Col. Jack E. Cunningham wrote: "It is the firm conviction of the author that the non-segregation policy can work successfully only if positive measures are taken to educate officers and airmen in order to erase or at least minimize their prejudice. . . . In terms of simple economy there is ample justification for this. . . . Eradication of a foolish prejudice and the granting of fair and equal treatment to all, should keep morale high. . . . Under these conditions, the Negro and the white can work together in the 'non-segregated' Air Force team."[164]

After the policy was implemented, the Pentagon learned of examples of how eager whites were to have blacks on the air force team. A San Antonio air base reported several attempts of white airmen trying, with their new friends, to end segregation in San Antonio. In August 1949 air force blacks and whites integrated Sommers' drugstores, resulting in a white protest. At first, three whites entered the store and ordered four sundaes, explaining that their buddy would join them momentarily. Once the ice cream had been served, the fourth, a black, joined them at the counter. This initially upset the white manager, but all four were able to eat and leave in peace. During later incidents drugstore officials refused to be integrated or else served the airmen while other whites walked out. The owner, Mr. Sommers, received threatening mail warning him that if his "policy is to serve niggers in your cafeteria as you did on Saturday night . . . you cannot expect white patronage." He also received a telephone call expressing the same view.[165]

During the drugstore integration attempts, other establishments were also visited by "salt and pepper" teams, with varying results. A sit-in took place at a Walgreen's drugstore later in August. An intelligence summary describing these events states that premeditation was indicated, and the entire report was based upon information provided by usually reliable sources and was therefore probably true.[166]

Jack Marr noted these events when he prepared a report summarizing the first year of air force integration. He said that there were more attempts of this kind—for example, whites trying to lessen the humiliation of segregation—than negative racial incidents. He did cite other problems. For example, blacks attempted to test integration in base barbershops by getting haircuts from white barbers. When bigoted whites tried to force blacks to stay in a corner of the barracks, appropriate action was taken to eliminate friction. Some whites stated that they would not reenlist if integration continued. Some parents requested transfers for their sons, but on the whole "parents appeared more concerned than the men." The command structure was more effective in the speeding of integration than was the geographic location. At the time Marr's report was compiled, there were 24 predominantly black units remaining in the air force, but the pace of change was encouraging. Social integration progressed slowly, and that too was becoming a reality. The men who worked and lived together also partook in recreation together. Marr said that all indications from confidential command reports and from outside observers showed that the program worked better than even the optimists had anticipated.[167]

Most major air commands during the first year of integration reported on the implementation of AFL 35-3 in their command histories. Thereafter all mention of blacks disappears until the 1960s. SAC demonstrated how the 25 percent black-white merger helped integration advance very satisfactorily, but the command noted that there were problems in social integration, especially in the NCO clubs. The practice was introduced of establishing branch clubs on the same base, and it was tacitly understood that one club was for whites and the other for blacks.[168]

The ATC on its own instituted a 10 percent quota to prevent bases from becoming overpopulated with blacks. The command also tried to ensure that the first blacks sent to previously white bases were of the highest caliber possible, to ease the shock of integration. ATC's history states: "A nucleus of high type, well trained and properly oriented Negro airmen would serve as a forerunner in establishing the confidence necessary to facilitate increased assimilation of Negro personnel."

The command at the same time refused to reassign blacks in large numbers, moving them in small groups to bases over a 30-to-60-day period to cushion the impact.[169]

The Ninth Air Force history records the Lockbourne breakup. The commander of the Ninth Air Force, Maj. Gen. Robert D. Old, discovered that blacks he knew were generally disappointed because they were not socially accepted even though on-the-job integration was completed. He remarked that the "intelligent Negro appears to feel that he would rather be in an all-Negro organization."[170]

The Ninth Air Force later played host to Dr. Mordecai Johnson, president of Howard University, who visited Langley AFB to evaluate the success of integration. Behind closed doors, he interviewed 50 black airmen picked at random. Johnson had been skeptical about integration but was pleased with what he saw and heard. He did take note of the fact that the NCO club was not fully open to blacks, but he was assured that the situation was being corrected. He also was discouraged by the small complement of black officers and the minuscule number of active pilots (30 in number).[171]

The air force record was good and a prod to the other services. The Fahy Committee commented favorably upon the air force's ability to integrate a large number of individuals (more than 20,000) and believed the navy could do better than it had, since most blacks in that service were still messmen and segregated. The air force had demonstrated to itself, to the Fahy Committee, and, by inference, to the other services that blacks had a wider range of abilities than anybody had thought. It also discovered that even with high enlistment standards, a large number of blacks were deemed qualified for air force service.[172]

The black press, which followed with great interest the air force's achievement, criticized the army for remaining segregated.[173] When the air force apparently decided not to bar black aviators from southern bases to placate southern representatives and senators who sat on appropriations committees, the *Pittsburgh Courier* applauded in a page-one headline: "Air Force Won't Give In to Dixie."[174] This journal and other leading black newspapers followed every phase of integration during the first six months. In a series of articles, a *Courier* reporter, Collins George, traveled throughout the United States to observe the extent of compliance of the armed forces with integration directives. He was not completely satisfied with the air force, but he found its policy well in advance of that of the army. His report was published on 28 July 1951 below a banner headline which proclaimed: "2 Calif. Bases Confirm Air Force Lead in Integration." George visited Travis and Hamilton and declared that these bases confirmed "the already well known fact that the Air Force so far out distances the other services in the manner of racial integration—both on the enlisted and officer level—that comparison is impossible." He observed: "When one sees the ease and efficiency with which the Air Force policy works, one wonders why the other services will not go into the integration with the same wholeheartedness, if only for the simple good of the services. It takes only a firm policy enunciated by top authority with equal firmness in seeing that the policy is carried out."[175]

At Williams AFB, Arizona, he noted that black pilots were fully accepted, and he labeled the air base the most dramatic of the air force bases he had visited. He was heartened by the fact that blacks and whites were being trained as jet pilots according to the same standards.[176] He found no segregation at Williams but complained bitterly about segregation in nearby Phoenix.

Maxwell AFB, Alabama, on the other hand, received no praise. George visited headquarters' Air University in April 1951 and wrote about what he saw. His story in the *Courier* was headlined: "Morale Is Extremely Low in 'Shantytown'" and "Segregated Unit Sore Spot at Maxwell Field Air Base." He blamed part of the problem on the vicious effects of nearby Montgomery, Alabama, the first capital of the Confederacy. He reported that the base did proceed to integrate (probably because the men were permitted to work alongside whites). But he found that the men were miserable. He scoffed at statements that blacks—described as "pent-up [with] discontent and dissatisfaction"—had voluntarily decided to segregate themselves. After talking with the blacks, he learned that the black area lacked proper equipment and other amenities. He attributed these unsatisfactory conditions to the base command element, which was dominated by southern officers, and he denounced them for their bias.[177] This unit, however, was fully integrated before the end of 1952.[178]

Unsympathetic whites at Brookley AFB near Mobile, Alabama, created problems. Concerned about having black civilians on the base, they protested the lowering of racial barriers. Some whites on three occasions bludgeoned blacks for drinking water out of fountains, and the whites were punished. The base commander subsequently warned all Brookley personnel that he would not tolerate such intimidation or coercion. All supervisors were required to sign statements that they were aware of Truman's executive order on equal opportunity.[179]

The move to an integrated service created diplomatic problems for the air force. Several foreign countries—Denmark, Canada, and Great Britain—refused to accept blacks at air bases provided to the United States in their various possessions. The air force asked the State Department to work out this problem. Although many months of diplomatic negotiations followed, the problem was eventually resolved, and these countries agreed to accept black airmen anywhere.[180]

Records in the National Archives and the Library of Congress contain little evidence of rabid protest or critical problems following the initial era of integration. One southern judge, opposed to air force integration, wrote to Secretary of Defense Johnson to inform him that forcing "white boys into armed services" with blacks was "crushing their spirits." He condemned Truman for dismantling segregation to garner the black vote and claimed the president was impairing the safety of the nation. He called Truman a "moral murderer" and said the president should be impeached. The judge concluded:

> I would not blame any white man forced to train, eat, sleep and be mixed with Negroes while sick to burn the cantonment buildings, shoot the insolent Negro officers and non-commissioned officers as the occasion arose and I believe they will shoot them when they are in battle. This country is going to lose any major war in which it depends upon Negro troops to win. . . . If you know anything, you know that the Negro soldier in the first and second world wars were not worth a damn, notwithstanding the propaganda and lies spread to the contrary by the administration in Washington, the Negro press and Negro politicians.[181]

Gov. J. Strom Thurmond (Dem., S.C.) complained to Secretary of the Air Force Symington—through Sen. Burnet R. Maybank (Dem., S.C.)—that 35 Clemson University ROTC cadets were housed with black ROTC cadets at Lowry AFB, Colorado, during their summer encampment. Thurmond predicted violence and demanded resegregation. Secretary Symington, however, cited the air force's successes in integrating officer training and its enlisted force.[182] An Alabama congressman complained to Assistant Secretary of the Air Force Eugene Zuckert that a constituent's son had protested sleeping and eating in the same areas with blacks and demanded a transfer. Zuckert, in turn, recommended a discharge for the unhappy white.[183] The success of air force integration in the year 1950 is attested by a Secretary of Defense file on "Negro Problems." It contained not a single paper on air force integration problems.[184] Clearly, the air force had succeeded in integrating with a minimum of friction, in a minimum amount of time.

The integration process advanced rapidly and smoothly. The air force inspector general did not mention integration in a lengthy report to the vice chief of staff that discussed major problems, although racial policy was reviewed. Apparently integration was not a problem.[185] Indeed, official air force unit histories written during the 1950s scarcely took notice of integration other than to mention that it had gone well. By the end of June 1952—during the Korean War—the last all-black unit disappeared without notice.[186]

In the late 1940s—a period without fierce racial tensions—it was possible to become sentimental about the achievements of integration. A review of air force integration from the perspective of that decade indicates that acceptance was not generally expected. Even the most sanguine of individuals had harbored fears, which made the trouble-free implementation of desegregation more than welcome. Its success reflected the views of a handful of pragmatists who were determined not to let racists stand in the way. Men like General Edwards and Lt. Col. Jack Marr helped to open a new chapter in air force history.

Lee Nichols commented extensively about the change in air force thinking. Having had access to air staff personnel reports that reflected a remarkable social change, he spread the good news. Whites who continued to oppose integration for air force blacks were quietly removed from their posts. Racial conflict seemed all but ended. At Lowry AFB, Colorado, an ATC installation, the base commander (a general officer) told Nichols he had no idea how many blacks were on this facility. This comment clearly reflected the progress the air force had made. The general reported that blacks performed as well as whites in various courses. He stated further that integration was the best policy for the air force, and "that's a southerner speaking."[187]

He did speculate momentarily that the military services might become a haven for blacks, who recognized that it was the best-possible situation for blacks, and he expressed concern that the services might become predominantly black in the future. Another commander at Keesler AFB, Mississippi, who told Nichols he was Virginia-born, stated that integration had been no problem. He admitted that he had been skeptical about mixing the races at first but had seen clearly that the policy was a correct one.[188]

Nichols also believed that the impact of integration would be as great or greater on America than it was on the military. A native of Biloxi, Mississippi, commented that the men leaving the service would be sure to retain at least some of their integration experiences with positive benefits. He added: "Our airmen who are discharged have different views in civilian life than they had before. It happens more and more every day. They are learning to live with Negroes." Anna M. Rosenberg, an assistant secretary of defense (1950–53), supported Nichols's contention. "In the long run," she noted, "I don't think a man can live and fight next to one of another race and share experiences where life is at stake, and not have a strong feeling of understanding when he comes home." The chief of air force chaplains told Nichols: "You can't turn a million guys into the military this year, and have them live and work together without segregation, without some impression when they return to their own communities. Integration is already having an impact, though not out in the open. It is working like yeast, quietly."[189]

Nichols also believed the military was having an impact on the nearby civilian communities. Some communities were altering their racial customs. Amarillo University accepted black airmen along with whites in their extension-course program. Previously, the school had been segregated. George L. B. Weaver of the Congress of Industrial Organizations (CIO) Civil Rights Committee credited military integration with improving industrial race relations because it firmly put the government on record as practicing what it said about equal opportunity.[190] Nichols praised the military for showing the country the way by demonstrating that it could be done and by molding men who were less bigoted than they were before entering the military service. He stated: "From all available evidence the great majority of men in integrated units took home a fresh slant on race free from the basic concept of segregation that once dominated the American scene. This type of experience was certain to influence not only the men themselves but also their families, friends, and casual acquaintances."[191]

Nichols watched with obvious pleasure the lowering of community racial barriers. Near one northern location, a local bar owner was told by base officials to serve all military personnel or his establishment would be declared off-limits. The owner integrated.[192] In this situation, however, Nichols was overly optimistic, for this became a serious problem area in the 1960s. Nichols in 1953 looked for the bright side, found a positive example, and who could fault him for broadcasting it? In February of that year, Col. James F. Olive, commander of Harlingen AFB near Brownsville, Texas, received the following letter from a white church in a tightly segregated community:

> It is with pleasure that we inform you of the following motion that was unanimously passed by . . . our church. . . . "That the commanding officer of the Harlingen Air Force Base be asked to invite all officers and airmen of the . . . Base, regardless of race or color, to attend any or all of our church services. . . ." We will appreciate any action you may take that will make the officers and airmen under your command, regardless of race or color, feel free to worship God with us in our church. We commend the actions of the Air Force in your program of eliminating race discrimination, and hope that our action may be at least a step forward in uniting our people as one under God.

Nichols believed that before this letter was sent, "probably no Negro had ever been admitted to a white Protestant church in Brownsville. . . . Racial integration in the military was exercising a powerful influence on civilian habits, it was inevitable it should."[193]

Once the air force had completed integration, USAF officials took less note of continuing problems, including prejudiced communities with which blacks were forced to interact, individual bigots in uniform who overtly or covertly discriminated against or humiliated blacks, and the changing racial climate in the United States. It was ironical that the air force, which had been well ahead of the civilian sector in the late 1940s and the 1950s, missed the tone and tempo of the black civil rights revolution of the 1960s. It may be significant to note that the original letter on equal opportunity (AFL 35-3) was revised in September 1950 and later issued as an air force regulation (AFR 35-78), but with few changes. It remained in force until 1955, when it was rewritten and its title changed to "Air Force Personnel Policy Regarding Minority Groups." The regulation admonished commanders to carry out the air force's policy of equal treatment and opportunity. It did not tell them how to do this and offered no guidance for eliminating the prejudiced service member or for improving the lot of blacks in nearby local communities.[194] When the regulation was superseded in 1964 by a very specific directive, it changed the whole face of air force race relations. But this came after the air force seemed to lose its interest in promoting equal opportunity for black airmen and officers on and off base.

4   Benign Neglect

y 1952 the air force had completely desegregated and concluded that integration had been completed. Those officials responsible for desegregation were transferred to other posts. In 1951 General Edwards was appointed commander at the Air University, Maxwell AFB, Alabama, and Colonel Marr was reassigned to a European post. Marr was not replaced and would have been the first to question the need for replacement. He and Edwards believed the problem had been resolved—since all-black units had disappeared and blacks were working and socializing with white airmen. In the early 1950s there seemed to be no disputing the fact that the air force was integrated. The black press, a leader in the integration campaign, seemed satisfied, and the air force became the model for the other services. When the army, the marines, and the navy desegregated during the 1950s, the race problem seemed to be resolved. Few spokesmen of prominence within the military or black community addressed at this time the problems of racial discrimination which most blacks faced within the civilian communities.[1] These problems were not addressed during the last years of the Truman administration, which found itself involved in a hot war in Korea.[2]

The Korean War
The Korean War (1950–53) underscored the fact of integration. The black press covered the war and wrote numerous news stories about individual air force blacks in the Far East and many favorable articles about air force integration. The disbandment of all-black units, however, made it more difficult to report on black airmen's achievements.

The *Pittsburgh Courier* headlined one edition: "Tan Fliers . . . over Korea." The paper reported that six blacks were flying in combat. The following week the *Courier* in a headline article reported that "25 Tan Fliers Battle Reds" but admitted that it was difficult to state precisely the number of blacks engaged in combat, since the air force did not keep records by race.[3] The black press focused on Capt. Daniel "Chappie" James, who gained prominence as a pilot of an unarmed reconnaissance jet, flying dangerous missions over North Korea. The articles usually stressed that a white airman operated a camera in the back seat of his aircraft.[4] Front-page coverage also was given to 1st Lt. Dayton Ragland, the first black to shoot down a MIG aircraft.[5] Ragland later was shot down and became a prisoner of war for the duration of the conflict.

The theme of most news accounts, however, was not of individual heroism but of the fact of integration. The *Baltimore Afro-American* said that war correspondents described integration in two words: "Air Corps." It added, "No one here will challenge their right to spell it that way."[6] The *Pittsburgh Courier* called Yokota Air Base, Japan, a "perfect model of race harmony" and noted that whites and blacks forgot about race and color and went about their "work and sociabilities in absolute harmony."[7] Yet the real story in Korea was not air force integration but army desegregation, for that war demolished forever a centuries-old tradition of separatism. For every black flyer the air force graduated, the army produced hundreds of black combat soldiers, and the black press began to report their exploits in 1950 and 1951.[8]

One item of disagreeable air force marginalia survived to indicate that the upbeat stories in the black press did not tell the full story. Lt. Gen. Earle E. Partridge, commander, Far East Air Forces (FEAF), decided to remove blacks from duty as forward air controllers after several had twice misdirected fire on friendly troops. He wrote in his diary:

> I discovered on the third of January, strikes were made in the Uijonbu area by Navy aircraft, operating under a Fifth Air Force controller. It developed that the controller was a Negro pilot. This makes the second time that a Negro controller has placed strikes on our own troops. I am forced to the unhappy conclusion that certain of these people are not temperamentally suited for such important assignments. Accordingly I issued orders . . . to quietly remove from Mosquito Squadrons all Negro pilots . . . when the Negro pilots with the TACP's [Tactical Air Control Party] finish the tour no more Negroes [will be] assigned to that type of duty.[9]

The numbers affected by the directive could not have been many, but it is significant to note that some military leaders continued to generalize about an entire race because of the poor performance of a few. Before the Korean War ended in July 1953, a new administration entered the White House, and blacks thereafter received less moral support from President Dwight D. Eisenhower than from his predecessor, Harry Truman.

Soon after the end of the Korean conflict, the last all-black units in the army disappeared. By 1952 military discrimination seemed a dead issue, although Eisenhower tried to capitalize on his role in integrating the U.S. Army in Europe. Neither political party in that year vigorously sought black votes. The ticket of Gov. Adlai E. Stevenson of Illinois and Sen. John J. Sparkman of Alabama could hardly afford to do so, and the ticket of Eisenhower and Sen. Richard M. Nixon probably did not want to. The black press conducted muted campaigns for the candidates, in contrast to 1944 and 1948. Although the black press took stands, there was little fire in the editorials. The *Pittsburgh Courier* endorsed Eisenhower in its edition on the eve of the election, but its coverage until then had been almost neutral. The newspaper headlined, "Ike and the 99th" and claimed that Ike had "kept them on 'Wings.'" In a breathless style the paper advised: "Now it can be told. . . . A decision which saw General Dwight D. Eisenhower going 'all out' for the first Negro fliers ever to soar into the skies against an enemy of this country." The article lacked names, dates, or other substantiating evidence, but the fact that the newspaper had to reach far back in time to say something nice about the Republican candidate is clear evidence of the poverty of the Republican Party's civil rights platform. In addition, the paper carried numerous photographs of Eisenhower and predicted his victory. Again, articles on the second page recounted how Eisenhower had fought segregation in the army.[10]

The *Baltimore Afro-American* endorsed Stevenson, apparently because the newspaper did not find Eisenhower strong on civil rights. The latter was attacked for his negative statements on military integration and civil rights prior to 1948, and one issue claimed, "Ike flunks initial tests on Civil Rights."[11] The paper in an October 1952 edition displayed a photograph of the home of his running mate, Nixon, with a photostat of the restrictive covenant Nixon and his wife had signed promising not to sell to any "person or persons of Negro blood or extraction . . . of the semitic race, blood or origin, which racial description shall be deemed to exclude Armenians, Jews, Hebrews, Persians, and Syrians." All of the above could be welcomed into the neighborhood as "servants."[12] On 11 October, the *Baltimore Afro-American* endorsed Stevenson, more it would seem for distaste of the Eisenhower-Nixon ticket than for fondness of Stevenson and his running mate, Sparkman.[13]

Eisenhower and Civil Rights

Eisenhower had no black constituency and did little for blacks. The 1954 Supreme Court decision on school segregation was another matter. In his memoirs, the former president did not claim any credit for this decision on school segregation. He admitted that he found the decision sound, emphasizing again that he had said nothing in its support originally but finally getting himself on record after almost a decade of silence.[14] Civil rights legislation during the Eisenhower years was not of a revolutionary nature and received little presidential backing. When the *Pittsburgh Courier* endorsed Eisenhower in 1956, it supported him for his conservative views and not for his leadership on racial matters.[15] Even the *Baltimore Afro-American* gave qualified approval of the Republican ticket, in the hope that a landslide might sweep away the Democratic senators opposed to integration.[16]

This is not to say that Eisenhower did utterly nothing but that he was passive when the tide of expectations was rising steadily. A journalist, Robert J. Donovan, who closely scrutinized the first Eisenhower administration, wrote, "When the administration took office . . . no one gave much thought to the special problems of the Negro, and practically nothing was done about this politically very sensitive matter." He concluded that in the early months of 1953 "the matter of civil rights was let slide." Unlike Truman, Donovan wrote, "Eisenhower had deliberately refrained from assigning anyone on his staff to a more or less full-time job of attending to the problems of minority groups."[17] But two years after taking office, Eisenhower issued an executive order establishing a President's Committee on Government Employment Policy. This committee reaffirmed and monitored the equal opportunity program within the civil service initiated by his predecessor, but it was not a dramatic gesture.[18] In 1956, however, the president requested civil rights legislation and won a victory the following year with the passage of the Civil Rights Act, the first such legislation in more than fourscore years.[19] He also sent federal troops into Little Rock to support the Supreme Court's 1954 school desegregation decision.[20] These presidential acts, however, did not retain the black vote for the Republican ticket in 1960.

An early Eisenhower executive action that did have impact on the armed services was his decision to integrate dependents' schools on military posts before the Supreme Court ordered general school integration. In March 1953 Eisenhower sent a memorandum to Defense Secretary Charles Wilson requesting data on segregated schools operating on military installations. Wilson advised the president that there were 21 schools operating on a segregated basis on military posts. He also informed Eisenhower that he wanted to end school segregation quickly and requested firm instructions to do so. The secretary of defense acknowledged that desegregating these schools would be difficult because they were operated by local authorities and therefore came under local laws which maintained racial segregation. He suggested that if the federal government dictated integration, teachers might leave the schools, accreditation problems might arise, and the federal government would probably have to provide more funds. Despite the anticipated problems, Wilson wanted to integrate. "I suggest," he wrote to the president, "that . . . this problem would be expedited if you were to direct that the procedures for integration are to be finalized so that the objectives can be accomplished not later than the school year beginning in the fall of 1955."[21] Even before Wilson's letter, Eisenhower had ordered the end of segregation at the Fort Benning elementary school beginning in September 1953. The school, unlike others on federal posts, was wholly supported by the government and did not depend on local funds for teachers' salaries or for operating costs.[22]

Eisenhower moved cautiously on the question of other segregated schools. Within his cabinet, the secretary of the Department of Health, Education and Welfare, Oveta Culp Hobby, advised deliberation. In a memorandum to the president, she recommended he act slowly and do nothing for the time being. She cited the problem areas noted by Wilson and introduced new issues which today do not appear to be too serious. There were, she wrote, small numbers of "local children . . . now attending the on-base schools," though they did not live on military posts. What was to become of these children? How would children be affected if after leaving military-supported integrated elementary schools, they were forced to attend segregated secondary schools? Finally, she advised Eisenhower that the best reason for delaying a decision was that the Supreme Court was then studying the entire question of segregated schools and that it would be helpful to have the "benefit of the Supreme Court's decision on the segregation issue" before taking executive action. She concluded by warning Eisenhower about the impact such a move would have on southern members of Congress. She recommended that he wait until more information could be gathered.[23]

It is difficult to evaluate Eisenhower's position during this internal debate. He does not appear to have taken a firm stand. Records in the Eisenhower Library indicate that the question was discussed. A draft letter from Sherman Adams, assistant to the president, to Congressman Adam Clayton Powell (Dem., N.Y.) contains a statement which would have committed the administration to desegregating schools on federal installations, but someone later removed the sentence from the final draft of the letter. It is impossible to establish with certainty who ordered the material deleted, but it does show indecision on this question.[24] Eisenhower's conservative supporters recommended he shun the issue. Gov. Allan Shivers of Texas urged the president to stay out of the entire school desegregation thicket and leave such matters to the people at the "local level."[25]

For all of the indecision, in late 1953—more than eight months prior to the Supreme Court integration order—the Defense Department announced its decision to desegregate schools on military posts within two years at the latest. If local school boards would not cooperate, the federal government would finance the schools. The two-year lead time would provide an opportunity to iron out all details.[26] On 12 January 1954 Defense Secretary Wilson directed the service secretaries to take "appropriate steps" to ensure that the operation of all schools on military posts was conducted on an integrated basis. Effective that date, no new schools opened were to be segregated, and all schools had to be integrated by the opening of the 1955 school term. Wilson also outlined a policy for operating the schools should the community fail to cooperate.[27] The Defense Department's program to desegregate was hastened after the Supreme Court *Brown* decision in May 1954. The elementary school at Maxwell AFB, Alabama, was integrated in the fall of 1954 without the cooperation of Montgomery school officials. The local superintendent wrote to Air Force Secretary Harold Talbott demanding the return of the school to city jurisdiction. Talbott advised him that he would get back the school once the state government had decided to desegregate the Maxwell school.[28]

Undoubtedly, the Supreme Court decision influenced the Department of Defense to act before September 1955, because the federal government had to appear to support the decision if it expected compliance with federal law. Richard M. Dalfiume argued in his important 1969 book, *Desegregation of the U.S. Armed Forces: Fighting on Two Fronts, 1939–1953,* that military integration had been an important factor influencing the Supreme Court in a positive manner. Dalfiume claimed that in "1954, before the epochal decision on school desegregation, members of the Court read in manuscript form . . . Lee Nichols' 1954 book, *Breakthrough on the Color Front. . . .* Desegregation of the military was indeed an important precedent for the Federal Government's new role in race relations."[29] An attempt to confirm Dalfiume's statement brought negative comments from Chief Justice Earl Warren and Associate Justice Thomas Clark. Warren stated that he had no recollection of Nichols's book, nor had he ever asked anyone on the bench to read it. Concerning Dalfiume's statement, Warren stated that the court was not "thinking in terms of the military at all. I have no recollection of it at all. I never heard of the book."[30] Clark also said in an interview that he had never heard of the book: "I know I never read it." He was aware of "armed forces integration, but it was not a factor. . . . Armed forces integration had no weight. I don't recall it being discussed."[31] Associate Justice Thurgood Marshall also was asked the same question because he had argued the case before the court. He wrote that he had not used the Nichols book in preparing his brief.[32]

One should not conclude that armed forces integration had no influence on the Court's decision. Had race riots accompanied military integration, the Supreme Court might have proceeded more slowly. Had Truman never moved into the civil rights field in 1946 and issued Executive Order 9981 in 1948, the national climate might not have supported a judicial school integration decision, although Justices Warren and Clark would have been among the first to deny that the unanimous decision was based on anything other than points of law. Thus, it seems that armed forces integration—despite Dalfiume's comment—influenced the court only indirectly, if at all. One must look elsewhere for an explanation.

The historic court decision did increase black militancy, and after 1954 complaints by black servicemen in the South increased. The files of James C. Evans, a civilian assistant in the Office of the Secretary of Defense, reveal many complaints, mainly from married servicemen who objected to being stationed in the South, where they were forced to send their children to segregated schools.[33] Rep. Adam Clayton Powell, trying to halt federal impact funds to systems that segregated in violation of the court decision, introduced amendments to two public laws that permitted civilian communities to tap federal funds if large government installations were nearby.[34]

Little Rock Air Force Base

The air force was drawn into the school controversy in 1958. The elementary school adjacent to Little Rock AFB, Arkansas, was built with federal funds exclusively for air force dependents and financed with impact aid but was open to whites only.[35] The base commander expressed the official air force position. He noted that the school was situated on Pulaski County property and not on the base and that the air force had to abide by the school board's decision not to integrate. It was Department of Defense policy, the commander added, to conduct "civil activities according to the customs and decision of local agencies in the area of military installations. . . . Although there is no segregation within the Armed Forces all military services have traditionally followed local civilian rules, regulations and customs with regard to segregation in their off-base activities."[36] The Eisenhower administration, however, reacted to this situation by buying the school from the county.

This controversy required staff activity within the air force secretary's office. The president wanted the question resolved in favor of black parents who were offended by federally supported segregation. Air Force Secretary Donald Quarles decided— after consulting with the attorney general—that the U.S. government should take over the elementary school by right of eminent domain. The school would then be operated as a federal school using Department of Health, Education and Welfare funds. The pain expressed by parents at having their children bused through the gates of the base, past a school built by the government for air force children, to another, older, and less-well-equipped school 11 miles away was too much for the president and his advisers.[37] Service children were caught up elsewhere in the ugly turmoil over school integration in the 1950s and in many cases became innocent victims in campaigns like Virginia's massive resistance fight. Service personnel, who seldom vote in states where they are stationed, lost out because local Virginia politicians preferred to shut down a school rather than integrate. In Congress, there was some sentiment to provide federal funds to schools which accepted service dependents if state officials closed the schools.[38] No action was taken on such a measure, however, until 1960.

In addition to the Little Rock situation, there were other scattered examples which reflected the civil rights sentiments of the Eisenhower administration. The president assigned a high-level administrator, Maxwell Rabb, who served as secretary to the cabinet and as associate counsel to the president, to deal with civil rights. Rabb received a complaint about segregated barbershops at Chanute AFB, Illinois. He solved the problem by ordering a consolidation of base shops.[39] Rabb received letters from various congressmen—among them, Representative Powell—who complained vigorously that blacks at West Point in 1954 were "rigidly jim-crowed, segregated, and discriminated against by being forced into categories of domestic servants."[40] He also learned that a black airman at Keesler AFB had requested a transfer because he had been ordered off a public beach near the base. The airman was advised the air force could not interfere "with the customs and laws of a civilian community." He was told further that he could not be transferred simply because of discrimination, since it was "practiced in many communities throughout the United States." To transfer personnel to bases where there was no discrimination would limit the bases to which such personnel could be assigned. According to Rabb, reassigning personnel on such a basis would make it impossible to man a unit properly and would be contrary to the policy of equality of treatment.[41]

The administration did react to some integration issues. For example, it transferred the 1957 Tulane–West Point football game from Louisiana to New York because black cadets would have been required to sit in segregated sections.[42] Such actions, however, were rare. There was no major effort attempted by the Eisenhower administration to deal with such questions, perhaps because there was no black constituency to respond to.

In 1957 James C. Evans, a civilian assistant in the Office of the Secretary of Defense, prepared a formal report for Rabb in which he summarized the racial gains made in the services. Evans's report was titled "Advances in the Utilization of Negro Manpower under Ten Years of Unification of the Armed Services." Almost all of Evans's brief report tracing the progress from segregation to desegregation was a condensation of various statements issued by the defense secretaries, from George Marshall to Charles Wilson. Secretary Wilson noted: "Combat effectiveness is increased as individual capabilities rather than racial designations determine assignments and promotions. . . . Above all, our National Security is improved by the more effective utilization of personnel regardless of race."[43] There was no hint from Evans that the job was less than fully done. Oddly, two years earlier he had prepared a progress report in pamphlet form for general distribution, which liberally praised the advances made by black servicemen. In his 1955 report, Evans had also claimed—without furnishing substantiating evidence—that the Defense Department had made gains for minorities that were "beyond the direct purview of the Department of Defense."[44]

Air Force Off-Base Discrimination

There is, however, no evidence that the Department of Defense ever worked for blacks off the post before the 1960s. Even if black airmen suffered no more than their civilian contemporaries, those in the service did not have the freedom to relocate when faced with poor facilities and open discrimination. Often they were required to live in areas which they would have avoided if given an option. Blacks would have been least likely to move to bases in the rural North, where many communities were every bit as segregated and hostile as those in the South. And their situation was made worse by the absence of legitimate recreational and social outlets because there were no nearby black communities. Indeed, blacks in the rural North suffered as much or more than those in the southern states.

In the South, the situation was less than idyllic for black airmen. Maxwell AFB, whose racial problems were typical of southern bases, was located in Montgomery, Alabama, the first capital of the Confederacy. The base became a captive of deep southern prejudices and a model for racial intolerance.[45]

It took Maxwell AFB officials, it will be remembered, more than two years to carry out the provisions of AFL 35-3 to integrate the installation. The problems black airmen faced in Montgomery were no worse than those endured by black civilians, but few airmen would have chosen to live there, given a reasonable alternative. Capt. Emmet S. Walden, Jr., an officer attending the Air Command and Staff College during the civil rights era, researched and wrote his staff college thesis about Maxwell and its peculiar institutions. The author, a southerner, began his research by adopting an unsympathetic attitude toward the racial activism of the Kennedy administration. At first, he believed that the military was being misused by President John F. Kennedy when the president tried to ensure equal rights to minority groups. After studying the issue, however, Walden changed his position. He examined the real problems blacks faced while attending the air force professional schools at Maxwell AFB, and he then reached difficult conclusions. He discovered, for example, that in order to invite a black classmate to his home, he had to go through a procedure that was both elaborate and demeaning.[46]

To begin with, interracial socializing in private homes was officially discouraged by both the base and the school officials. Captain Walden was told: "There are no local laws which prevent . . . voluntary off-base association between white and Negro military personnel or their dependents. Local police officers have on occasion warned persons about their safety where whites and Negroes were associating but no charges were made. The local custom against social associating of whites and Negroes is very strong. A white person associating socially with a Negro can expect general community disapproval and ostracism. . . . A Negro visiting a white residence for social purposes would arouse the greatest local resentment."[47] Students who still desired to entertain or study with black classmates were told to inform their neighbors that a fellow student, a black, was coming to call and were advised to be sure that the whites knew just "who he is and why he is coming." Blacks visiting whites were counseled to wear their uniforms.[48]

From the 1940s into the 1960s, youth activities offered to dependents at Maxwell AFB that were in any way involved with off-base groups—such as the Little League and Boy and Girl Scouts—were strictly segregated because the civilian community would not tolerate integrated recreational and social activities. One Air University commander explained that "long standing customs, tradition," and laws made it a "breach of the peace to mix the races." He stated that all relationships "with the civilian community must conform or risk inciting riots and arrest of all participants. . . . Air Force youth activities cannot participate with their counterparts in the Montgomery area if any Negro participants were included." He added, "Likewise all the civilian community activities that participate with like Air Force activities were strictly segregated." This meant that adult groups such as the Toastmasters and Kiwanis also were segregated. Some organizations used Maxwell facilities—the gymnasium, clubs, and athletic fields—giving the base the appearance of sanctioning segregation. If there were no black organizations that corresponded to a segregated activity, blacks were barred from all participation. While membership or participation in any of these organizations had "not been denied any person because of race . . . the local customs and ordinances for mixing the races are well known by all," and blacks did not apply for membership.[49]

The practice of segregating recreational activities, which continued into 1962 and 1963, had been ratified by Maj. Gen. Truman Landon, deputy chief of staff for personnel. To do otherwise would have deprived the vast majority, that is, the whites, of needed recreational activity, and a demand for racial integration would seriously damage the relationship Maxwell had painstakingly built with the town. Blacks did not join Maxwell athletic teams until 1963, and when several blacks joined a basketball team, the local YMCA immediately withdrew its permission for Maxwell to participate in its leagues.[50]

Other functions were also segregated at Maxwell. As late as the early 1960s, cab service to and from the air base, the base-community council, housing lists, and mortuary service were segregated.[51] From time to time the base commander had considered it necessary to instruct blacks to stay out of Montgomery except when on important business, which in effect placed the city off-limits to blacks. He exercised his option during periods of tension, which became increasingly more common in the early 1960s. Congressman Charles Diggs (Dem., Mich.) sent an inquiry to the air force inspector general and was told that the base commander had indeed at times directed black personnel to avoid Montgomery.[52]

The inspector general's letter to Diggs included a summary of recent incidents involving black officers and airmen at Maxwell. For example, in March 1960 a black air force major was arrested while accompanying two Ethiopian officers and an air force captain to a downtown barbershop. The Air University students were stopped and searched at gunpoint, and because the trunk of the car contained a carpenter's hammer, the police hinted that the major might be booked for possession of a dangerous weapon. He was, instead, booked for reckless driving and fined $25, in addition to court costs. Such hostility, the inspector general said, was reason enough for the base commander to caution blacks.[53]

A more violent confrontation took place the same month. A black airman in uniform was arrested and charged with assaulting a police officer with intent to murder and with carrying a concealed weapon, a straight razor. The police officer testified that the airman became abusive while being questioned on a routine matter. According to the officer, the airman struck him, knocking his revolver to the ground. The airman seized the gun and allegedly fired at the officer at point-blank range but missed. But the airman told a different account. He testified he was quietly waiting for a bus when the policeman approached and made derogatory remarks about his race. He said the officer struck him with a nightstick, whereupon the airman grabbed the gun and in the process fired it into the ground. An eyewitness corroborated the airman's story.[54] Maxwell military police officers interviewed the airman in the local jail that same day, observing that he was uninjured except for a small bump on the head where he had been struck by the nightstick. The next day the airman showed signs of a physical beating. He had suffered a laceration above the right eye requiring clamps, a swelling on the right side of the face, and another lump on the head. The Alabama court assessed the airman more than $600 in fines and court costs but did not try him for attempted murder as had been threatened.

The inspector general informed Diggs that the air force was most interested in the morale, health, welfare, and security of all its personnel and deeply believed in equal opportunity but that air force authority in this matter was "restricted to the limits of Air Force jurisdiction. Beyond these limits civilian jurisdiction prevails, as determined by civil law and local custom." The letter further stated: "There is little basis to expect that any member of the Air Force will receive more favorable treatment from the civilian community than he would receive as a civilian under the same circumstances. Nor does the Air Force have authority to use any measure of force or coercion to change or influence local law or custom which does not agree with official Air Force policy."[55]

The air force, in effect, had sent its black airmen into a segregated community which air force officials surely knew would abuse and demean them whenever they ventured off the base. The Air University, established in 1946 before integration, began a $5 million building program at Maxwell to house an Air War College and the Air Command and Staff College in 1955, well after integration.[56] At the time no one paid attention to the situation that black airmen sent to Maxwell might face while attending the schools there.

Their problems were manifold. For example, it was difficult if not impossible for black airmen to find decent lodging, restrooms, restaurants, homes, and schools to educate their children. Maj. Alfred E. McEwen, who attended the Air Command and Staff College in 1965–66, examined these issues in his thesis, "Permanent Change of Station: A Continuing Problem for Negro Airmen." McEwen described automobile travel through the South as a nightmare. Blacks generated white hostility, he wrote, for simply owning a late-model automobile.[57] The blacks were forced to plan all journeys in the South with care to avoid trouble from hostile whites on the road. Even after arriving at Maxwell, they faced the danger of physical attacks if they tried to socialize with white servicemen. "Fear," McEwen wrote, "is constantly a companion of the Negro airman. He suffers from fear anytime he departs the confines of the base to which he is assigned in the Deep South." Frustrations followed blacks. On the base, they were treated as professionals; off the base, they were humiliated daily. Forced to live in the least-desirable parts of the city of Montgomery, they were unable to offer their families amenities enjoyed by their white associates. This conflict drained their energies and led many to react defensively and aggressively and to display antisocial behavior.[58]

The danger of being stationed in the South is well illustrated by the case of Lt. Titus A. Saunders, Jr. In the spring of 1955, Saunders was a passenger in an automobile involved in a minor accident in Mississippi, where he was stationed. Although he was not the driver of the car, he rolled it off the highway after the accident to prevent blocking traffic. He was promptly arrested and charged for driving while under the influence of alcohol, was fined $500, and was sentenced to serve six months on the state's chain gang. He appealed his sentence, and after he had served one day on the gang, the air force reassigned him to Ohio. The governor of Mississippi demanded Saunders's extradition, but Ohio Gov. Frank Lausche (Dem.) refused to return him, calling the conviction "unjust." One of Mississippi's senators wrote a letter to Air Force Secretary Donald Quarles demanding Saunders be discharged from the air force because he was a convicted felon and air force regulations called for the discharge of those so convicted. Reacting to this political pressure, Quarles gave Saunders the choice of resigning or receiving a less-than-honorable discharge. The secretary said that it "was not the responsibility of the Air Force to determine the adequacy of the evidence. It was sufficient for the Air Force . . . that Lieutenant Saunders had been convicted and that the conviction had been upheld upon review by the Mississippi Supreme Court."[59]

The Problem in the North
Blacks in North Dakota, South Dakota, Montana, northern Michigan, Maine, and elsewhere in the rural North suffered as many indignities or more than those in the South. Blacks stationed in the rural North might not be able to document a case

history as dramatic as Titus Saunders's, but they also were badly treated. Black airmen stationed at Ellsworth AFB, South Dakota, were rejected by the local communities, and base officials seemed to be indifferent to their plight. Many business establishments were closed to blacks, all taverns were segregated, and housing for blacks was extremely limited, substandard, and exceptionally expensive.

In 1962 the NAACP complained to the air force inspector general. It was told that the air force was "extremely limited in the extent to which it may exert its influence in the local civilian community." The NAACP then wrote to the commander of the air division at Ellsworth suggesting that the town could be opened to blacks if the commander declared segregated facilities off-limits to all military personnel. This, said the NAACP, would "almost immediately bring the desired results."[60] The air force replied that the community of Rapid City had to solve its own problems and that, in any case, its authority was "restricted to the limits of the base."[61]

Most senior air force officials were probably aware of the misery that accompanied blacks in such assignments, but they were restricted to a policy of nonintervention. Frequently in the 1950s and 1960s, Congressman Diggs complained about the situation, only to be informed that living conditions, while deplorable, were not an air force problem. Black airmen complained they had been called "niggers" and "darkies" by whites in the communities surrounding Finley Air Station, North Dakota, and that they also were routinely barred from dances. Maj. Gen. Joe W. Kelly, USAF, in responding to Diggs's request for information, told the Michigan lawmaker that a "major difficulty lies with community sentiment concerning Negro airmen." Most of the local citizens were Norwegians who had never associated with blacks prior to the establishment of the air station. This unfamiliarity "coupled with the total absence of a Negro civilian populace within a hundred miles presents a difficult problem for colored airmen and their families as concerns social status, freedom of action, and entertainment facilities." Kelly informed Diggs that the town of Mayville, North Dakota, about 30 miles from the base, was especially hostile toward blacks. He added, "Emphasis is made by the police department and prominent citizens that Negro airmen are not wanted in the town, and neither are white airmen who choose to associate with Negroes."[62]

Blacks stationed in Montana were no better off. In December 1948 General Kuter wrote to General Edwards about the off-base situation at Great Falls. Kuter wanted to reduce the number of blacks to a maximum of 50 and to limit their tour on the post to 18 months.[63] The situation, furthermore, did not improve following integration. A year later James L. Flaherty, the director of the Larger Montana Chamber of Commerce, asked General Vandenberg to bar blacks from Great Falls. Vandenberg refused.[64] Edwards shortly thereafter wrote to Kuter, stating that the problem still continued and that he could not consider a quota on blacks or a shortened tour. General Edwards suggested to Kuter that the economic benefit that accrued to Great Falls should make them grateful for the air base and require them to accept the "minor inconveniences inherent in the situation."[65] But the people of Great Falls were unyielding. Blacks found they could not purchase hamburgers from local food concessions and had difficulty buying gasoline—restrictions not found even in the South. The only restaurant in town open to blacks was also a house of prostitution.[66] After repeated complaints from the air force, many town establishments agreed to remove the offensive signs barring blacks, but some still refused to serve them. One investigator summing up the situation wrote:

> The lack of a Negro Community with normal outlets in restaurants, hotels, recreation and religious services, and the utter and deplorable scarcity of housing for Negro married personnel will always make Great Falls an undesirable place for the assignment of Air Force personnel. . . . Great Falls is probably above the standards of most western communities of Air Force personnel except those on the Pacific Coast in its acceptance of Negro personnel in uniform. . . . The Great Falls situation is another example of the impossibility of providing any substitute for a Negro community. . . . The problems of western and northwestern cities where some of the worst discrimination now exists are mainly those of a lack of Negro citizens and services.[67]

In July 1953 Brig. Gen. John Ives, the director of military personnel, wrote to an assistant secretary of the air force that discrimination in Montana persisted. The situation in Great Falls presented a dilemma. Air force personnel policy could not bar blacks from such stations, General Ives claimed, and closing the base would be too costly and a poor policy. He recommended working with the more influential elements in Great Falls to find a suitable place for blacks.[68] Trying to gain cooperation from the town fathers for better treatment of blacks was the best the air force could do.

Glasgow, Montana, was another difficult place for blacks. For years the NAACP had complained about the problems in the community. In 1961 Sen. Philip Hart (Dem., Mich.) wrote to Secretary of the Air Force Zuckert about discrimination in Glasgow. He said, "Most serious consideration should be given to a policy whereby base commanders could declare private establishments which refuse service to uniformed members of the armed services because of race, to be 'off-limits.'" Hart told the secretary that Glasgow profited from the base and that, by wielding economic power, the air force could end the continuing embarrassment and disgrace suffered by blacks in uniform. He complained that towns like Glasgow had discriminated for years but that the air force had done nothing to solve the problem. It was time, he said, for a change.[69]

Blacks stationed at an air base in upper Michigan fared no better than those at Great Falls or Glasgow. The men were completely integrated on the job, but the towns in the area were so hostile to blacks that black airmen believed they were imprisoned and lived in fear because of local hostility. Barbershops refused to cut their hair, and most restaurants and taverns refused them service. There was a United Service Organizations (USO) in one of the towns, but it provided little comfort. Housing, furthermore, was nearly unavailable.[70]

The air force, while aware of the situation, was short of solutions because of its reluctance to challenge community customs, mores, and laws. A two-year study of its recreational problems suggested that the promise of equal opportunity expressed in Air Force Regulation (AFR) 35-78 was incomplete so long as the matter of off-base discrimination remained a problem. The air force recognized, the investigator wrote, that it had no "power of right to insist on a change of local community practices with respect to racial segregation. . . . Where segregation is required by law in the community, the base has an obligation to stimulate activities on behalf of its Negro personnel among the Negro community, just as it does for its white personnel in the white community." The report recommended the base sponsor more interracial activities with the town. It was hoped that people would end their racial hostility once a common meeting ground was found in recreation. The program skirted, however, the more basic problems, such as housing and schools.[71]

Throughout these years James C. Evans, monitoring the affairs of blacks in the military, did what he could to interest the Department of Defense in the plight of black personnel. He was especially concerned about housing problems, schools, and off-base social discrimination. He further analyzed promotion complaints, courts-martial, and cases where blacks were separated with less-than-honorable discharges. Evans found that blacks generally were pleased with their on-base treatment but critical of civilian discrimination. An example of the latter was the case of Capt. Joseph B. Williams, USAF, a B-58 navigator, who made arrangements to move into a house in Kokomo, Indiana, near Bunker Hill AFB. When he suffered personal abuse and public hostility, the air base officials attempted to persuade him not to move into the community because of the damage this might do to the base's relationship with the town.[72]

Evans studied school complaints, including those from a staff sergeant at Charleston AFB, South Carolina, who regularly reported his grievances. Fearing reprisals, he asked Evans not to identify him in correspondence. At issue was the question of two schools built with federal funds 50 and 250 yards outside the base perimeter fence to educate base children. Holes had been cut into the fence to provide access to the schools which, however, were attended solely by white dependents. The black airman complained that the air base had "eighteen Negro military children" who were forced to attend segregated schools because they were not permitted to "attend schools which were constructed for the sole purpose of *educating military dependent children*." He stated that the children were bused "between 11 and 22 miles" to their segregated schools. The final correspondence on this subject, dated September 1964, indicated the problem had not been solved by that date.[73]

There is a paucity of material in the Evans files from individuals complaining about military discrimination. This did not mean that the air force had miraculously succeeded in eliminating individual bias and prejudice and that it had become a paradise for blacks. But the air force did provide better career opportunities for blacks than almost all civilian institutions, and blacks responded with reenlistment rates that exceeded the white rate by a large margin. The air force, furthermore, had a mechanism in the office of the inspector general for acknowledging complaints that most civilian institutions lacked. Blacks did not frequently turn to the inspector general, but when they did, he proved to be a powerful investigative force.

Evans and the inspector examined examples of military discrimination. For example, "Sgt. S. L." repeatedly found cases of discrimination since 1950, and the inspector general regularly investigated these. As early as 1952 Evans had gone on record indicating that S. L.'s grievances had no substance, but that did not end the complaints. In 1957, S. L. again complained to the NAACP that he had "noticed overt acts of racial violence, racial segregation, racial discrimination, and intimidation at Wright Patterson Air Force Base." S. L. informed the NAACP that he had previously brought matters to the attention of the Defense Department and his congressmen but had not received satisfaction. He claimed that he was being threatened with reprisals.[74] Despite S. L.'s record as a chronic complainer, the air force conducted an investigation.

Because S. L. raised the question about "cross-burnings" and "every other kind of racial violence" at the Ohio base, the air force moved quickly. When inconsistencies appeared in his stories, the air force interviewed ten blacks within his organization to see if any of the complaints were justified. The investigator reported that S. L. had consistently misrepresented facts, given erroneous information, and "failed to cite positive examples in support of his claims when requested to do so by investigative personnel." When pressed about his claims of cross-burnings and racial violence, he stated that he had not meant these things in a literal sense but that there were great pressures, adverse feelings, and negative attitudes. S. L. had been stationed in Louisiana, New Jersey, Kansas, and Ohio. But wherever he served, he had complained of mistreatment and could not support his allegations. In 1957, he accused air force officials of segregating airmen in the barracks and chapel. He claimed his phone was tapped and charged that he had not been promoted to warrant officer because of discrimination. Despite this charge, he had a white roommate, and no other blacks supported his claim of segregation in the chapel. In fact, many blacks were members of the interracial chapel choir.[75] S. L.

persisted in raising unsubstantiated charges into the next decade. Perhaps he employed this method to guard against bias, and if his rank was any indication, he was successful; S. L. was promoted to master sergeant in his twelfth year, a promotion rate which any white would envy.

The air force did give complaining individuals a hearing. Even if the complaint was outrageous, as in S. L.'s case, it was not a bar to promotion. Investigators in the Kennedy years further examined internal air force personnel problems, but they were minor and few in comparison to off-post difficulties. When confronted with questions of bias outside of its direct domain, the air force was in a quandary about how to respond. For example, during the 1950s the air force sent personnel to technical training schools under civilian contract. Some of these schools were in states which practiced segregation. When blacks were assigned to such schools, the individual had the option to choose whether he wanted to attend a segregated school or not go at all.[76] This was not much of a choice for the blacks, who could choose humiliation or refuse the opportunity for advancement.

The off-base problems encountered at Great Falls, Glasgow, Montgomery, and other stations affected black morale overseas as well. In France, blacks complained that white servicemen had poisoned the social atmosphere against them, making recreation and housing scarce. Rep. Adam Clayton Powell investigated and found that white airmen used economic pressure to force bars and dance halls to discriminate and landlords to refuse to rent to blacks. Powell also discovered that when a club entertained blacks, it soon became an all-black facility because the air police and others discouraged whites from entering such entertainment centers. He also discovered that the French were not anti-black but were hostile to American blacks whereas they were cordial to black Africans. Powell asked the president to declare off-limits any establishment that discriminated.[77] Elsewhere, the *Chicago Defender* reported that whites and blacks brought their racial tensions with them to Germany. Most bars in that country were established exclusively for one race or the other.[78]

Representative Diggs, after traveling to U.S. bases in Asia, found the situation similar to that in Europe. He argued that Executive Order 9981 had not been fully implemented because of rigid segregation in communities outside military installations. He visited Okinawa, Japan, and the Philippines and noted discrimination in each of those countries. He also discovered that housing problems for blacks were as severe overseas as they were in the United States, with much of the housing being controlled by the service to which it was leased. He noted social segregation as well and argued for off-limits sanctions to end this humiliation.[79] The *Chicago Defender* reported a similar situation in Newfoundland, finding that white Americans had infected the local populace with the disease of racial prejudice.[80]

Blacks stationed near Misawa City, Japan, decided to employ sit-ins to end discrimination in the bars and cabarets of that city. Of the 45 such businesses in the city, 42 refused service to blacks. Black airmen then sought service at white bars but were repeatedly refused. The Misawa base commander advised Japanese bar owners that if "problems were to arise from this situation, he would be required to place the bars and cabarets in Misawa City Off-Limits." The bar owners, in turn, threatened to import thugs to eject the blacks. Local newspapers carried accounts about the sit-ins, but in the end, the bar owners relented and extended their services to all.[81]

Off-base discrimination and subtle personal discrimination came to the attention of Lee Nichols. In the early 1960s he spoke of updating his study, *Breakthrough on the Color Front,* and he traveled throughout the United States and overseas to perceive the changes instituted since 1954. He found "complete official acceptance of racial integration at all command levels with no indications of any thought of reverting to the former segregated system." He talked with many blacks who were "fully satisfied with their rate of advancement and apparently respected by their peers, their superiors, and their subordinates." Nichols noted that no one objected to shared facilities on base such as gyms, mess halls, theaters, and clubs. He did discover, however, a "lack of sensitivity on the part of most commanders to some of the ramifications of segregation which are manifested in both off-post and to some extent on-post circumstances." He was particularly distressed with overseas discrimination and the unwillingness of the military to eradicate it. He reported that the off-post bias he encountered in Germany, France, Korea, and Japan was "caused primarily by the pressures and actions of white GIs, not by the wishes of the local proprietors." He concluded that American racial prejudice had circumscribed the overseas housing market for blacks. Suggestions made by Nichols to local commanders to do something about off-post discrimination brought only negative responses.[82]

The services obviously could not eliminate all forms of racial prejudice among their diverse personnel. Consciously or unconsciously, for example, blacks were rated slightly lower than whites, which led to lower promotion rates for the former. By the early 1960s, after the air force had had blacks within its ranks for more than two decades and after more than a dozen years of integration, blacks accounted for 9.2 percent of the enlisted force, but only 0.8 percent of the highest enlisted grade, Chief Master Sergeant (E-9), was black. Less than 2 percent of the next-highest category, Senior Master Sergeant (E-8), was black. The officer total was equally bleak.[83] Even Kennedy administration investigators were unable to grasp fully the indistinct tracing of such bias and concentrated rather on the more obvious form of discrimination, that is, the problems blacks faced in the civilian communities.

Eleanor Roosevelt and C. Alfred ("Chief") Anderson. In the spring of 1941, before the first officers and cadets arrived at Moton Field in Tuskegee, Alabama, the first lady flew with "Chief" Anderson, an instructor pilot in the Tuskegee Institute Civilian Pilot Training Program. Anderson was a pioneer aviator who taught himself how to fly because white flying schools refused to instruct him. This flight, of course, was symbolically significant (because the photo was widely published) and typical of Eleanor Roosevelt, always a friend of black Americans. (C. Alfred Anderson)

Tuskegee Army Air Field, Alabama. The white officer in the center of this photo is Lt. Col. Noel F. Parrish, Tuskegee Army Air Field commander from 1942 to 1946. Parrish treated the Tuskegee Airmen with respect and vastly improved the morale of the trainees over what it had been under the previous commander. His leadership contributed mightily to the wartime success of the 99th Pursuit Squadron and the 332d Fighter Group. Parrish's memory is hallowed by the Tuskegee Airmen. (Schomburg Center for Research in Black Culture, New York Public Library)

Top: Armorers carrying belts of .50-caliber machine-gun bullets for P-40 aircraft at the AAF range in Oscoda, Michigan. The Tuskegee Airmen trained at several ranges, most often either at Oscoda or Walterboro, South Carolina. The civilian surroundings in Walterboro were never friendly. It is important to note that all of the enlisted technicians who armed and maintained the aircraft of the 99th, the 332d, and the 477th were black. All of these units had normal in-commission rates (that is, they were equal to the rates of white outfits). Left to right: Leon Strong, Allen Norton, John T. Fields, unknown. (U.S. Air Force) *Bottom:* Twelve of the 26 members of the original 99th Pursuit Squadron before it deployed to North Africa. Bottom row, left to right: Charles B. Hall (who scored the first Tuskegee Airman victory), George R. Bolling, H. V. Clark. Center: Paul G. Mitchell, Spann Watson, Willie Ashley, Louis R. Purnell, Erwin B. Lawrence. Top: Allen Lane, Graham Smith, William A. Campbell, Faith McGinnis. All of these men had been cadets and were commissioned upon receiving their wings as AAF pilots. (Elmer D. Jones)

Top: Left to right: Capts. Elmer D. Jones and Graham Smith on the *Mariposa* at sea in the spring of 1943 en route to North Africa. Jones was the first maintenance officer assigned to the 99th. He supervised dozens of enlisted men who kept the 99th flying. He remained in the air force after 1945, eventually retiring as a colonel after a distinguished career. After the air force integrated, Jones was one of the earliest of the Tuskegee Airmen to supervise whites. (Elmer D. Jones) *Bottom:* Sidney Brooks next to his P-40 Warhawk, *El Cid.* Brooks was killed in action over Sicily in the summer of 1943. There were 66 Tuskegee Airmen killed in action during World War II in the combat theaters. (Elmer D. Jones)

Top: Col. Benjamin O. Davis, Jr., in the cockpit of a P-51 Mustang at Ramitelli Air Base, Italy. Davis, class of 1936, U.S. Military Academy, was the first commander of the 99th and brought the 332d Fighter Group to Italy in January 1944 as its commander. The Mustang was his fourth combat aircraft. He had previously flown the P-40, P-39, and P-47, in that order. The P-51 was used by the Tuskegee Airmen primarily as escort fighters, that is, to protect B-17s and B-24s on bombing missions. The P-40 and the P-39 were ground attack aircraft (the latter solely). Davis's 332d was uniquely successful in its escort role—the Tuskegee Airmen never lost a bomber to an enemy fighter in 200 escort missions, approximately 10,000 combat sorties. No white group that escorted bombers with as many missions could make the same claim. (Benjamin O. Davis, Jr.) *Bottom:* The supervising officers of the 332d Fighter Group next to a P-51 at Ramitelli Air Base, Italy. Bottom row, left to right: Edward C. Glead, Nelson Brooks, Benjamin O. Davis, Jr., unknown, George S. ("Spanky") Roberts, Thomas J. Money. Top: Denzal Harvey, Cyrus W. Perry, Roy B. Ware. Edward Glead and Spanky Roberts were Davis's two most trusted officers. The latter took over the 99th when Davis returned to command the 332d; Roberts retained command for almost a year and also during the squadron's most successful missions over Anzio Beach in early 1944. He also became commander of the 332d when Davis returned to take over the 477th. Roberts completed a distinguished career as a colonel. (Benjamin O. Davis, Jr.)

Benjamin O. Davis, Jr., at Ramitelli Air Base briefing his pilots before the 200th escort mission. The Tuskegee Airmen flew 200 escort missions—about 10,000 combat sorties—and thousands of ground attack sorties. Frequently after the pilots completed the escort portion of one of their missions to protect bombers, they would return to Ramitelli Air Base at low altitude, destroying German war and transportation equipment along the way. (U.S. Air Force)

Capt. Andrew D. Turner (left) and Lt. C. D. ("Lucky") Lester returning from a P-51 air combat mission at Ramitelli Air Base. Turner was killed in an aviation accident after World War II. Lester received his nickname before becoming a Tuskegee Airman. (U.S. Air Force)

Lt. Gen. Carl A. Spaatz visiting Col. Benjamin O. Davis, Jr., commander of the 332d at Ramitelli Air Base, Italy. Spaatz was the senior AAF commander in Europe. He became commander of the AAF in late 1945 and the first chief of staff of the air force in 1947. (Benjamin O. Davis, Jr.)

Lt. Lee A. Archer in his P-51 cockpit. Archer is the Tuskegee Airman credited with the most victories: four and one-half. The Tuskegee Airmen are credited with destroying 111 enemy aircraft in air-to-air combat and another 150 on the ground. Archer completed his air force career as a colonel. (U.S. Air Force)

John T. Fields, an enlisted armorer at Ramitelli Air Base, Italy. The P-51s were also capable of dropping bombs but produced a withering rate of fire with eight machine guns. The P-51 was the fighter aircraft with the longest range (by the end of the war it exceeded 1,500 miles). The airplane was sleek, rugged, fast, and maneuverable, and it could escort American bombers from England (or Italy) to Berlin and back. In fact, in the spring of 1945 the Tuskegee Airmen did just that, escorted bombers from Italy to Berlin. (U.S. Air Force)

Lt. C. D. ("Lucky") Lester with his P-51 crew chief, name unknown. The painting on Lester's aircraft signifies his three victories, all of which were shot down on the same mission. This reinforced his nickname. (U.S. Air Force)

Col. Benjamin O. Davis, Jr., receiving the Distinguished Flying Cross from his father, Benjamin O. Davis, Sr. The latter was the first black officer to be promoted to the general officer ranks, and his son was the second to be so promoted. The elder Davis's career was terribly stunted by the racial policies of the interwar army; he was usually shuttled between ROTC units at black colleges. The younger Davis's career began the same, but racial integration rescued him. His performance in World War II, and that of the units he commanded, helped bring about racial integration. (Benjamin O. Davis, Jr.)

Five crewmembers of the 477th Bombardment Group (M) (Colored) planning a mission. Segregation and command bigotry barred the 477th from combat. Many of the officers in this unit mutinied in April 1945 rather than tolerate illegal orders segregating them beyond what War Department regulations required. The slogan of the NAACP in World War II was the "Double V"— victory over our enemies abroad and victory over our enemies at home. These men fought the latter fight, risking their lives and careers—present and future—to make the point that illegal segregation while they were training to fight a war was intolerable. (Joseph Hardy)

A 477th Bombardment Group (M) waist gunner. The B-25 carried a large crew: two pilots, a navigator, a navigator bombardier, a radio operator, and at least two gunners. (Joseph Hardy)

Maj. Gen. Elwood (Pete) Quesada visiting Col. Benjamin O. Davis, Jr., commander of the 477th Composite Group at Lockbourne Army Air Field, Ohio, in 1946. Davis was the base commander in addition to being the flying unit commander. Davis was the first black to command a base inside the United States, and all of the civil servants at Lockbourne were white. This employment situation was unique. When it was announced by the AAF that blacks would be moving to Ohio from Kentucky, the Columbus, Ohio, press complained bitterly. It took all of Davis's professionalism to overcome the bigotry in the North. (Benjamin O. Davis, Jr.)

The 477th Composite Group at Lockbourne Army Air Field, Ohio, Benjamin O. Davis, Jr., commanding. The 477th had a B-25 squadron (the airplane in the background) and a P-47 squadron. Later the unit became the 332d Fighter Group, dropping the B-25s, and later yet the 332d Fighter Wing. It was so designated when the air force integrated in 1949. (Benjamin O. Davis, Jr.)

Lt. William E. (Earl) Brown mounting his F-86 Sabre jet in Korea in 1953. Brown retired as a lieutenant general (three stars). Brown was the only black pilot in his unit. (U.S. Air Force)

The President's Committee on Equality of Treatment and Opportunity in the Armed Services, usually called the Fahy Committee after its chairman, Charles Fahy. This committee was called for by President Harry S Truman's election campaign–inspired Executive Order 9981, in July 1948, but was not appointed until Truman was safely elected. The committee took as its mandate to integrate the armed forces, but it was terminated before the U.S. Army and Marine Corps did so. Seated, left to right: James V. Forrestal, secretary of defense and not a committee member (Forrestal was a supporter of racial integration and had brought token integration to the navy in 1945, but after he departed as navy secretary the navy stayed frozen until well into the next decade), President Truman, and Alphonsus J. Donahue. Standing: John H. Sengstacke, William E. Stevenson, Kenneth R. Royall, secretary of the army and not a Fahy Committee member (Royall was an ardent foe of racial integration, and he and his successor fought the Fahy Committee to a standstill over the issue), Stuart W. Symington, secretary of the air force and not a Fahy Committee member (Symington was a steadfast supporter of racial integration), Lester B. Granger, Dwight R. G. Palmer, John L. Sullivan (not a Fahy Committee member and not a friend of racial integration), and Charles Fahy, committee chairman and an advocate of racial integration. (U.S. Air Force)

Col. Benjamin O. Davis, Jr., commander, 51st Tactical Fighter Wing, Suwon Air Base, Korea, in 1953 in front of his fighter jet. The two subordinates are unknown. This is the integrated air force. Davis attended the Air War College after the 332d was broken up and the men were assigned to white units. He then went to the Pentagon, where he held an exceptionally responsible position in the Operations Directorate. He was assigned to command the 51st while the war was raging, but the truce was signed shortly before he arrived. By choosing Davis to command a fighter wing, the air force leadership signified it was testing Davis for promotion to brigadier general. He passed the test. (Benjamin O. Davis, Jr.)

The integrated air force at Bien Hoa Air Base, Vietnam. Left to right: Capt. James T. Harwood, Lt. James H. Pauly, Capt. Robert H. Tice. All three were A1E Skyraider pilots. (U.S. Air Force)

The integrated air force in Vietnam: two F-4C Phantom pilots, Capt. Everett T. Raspberry (left) and Lt. Robert W. Western, after shooting down MIG-21s in a dogfight. (U.S. Air Force)

Col. Fred V. Cherry getting a light from Lt. Col. James Warren. In the photo, Cherry has just landed after being picked up by an air force C-141 in Hanoi, where he was a prisoner of war for many years. Cherry had been an F-105 pilot. Warren was the navigator on the C-141, the first American flight into Hanoi, and had been a member of the 477th Bombardment Group (M) during World War II. He had been arrested for disobeying the orders and regulations established at Freeman Field, Indiana. His book, *The Freeman Field Mutiny*, was published in 1995. Cherry's account of his ordeal as a prisoner of war can be found in Wallace Terry's *Bloods: An Oral History of the Vietnam War by Black Veterans* (1985). (U.S. Air Force)

The integrated air force in Vietnam: three crewmembers of an HH-43F rescue helicopter. The copilot (with his head turned) is Capt. Leslie E. Johnson. The wounded man who has been recovered is unknown. The flight mechanic (middle) is A/1C Archelous Whitehead, Jr. He is assisting A/1C Larry Nicholson. The Vietnam War was the first U.S. war in which all of the services were integrated from beginning to end. (U.S. Air Force)

Gen. Daniel Patrick ("Chappie") James at a press conference after his promotion to four-star general and elevation to commander in chief, North American Air Defense Command, in August 1975. James was the first black to be promoted to four stars. He was the last born of 19 children in a racist Deep South community. Of all the Tuskegee Airmen who went far, nobody else had a humbler beginning than James. (U.S. Air Force)

Col. Daniel Patrick ("Chappie") James, vice commander, 8th Tactical Fighter Wing, Thailand, in front of his F-4 Phantom. James, an original Tuskegee Airman (instructor and B-25 pilot), flew more than 60 missions over North Vietnam. (U.S. Air Force)

Col. Daniel Patrick ("Chappie") James briefing President Lyndon B. Johnson at the White House. (U.S. Air Force)

Captain Lloyd ("Fig") Newton, first black pilot to fly as a member of the Thunderbirds, the air force aerial demonstration team. Newton is currently a four-star general and commander of the Air Force Air Education and Training Command, the largest major command in the air force. (U.S. Air Force)

Astronaut Charles F. Bolden beside his T-38 aircraft, used to keep the astronauts proficient. Like all other black astronauts, Bolden recognized that this ascent into space began with the Tuskegee Airmen, who proved that they could fly with and fight against the best pilots in the world. (National Aeronautics and Space Administration)

5 *The Kennedy Era*

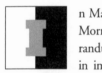n March 1960, in the twilight of the Eisenhower presidency, E. Frederic Morrow, the president's "black man in the White House," wrote a memorandum on the emerging civil rights tide. "The Greensboro incident grows in importance," he noted of the first black sit-ins, "because of the accumulating evidence that Negroes throughout the South saw in its example a means of release from discrimination and slights. . . . The South is in a time of change, the terms of which cannot be dictated by one race." Morrow concluded that segregation could no longer be maintained except by "continuous coercion." He saw a new trend emerging, one of "direct action," and predicted that if the South tried to preserve segregation in the face of this movement, it would invariably encounter violence.[1]

The civil rights revolution advanced through the 20th century in an irregular ascent to ever higher plateaus as if catching its breath after each exertion to climb to another level. The high ground reached with the 1954 Supreme Court decision that school segregation laws in the South were unconstitutional was not surpassed until massive efforts, beginning in February 1960 with the Greensboro sit-ins, led to enactment of the Civil Rights Act of 1964 and the Voting Rights Act of 1965. The black press paid little attention to civil rights news between 1954 and 1960. Its coverage of the Civil Rights Act of 1957 was thin at best.[2] Much space was given to the crisis over President Eisenhower's 1957 decision to send federal troops to integrate the public schools of Little Rock, Arkansas, in accordance with the Supreme ourt's ruling. But during the next two years the black press spent most of its time reporting sensational news, for example, recording the tax problems of wealthy blacks, lurid divorce cases, and marital strife among black celebrities. It took the sit-ins of 1960 to awaken the black press from its slumber and to reorient the focus of its attention. After March 1960 the front pages were given over to civil rights stories and to the revolution that found its footing with the courageous college students in Greensboro.[3]

The struggle for civil rights spilled over into the 1960 presidential election contest between the major candidates, Sen. John F. Kennedy and Vice President Richard M. Nixon. Senator Kennedy was not the first choice of the black leadership because some believed he was not committed to civil rights. Once nominated, however, he did receive support from most black papers and organizations.[4] The *Baltimore Afro-American* and the *Chicago Defender* fell into line after he won the nomination. The *Pittsburgh Courier,* for the first time in the 20th century, failed to endorse either candidate.[5]

After the election, all three of the leading papers interpreted the campaign as a replay of 1948, with blacks playing a decisive role in Kennedy's victory. The *Pittsburgh Courier* claimed that blacks had put the Bostonian into the White House and anticipated full citizenship for blacks as a reward for their support. The paper further argued that the margin of victory in the black wards of Philadelphia and Pittsburgh carried Pennsylvania, that the black wards of Detroit and Cook County carried Michigan and Illinois, respectively, and that the voters of Watts, California, carried the state. (The paper was in error about California, which Nixon won.) The *Courier* claimed Kennedy deserved to win the black vote because he had solicited it, whereas Nixon had refused to do so.[6] The *Chicago Defender* reported that Kennedy had received huge pluralities in the black wards of Philadelphia (80 percent), New York City (75 percent), Chicago (80 percent), and Cleveland (75 percent), giving him the margin for victory in Pennsylvania, New York, Illinois, and Ohio.[7] The *Baltimore Afro-American* cited the same statistics and also pointed out that Kennedy won only 7 of the 21 counties in Maryland, yet he won in the black wards of Baltimore a huge plurality that carried the state for him.[8]

President Kennedy, like Truman, resorted to executive action in the area of civil rights. He saw the military as probably the most fertile ground to plow.[9] Less than two months after his inauguration, he issued Executive Order 10925 forbidding the armed forces from encouraging segregation or other forms of discrimination. The military was told that it was not to permit organizations that practiced race, religious, or other forms of discrimination to use military facilities. The air force inspector general, acting on this order, declared that air force facilities—including those financed through nonappropriated funds—could not be made available to segregated organizations. The air force required all commanders to certify in writing that they had read and understood the Department of Defense memorandum implementing the president's executive order. The inspector advised commanders that he intended to make compliance a special matter of interest.[10]

Kennedy's executive order was followed several months later by a memorandum written by Deputy Secretary of Defense Roswell L. Gilpatric, dated 19 June 1961. It dealt with the subject of the availability of facilities to military personnel. It reaffirmed the policy of equal treatment for all personnel and asked the services to assist minorities in securing integrated quarters. Where unsegregated facilities were not readily available to all members of the service, Gilpatric instructed the military to provide facilities on the post. Local commanders, furthermore, were told "to make every effort to obtain such facilities off base for members of the Armed Forces through command community relations committees." The memorandum also warned that the military police should not be used to enforce segregation or other forms of racial discrimination. Finally the memorandum called on the services to provide legal assistance to ensure that members of the armed forces were afforded due process of law.[11]

The Gesell Committee

On 24 June 1962 President Kennedy followed up by establishing a Committee on Equal Opportunity in the Armed Forces, headed by Gerhard A. Gesell, of Washington, D.C.[12] The president asked the Gesell Committee to look into the general problem of equal opportunity for members of the armed forces and their dependents in the civilian community, particularly with regard to housing, education, transportation, recreational facilities, community events, and other activities.

Not surprisingly, a number of members of the House and Senate reacted to the initial report of the Gesell Committee as a threat to the republic and denounced it on the floors of Congress. Most of the committee's recommendations, however, bore fruit, although it took the unusual events of the late 1960s and early 1970s to finally implement all of its suggestions. Adam Yarmolinsky, a deputy assistant secretary of defense for international affairs under Defense Secretary Robert S. McNamara, has stated that he invented the Gesell Committee.[13] His claim of authorship, however, can be challenged. In February 1962 Congressman Diggs, long an advocate of military civil rights, wrote to Secretary of Defense McNamara, urging him to investigate the conditions of servicemen at home and abroad. Diggs claimed he had received more than 250 complaints during the previous 60 days. He called attention to an August 1961 letter he sent to McNamara, reiterating his demand that a "Citizens Committee be invited . . . to investigate the current status of integration in the Armed Forces." Diggs attached a summary of racial incidents, the bulk of which dealt with off-base discrimination.[14] Early Kennedy administrative correspondence on what subsequently became the Gesell Committee referred to this body as the "Civilian Committee" or "Citizens Committee."[15]

No matter who initiated formation of the Gesell Committee, President Kennedy on 24 June 1962 reestablished the President's Committee on Equal Opportunity in the Armed Forces and asked Gesell "to make a thorough review of the current situation both within the services and in the communities where military installations are located to determine what further measures may be required to assure equality of treatment for all persons serving in the Armed Forces." The committee was directed to study the fact that there was "considerable evidence in some civilian communities . . . [that] discrimination on the basis of race, color, creed or national origin is a serious source of hardship and embarrassment for Armed Forces personnel and their dependents." The president asked for recommendations that would improve the lots of servicemen and their families "in the civilian community, particularly with respect to housing, education, transportation, recreational facilities, community events, programs, and activities."[16]

The services were upset by the findings of the Gesell Committee. As the investigation process lengthened and direction of the study became clear, fears increased among both uniformed and civilian defense leaders. The air force liaison to the committee, Col. John Horne, of the Directorate of Military Personnel, wrote to his chief to complain that the committee's efforts—which he believed (falsely) were only to be a "survey"—had turned into an "investigation." He stated that the committee was helping to initiate "racial problems" with its studies and suggested the air force threaten to withdraw its support of the study if it was not given an "opportunity to review and comment" on the committee's findings. Horne also complained that much of the data sought by the committee was unavailable because the air force did not maintain records by race, since it had been under "strong pressure . . . to keep racial designations off records." When some committee members expressed displeasure over the timidity of southern base commanders in seeking equal off-post facilities for blacks, Horne defended the commanders: "It is not possible for these commanders to go to local community officials in Alabama, Texas, and Georgia, regarding their off-base problems, with the same aggressiveness as their northern and western brothers. If they did, good community relations which have been maintained for years could be ruined in a matter of minutes." Horne wished to persuade the committee to turn to the Commission on Civil Rights or to the Department of Justice or the Department of Health, Education, and Welfare to gather information about racial problems around southern bases rather than to force the services to report such information.[17]

James Goode, deputy assistant secretary of the air force for manpower policy, attended a Gesell Committee session and later reported that answers provided by five air force base commanders were inconsistent. Two from the Deep South stated that it was not their job to influence civil leaders on racial matters. When committee members suggested they use off-limits sanctions as a solution for off-base discrimination, the five commanders balked. Several stated that they did not have the power to take such actions, while others said they would not place community facilities off-limits to benefit a few while the white majority suffered. All five claimed to have good relations with the nearby communities. This statement brought forth the ire of Whitney Young against those base commanders who preferred good relations at the expense of the suffering blacks. The Maxwell AFB commander told the committee it was air force policy not to assign blacks to that base.[18]

In addition to interviewing personnel, the committee requested an enormous amount of data from the services. The air force was asked to answer 30 questions, most of them statistical in nature. The first question dealt with how the air force handled discrimination complaints. Had there been a lessening of problems in segregated communities because of air force efforts? Did the air force provide guidance to commanders in such areas? Other questions dealt with schools, recruiting, housing, commissioning programs, and promotion.[19] The answers to these questions provided much of the raw material for the committee's initial report, published 13 June 1963.

Release of the Gesell Committee report brought down a storm of protest, and perhaps for that reason it was never widely publicized. Yet it can be demonstrated that nearly all of its major recommendations were implemented by the 1970s. Unlike the reports of the Fahy Committee, Truman's Civil Rights Committee, or the Commission on Civil Rights, the Gesell Committee report was not published in a form accessible to the public. Nonetheless, it was placed in the *Congressional Record* by a hostile congressman.[20]

Blacks, the report noted, served in the armed forces in slightly smaller numbers than their proportion of the population, but they held only a small percentage of the higher officer and enlisted ranks. In fact, the officer corps of each service was overwhelmingly white. The army reported that more than 3 percent of its officer corps was black and the navy less than 1 percent. Black gains since 1949 were meager, and much still remained to be done to provide equal opportunity. "Promotion selection," the report complained, was "made primarily by white officers." The committee recommended removal of all racial data from promotion folders, including photographs, to prevent selection bias among board members. The report also recommended adoption of a conscious policy of assigning blacks to promotion boards and choosing whites "whenever possible . . . who have more than casual experience serving with Negro officers and enlisted men."[21]

The keynote of the report was sounded early. Blacks in the military and their families were "daily suffering humiliation and degradation in communities near bases at which they are compelled to serve, and a vigorous, new program of action is needed to relieve the situation."[22] This was the report's theme throughout. It stated:

To all Negroes these community conditions are a constant affront and a constant reminder that the society they are prepared to defend is a society that depreciates their rights to full participation as citizens. This should not be. . . . Homes are broken up by these conditions as Negro families coming from parts of the country which are relatively tolerant of color differences find themselves facing a situation which is both new and frightening. For them, the clock has turned back more than a generation. To protect their children and to maintain some degree of dignity they return home, and the husband is left to work out his service obligation alone . . . the indignities suffered in the community place a load upon his service career affecting both his interest and performance.[23]

The committee discovered that base commanders lacked specific directives to guide them in helping blacks and that for the most part military leaders believed that "problems of segregation and racial discrimination in the local community" were not their legitimate concern. The committee, however, designated the base commander as the individual primarily responsible for "solving local problems."[24]

Finding litigation too slow, the committee opted for a more rapid solution. It declared:

Segregation and other forms of discrimination in facilities in a given locality, detrimental to the morale of Negro personnel . . . must cease. The commander should . . . attempt by means available to him—community committees, persuasion, emphasis on the base's importance to the local economy—to eliminate such practices. In situations in which these efforts are unsuccessful, the commander should develop a plan under which military personnel of all races would be permitted to patronize *only* those facilities which receive his express approval. One of the requirements for such approval should be the guarantee from the proprietor that the establishment will be open to all servicemen and their dependents without regard to race or color.[25]

As indicated above, private citizens and some members of Congress had earlier suggested the use of sanctions. The Gesell report, however, represented the first attempt by a high-level committee to endorse the method. The committee went even further: "Should all other efforts fail, the Services must consider a curtailment or termination of activities at certain military installations near communities where discrimination is particularly prevalent. . . . The objective here should be the preservation of morale, not the punishment of local communities which have a tradition of segregation."[26] In the report the committee complained that the services had not given emphasis to this factor when selecting base locations and recommended more attention be given to such details in the future.[27]

The mechanism which blacks might employ to air their sentiments against discriminatory practices was also open to committee criticism. No one was charged with responsibility to listen to equal opportunity complaints. Given the absence of such an apparatus, blacks often took their complaints out of channels—to members of Congress, to the NAACP, and even to the president. The inspector general, the committee believed, was a "fruitless" channel because he was not "geared to handle such problems." Blacks, furthermore, feared "reprisals if they raised matters of this kind." The committee recommended the appointment of "an officer . . . to receive such complaints." This officer would have to have "free access to the base commander . . . for the purposes of communicating and discussing complaints of discrimination." Every black was to be free to contact this officer "at any time, without the consent, knowledge or approval of any person in the chain of command." The committee further recommended that such complaints were to be privileged, and service regulations were to "prohibit the disclosure of such communications without the serviceman's consent."[28]

With the aid of a specially appointed equal opportunity monitoring officer and armed with off-limits sanctions, base commanders would be required to improve the racial climate on and off the installation. The committee advocated a new policy and mission for the chain of command, from the service secretaries down to the base commander, not only to "remove discrimination within the Armed Forces, but also to make every effort to eliminate discriminatory practices as they affect members of the Armed Forces and their dependents within the neighboring civilian communities." To ensure active compliance on the part of local commanders, the report suggested that base commanders be rated on their performance in these areas. It declared:

> It must be made clear to base commanders and others concerned with these problems that they will be measured in terms of their performance. A regular system of monitoring and reporting on progress should be instituted. It should be made clear that officers showing initiative and achievement in this area will enhance their performance ratings and career advancement. It is especially important that such officers be assured that they will not run the risk of official disfavor for their efforts, and they will receive the support of all echelons of command if their programs are attacked by local interests.[29]

To acquaint future base commanders with the problems confronting blacks, the committee recommended that the "history of Negro participation in the armed forces and the problems which he confronts in the services must be emphasized and made a definite part of the curriculum at all levels of officer and command training." It suggested that the military must "insure that men reaching the position of base commander are familiar with the requirements of the Constitution and the history of the Negroes' struggle to achieve equality of treatment and opportunity."[30]

Another recommendation dealt with discrimination in NCO and service clubs. The report noted that bases with branch clubs often had *de facto* segregation and that base commanders had chosen to ignore this fact. Hostess recruiting for club dances also created tensions because there were "instances when too few or no Negro girls" were brought to a base. The committee also provided evidence that "civilian hostesses . . . imported onto the base from the civilian community [exhibited racial] attitudes which are inconsistent with Department of Defense policy." More efforts had to be made to secure unbiased hostesses, and more black girls "should be secured for dances." In any case, "greater care should be taken in the selection and training of hostesses and other civilian personnel operating Service Clubs."[31]

There were other recommendations: base commanders were told to appoint biracial citizens' committee to assist in maintaining good town/base relationships;[32] Defense Department funds should not be spent on schools that were segregated, nor should such schools retain ROTC programs;[33] segregated cabs and buses must not be permitted on military posts;[34] base commanders should not urge compliance with local segregation requirements;[35] the military should not permit its name to be used in sponsoring segregated athletic, social, or other functions; the military police must not be segregated in town patrol duties; and above all, the military, from the Pentagon down to the recruit, must set the example for the community and country. The report concluded: "The Committee is mindful that the Armed Forces are an ever present symbol of our democracy. Both at home and abroad, they must be leaders rather than followers in establishing equal opportunity. To the extent they practice and preach equality without regard to race, creed, color or national origin, they provide a standard by which communities at home may measure their own conduct and against which citizens of other lands may judge our adherence to the principles we advocate."[36]

Kennedy wrote to Gesell, thanking him and informing him that his recommendations would have the immediate attention of Secretary McNamara, who was required to report to the president within 30 days.[37] McNamara issued a directive which summarized the main Gesell Committee points. Department of Defense Directive 5120.36, dated 26 July 1963 and titled *Equal Opportunity in the Armed Forces,* called upon the uniformed services to "issue appropriate . . . manuals and regulations" to implement equal opportunity. The directive also created a civil rights office within the secretariat. The heart of the directive is contained in the final paragraph: "Every military commander has the responsibility to oppose discriminatory practices affecting his men and their dependents and to foster equal opportunity for them, not only in areas under his immediate control, but also in nearby communities. . . . In discharging that responsibility a commander shall not, except with the prior approval of the Secretary of his military department, use the off-limits sanction in discrimination cases arising with the United States." Never had the use of off-limits sanctions in discrimination cases been considered in an official directive, and even if the power to use such tactics was hedged, its possible adoption was a significant new tool in the integrationist's hands.[38]

A week earlier, McNamara's nominee for the civil rights office, Alfred Fitt, prepared a long memorandum for the secretary outlining the service's objections to the Gesell report. Fitt commented on the military criticisms and offered his own recommendations for action by McNamara and Kennedy. Fitt explained that most of the service opposition was concerned with the Gesell Committee off-base proposals. Although not all of the recommendations for on-base improvements were well received, the services were nervous about those suggestions that might destroy their relationships with the surrounding community. There was in addition strong opposition to the appointment of an equal opportunity officer. On this point, Fitt concluded that the real problem was in communication; the committee perceived the military had to improve communications, but if that was done, there would then be no need for the establishment of new communication channels because several already existed. If communications then were not encouraged, the newly assigned equal opportunity officer would prove ineffective in the performance of his functions. Fitt, therefore, recommended a lesser course: that establishment of equal opportunity officers be voluntary at the base level.[39]

While the services objected to the idea of rating commanders on their success in achieving equal opportunity for service personnel, Fitt agreed with the need for such evaluation. He believed that men were more industrious when they were graded. He did not, however, agree with all of the report's major recommendations; of most concern to him was the use of off-base sanctions. He wrote:

> This is unquestionably the most controversial of the Gesell recommendations. The services have slowly accepted the idea that their responsibility for equal treatment extends off-base, but they have no stomach for the kind of fight which they think use of the off-limits sanctions will mean.
>
> There is a melange of reasons for the service reactions. One is that the connection between off-base discrimination and on-base reduction in military effectiveness is no-where so direct as in the instances of prostitution, illegal gambling, lack of sanitation and the like.
>
> The services are also troubled by enforcement problems, particularly those arising out of a serviceman's desire to be with his dependents. Military officers understandably prefer not to start battles unless they see a prospect of winning.
>
> Finally, there are vexing line-drawing aspects in carrying out the Gesell recommendations, many of which would be eliminated if only Congress would prohibit discrimination in public accommodations, and so they ask why not wait for Congress to act?
>
> My own judgment is that the off-limits sanctions is a severely limited weapon, to

be used only after negotiations make clear that a community is unwilling to end objectionable practices involving servicemen and their families.

Hatred violence and murder are part of the struggle for civil rights. We must not forget that we, not they themselves, have put Negro servicemen at bases in the South. We owe them a duty not to exacerbate the hostility they already face when venturing off-base.

He gave only "guarded approval" for the use of sanctions and the imposition of "severe restraints in actually using it, and then only with Office of the Secretary of Defense's approval of a specific program."[40]

Reaction to the Gesell Report

The military objections raised in Fitt's memorandum were only the sound of a falling stone before the rumble of an avalanche. With the publication of McNamara's directive—demonstrating that the Department of Defense took the Gesell report seriously—the opposition mounted. Many in the military who disliked the report had strong allies in Congress. Although a certain amount of criticism in Congress was regional, many of the criticisms represented an open fear that the armed services were being misused for political and social purposes. Was it the province of the military to intrude into the domestic and political affairs of the nation? Should the armed forces become the tool of a president who desires to improve the social and economic plight of a segment of his constituency? Congressman Melvin R. Laird (Rep., Wis.), argued on the floor of the House that the McNamara directive went far beyond the equal opportunity provisions for all citizens which he and all Republicans had always supported.

Another congressman, J. D. Waggoner, Jr. (Dem., La.), asked if the military was being used for "a purpose" for which it was "never intended." Would not the military be "misused" if it helped to implement this report? Many other members of Congress also asked the same questions. But what McNamara perhaps saw as a legitimate morale question, members of Congress interpreted as a legislative prerogative to be discussed in the halls of Congress, and the military did not have a right to partake in the debate. Congressman Thomas G. Abernethy (Dem., Miss.) declared he was "deeply shocked to find that the executive branch of our government is diverting the serious mission of the Department of Defense and is now using it for the purpose of molding the social and political life not only of the country but of the military itself." Implementing this report, he claimed, would lower "our standard of national defense."[41]

There were other serious charges. Adam Yarmolinsky claimed that the entire thrust of the off-limits sanctions was not to punish segregators but to effect a "direct military benefit." The Department of Defense wanted to "do the best" it could for men and women in the military. The idea of using the military as leverage in the South was never a discussion topic, Yarmolinsky claimed, but if the military was to be the vanguard of society at large, so be it. Something had to be done for blacks because they did not choose their situation. Yarmolinsky asserted, "Laws binding them to segregation were unconstitutional to my mind, and would not have stood up under a court test so we were not involving them in law breaking."[42]

Most military leaders, however, disagreed with Yarmolinsky and feared that McNamara was leading the armed services into domestic controversy and that this was politically motivated. McNamara admits in a book, written after he left office, that he used the military to attack "tormenting social problems." He justified this action by arguing that "poverty and social injustice" could "endanger our national security as much as any military threat." His only reference to the Gesell Committee was the housing recommendations, but the entire thrust of his chapter called "New Missions" was to elaborate upon several examples of military efforts to solve social and economic problems.[43]

Eugene Zuckert, air force secretary during the Kennedy administration, was familiar with Democratic Party programs and no foe of civil rights. He found the Gesell Committee recommendations and McNamara's implementation of them "transparent" attempts "to make a significant advance in the battle against segregation." Zuckert added that if his sole job was integration of the air force, he would have regarded the Gesell Committee recommendations as "a very useful and effective way of going about the job." Racial integration, however, "wasn't my job, I had to balance a lot of other considerations." He did not necessarily believe that using off-limits sanctions was a "bad move," because he was fundamentally in sympathy with the approach; as air force secretary, he did not, however, favor it. He said: "Yarmolinsky and company were social movers, and this was an instrument which they thought would be very effective for their purposes. I don't say that with any rancor at all. I think that the net result has been great. But at that time, with my responsibility, at least I thought that they were adding to my problems and not helping me with them." He also discovered that air force general officers were unanimously "very much opposed" to imposing the Gesell Committee off-limits sanctions.[44]

Though Zuckert was fundamentally in tune with the administration, he saw the program as a misuse of the military. Other people—senators and representatives—were less friendly. Sen. J. W. Fulbright (Dem., Ark.) wrote to McNamara complaining that the military was being thrust into a political conflict and that it did not belong there. The military, he believed, was too powerful to be used in domestic affairs, and the potentialities for abuse were great. He elaborated: "My concern about the dangers of military intervention in civil and political affairs is not satisfied by the fact that such intervention may be done under the authority of civilian superiors. The more important question is, what is the proper role of the military in our national life?" Using the military to intervene in the affairs of local communities, he held, established a "very bad precedent."[45] Other congressional critics were more vitriolic in their criticism of the report and the McNamara directive.

A flood of acidic editorials and essays inserted by hostile members of Congress filled the pages of the *Congressional Record.* Watkins Abbit (Dem., Va.) placed into the record an editorial from the *Lynchburg News* titled "Our Coming Battle with the Military," in which the commentator foresaw communities near military bases "under a degree of martial control through the power of economic boycott." He said that Pentagon statements to the effect that these steps were being taken to protect military men and not for the purpose of racial integration were "at best" lies. The editorial predicted dire consequences if the Gesell Committee recommendations were fully implemented.[46]

Rep. F. Edward Hébert (Dem., La.) also read into the record a resolution from the Veterans of Foreign Wars (VFW) which condemned "this forced interference by the Armed Forces into domestic affairs." The VFW feared that the advice would lead to an undermining of general morale and discipline, and the organization "vigorously" opposed implementation of the report.[47] Hébert added another editorial, from the *New Orleans Times-Picayune and States Item,* which labeled the Gesell Committee recommendations a "radical takeover" of the defense establishment. The editorial further claimed this would lead to a "virtual transformation of the armed services of the United States into an instrument of domestic sociological pressure" and to the "prostitution of a vital national institution."[48]

Hébert was vocal in his opposition and initiated a personal correspondence with Gesell and Horton Smith, an old law partner of Gesell's and a personal friend of Hébert's. The exchange began when Smith wrote to Gesell stating that it was "shocking" that the latter would lend his name "to a document recommending the use of our armed forces for political purposes. Regardless of the civil rights, it is a most improper use of the military establishment and could certainly lead to greater abuses, even to influencing elections." Smith included in his correspondence a number of articles, letters, and editorials from the *New Orleans Times-Picayune and States Item,* claiming also that someone in the Department of Defense had leaked the report to a hostile press. He believed that New Orleans was more integrated than New York City and was too sophisticated to be concerned with the race question; therefore, he maintained the editorials were prompted by a genuine concern for the civil-military issues involved. "Gerry, I think you've been taken," was Smith's parting shot.[49] Apparently, Gesell wrote to Smith and attempted to calm his fears because when Hébert first wrote to Gesell, he was aware of both Smith's letter and Gesell's answer.

Hébert knew, he wrote, that Gesell "did not write the report which bears your

name, but at least I thought you read it." The congressman further condemned the
use of the military "to advocate and influence social reforms off base." He admitted his point of view might be suspect because of the "geographical location of my
district," but he did not "approach" his criticisms on the basis of "segregation or
integration. . . . I criticize the report and assail it because of the misuse of the Department of Defense and its military components in putting into effect that which
has not been authorized by Congress." Hébert claimed that he had not found a
single officer in any branch of the service who favored the report or concurred in
its recommendations. And he added, "Every man in uniform that I have talked
with is horrified and shaken by the use [to] which the military is being put." Military men to whom he had spoken perceived preferences given to blacks in future
terms, and Hébert had "never known the morale of the military to be so affected
negatively by a proposal as in this instance. It is the most destructive document
that has ever been issued," and its effect upon the military was "appalling." Because
Gesell had apparently told Smith that the services, specifically the navy, were not
in opposition to the report, Hébert concluded his letter with a series of comments
concerning the navy's attitude toward the Gesell report. The congressman wrote
that the army and the air force shared the navy's negative attitude, and he told
Gesell that the quoted objections came from internal Pentagon correspondence.
He elaborated further:

> The Navy rejects the contention that Negro officers had been discriminated against
> when it came time for promotion. . . . The Navy rejects any implication that officers
> serving on a promotion board would, contrary to their statutory oaths, practice bias.
> The Navy rejects the committee's recommendation that photographs and racial des-
> ignations be eliminated from officer's record jackets. . . . The Navy rejects the con-
> tention that new techniques be developed to assure that promotion board members
> are free from bias. . . .
>
> The Navy rejects the committee's suggestion that special consideration for promo-
> tion and career advancement be given to officers who promote integration. . . . The
> Navy rejects the recommendation that the history of Negro participation in the
> Armed Forces and the alleged problems he confronts be made a part of the curricula
> of all levels of officer and command training. . . .
>
> The Navy rejects the suggestion that economic sanctions be leveled at off base es-
> tablishments which practice segregation . . . .
>
> The Navy flatly rejects the suggestion that curtailment or termination of activities
> at certain military installations be considered as an ultimate lever of force. . . .
>
> The Navy rejects the recommendation that offices be established in each service
> for the purpose of handling cases of alleged discrimination.

And finally, the navy rejected all of these recommendations because it denied that
there was an equal opportunity problem, according to Hébert.[50]

One of the most bitter critics of the committee was retired Army Lt. Gen. Edward M. Almond. His remarks were inserted into the *Congressional Record* by Representative Abbit. Almond condemned the report because it was biased and would deny "essential information to promotion boards in the military services," especially by withholding photographs. He complained that the report demanded a "higher percentage in Negro promotions" than those qualifying by "merit." Almond was upset further because the report sought racial integration for the "amalgamation of the races" and not for military purposes. He was concerned that it required commanders to use "blackmail" as a weapon to force integration on civilian communities. Almond also castigated the report for its recommendation to establish equal opportunity offices. This, he argued, would permit blacks to make accusations through "secret testimony without the person accused being given the source of the accusation." He chided the report for not permitting a "real evaluation of the individual Negro based on merit," because the report consistently spoke of evaluating the "latent skills inherent in the Negro. . . . It seems never to have occurred to the authors of such projects that there may be a slight difference between the average white and the average Negro in his ability to absorb information and to deliver a satisfactory performance." The committee, he protested, was trying to introduce a "spy system to be called monitoring with an especially sympathetic monitor throughout the range of troop levels . . . to report on responsible commanders as [to] how they carry out their function." Almond grumbled, "Three of the members of this committee are Negroes and the other four have a long career as racial agitators working with the ADA [Americans for Democratic Action], ADL [Anti-Defamation League], and the NAACP [National Association for the Advancement of Colored People]." These people were trying to impose a Soviet political commissar system on the United States military, and this was both "shocking and revolting." Finally, Almond alleged the report sought to "pervert the Armed Forces' mission from that of maintaining the defense and security of the United States for the sake of one small segment of its personnel. An example of this . . . internal turmoil is the requirement of local military commanders to prevent the practice of Negroes gravitating by choice to one post service club and whites to another. This is intolerable interference with the off-duty rights of any American."[51]

Almond's perception of an equal opportunity officer as a page out of Leon Trotsky's book was also seen by others. Congressman John J. Flynt (Dem., Ga.) read an essay into the *Congressional Record* which called attention to the fact that the greatest problem besetting the Russian military was the "political officer" in each unit, because one cannot have politics in the armed forces and efficiency too. The newspaper warned that the next step in the process would be to order the men to vote for certain candidates in presidential elections.[52] Senator Thurmond of South

Carolina struck a similar chord. An editorial, written by Truman Sensing, was inserted by the senator. It lashed out at the attempt to "create a commissar system in the United States subject to the political order of military base commanders." It was clear that the "aim of the Kennedy administration" was to "use the military bases to force radical social change in this country. As in the Communist armies, political commissars ride herd on officers and men alike." In the future, the editorial noted, officers would be required to "hold the political opinions of the administration." This is the "kind of setup one finds in the Red Army." The editorialist ended by calling the report a "national shame." The armed forces "do not exist for the purpose of pushing the Kennedy's pet social theories or for helping the Kennedy administration win more Negro votes in the 1964 elections."[53]

Perhaps the most significant negative response to the Gesell report was an attempt by Rep. Carl Vinson (Dem., Ga.), chairman of the House Armed Services Committee, to nullify by legislation all of the key recommendations contained in the report. His bill would have made it a court-martial offense for any base commander to invoke off-limits sanctions or similar means to prevent segregation of military personnel. Vinson claimed his bill had nothing to do with "segregation or integration"; it was aimed at keeping the "military in the business of defending the nation." He wanted "Congress, the courts, the states and the people [to] worry about social reform." The congressman also would have made it a court-martial offense for any officer who sought to "direct or control in any way the manner in which a member of the Armed Forces lives off military base. Any base commander who because of race, color, or religion tries to prohibit a member of the Armed Forces from making purchases for goods or services or renting housing accommodations or engaging in recreational activities or any other similar activities would be subject to court-martial. Any commander who directs, implements, or requests use of an off-limits sanction because of race, color . . . will also be subject to court-martial." His bill made it illegal as well for anyone to make any "notation on a fitness report, or other written report, with respect to the manner in which a member of the Armed Forces, because of race, color, or religion, attempts to influence or fails to influence" the off-base activities or conduct of any member of the armed forces.[54]

Air Force Opposition

The air force's opposition to the report was very strong but at the same time muted. Air force internal correspondence reflects an enormous dislike for nearly all provisions of the report, but in a communication that it sent to the Department of Defense, its repugnance is couched in philosophical and diplomatic language. Harris Wofford, who was President Kennedy's chief civil rights adviser, said that the military had been given the "hardest" tasks because the armed services were asked to operate outside of their own element. This, he believed, could cause nothing but apprehension.[55] Beyond that, the military had been told abruptly to change direction. Heretofore, the services had been indifferent to off-base discrimination, but they were now told to shift gears. James Goode wrote to Zuckert, pointing out that there had been a "traditional military reluctance to take positive steps insofar as off-base problems" were concerned.[56] He had written earlier to the air force secretary, in late 1962 (when the main points of the Gesell Committee recommendations were being solidified), and declared that it was undesirable to relocate bases primarily because of civilian discrimination. Goode, furthermore, did not believe that the off-limits authority should be used to achieve "social reform." He suggested that the courts should handle such matters. But he did believe that base commanders could be more active than they had been in the past and that they might seek assistance from the Justice Department if laws were being broken. He advised Zuckert that servicemen should not consider a ban on participating in test cases as an order to submit to segregation. Goode wrote: "In my opinion, colored military personnel should not be directed to comply with segregation laws under any circumstances. They may, of course, be advised of local difficulties they may get into in the event they should force a peaceable test of their constitutional rights, but this should be a privilege which should not be curtailed by military fiat."[57]

Prior to the publication of the Gesell report, the air force created a Committee on Equal Opportunity to review all policies and procedures concerning antidiscrimination. This was an obvious reaction to the Gesell Committee's probings, and Zuckert appointed leading members of the air force to this body—Under Secretary Brockway McMillan was designated chairman—and the membership included the deputy chief of staff for personnel, the inspector general, the judge advocate general, the director of information, the director of legislative liaison, and others. The committee had the responsibility to ensure that air force programs were in agreement with Defense Department policies and that Defense Department directives were properly disseminated and "clearly understood by all commanders." The committee, furthermore, was to recommend equal opportunity measures to improve the racial climate within the air force.[58] The minutes of its fourth meeting reveal that the Gesell report was discussed and an attempt was made to fashion an air force position. At the same time, the judge advocate general, the chief lawyer of the air force, advised that the off-limits sanctions suggestion was of "doubtful legality" and argued further that the other service judge advocates held the same opinion. They believed that the impetus for such moves clearly had to come from the president or from the civilian heads of the Department of Defense. The committee hoped that all actions would be deferred "pending final passage of civil rights legislation."[59]

Zuckert responded to a letter from McNamara that had requested official opinions on the Gesell report. Zuckert's answer was temperate in tone. He stated that the air force agreed that the "full equality of treatment and opportunity is of the greatest importance to the welfare and morale of the personnel in the Armed Forces." While the Gesell report contained "many thoughtful recommendations," and the air force intended to move into those areas where its responsibility and authority were clear, certain recommendations required further study. He elaborated:

> First, I would expect that the Department of Defense establish and maintain closest coordination with other Federal agencies which have an interest, or could assist in these matters. I would also expect that the military services would defer action in those areas where such agencies as the Department of Justice, Department of Health, Education, and Welfare, and Home Finance Agency have the primary responsibility and authority. My last point concerns service action in the local communities which must be guided by the civil rights legislation now under consideration in Congress. Pending the final outcome of this legislation, I recommend the Services continue to plan, but defer implementation of such plans where questions of law will subsequently determine the extent of authority which can be exercised in the areas of public accommodations and the rights of individual servicemen, their dependents, and local proprietors of business establishments.[60]

Zuckert's recommendation to delay all off-base action until congress had acted was cautious, diplomatic, and seconded by the uniformed leadership. His reply, however, was not fully indicative of the hostility the generals and colonels harbored.

More demonstrative was a memorandum prepared in July 1963 by the air force to place before the Joint Chiefs of Staff the question of the Gesell report. The major issue, as viewed by the air force leadership, was the nature and extent "of involvement of active military establishments in the enforcement, by base commanders, of sanctions against communities and off-base business establishments which continue to engage in discriminatory practices." The memorandum appears to have been prepared following discussion at high levels, because it claimed that the "Joint Staff and the Services have expressed considerable concern over the proposed use of the military in coercing compliance with civil rights edicts." The air force was uneasy because it was not entirely clear that off-limits actions were legal and because the ramifications of closing or relocating installations based on civilian discrimination practices had not been thoroughly researched. What would be the reaction, furthermore, of the local public if the base interfered in civil affairs beyond showing a concern for the health and welfare of its troops? The air force insisted that there must be "complete coordination in these matters with *all* governmental agencies," and if the services were required to engage in off-limit sanction actions, there must be "well publicized guidance from the Department of Defense of any responsibilities which may be assigned base commanders in these matters." Clearly, the air force feared becoming the vanguard of this explosive issue. The air force expressed other concerns too. Would standards be lowered by assigning personnel for reasons other than qualifications or experience? Was it wise or proper to establish a "special complaint officer . . . outside the existing inspector general procedures and channels"? Would overall morale be lowered if the air force tried to raise the morale of blacks by "extending their plight to all of their military associates"? Why should commanders be rated on their ability to cope with deep-rooted emotional problems? How would one compare a man who might fail in Mississippi with a man who had succeeded in a more salubrious climate? The air force sought to adopt the stand of "firm opposition to (the) use of the military as proposed in the Gesell Report as an instrument of public policy in current civil/domestic issues."[61]

Gen. William McKee, vice chief of staff during this period, expressed his opinion of the Gesell Committee's recommendations during a personal interview. He stated:

> The Air Force, at least I was and I am sure that the leadership's view was, that the Air Force . . . should not be used as a tool for national integration, that it was not up to the Air Force to do this. I took a very strong stand. There were lots of pressures for the Air Force to put towns off-limits, to force integration in the South even to the extent urged by some people of closing up a base or moving it away. And the Air Force took the position that this was a national problem and a national enforcement problem and not one, repeat, not one to be enforced on a national scale by the services and I still feel that way.

When asked if the air staff and Chief of Staff Curtis LeMay shared his opinion, he answered: "We all felt that way very strongly. We were not in the business of being a police force to enforce integration . . . in communities. We didn't feel it was up to us to fight with the local communities, to threaten the local communities. . . . [The Kennedy advisers] obviously were trying to use the military as an aid, as a major aid in the fighting. I didn't think that was possible. . . . I didn't find a single person, or remember a single person, in the entire leadership of the Air Force that felt the Air Force ought to be a police agent to enforce the recommendations of the Gesell Committee."[62]

The *Air Force Times,* in its editorial of 10 July 1963, expressed its views on this subject. The newspaper had warmly supported racial integration in the 1940s in its news coverage and found many good points to comment on in the Gesell report. It also believed that some of the Gesell Committee recommendations were unwise. The *Times* did not approve of the appointment of a special equal opportunity monitor (the paper referred to him as an "integration officer"), arguing that "this could create more problems than it solves." The newspaper found that the off-limits sanctions suggestion was "fraught with problems, regardless of how worthy the principle behind it. So is the suggestion to close bases in communities which do not integrate voluntarily."[63]

A month later, however, the *Air Force Times* reversed itself and published a lengthy article calling on the services to take the lead in the nation's integration battle; it became the first service journal to favor the Gesell Committee's affirmative action program. Blacks suffered terribly, the newspaper stressed, and "any reasonably sensitive person can appreciate the injustice of this situation." If blacks were permitted to choose their assignment stations, the article maintained, there might be no serious basis for complaints of off-post discrimination. "But," the *Times* noted, "they are not able to do so." It added: "While under . . . orders they are often forced to live under severely degrading conditions. . . . The national interest is not served when military personnel are seriously demoralized by the actions of the communities adjacent to our bases." The *Air Force Times* admitted that there were serious problems on and off base; there was a communications gap between officers and blacks; there were some segregated (by custom) clubs; there was studied ignorance of off-base discrimination; interracial association was discouraged in some parts of the country; no action was taken in housing discrimination; and there were segregated schools and school buses. The article cautiously endorsed the findings of the Gesell Committee.[64]

But once the problems had been systematically defined, solutions had to be considered. No longer was it sensible to argue that the dimensions of the problems were known and obvious and do nothing to resolve them. For weeks thereafter in the "letters to the editor" section of the *Air Force Times,* responses to the Gesell report arrived from interested airmen. No other subject in the history of the *Air Force Times* ever garnered such a reaction. White airmen expressed fears that blacks might receive preferential treatment, and in the intense competition for promotions no one wanted the other fellow to be in a favored position. The *Air Force Times* had raised the favoritism argument by showing that blacks made up 9 percent of the air force enlisted corps but only 0.83 percent of the E-9's and less than 2 percent of the E-8's. Immediately, a correspondent asked if blacks had the native ability to deserve more.[65] Most whites disliked the idea of an "integration officer" to hear complaints from blacks outside of normal channels.[66] White airmen complained about the off-limits sanctions, arguing that their morale was not being considered.[67] Some blacks were distressed over the new attention they were receiving, stating that they believed they had equal opportunity and wished no preferential treatment.[68]

Actually, the period from mid-1963 to the end of 1964 was a time of introspection. The air force had begun to confront the issue before the Gesell report was published, simply because it could read the unmistakable signs. The air force house was not in order, and the post-1949 period of self-congratulation over its success at integration had to be replaced by one of self-examination.

Air Force Equal Opportunity Efforts

In December 1962 Acting Secretary of the Air Force Joseph Charyk issued a memorandum for air force commanders which Secretary McNamara believed was worthy of emulation by the other services. Charyk designed a program to implement antidiscrimination policies, and McNamara asked the other services to develop similar programs. It was obvious to the air force secretariat that studies by two government bodies were a clear sign that something had to be done, and it was also clear that Charyk's memorandum was intended to have the air force take positive action to solve the long-standing problems. Charyk recommended the following minimum actions: "All existing directives and policy guidance which have been transmitted to field activities as Air Force policy should be reviewed to insure that they are consistent and clear with the guidance furnished by the Secretary of Defense and the Commander in Chief." The deputy chief of staff for personnel, furthermore, was to review all existing curricula in the various air force schools (the Air University, Air Force Academy, Air Force ROTC, Officer Training School) to "insure that appropriate allocation of time consistent with the length of the course is prescribed for education of the students on anti-discrimination policy." Charyk directed that basic course textbooks be developed to that end. No officers hereafter would be assigned as base commanders who had not been educated in detail on the provisions of air force equal opportunity policy; and they also had to have acceptable efficiency ratings in compliance with such policies. He continued, "Military commanders will be expected to show some positive efforts to improve conditions where off-base prejudices exist." Unsuccessful commanders were to "apprise higher headquarters of difficulties experienced in the treatment" of minorities and request assistance from other governmental agencies. If there was no progress at all, commanders could request funds to build facilities on base to compensate for their absence in the community.[69]

General LeMay, air force chief of staff, received this memorandum. But no implementing directives were sent to the field, probably because Maj. Gen. John K. Hester advised LeMay not to do anything until the Gesell Committee had published its report. Hester informed LeMay that he did not want the air force to be in the forefront on the issue.[70] Gesell himself did not believe the air force would spearhead a revolution with the publication of Charyk's memorandum. And Gesell found many of the suggestions "premature, inadequate and ill-defined."[71]

To ensure coordination on equal opportunity problems within the air staff, an Equal Opportunity Group was created within the Directorate of Personnel Planning, an office subordinate to the deputy chief of staff for personnel. The new group began operating on 1 July 1963, and its membership included Col. Ray R. Koontz, Lt. Col. K. M. Farris, Charles Doane, and two civilian clerks. The directorate's history records, "With the establishment of this staff activity, all matters relating to equal opportunity in the Air Force were forwarded to the Equal Opportunity Group for action." Thus, this group was primarily an answering service for complaints focusing on questions of housing, assignments, promotions, contracts, disciplinary actions, education, community relations, and the like. If a congressman wrote to the air force complaining about the mistreatment of a minority constituent, the new unit would research the matter and would either answer the question or write a response for a senior officer's signature. Additionally, the group would have the function to advise the deputy chief of staff for personnel and through him the chief of staff and others on equal opportunity matters. It was charged with coordinating all air force staff agencies on equal opportunity matters and with maintaining liaison with other services on such matters. Furthermore, it was to advise the deputy chief of staff for personnel on "racial incidents involving military personnel." The group was the air force's point of contact with the U.S. Commission on Civil Rights and with the Gesell Committee. It was the executive secretary and recorder for the Air Force Committee on Equal Opportunity. Finally, group members were charged with the responsibility to formulate, coordinate, and publish air force equal opportunity policy and to implement defense directives on the same subject.[72] In reality, however, the group formulated little policy and spent much of its time investigating alleged incidents for members of Congress and generals.

Air force staff agencies maintain *Read-Files,* which contain copies, chronologically organized, of correspondence generated by the office. The files serve as a useful reference for those who have been gone for short periods of time and who desire to familiarize themselves with the latest activity. The group read-file reveals that attention was given to answering complaints from politicians, superior officers, concerned air force personnel, and interested civilians. For example, Colonel Koontz replied to a lieutenant at Shaw AFB, South Carolina, asking the young officer to be more understanding and patient with his base commander's problems with that state. The lieutenant had apparently written out of normal channels to gain some improvement in the off-base situation. Koontz advised him to appreciate his "commander's tasks in this area," because it was "not an easy one." The lieutenant had expected the base commander to make improvements, even though the military lacked the authority to direct changes within the community. Koontz noted as well: "The letter-writing campaign being conducted by you and your associates is of little benefit to your base commander. He is subject to periodic reports on this subject and needs your loyal support and cooperation if benefits are to be gained."[73]

At the same time, however, Koontz prepared for Maj. Gen. James Moore's signature a letter to the commander of TAC admonishing him that more was expected of the command than waiting for the community of its own volition to alter its customs and mores. Koontz added: "Military commanders must concern themselves with the off-base treatment of military personnel and dependents. . . . They should not confine their efforts on behalf of military personnel to those changes that the community is willing to make for all its minority group residents." Then Koontz softened the blow: "The lack of guidance that you have received on this subject is recognized. Proposed Air Force directives to implement the Defense Directive on this subject are awaiting the Department of Defense approval."[74]

Other correspondence reveals that the group tried to get another institution of higher learning to replace the University of Mississippi, which decided to stop teaching at Keesler AFB because the air force asked it to desegregate its base extension classes. A Jesuit college, Spring Hill, and American University volunteered to offer programs of study.[75] Elsewhere, SAC requested and received permission from air force headquarters to deny the NAACP meeting space for its gatherings on Ellsworth AFB.[76] The group was also involved in an exchange of correspondence with NAACP state and national offices, answering their complaints and providing information.[77] There were also letters from the group to other organizations soliciting information for the air force leadership.[78] One particular piece of correspondence by Colonel Koontz is sarcastic. In a letter to a general in air force personnel, Koontz wrote that Selma's sheriff, Jim Clark, was "effective" in his dealings with blacks, while "his methods are not always universally acceptable."[79] An air force officer most familiar with the Selma, Alabama, scene called Jim Clark a "sadist."[80]

Over the next year, the group's mission changed little. When Koontz left in mid-1964, he was not replaced, but the activities changed not at all. In 1964 the office published a major revision to AFR 35-78 but went no further than Department of Defense directives. The group mainly investigated complaints and tried to stay on top of the problems. The Defense Department floated a trial balloon in the form of a draft memorandum that would have denied the right of air force moonlighters to work for employers discriminating against military personnel and their dependents because of race, color, religion, or national origin. The group prepared an air force negative answer to the proposal.[81] A proposed directive prepared by Alfred Fitt is a measure of the control some members of the Kennedy administration believed they had over uniformed personnel. Fitt asked McNamara to consider adding the following passage to Defense Directive 5000.7, then in draft: "No member of the Armed Forces on active duty may engage in off-duty employment with an employer who, although ostensibly dealing with the public at large, conducts his business in a fashion which results in discrimination on grounds of race; creed, color or national origin against members of the Armed Forces or their dependents." Fitt wanted the proviso added because there had been instances whereby black servicemen were refused service by off-duty white military personnel.[82] The idea was not accepted, but enforcing such a regulation would have introduced all manner of problems. The proviso probably would have caused enormous resentment, since moonlighting servicemen work a second job to earn money and not to humiliate fellow soldiers.

In a positive vein, the air force banned attendance of its personnel at schools which would not accept them regardless of race. This provision was effective only if the air force furnished any part of the tuition for an airman. The service permitted attendance at segregated graduate schools, but only if the program was unique.[83] The air force also prohibited its personnel from speaking at segregated affairs.[84]

Passage of the Civil Rights Act

The major story of 1964 was the passage of the Civil Rights Act and the promulgation of the revised and expanded AFR 35-78. The landmark legislation opened public accommodations to blacks and appeared to be a life buoy for the air force.[85] Prior to the enactment of the legislation, the air force and the other services were placed between a "rock and a hard place" by the Gesell Committee and the Kennedy administration. Even if Adam Yarmolinsky was not attempting to use or misuse the military as a lever to coerce recalcitrant southern communities into line, it so appeared to senior military officers and to many politicians. What the Civil Rights Act did was to place the law on the side of a commander who desired to assist his personnel in solving problems with the civilian community. The air force and the other services did not delay in publishing regulations taking advantage of their strengthened position. In a talking paper prepared for the air force chief of staff by Lt. Col. Farris, the message was clear:

> The passage of the Civil Rights Act of 1964 gives added emphasis to the requirement for commanders to take affirmative action in fostering equal opportunity and treatment for all military personnel and their families in off-base communities.
>
> We are no longer engaged in a social reform program that has a debatable basis in law. We are now engaged in a program to provide for all of our people the basic rights that are guaranteed by the Constitution and the Civil Rights Act and to support them in the lawful assertion of those rights. . . . Military personnel must be informed of these rights and be informed of the type of support that the Air Force can and cannot provide.[86]

The *Air Force Times* informed its readers in bold headlines that read "Defense Hits Hard at Bias" and "Commanders to Act." The Civil Rights Act had given the air force the power to strike at discrimination. Pentagon memoranda appeared daily, noted the newspaper, assisting the services to do all they could to help servicemen counter off-base discrimination.[87] In *Supplement to the Air Force Policy Letter for Commanders,* McNamara advised:

The Civil Rights Act of 1964 is an immensely important and historic expression of this nation's commitment to freedom and justice. It has special meaning for the members of our Armed Forces, all of whom have already given a personal commitment to defend freedom and full justice in their own country.

The President has made it very clear that he expects each Department to move with dispatch within its areas of concern in developing programs and policies which will give full impact to the Civil Rights Act.

In the Department of Defense this means, primarily the vigorous, determined, sensitive commitments by military commanders to a program of fostering and securing equal opportunity for all their men, and their families off-base as well as on. . . .

This Department was created to defend the freedom of the United States. The denial of the rights of members of the Armed Forces is harmful to the very purpose in which we are engaged, for discrimination against our people saps the military effectiveness we strive to maintain.

His statement is followed by one from Norman Paul:

The Civil Rights Act of 1964 includes provisions of major importance to the Armed Forces. Of particular significance are the sections banning discrimination in privately owned facilities of the kind frequently patronized by servicemen and their families: hotels, motels, movie theaters, gasoline stations, restaurants and all other places principally engaged in selling food for consumption on the premises.

The act creates a specific judicial remedy for individual victims of discrimination in most privately owned public accommodations, and it empowers the Attorney General to bring such suits as well. . . .

It is important that military personnel be acquainted with the pertinent provisions of the Civil Rights Act, and be advised of their rights there under. . . .

It is also important that responsible military officials understand that the passage of the act . . . is of itself not going to bring an end to the problem of unequal treatment off-base for members of the Armed Forces. . . . Consequently, it is more important than ever that base commanders initiate or continue discussions with community leaders designed to bring about the peaceful, proper and prompt implementation of the Civil Rights law as it affects servicemen and their families.[88]

The *Air Force Times* spread the message further: "When the President signs the Civil Rights bill, . . . 200,000 Negro servicemen will have a federal law supporting them when seeking access to off-base public accommodations and other facilities." The newspaper pointed out that new equal opportunity regulations were being prepared.[89]

The new directive, titled "Equal Opportunity and Treatment of Military Personnel" and published 19 August 1964, was quite explicit. A draft of the regulation had first been prepared a year earlier, and with passage of the Civil Rights Act, the regulation was published. The impact, then, of the legislation on the regulation is clear.[90]

The new regulation advised air force personnel how to go about changing the situation for blacks and other minorities. The order stated:

> It is the policy of the Air Force to conduct all of its activities in a manner which is free from racial discrimination, and which provides equal opportunity and treatment for all uniformed members irrespective of their race, color, religion, or national origin. . . . The equal and just treatment of all personnel is a well established principle of effective personnel management. Such treatment is essential to attaining and maintaining a high state of morale, discipline and combat readiness.
>
> Discriminatory practices directed against military personnel, all of whom lack a civilian's freedom of choice in where to live, to work, to travel and to spend his off-duty hours, are harmful to military effectiveness.

The policy expressed in the regulation applied worldwide and as well to the Air Force Reserve but not to the Air National Guard, except when the latter was on "active duty in a Federal status."[91]

Commanders were responsible for ensuring that the policy was "implemented in all on-base activities"; for orienting personnel on the new policy; for apprising personnel "of the provisions of Titles II, III, and IV of the Civil Rights Act of 1964 . . . ; and for processing requests for suit by military personnel for action by the Attorney General." For the first time, commanders were made directly responsible for fostering "equal treatment of military personnel and their dependents in off-base civilian communities." Commanders were now required to provide "unsegregated accommodations" for personnel "attending or participating in command sponsored meetings, conferences, or field exercises." The regulation required that all service members "regardless of race, color, religion or national origin" be accorded equal opportunity for "enlistment, appointment, advancement, professional improvement, promotion, assignment, and retention."[92]

But the regulation hedged on the question of off-base implementation. Because military commanders had no "direct control" over civilian communities, the regulation claimed that there could be no "complete uniformity" in procedures for off-base programs. The final resolution of difficulties was left to the individual communities. Commanders, however, could assist urban centers in solving their problems. Military heads might use the base-community council as a means of resolving local discriminatory practices. Commanders could meet with local trade associations to solicit cooperation and with realtors and others involved in the sale and rental of housing to ask for equal opportunity. The chief officers could establish a "local liaison" with other federal agencies in an attempt to adopt a common policy toward civilian community problems. The former could request local cooperation from the community so that service members and their dependents would have access to all public accommodations and facilities, would be served in all business establishments, would be admitted to local sporting events on a non-segregated basis, and would be admitted to all "community controlled public facilities." Commanders were directed to publicize the success of on-base integration and to take advantage of any state or local antidiscrimination laws that might benefit military personnel. Finally, the military chiefs were to ensure that no "actual or tacit support" was given to community discriminatory practices.[93]

The regulation devoted considerable attention to those means that would assist blacks in bringing an end to housing discrimination. In addition to forbidding housing bias on station, the regulation directed commanders to use their "good offices" to achieve the same goal in the community. No sale or rental listings were to be posted by the housing or family services office that did not make residences available to all without regard to race, color, or national origin. Commanders were empowered to investigate any housing projects constructed with the aid of federal funds and to help ensure that they were available to all without discrimination. The military heads could use their judge advocates to assist personnel to file complaints against realtors or builders who acted in violation of federal, state, or local laws. All housing leased by the government was to be available to all service members without regard to race, color, religion, or national origin.[94]

The regulation codified previous departmental rulings on education and further stated:

> Military personnel will not be sponsored or subsidized from Air Force funds while attending civilian educational institutions in the course of such programs as Operation Bootstrap, tuition assistance, and permissive TDY [temporary duty] if the educational facility discriminates on the basis of race. . . . The Department of the Air Force supports the right of dependent children of military personnel to be assigned to and to attend public schools without regard to race, color, religion or national origin. Where deviations from this policy are practiced with respect to dependents of military personnel, commanders will make appropriate efforts on behalf of military children to eliminate these deviations.

Equally important, commanders were directed to transfer the registration of children from segregated to nonsegregated schools and to assist parents in providing children with an unbiased education.[95]

The regulation called it "inappropriate" for military personnel to participate in civil rights demonstrations. It limited the rights of personnel to do so but did not forbid it under all circumstances. Air force personnel could not participate in demonstrations when on a military reservation, when breaking a law, when violence was attendant, when required to be present for duty, when in uniform, or when in a foreign country. The regulation advised airmen that an attempt to exercise a "right conferred or protected by the civil Rights Act of 1964" was "not in itself a civil rights demonstration. Commanders are to support military personnel and their dependents in the lawful assertion of such rights."[96]

The regulation forbade military personnel from attending or speaking at segregated meetings in an official capacity. It stated: "Care must be exercised that acceptances of speaking engagements and participation in conferences by military and civilian officials are consistent with this policy. Officials should not participate in conferences or speak before audiences where any racial group is segregated or excluded from the meeting or from any of the facilities used by the conferences or meetings. . . . The Air Force will not sponsor, support, or financially assist, directly or indirectly, any conference or meeting held under circumstances where participants are segregated or are treated unequally because of race." Commanders were directed to report promptly all racial incidents on or off base and to process rapidly complaints of racial discrimination. They were also asked to assist their personnel in filing complaints with the attorney general. Included in the regulation was an attachment that explained how to process complaints under the provisions of the Civil Rights Act of 1964, reading as follows: "The purpose of this attachment is to promote the Air Force policy of fostering equal treatment for military personnel and their dependents by describing policies and procedures for processing of requests for civil rights suits by military personnel electing to utilize command assistance in forwarding such requests to the Attorney General." Commanders were told to inform their personnel of the provisions of Titles II, III, and IV of the law and of the "remedies" provided in these titles. They also were to ensure that legal assistance offices serving the commander were available to "advise personnel eligible for legal assistance." Commanders were instructed to seek cooperation from discriminating facilities before allowing the judge advocate to move the case through the federal government to the attorney general.[97]

Finally, the off-limits sanctions provision was seriously circumscribed. Yet it must be remembered that no previous air force regulation had even hinted at the use of this weapon. The regulation read, "Commanders will not use the off-limits sanction in discrimination cases without the prior approval of the Secretary of the Air Force and then only after all reasonable alternatives have failed to achieve the desired effect."[98]

When in August 1964 the *Air Force Times* publicized the new AFR 35-78, it pointed out the regulation's shortcomings. Since the directive indicated that uniform success could not be anticipated, the newspaper theorized that off-limits sanctions were "unlikely to be granted" by the secretary. The paper also pointed out the absence of a provision for the appointment of an antidiscrimination officer. Finally, the newspaper took note that the regulation had no impact on the Air National Guard until one of its units federalized.[99] The regulation did mark an advance in civil rights questions, however, because it transposed air force official policy from one of benign neglect to one of open support for winning rights for black personnel under the Constitution and federal statutes. In reality, the new regulation meant little by itself. It could serve as a platform for more aggressive actions if the leadership saw need for such action.[100]

The Air Force Marks Time

With the passage of the law and publication of the regulation, the air force seemed to accept its new role in granting equal opportunity to all of its personnel. Black airmen had reached another plateau and remained there until a series of race riots occurred on military bases early in the next decade. But in the meantime, a new wave of civil disturbances, many racially inspired, struck the United States in the mid-1960s. These riots ushered in a new way of looking at the race question and precipitated attempts for the first time to try to educate all military personnel on racial policy and on the history and sociology of the race problems in America. A new perspective was needed probably because the race issue seriously affected the military's ability to fight. The civil and later military riots were caused by minority frustrations after the promises of the Civil Rights Act and of the new service regulations were not fulfilled rapidly enough. The riots that tore apart sections of New York, Los Angeles, Cleveland, Washington, Baltimore, Boston, and a dozen other cities occurred after the passage of the most important piece of civil rights legislation in this country. Revolutions take place when life is improving but not advancing rapidly enough for some segments of society. The air force experienced a Watts-like riot at Travis AFB in 1971 for the same reason that the United States suffered the Watts riot in 1965.[101]

Unfortunately the air force, more and more distracted by the war in Vietnam, overlooked the lessons of the racial explosions in the 1960s. When Colonel Koontz left the Equal Opportunity Group in 1964, no one replaced him to continue to keep an eye on racial questions. He left in the same year as the bloody race riots in Bedford-Stuyvesant and Harlem.[102]

Lieutenant Colonel Farris continued to carry on the functions of the office, answering correspondence to higher air force levels, to various members of Congress, and to influential organizations. Sen. Allen Ellender (Dem., La.) complained of an integrated air force funeral procession for a white airman, but he was told that the air force could no longer honor requests for all-white color guards or funeral parties.[103] The group replied to correspondence from Congressman Diggs and Sen. L. Saltonstall (Rep., Mass.) on behalf of their constituents.[104] There was a great exchange of traffic between the office and Col. Richard Ault about problems at Craig AFB, near Selma, Alabama.[105]

In a personal interview, Ault revealed that he had not received much genuine guidance from the Equal Opportunity Group. He said the office had been a link between the field and the air staff and intended to keep each informed of the other's situation. The Equal Opportunity Group seldom offered Ault advice except to tell him to continue to walk his narrow course ("tight-rope" walking according to General LeMay) between the Department of Defense and the denizens of Selma. Without any help from the air force, Ault was able to get the local Selma Housing Authority, a city organization, to integrate its Nathan Bedford Forrest Homes by giving complete assignment control to Craig AFB personnel. This significant victory was not commonly known because both Ault and "the Selma Housing Authority had agreed that there should be absolutely no publicity about this agreement."[106] The housing unit was built for and used solely by air force personnel but was segregated because it came under the jurisdiction of Selma.

Ault worked continuously for equal opportunity issues, and integration of the housing project named for the founder of the Ku Klux Klan was one of his triumphs. He readily admitted that momentum was gained after the passage of the Civil Rights Act, although the housing victory had come earlier. While Ault received few complaints, he was aware of the problems blacks encountered in the community, and he created a biracial military committee to "serve as a form of sounding board for black troops." His chief problems with Selma between 1962 and 1964 were caused by a "traditionalist" southern mayor and his "sadistic sheriff . . . Jim Clark," who would not budge on racial matters. Ault admits that he did not "get very far with these people, although I tried." After the appearance of the Civil Rights Act, an election brought a change in Selma's administration. A new mayor, Joseph Smiterman, and a new sheriff, Wilson Baker, took office, and they undertook to improve conditions. Hereafter, Ault made headway, but even then he was unable to advertise publicly the formation of an interracial base-town committee. When he left Selma in 1966, however, it was a completely changed community, "much, much for the better—a whole other world."[107] Yet, he accomplished much on his own because the Equal Opportunity Group was not geared or manned to assist.

By July 1965 the group had declined in importance and thereafter disappeared entirely as a separate operating agency;[108] it was merged with the Flying Status and Entitlements Branch of the Personnel Plans division. The remnant was manned by only one officer with no clerks until the Travis AFB riot in 1971. The office then expanded to a size even larger than it had been in 1963. During the years of decline, the office primarily answered congressional inquiries and interpreted its chief regulation for the field.[109] A secretary of the air force investigation of race relations completed on 17 September 1968 found that the air force had no equal opportunity program at all, although it had a regulation, and the investigators were unable to locate the Office of Equal Opportunity anywhere in the Pentagon except by accident and after many fruitless calls.[110]

The fact is the air force no longer acted as it had in 1949. In that earlier time, the air force hatched its own plan in a huddle before the commander in chief sent in a play. When given the ball, the air force ran with it until it scored its own goal. After 1964 and for the next seven years, the air force received passes thrown by the Department of Defense, dropping some and downing the ball immediately on those caught. There is nothing in AFR 35-78 or in air force policy that was produced from within. What the air force accomplished in race relation matters, it was told to do. Making innovative social change in civilian communities probably is not a proper air force mission, but seeing that the morale of its personnel was not adversely affected by discriminatory practices now became one of its responsibilities. Some progress was made, however, in housing, promotions, and off-base accommodations. Black officer procurement in the air force increased by 50 percent between 1961 and 1965—from a strength of 1,300 to 2,026—but the percentage of black officers in the latter year was still less than 2 percent of the officer corps.[111]

Herein lies a clue to the question: Why could the air force not avoid the problems of general society even if it had regulations that tried to guarantee equal opportunity? The air force was a part of the national milieu, and unless it attempted to stay ahead of society's problems, it would become enmeshed in them. That the air force was not confronted with race riots until the events at Travis in 1971 may be attributed to the fact that it provided greater equality than society at large. There were blacks in supervisory positions, and they received essentially equal treatment on the base. In contrast to some civilian communities during this period, the air force may have looked wonderful.

But even if the air force was utterly free of racism, and no one would be so naive to claim that it was, progress appeared suspiciously slow. By 1965 all vestiges of official racism had disappeared; what remained was personal bias and prejudice and residual problems off base. When the air force decided in 1964 not to establish an on-base equal opportunity officer, it eliminated the one communication link that might have prevented the riots at the beginning of the next decade. When the air force permitted the Equal Opportunity Group to atrophy, it ensured that it would not hear the unpleasant racial news from the field. The air force believed it had the problem resolved, yet saw to it that the mechanism for telling the truth was still-born.

The air force had progressed far from the prejudicial attitudes of the 1920s and 1940s. This can be demonstrated by quoting from several theses written at the Air University, perhaps appropriate since this narrative began with a study prepared in 1925 at the Army War College. Vergil M. Bates, an Air War College student in 1964–65, wrote that military commanders had new roles: "A man whose family is feeling the effects of discrimination will not be keenly attuned to his team members' goals as his mind will be searching for the answer to his own problems. In welding his troops into a homogeneous fighting force, the commander must strive to eliminate discrimination and social prejudice both on-base and off-base."[112] Another work, prepared at the Air Command and Staff College by Don G. Harris, shows the willingness of military men to adapt to the new demands placed upon them. He wrote:

> Off base equal opportunity for Negro military personnel is necessary. The use of the Air Force, and the other services, as leaders in social reform to reduce discrimination is unprecedented in United States History. However, this bold course of action established by President Kennedy is justified by the United States constitution and current federal law. At one time this use of military institutions to lead social reform may have been assessed correctly as a purely political maneuver to achieve political objectives. However, present day social attitudes and democratic ideals reflected in congressional legislation and judicial decisions support the use of military institutions as leaders in social reform. . . . The man who commands an Air Force base plays the key role in determining success or failure of Air Force off- base equal opportunities and community relations policies. Ability to resolve local problems without outside publicity and interference is required of every base commander. . . . He must have a firm concept of human relations and why human relations is important in military management. . . . The Air Force [should] use careful and prudent judgment in selecting officers as base commanders, keeping in mind those managerial and communicative abilities required to skillfully cope with problems by this conflict of responsibility.[113]

Such attitudes moved the air force to react positively when the Travis AFB conflagration turned its nightmare into reality. Henceforth, the air force put into effect the remaining Gesell Committee recommendations, enforced an improved AFR 35-78, required all service personnel to attend courses in race relations, and, with the other services, moved up to another plateau of consciousness. If this plateau is seen as the last height to be reached, or if the air force relaxes its efforts again and fails to keep a watchful eye for racial injustices and discrimination, the events at Travis might repeat themselves.

Epilogue

he purpose of this epilogue is to highlight only the most significant events involving blacks in the air force between 1964 and the late 1970s. (The preface brings this story up to the mid-1990s.) Between the mid-1960s and the early 1970s, the service did act to improve the internal racial climate. The record reflects an increased awareness and sensitivity among USAF officials on the subject, but it also indicates that they did not fully grasp the depth of black frustrations. The reforms instituted earlier by the air force proved insufficient to prevent a major riot by black airmen at Travis AFB, California, in May 1971 and other serious (but less violent) altercations that followed. Thus, despite the substantial gains won by black airmen after 1964, they did not fulfill their expectations of equal treatment. There is little doubt that the air force failed to keep abreast of sentiments within the black community. Had it acted earlier to establish equal opportunity offices at all command levels to respond to black airmen's grievances, the problems of 1971 might have been avoided. Although such offices were set up in December 1970, they came too late to avert the Travis riot. The disorder led to a wave of change in the air force, which seemingly inaugurated a new period of racial stability.

Positive Programs between 1964 and 1971

A significant step was taken in 1969 with the publication of AFR 35-11, "Equal Opportunity for Military Personnel in Off-Base Housing Programs." This directive, which implemented a Department of Defense policy, had as its goal the elimination of all discriminatory practices against military personnel in securing off-base housing. The James C. Evans files are replete with black complaints about housing. Defense Secretary Robert McNamara had initiated voluntary programs to encourage realtors and others to offer housing on a nondiscriminatory basis, and segregated housing listings had been banned from base files. The changes brought about at the end of the 1960s included a provision that forbade military personnel from leasing or renting housing which was not open to all service personnel. This restriction put economic pressure on housing facilities located near military bases. The goal of the regulation was not simply to find housing for blacks in a nearby black district but to locate housing anywhere in the surrounding area that would not force the black servicemen to suffer indignities and humiliation because of their race.[1]

In 1970, Headquarters, U.S. Air Forces in Europe (USAFE), demonstrated an awareness of rising racial frustrations and published *Commanders Notebook on Equal Opportunity and Human Relations.* This pamphlet was an adaptation of a similar publication printed by the United States Army, Europe (USAREUR). The USAFE *Notebook* explained that the air force was "fully committed to a policy of fostering equal opportunity for all its members regardless of their race, color, religion or national origins." The authors of the text believed that failures in communication precipitated racial problems. They hoped to "provide an insight into the factors leading to racial tension and to provide guidance for a continuing program that will improve human relations and assure equal opportunity and treatment."[2]

The study also observed that one of the "strongest convictions held by the black military member is that he does not have the same opportunity for advancement as his white counterpart. Statistics tend to support this belief." The data included in the *Notebook* show that the percentage of black air force officers increased from only 1.6 percent to 1.8 percent between 1965 and 1969. While the percentages of blacks in the top three enlisted grades had doubled in the same period, blacks, constituting 11 percent of the enlisted corps, made up less than 3 percent of the Chief Master Sergeant (E-9) ranks, only 4 percent of the Senior Master Sergeant (E-8) grades, and less than 6 percent of the Master Sergeant (E-7) echelon. The *Notebook* reported that 80 percent of the blacks surveyed in April 1970 did not believe they enjoyed equal opportunity in the air force. The authors stressed that their attitude could be based on either fact or perception, but the evidence of mass frustration was apparent, whatever its cause.[3]

The study further discussed at some length racial irritants and grievances. Blacks were upset with bar and tavern owners who overcharged them, refused them service, or created private clubs that excluded them. Blacks were irritated at similar practices in hotels and motels. They resented discrimination in housing through overcharging or an outright refusal to rent. Blacks resented the custom in the German press to refer to black crime suspects as "black Americans" instead of merely Americans. Blacks had grievances regarding off-duty employment opportunities, unequal punishments for offenses, an inordinate share of menial duties and details, poorer training opportunities, unequal on-base dependent employment opportunities, little choice in NCO and service club entertainment activities, no opportunity to pick one's roommates (supervisors arbitrarily assigned whites and blacks to bunk together to ensure that integration worked), and being the targets of derogatory names (like "boy" and "spook"). Blacks often complained that barbers were not qualified to cut their hair and that there were inadequate stocks of their special needs in the base exchange, commissary, and newsstand. Blacks believed they were ineffective in having prejudiced officers and NCOs removed from supervisory positions and were usually branded as "militants" or troublemakers if they voiced grievances on racial subjects. Black airmen believed that they were underrepresented on club advisory boards, there were too few of their race teaching in overseas public schools, few black studies courses were offered in extension programs, little publicity was given to black entertainers, only minimal recognition was given for meritorious achievements, and too little black literature was found in the base libraries. They resented the hostility and bigotry displayed toward black dependents by white families.[4] The *Notebook* played down none of these irritants, because its authors knew that troubles brew from an accumulation of grievances, no one of which might be considered terminal in itself but any one of which, when combined with a plethora of other morale-depressing hurts, could ignite a riot.

The study also listed indicators of racial unrest and evaluated several incidents for the lessons that might be learned. It stressed, "Lack of communication between commanders, supervisors and lower grade airmen was one of the most significant factors leading to racial disharmony and tension." As a means of suggesting methods for improving communications, the *Notebook* produced descriptions of formal and informal groups created at various military installations which had been established to air grievances, squelch rumors, and improve situations that were injurious to morale. The study's writers called on bases to establish equal opportunity seminars to heighten sensitivity to racial questions and to discuss problems before they became serious.[5] This was a forerunner of the Defense Race Relations Institute program, which will be discussed below.

In addition to the heightened awareness as demonstrated by one major air command in the USAFE *Notebook,* Headquarters USAF implemented a controversial Gesell Committee provision—the appointment of an equal opportunity officer to the commander's staff. He was to be a conduit of information between the community and the commander, or between the field and the Pentagon, ensuring that the local commander and the air staff were aware of the racial problems. The directive stipulated:

Each major commander will appoint a command equal opportunity officer. The officer should be of field grade or comparable civilian grade. . . . The role of the command equal opportunity officer should be that of the major commander's personal representative for monitoring, guiding, and evaluating the command equal opportunity program. . . . Normally, the command equal opportunity officer duties are assigned as additional duty to an officer or civilian assigned to the personnel function. However, a commander may appoint a fulltime equal opportunity officer from within his manpower resources when he determines that this is required to maintain adequate control of the program. Commanders of all Air Force installations with a military population of 500 or more will appoint, on an additional duty basis, a base equal opportunity officer. . . . Officers assigned to the position of senior base Chaplain, senior base Judge Advocate, Inspector General, and Chief Security Police will not be appointed base equal opportunity officer. The role of the base equal opportunity officer should be that of an informal counselor who has direct access to the installation commander on equal opportunity matters and who is in a position to obtain assistance of the staff activities concerned in resolving allegations of discrimination on an informal basis. In all cases, he should strive to resolve issues at the lowest level of command.[6]

The above text appeared as a change to AFR 35-78 in late 1970. It called upon commanders to establish effective lines of communication to ensure good human and race relations and to maintain an "open door policy."[7]

Fewer than six months later, the air force again rewrote the regulation. The new text called for more affirmative action on the part of the leadership. Published a week before the Travis riot, the regulation called on commanders to "initiate action to oppose and overcome discriminatory treatment" of personnel and their dependents on and off base. The 1964 version had simply called for commanders to foster an atmosphere of equal opportunity. The new revision also added a provision asking "rating and indorsing officials" to "consider the quality and effectiveness of an individual's leadership or support of the Air Force equal opportunity and treatment policy." The regulation, however, did not require a statement to this effect on all effectiveness reports. The new version also removed the requirement for commanders to seek the approval of the secretary of the air force before imposing off-limits sanctions against all segregating establishments. The directive simply stated, "Commanders will impose off-limits sanctions against all business establishments . . . that discriminate against military personnel and their dependents."[8]

Despite the evidence incorporated in the USAFE *Notebook* and the revisions of December 1970 and May 1971 to AFR 35-78, the air force was largely unaware of the dimensions of its racial problem. This is evidenced by the size of the Equal Opportunity Office in the headquarters—still a one-man operation until the Travis riot. At the same time, the army also faced a number of race riots, but it began to focus on the problem before the air force. The army first experienced bloodshed at Fort Bragg, at Fort Dix, and at various camps and cantonments in Germany, Korea, and Vietnam. The air force, however, was relatively unscathed until May 1971, when Travis AFB erupted. This riot shattered the air force's complacent attitude and provoked probing reappraisals. At first, air force leaders believed that the Travis riot was a mere spillover from the "steam of racial prejudice" that had infected society at large. They were to discover, however, that the riot had been caused by a failure in leadership, which had led to a "critical breakdown in communication."[9]

The Travis Riot

The *Air Force Times* reported that the Travis riot was caused by an accumulation of "little things." Representative of black grievances was the practice of imposing nonjudicial punishment on blacks for offenses for which whites received counseling or reprimands. Blacks were equally disturbed that the base commander had apparently refused to place off-limits an apartment complex in the nearby community which allegedly refused to rent apartments to blacks. The base commander stated that he did not place a ban on the apartment project because he had not received a fully substantiated report. He noted: "I do not administer social justice. I need a complaint. . . . I do not wander around the community looking for social injustices."[10] Blacks were also disturbed because the predominantly black staff at the NCO club was fired, allegedly because an audit showed funds and property missing. They believed as well that the base commander demonstrated insensitivity when he forbade the clenched-fist salute at Travis. When asked by a reporter if he would relax this prohibition, the commander said: "Absolutely not. It will never be [permitted] as long as I'm a military officer." Blacks also alleged that there was discrimination on the air base in duty assignments, leave, and promotions. There was also a lack of recreational facilities suited to the tastes of young blacks. And finally, they claimed that the civilian personnel office and the base exchange discriminated against them and their dependents in its hiring practices.[11]

These "little things" provided the fuel for a four-day riot which occurred between 21 and 24 May 1971. The spark igniting the outburst was a fight between a white and a black over the high volume of a phonograph played during a party to which only blacks were invited. When news of their confrontation spread, whites and blacks spilled out from nearby barracks and joined in general fighting. Security police successfully broke up the barracks area fight only to encounter a new outbreak at the NCO club. Later, another struggle broke out in a base cafe when blacks ordered all whites to vacate the building. At one stage police in riot gear battled "200 brawling airmen." When the security forces tried to arrest a black who had made obscene gestures and remarks to the base commander, a mob of blacks intervened and the airman escaped. Later during the rioting, 60 blacks moved on the base jail to free some arrested airmen, but they were turned back by the security police. The mob then attacked some nearby whites and later moved on to the barracks area and assaulted whites along the way, smashed windows, and damaged automobiles. A white lieutenant colonel near the barracks area was beaten by the mob and suffered lacerations and bruises. At times the security police had to use high-pressure fire hoses to disperse the mobs. In all, 135 were arrested (including 25 whites), and 89 of this number were detained for the night. More than 70 civilian lawmen from neighboring communities had to be brought onto the base to help restore order. There was one recorded death during the rioting—a civilian firefighter died of a heart attack while helping to extinguish a fire set in the transient officers quarters. More than 30 airmen and officers were treated at the base hospital for riot-related injuries.[12]

The Travis riot shocked the air force into a vast expansion of the Equal Opportunity Office within the Directorate of Personnel Planning. It further precipitated a restructuring of all programs dealing with equal opportunity. A new Social Actions Directorate was created within the headquarters to monitor all social problems—race relations, human relations, drug abuse, and alcoholism—and this organization was copied by all bases within the air force.[13] A most significant innovation was the introduction of mandatory race relations education for all personnel. In light of the increasing amount of racial friction among the military, an all-service study group was formed to investigate the problem. The group recommended the establishment of a Defense Race Relations Institute (DRRI) to prepare personnel as instructors to teach race relations at the base level to all people in the services. The air force soon published AFR 50-26, titled "Education in Race Relations," which described in detail a program "intended to improve and achieve equal opportunity within the USAF and to eliminate and prevent racial tensions, unrest and violence." The directive prescribed classes, comprising 18 to 25 participants, to reflect the rank composition of the base at large. The course was to be 18 hours in length. All officers and airmen were required to attend during regular-duty time, and training was to be accomplished beginning with the highest-ranking officers and airmen. While order was to be maintained in the classroom, an atmosphere of "free discussion" was encouraged. All personnel sent to DRRI to become race relations instructors were to be true volunteers. Finally, the regulation called for the establishment of formal race relations courses at all military schools.[14]

Soon after the publication of the regulation, military personnel undertook courses designed to broaden their ability to communicate across racial and ethnic barriers, to heighten their awareness of the minority contribution to American history, and to assure all personnel that the air force was serious about improving race relations. Students were informed how institutional and personal insensitivity, personal prejudice, and unconscious bigotry created racial problems. These would no longer be tolerated. If the program did nothing else, it did convince most airmen of head-quarters' intent to eliminate friction which hindered mission accomplishment.

Brig. Gen. Lucius Theus, air force representative on the study group which recommended the formation of the DRRI (he later became chief adviser to the deputy chief of staff for personnel on racial matters), maintained that the program was established to modify behavior. A change in attitudes was to be desired, but it was almost too much to expect from a short course. He assumed that the program could convince all personnel that it was in their "best interest" to conduct their affairs in a nondiscriminatory manner: "We want to explain the standards to you and demand compliance with those standards."[15]

Another innovation which was introduced after the Travis riot was the mandatory requirement for all officers to be rated on their "Equal Opportunity Participation." Although AFR 35-78 of 1971 had called for rating in this area, the manual governing effectiveness reports did not make this obligatory until late 1974. Under most circumstances, if an individual being rated was not a commander or supervisor of blacks, no remark was required until the latter date.[16] With this addition to the effectiveness report, the last unfulfilled major recommendation of the Gesell Committee was implemented. And with the establishment of the Race Relations Education Program, the air force finally decided to attempt an attack on the one remaining area of difficulty upon which it had refused to focus since 1949—the individual. If beliefs, attitudes, and inner prejudices could not be modified, perhaps behavior could be.

Soon after the military began to conduct race relations courses, Secretary of Defense Melvin Laird appointed a biracial task force to study the administration of military justice. This group published a four-volume study in the fall of 1972 that ranged well beyond military justice. The task force determined that there were two forms of racial discrimination within the military: intentional and systemic. The former was described as individual bias with the intent to affect minorities negatively, and the latter referred to "neutral practices or policies which disproportionately impact harmfully or negatively on minorities." A major example the task force offered of systemic discrimination was aptitude testing which frequently determined an individual's entire service career pattern almost before the career had begun. Minorities were frequently ill-prepared by civilian society to take these tests and often found themselves locked into unsatisfying specialties because of their poor educational preparation. The task force reported that some discrimination was purposive, but "more often it is not. Indeed it often occurs against the dictates not only of policy but in the face of determined efforts of commanders, staff personnel, and dedicated service men and women."[17]

The main body of the report was concerned with military justice. The task force admitted that it had too small an air force sample upon which to base conclusions and, instead, used courts-martial data in the army and marines. The report demonstrated that 23.3 percent of the whites on army posts received counseling short of the punishment to correct behavior, while only 8.3 percent of the blacks did for the same offenses. While 71.7 percent of army blacks received nonjudicial punishment for short-term Absence Without Leave, only 63.1 percent of the whites did. Blacks served longer pretrial confinement than whites for the same offenses. Most revealingly, blacks had a higher proportion of "not guilty" pleas than whites (47.6 percent to 35.5 percent) and were acquitted 47.8 percent of the time as compared with an acquittal rate of only 22 percent of whites. This indicated to the task force that blacks were more often falsely accused than whites. The report also noted that blacks were much less likely to receive an honorable discharge after conviction than whites for the same offenses. The task force discovered that those individuals with the less satisfying or more menial jobs were more likely to commit offenses drawing punishment than those personnel in more challenging specialties. Since blacks, because of poor showing on aptitude testing, were more likely to be relegated to these less satisfying positions, their offense and confinement rates were out of proportion to their percentage of the service population.[18]

Because personnel with deprived educational pasts were more likely to have problems in the military, the task force called on the Department of Defense to lend its considerable weight to a national movement to improve and upgrade educational opportunities. The task force also made several other recommendations. The position of Deputy Assistant Secretary of Defense (Equal Opportunity) should be upgraded to an assistant secretary position with a commensurate increase in staff. Equal opportunity staffs should be added to inspector general offices and to judge advocate general offices. A course in military discrimination should be added to the curriculum at the DRRI. Armed Forces Qualification Testing programs should be reevaluated, and service personnel interest and preference should be added to tested aptitude as criteria for determining specialties. Personnel ought to be periodically rotated out of low-status jobs. Haircut and dress standards should be relaxed. A "specific punitive article prescribing discriminatory acts and practices ought to be included in the Uniform Code of Military Justice in order to provide a more visible focus on detection and elimination of discrimination."[19]

Probably the appointment of the task force and the publication of its report can be taken as positive signs that the military had become more conscious of its responsibilities in the area of race relations. As indicated above in chapter 5, the air force apparently reached a new level of awareness following the Travis riot. As long as communications remain open and there are mechanisms which blacks trust to bring grievances to the attention of the leadership; as long as there are devices by which the situation can be effectively changed; as long as there are programs which attempt to modify negative behavior; as long as there are leaders who are willing to trade the prejudices of the past for sensitivity and a desire to increase racial harmony and, through it, mission effectiveness; as long as there is no relaxation of these efforts while America at large still has a race problem, the air force can expect to continue to enjoy the relative racial peace it has experienced in the period between 1971 and 1998.

Table 1

Blacks in the Air Force

Date	Total	Blacks	Percentage of Total
Jan. 1943[1]	1,696,866	88,302	5.2
Jan. 1944[1]	2,400,151	144,593	6.0
Jan. 1945[1]	2,345,068	137,817	5.9
Aug. 1945[1]	2,253,182	139,599	6.2
Jan. 1946[2]	733,786	60,663	8.3
June 1946[2]	455,515	42,980	9.4
Dec. 1946[2]	341,413	29,983	8.8
Jan. 1947[3]	327,404	25,759	7.9
June 1947[3]	305,827	21,243	6.9
Dec. 1947[3]	339,246	23,181	6.8
Jan. 1948[4]	353,143	24,554	7.0
June 1948[4]	387,730	25,855	6.7
Dec. 1948[4]	412,312	23,636	5.7
Jan. 1949[5]	415,576	22,763	5.5
June 1949[5]	419,347	22,092	5.3
Dec. 1949[5]	413,286	25,881	6.3
Jan. 1950[5]	415,004	25,702	6.2
June 1950[5]	411,277	26,604	6.5
June 1951[6]	788,381	39,114	5.0
Dec. 1951[7]	897,366	49,270	5.5

Continued on next page

Table 1 continued

Blacks in the Air Force

Date	Total	Blacks	Percentage of Total
June 1952[7]	974,474	61,124	6.3
Dec. 1952[8]	957,603	68,031	7.1
June 1953[8]	977,593	70,958	7.3
Dec. 1953[9]	912,537	66,998	7.3
June 1954[9]	947,918	72,119	7.6
1962[10]	613,741	47,884	7.8
1964[10]	829,057	71,769	8.7
1965[10]	811,853	74,958	9.2
1966[10]	899,768	81,766	9.1
Dec. 1967[11]	887,347	80,414	9.1
Sept. 1969[12]	857,163	78,859	9.2
Mar. 1970[13]	802,284	76,217	9.5
Mar. 1971[14]	754,331	76,961	10.2

Sources (all statistical data in author's possession):

[1]Office of Statistical Control, *Army Air Forces Statistical Digest: World War II*, tables 4, 10.

[2]Statistical Control Division, *Army Air Forces Statistical Digest: 1946*, tables 8, 16.

[3]Director of Statistical Services, *United States Air Force Statistical Digest: 1947*, tables 8,11.

[4]Statistical Services, *United States Air Force Statistical Digest: 1948*, tables 36, 38, 54, 55.

[5]Statistical Services, *United States Air Force Statistical Digest: Jan. 1949–June 1950*, tables 20, 21, 23.

[6]Statistical Services, *United States Air Force Statistical Digest: Fiscal 1951*, tables 215, 216.

[7]Statistical Services, *United States Air Force Statistical Digest: Fiscal 1952*, tables 15, 16.

[8]Statistical Services, *United States Air Force Statistical Digest: Fiscal 1953*, tables 195, 196, 202.

[9]Statistical Services, *United States Air Force Statistical Digest: Fiscal 1954*, tables 111, 112, 118. Statistics were not kept on blacks between 1955 and 1962. *Statistical Digests* since 1962 were still classified as of 1975.

[10]Office of Civil Rights, Department of Defense, "Negro Participation in the Armed Forces," (AGC), months not given. This is simply a fact sheet.

[11]Office of Civil Rights, Department of Defense, "Negro Participation in the Armed Forces," (AGC). This is also a fact sheet.

[12]Office of Civil Rights, Department of Defense, "Negro Participation in the Armed Forces," (AGC). The total figure was extrapolated from the number of blacks and their percentage of the total.

[13]Office of Civil Rights, Department of Defense, "Negro Participation in the Armed Forces," (AGC). The total figure was extrapolated.

[14]Department of Defense, *Commanders Digest*, 15 July 1971, 5.

Table 2

Black Air Force Officers

Date	Black Officers	Total Officers	Percentage of Total
Aug. 1942[1]	78	82,130	.09
Dec. 1942[1]	129	127,267	0.1
Dec. 1943[1]	636	274,347	0.2
Dec. 1944[1]	1,303	375,973	0.3
Aug. 1945[1]	1,533	368,344	0.4
Dec. 1945[2]	1,050	164,004	0.6
Dec. 1947[3]	247	49,529	0.5
Dec. 1948[4]	308	53,928	0.6
June 1949[5]	319	57,851	0.6
Dec. 1949[5]	368	60,770	0.6
Dec. 1950[6]	411	69,901	0.6
Dec. 1951[7]	731	121,085	0.6
Dec. 1952[8]	1,036	130,445	0.8
Dec. 1953[9]	1,262	123,444	1.0
June 1954[9]	1,394	129,752	1.1
1962[10]	1,320	106,692	1.2
1964[10]	2,050	134,613	1.5
1965[10]	2,096	130,604	1.6
1966[10]	2,284	131,991	1.7
Dec. 1967[11]	2,417	136,667	1.8
Sept. 1969[12]	2,377	135,600	1.8
Mar. 1970[13]	2,267	135,600	1.7
Mar. 1971[14]	2,216	126,958	1.7
June 1972[15]	2,124	118,671	1.8

Sources (all statistical data in author's possession):

[1] *Statistical Digest: World War II*, tables 4, 10.

[2] *Statistical Digest: 1946*, tables 8, 16.

[3] *Statistical Digest: 1947*, tables 8, 11.

[4] *Statistical Digest: 1948*, tables 36, 54.

[5] *Statistical Digest: Jan. 1949–June 1950*, tables 20, 21, 23.

[6] *Statistical Digest: Fiscal 1951*, tables 215, 216, p. 403.

[7] *Statistical Digest: Fiscal 1952*, tables 15, 16.

[8] *Statistical Digest: Fiscal 1953*, tables 195, 196.

[9] *Statistical Digest: Fiscal 1954*, tables 111, 112.

[10] "Negro Participation in the Armed Forces" (AGC), months not given.

[11] "Negro Participation in the Armed Forces" (AGC).

[12] "Negro Participation in the Armed Forces" (AGC), total figure extrapolated.

[13] "Negro Participation in the Armed Forces," (AGC), total figure extrapolated.

[14] *Commanders Digest*, 5.

[15] Department of Defense, *Report of the Task Force on the Administration of Military Justice in the Armed Forces*, 4 vols. (Washington, D.C.: Government Printing Office, 30 November 1972), 1:54–58.

Table 3
Black Enlisted Men, July 1948

Grade	Blacks	Total	Percentage
E-1	3,526	42,181	8.4
E-2	10,363	96,979	10.7
E-3	6,027	62,789	9.6
E-4	3,329	56,784	5.9
E-5	1,780	46,297	3.8
E-6	381	20,785	1.8
E-7	402	22,758	1.8
Aviation Cadet[1]	14	1,526	0.9

Source: Statistical Digest: 1948, tables 38, 25.

[1] Aviation cadets were nonofficer students at flying schools who would be commissioned if they earned wings.

Table 4
Black Enlisted Men, June 1949

Grade	Blacks	Total	Percentage
E-1	3,843	27,497	14.0
E-2	6,999	102,590	6.8
E-3	4,975	67,604	7.4
E-4	3,097	59,365	5.2
E-5	1,959	55,891	3.5
E-6	528	25,571	2.1
E-7	365	21,118	1.7
Aviation Cadet	16	1,860	0.9

Source: Statistical Digest: Jan. 1949–June 1950, tables 10, 13.

Table 5

Black Enlisted Men, June 1950

Grade	Blacks	Total	Percentage
E-1	4,308	46,109	9.3
E-2	7,953	76,356	10.4
E-3	6,555	76,935	8.5
E-4	4,191	63,482	6.6
E-5	2,236	57,535	3.9
E-6	587	27,701	2.1
E-7	394	21,361	1.8
Aviation Cadet	27	2,186	1.2

Source: Statistical Digest: Jan. 1949–June1950, tables 10, 13.

Table 6

Black Enlisted Men, June 1954

Grade	Blacks	Total	Percentage
E-1	3,995	46,109	8.7
E-2	22,421	154,585	14.5
E-3	23,690	206,500	11.5
E-4	10,016	167,191	6.0
E-5	7,611	129,662	5.9
E-6	2,062	57,285	3.6
E-7	869	47,762	1.8
Aviation Cadet	61	9,072	0.7

Source: Statistical Digest: 1954, tables 113, 115.

Table 7

Black Enlisted Men, 1962

Grade	Blacks	Total	Percentage
E-1	597	3,476	17.2
E-2	6,951	67,921	10.2
E-3	11,505	124,158	9.3
E-4	14,321	114,158	12.5
E-5	10,287	110,152	9.3
E-6	2,115	50,374	4.2
E-7	616	24,029	2.6
E-8	140	8,358	1.7
E-9	32	3,813	0.8

Source: "Negro Participation in the Armed Forces" (AGC).

Table 8

Black Enlisted Men, 1966

Grade	Blacks	Total	Percentage
E-1	3,311	48,927	6.8
E-2	13,223	153,370	8.6
E-3	19,348	161,263	12.0
E-4	19,077	130,198	14.7
E-5	17,223	143,421	12.0
E-6	4,946	75,370	6.6
E-7	1,512	39,001	3.9
E-8	270	10,803	2.5
E-9	82	5,424	1.5

Source: "Negro Participation in the Armed Forces" (AGC).

Table 9

Black Enlisted Men, December 1970

Grade	Blacks	Total	Percentage
E-1	2,338	12,794	18.3
E-2	6,969	46,959	14.8
E-3	13,002	110,148	11.8
E-4	17,145	159,555	10.7
E-5	21,507	146,296	14.7
E-6	8,633	85,345	10.1
E-7	2,801	46,470	6.0
E-8	559	12,842	4.4
E-9	193	6,413	3.0

Source: Air Force Times, 10 February 1971, 1, 4.

Table 10

Black Officers, July 1948

Rank	Blacks	Total	Percentage
O-1	40	2,038	2.0
O-2	153	19,860	0.8
O-3	84	14,682	0.6
O-4	13	6,589	0.2
O-5	2	3,213	0.1
O-6	1	1,525	0.1
O-7–O-10	0	181	0.0

Source: Statistical Digest: 1948, tables 36, 54.

Table 11

Black Officers, June 1949

Rank	Blacks	Total	Percentage
O-1	30	2,908	1.0
O-2	161	21,050	0.8
O-3	102	18,900	0.5
O-4	14	7,054	0.2
O-5	2	3,760	0.1
O-6	1	1,894	0.1
O-7–O-10	0	201	0.0

Source: Statistical Digest: Jan. 1949–June 1950, tables 10, 13.

Table 12

Black Officers, December 1952

Rank	Blacks	Total	Percentage
O-1	311	25,992	1.2
O-2	317	31,032	1.0
O-3	256	37,024	0.7
O-4	82	19,791	0.4
O-5	8	8,181	0.1
O-6	4	3,938	0.1
O-7–O-10	0	382	0.0

Source: Statistical Digest: Fiscal 1953, tables 193, 197.

Table 13

Black Officers, 1962

Rank	Blacks	Total	Percentage
O-1	170	11,664	1.5
O-2	317	20,292	1.6
O-3	615	35,180	1.7
O-4	124	20,395	0.6
O-5	67	12,337	0.5
O-6	6	4,066	0.1
O-7—O-10	1	347	0.3

Source: "Negro Participation in the Armed Forces" (AGC).

Table 14

Black Officers, 1966

Rank	Blacks	Total	Percentage
O-1	369	14,320	2.6
O-2	629	26,568	2.4
O-3	797	42,936	1.9
O-4	365	22,745	1.6
O-5	83	16,733	0.5
O-6	17	6,474	0.3
O-7–O-10	1	436	0.2

Source: "Negro Participation in the Armed Forces" (AGC).

Table 15
Black Officers, December 1970

Rank	Blacks	Total	Percentage
O-1	190	14,857	1.3
O-2	235	16,199	1.4
O-3	1,108	49,389	2.2
O-4	449	25,903	1.7
O-5	185	14,933	1.2
O-6	25	6,133	0.4
O-7–O-10	1	429	0.2

Source: Air Force Times, 10 February 1971, 1, 4.

Table 16
Blacks as Percentage of Enlisted Personnel in Occupational Groups,
by Length of Service, 1962

Occupational Group	Length of Service (Years)					Total
	0-4	5-8	9-12	13-20	Over 20	
Electronics	3.0	8.0	6.9	3.7	1.6	4.8
Other Technical	14.9	8.4	10.7	5.2	2.5	6.5
Administrative and Clerical	14.5	19.3	17.6	8.6	5.4	14.2
Mechanics and Repairmen	4.2	7.1	6.9	5.0	2.2	5.3
Crafts	8.7	14.8	16.0	7.8	4.7	10.7
Services	13.9	15.0	20.9	15.2	10.8	15.4
Total	8.5	11.6	11.9	7.1	4.0	9.2

Source: Memorandum, William Gorham to Norman Paul, 16 July 1963, table 42 (AGC).

Table 17

First-Term Reenlistments by Race in Selected
Occupational Groups, 1962

Occupational Group	Blacks	Whites
Electronics Maintenance Technicians	57	36
Medical and Dental Technicians	50	38
Aircraft and Engine Mechanics	57	35
Automotive Mechanics	34	60
Utilities Men	49	29
Food Service	61	32

Source: Memorandum, William Gorham to Norman Paul, 16 July 1963, table 8
(AGC). The rate was computed by dividing the enlistees into the number of
separatees eligible to reenlist. The white column includes members of all ethnic
groups who were not black.

Notes

Chapter 1: Flying on Clipped Wings

1. The standard work on black troops in World War II is Ulysses Lee's book, *The Employment of Negro Troops* (Washington, D.C., 1966). It is one of a multiseries of histories dealing with the U.S. Army in World War II. Lee does not mention the Freeman mutiny, although many other racial altercations of less significance are noted. The air force had denied Lee the relevant documents by illegally keeping them classified beyond Lee's clearances.

2. John Slonaker, *The U.S. Army and the Negro* (Army War College, Carlisle, Pa., 1971), 12–13.

3. Lee, *Negro Troops*, 32–35. Lee quotes extensively from the 1922 plan and the study that supported it.

4. This document is deposited at Carlisle and in the Alan Gropman Collection (AGC), Albert F. Simpson Historical Research Center (AFSHRC), Maxwell AFB, Ala.

5. Office of the Commandant, Army War College, "Memorandum for the Chief of Staff: The Use of Negro Manpower in War," 30 Oct. 1925, 1–2 (AGC).

6. Ibid., "Supporting Documents," material on "Mental Capacities," pages unnumbered. The source of the comments on cranium size and brain weight are not documented.

7. Ibid., "The Negro Officer."

8. Ibid., "Morale."

9. Ibid., "Social."

10. Ibid., 1–2.

11. For consideration of the treatment of the American black trooper after his return from World War I, see especially John Hope Franklin, *From Slavery to Freedom: A History of Negro Americans,* 3d ed. (New York, 1969), 477–97. For other minorities, see Maldwyn A. Jones, *American Immigration* (Chicago, 1960), 247–77. Popular writers like Kenneth L. Roberts warned of America's mongrelization. See his *Why Europe Leaves Home* (New York, 1922), 21. See also Madison Grant, *The Passing of the Great Race in America,* 4th ed. (New York, 1923), xxvii–xxxiii.

12. Office of the Commandant, "Memorandum for the Chief of Staff" (1925): "Supporting Documents," "Performances in Past Wars"; Franklin, *Slavery to Freedom,* 125–44, 168–81, 271–96, 418–25;

Irvin H. Lee, *Negro Medal of Honor Men,* 3d ed. (New York, 1969), 139–41. Blacks were awarded no Medals of Honor for either world war until the 1990s.

13. Lee, *Negro Troops,* 25, 28–29.

14. This fascinating man tried without success to join the air service after the United States entered the war. He had fought with the French as an infantryman before earning his wings. He returned to America after the German conquest of France in 1940 and ended up working as an elevator operator in Rockefeller Center, New York. A photograph of Bullard taken on the *NBC Today Show* displays his numerous medals. See P. J. Carisella and James W. Ryan, *The Black Swallow of Death* (Boston, 1972), 256.

15. Lee, *Negro Troops,* 49: see further the statement by the army chief of personnel, Oct. 1939.

16. Ibid., 49–50, 82–84. See also "War Department Policies Governing the Employment of Negro Personnel upon Mobilization," G-3/6541-527, 3 June 1940. Such documents may be found in the Center of Military History Collection, Washington, D.C.

17. Ltr., Maj. Gen. Robert Olds to members of First Bomb Wing, 10 July 1943, found in Wg-1-Hi 1943, AFSHRC.

18. AG 291.2 (10-9-40) M-A-M, 16 Oct. 1940, Center of Military History. Also Lee, *Negro Troops,* 75–76.

19. Lee, *Negro Troops,* 55. See *The Crisis,* July 1940, 1. It displays airplanes in flight with the caption reading: "WARPLANES—Negro Americans may not build them, repair them or fly them, but they must help pay for them." On p. 199, *The Crisis* discussed the meaning of the cover. See also *The Crisis,* Dec. 1940, cover, which displays an air corps trainer over Randolph Army Air Field; the caption states: "For Whites Only."

20. Lee, *Negro Troops,* 56.

21. Ibid., and Lawrence J. Paszek, "Negroes and the Air Force, 1939–1949," *Military Affairs,* spring 1967, 1–9.

22. Lee, *Negro Troops,* 56; Paszek, "Negroes and the Air Force," 1–9; Richard M. Dalfiume, *Desegregation of the U.S. Armed Forces: Fighting on Two Fronts, 1939–1953* (Columbia, Mo., 1969), 28–29; and Patricia Strickland, *The Putt-Putt Air Force: The Story of the Civilian Pilot Training Program and the War Training Service (1939–1944)* (Washington, D.C., [1971]), 39–47.

23. Dalfiume, *Desegregation,* 28–29; and Charles E. Francis, *The Tuskegee Airmen: The Story of the Negro in the U.S. Air Force* (Boston, 1955), 11–18.

24. Lee, *Negro Troops,* 89, 117–18; and Francis, *Tuskegee Airmen,* 11–18.

25. Strickland, *Putt-Putt Air Force,* 39–47.

26. The most articulate statement on the point of view expressed here is Dalfiume, *Desegregation,* 28–29.

27. Quoted in ibid., 57, diary entry, 20 Sept. 1940.

28. Dalfiume, *Desegregation,* 32–33, 36–37.

29. Lee, *Negro Troops,* 79; and Dalfiume, *Desegregation,* 41. In Apr. 1941, Brig. Gen. W. R. Weaver wrote to Maj. Gen. George H. Brett reporting that the "Negro race is taking a tremendous amount of interest" in the building of Tuskegee Army Air Field. "These Negroes," he wrote, "are wonderfully well-educated and as smart as they can be, and politically they have back of them their race composed of some eleven million people in this country." Weaver advised Brett that this new policy affected the "entire Air Corps" because of its "political significance." Ltr., Weaver to Brett, 24 Apr. 1941 (AGC).

30. Dalfiume, *Desegregation,* 26, 27, 110–12. See *The Crisis,* Jan. 1942, 7. The editorial is titled: "Now Is the Time Not to Be Silent." With the country at war, the publication declared that "now is the time not to be silent about the breaches of democracy in our own land." *The Crisis* pledged loy-

alty to the idea of American democracy, but not to "many of the practices." Fight not only Hitler, it exclaimed, but Hitlerism—"a world in which lynching, brutality, terror, and humiliation and degradation through segregation and discrimination, shall have no place—*either here or there*." If "forced labor is wrong in Czechoslovakia, peonage farms are wrong in Georgia. If the Ghettos in Poland are an evil, so are the Ghettos in America."

31. Lee, *Negro Troops,* 37.

32. Ibid., 239–74, contains an outstanding explanation of the AGCT. On aviation squadrons, see 113–14; and Paszek, "Negroes and the Air Force," 4–5.

33. Lee, *Negro Troops,* 93, 94, 241–46; and William H. Hastie, "On Clipped Wings: The Story of Jim Crow in the Army Air Corps," NAACP pamphlet, 1 July 1943, 4.

34. WD Pamphlet No. 20-6, *Command of Negro Troops* (Washington, D.C., 1944), 4.

35. Wesley Frank Craven and James Lea Cate, eds., *The Army Air Forces in World War II,* vol. II, *Europe-Torch to Pointblank, August 1942 to December 1943* (Chicago, 1949), 655–56. In volume VI, published in 1955, the editors noted that the section on blacks was too limited. They noted, "The whole subject of Negroes in the armed services is important enough to deserve a more careful study" (pxxxi).

36. *Reader's Digest,* Sept. 1965. See also the testimony of Col. Benjamin O. Davis, Jr., before the Gillem Board. The Gillem Board Papers are deposited at the Army War College, Carlisle Barracks, Pa.

37. Lee, *Negro Troops,* 162–68, 175, 177; Hastie, *On Clipped Wings,* 4; "History of the 2164th AAF Base Unit, Tuskegee Institute," 1 Jan.–14 Apr. 1945, 13, and 1 Sept.–31 Oct. 1945, Supporting Docs., chart on numbers of men trained, unpaged. These and all other unit histories cited may be found in the AFSHRC.

38. Lee, *Negro Troops,* 162–68, 175, 177; Dalfiume, *Desegregation,* 83–84; and Hastie, *On Clipped Wings,* 1–10.

39. Hastie, *On Clipped Wings,* 10–12.

40. *Pittsburgh Courier,* 7 Oct. 1944, 9.

41. Lee, *Negro Troops,* 177; intvw, author with Noel F. Parrish, San Antonio, Tex., Mar. 1973; and intvw, author with Marion R. Rodgers, Colorado Springs, Colo., Jan. 1973. Rodgers was a Tuskegee Airman.

42. Noel F. Parrish, "The Segregation of Negroes in the Army Air Forces," Air Command and Staff school research study, Maxwell AFB, Ala., May 1947, 1, 2, 3, 8, 9, 11–13. The report can be found in the Maxwell AFB Library and in several Record Groups in the National Archives, including NARG 340, Secretary of the Air Force Papers. Those men responsible for integrating the air force read and appreciated Parrish's report. Intvw., author with Jack Marr, Cobbs Creek, Va., Feb. 1973. In 1949, Marr helped implement air force integration.

43. Parrish, "Segregation," 33, 48–50.

44. Craven and Cate, *The Army Air Forces in World War II,* II:424; and Lee, *Negro Troops,* 451–53.

45. Francis, *Tuskegee Airmen,* 41–44.

46. Lee, *Negro Troops,* 453–54.

47. Ibid., 454–61.

48. Ibid., 454–64, 467.

49. Ibid.

50. Ibid., 406.

51. "History of the 2164th AAF Base Unit," 1 Sept.–31 Oct. 1945, 1; Paszek, "Negroes and the Air Force," 6; and Lee, *Negro Troops,* 465.

52. A study made after the war compared 815 white West Point cadets with 356 black flying cadets in terms of flying aptitude and determined that the air corps testing methods were valid in predict-

ing on a "pass-fail" basis. The air corps had a valid device. See William Burton Michael, *Factor Analysis of Tests and Criteria: A Comparative Study of Two AAF Pilot Populations* (Washington, D.C., 1949).

53. Blacks were trained at Hondo Army Air Field, Hondo, Tex. See "History of Hondo Army Air Field," 1 Jan.–28 Feb. 1945, 44–47 (AFSHRC).

54. "History of the 477th Bombardment Group (Medium)," 15 Jan.–5 May 1944, Selfridge Field, 6 May–15 July 1944, Godman Field, 1, 2, 5, 6 (AFSHRC).

55. Ibid., 1, 2, 10, 12.

56. Ibid., 14, 15.

57. [Lyon, Earl D.], "The Training of Negro Combat Units by the First Air Force," vol. I, Text Copy 1, May 1946, 140, 141, 149 (vol. I hereafter cited as "Training, First Air Force"). This history with its accompanying volume of documents is a major source, not known to have been previously used. Nearly all of the history and its collection of documents concerns the Freeman Field mutiny. It includes direct transcriptions of telephone conversations between First Air Force Headquarters and the 477th Headquarters, as well as between high Pentagon officials and First Air Force Headquarters. Lyon also collected the transcripts of phone conversations as well as numerous documents to verify his account. Both volumes are in the AFSHRC.

58. *Chicago Defender*, 22 July 1944, 11.

59. "History of the 477th Bombardment Group (Medium)," 16 July–15 Oct. 1944, 72.

60. Ibid., 3, 23, 29, 30, 33, 56.

61. Ibid., "Freeman Field, Ind.," 16 Jan.–15 Apr. 1945, 2, 9, 22, and "Training, First Air Force," 75.

62. "History of the 477th Bombardment Group (Medium)," 16 Apr.–15 July 1945, 13–17. The lack of comment on the mutiny suggests possible censorship. There was much to be learned from this incident, but the story was not told until Lyon wrote of it more than a year later. His account was classified "Secret" and was not declassified until 1973.

63. Quoted in "Training, First Air Force," 114. Lyon's work is primarily documentary.

64. Ibid., 145. Lyon included the entire conversation.

65. This phone conversation took place on 29 June 1944 and is recorded in [Lyon, Earl D.], "The Training of Negro Combat Units by the First Air Force," vol. II, Docs., App. E (vol. II hereafter cited as "Training, Documents"). Phone transcripts and documents are chronologically arranged in this volume.

66. Telephone conversation between General Giles and General Hunter, 1 July 1944, in "Training, Documents," App. E.

67. This can be found in an article written by Truman Gibson in the *Pittsburgh Courier*, 26 June 1946, published under the headline, "Army Inspectors Attempted Whitewash of Freeman Field," 12. One suspects Gibson wrote the reprimand and took a copy when he left the Pentagon.

68. Telecon, General Hunter and Brigadier General Harper, 12 Apr. 1944, in "Training, Documents," App. E.

69. Par. 19, Army Regulation 210-10, 20 Dec. 1940.

70. WD Pamphlet No. 20-6, 29 Feb. 1944, 12–13.

71. Quote is in Lee, *Negro Troops*, 219. In a summary of the study, titled "Participation of Negro Troops in the Post-War Military Establishment" (prepared in mid-1945), the white-over-black hierarchy was cited as the major reason for the mutiny. The unnamed author wrote that the "basic cause" of the mutiny "derived from the resentment harbored by the Negro officers against white supervisory personnel. . . . The white supervisory personnel occupied the key positions and colored officers considered that their opportunities for promotion and advancement were denied as a result." See App. U, Summary, Air Adjutant General Mail and Records, File 291.2, NARG 18. Spann Watson,

a member of the 477th, stated in an interview, "You know that's what the trouble at Freeman was all about; it was position and promotion, it wasn't that damn club at all." Intvw., author with Spann Watson, Washington, D.C., Apr. 1973.

72. "Chronological Summary of Events at Freeman Field," n.d., File 291.2, NARG 18. This document was marked in pencil as approved by the inspector general.

73. Ibid.

74. "Training, First Air Force," 184–86.

75. "Training, Documents," App. E, "Rpt. of Racial Situation, Freeman Field, 31 Mar 45." This covers the period from 19 to 29 Mar. 1945.

76. See newspaper clipping from the *Indianapolis Recorder,* 17 Mar. 1945, File 291.2, NARG 18.

77. *Pittsburgh Courier,* 31 Mar. 1945, 2. This newspaper was by far the most widely circulated black newspaper, having expanded from a circulation of 126,962 copies in 1940 to more than 286,000 in 1947. In both those years, its circulation was larger than that of the next two largest black newspapers combined. The *Courier* was considered so powerful that the War Department tried to bar its distribution, and that of other black journals, from military posts. Stimson, McCloy, and others in the War Department blamed the black press for bad morale among black troops. Emanating out of the Justice Department were threats to try members of the black press for sedition, with some officials proposing to withhold newsprint from them. See Ronald E. Wolseley, *The Black Press and U.S.A.* (Ames, Iowa, 1971), 6, 49; and Dalfiume, *Desegregation,* 86, 87, 124, who discusses the War Department's attitude toward the black press.

78. "Chronological Summary of Events at Freeman Field," File 291.2, NARG 18. Spann Watson indicated in an interview with the author that he was contacted on the day of the mutiny by 477th members who stated: "We are going to the club tonight. Are you with us or against us?" They planned to go "as an orderly group." Watson was arrested that night. Watson intvw.

79. "Memo for the Air Inspector," File 291.2, NARG 18.

80. Telecon between Brig. Gen. Ray L. Owens and General Hunter, 6 Apr. 1945, in "Training, Documents," App. E.

81. An intelligence report, 7 Apr. 1945, stated that blacks had entered "Officers' Club and Mess #2 (White)." In "Training, Documents," App. E.

82. Chronological Summary of Events at Freeman Field," File 291.2, NARG 18. See also same file, "Memo for the Air Inspector." See Reg. No. 85-2, HQ, Freeman Field, subj.: "Assignment of Housing, Messing and Recreational Facilities for Officers, Flight Officers, and Warrant Officers," 9 Apr. 1945. See File 291.2, NARG 18, and "Training, Documents."

83. Telecon between Colonel Selway and General Hunter, 14 Apr. 1945, in "Training, Documents," App. E; "Chronological Summary of Events at Freeman Field," and "Memo for the Air Inspector," File 291.2, NARG 18.

84. Telecon between General Kuter and General Hunter, 13 Apr. 1945, in "Training, Documents," App. E.

85. Draft ltr., Col. John E. Harris to Secretary Stimson, n.d., in File 291.2, NARG 18.

86. Telecon between Colonels Selway and Harris and General Hunter, 13 Apr. 1945, in "Training, Documents."

87. Telecon between Air Inspector's Ofc. First Air Force and 477th Headquarters, 11 Apr. 1945, in "Training, Documents," App. E.

88. Container 326, NAACP Papers, Library of Congress, Washington, D.C.

89. Telecon between Brig. Gen. L. H. Hedrick and General Hunter, 16 Apr. 1945, in "Training, Documents," App. E. See WD Pamphlet 20-6, 14. Hunter did not use this document as justification in previous conversations, and it does not appear in correspondence prior to mid-April. It was prob-

ably thought of after the fact. The paragraph that Hunter counted on was ambiguous, and the pamphlet made it clear that blacks hated segregation.

90. Ltr., Hedrick to Hunter, 16 Apr. 1945, in "Training, Documents," App. E.

91. Ltr., Harold D. Gould to William A. Rowan, 17 Apr. 1945, File 291.2, NARG 18.

92. Ltr., White to Stimson, 17 Apr. 1945, Container 326, NAACP Papers.

93. Telecon recorded in "Training, First Air Force," 216–17. Two days earlier Brigadier General Welsh, air corps chief of staff for training, and Colonel Stewart, Hunter's acting chief of staff, talked on the phone. Stewart believed the rights of the whites had been slighted during the Freeman altercation. Welsh agreed: "I have maintained all along that it's the whites that are being discriminated against in the army and not the colored." Welsh also told Stewart that trouble should be avoided because First Air Force headquarters was very near to Harlem and "what I'm afraid of is this, if this thing gets out of hand you may have some of the 'jig-a-boos' up there dropping in on you at Mitchell Field." See telecon, 18 Apr. 1945, in "Training, Documents," App. E.

94. Memo for Asst Chief of Staff, 19 Apr. 1945, File 291.2, NARG 18.

95. Telecon between Glenn and Owens, 10 May 1945, in "Training, Documents," App. E.

96. Lee, *Negro Troops,* 157, 161.

97. Summary Sheet, 5 May 1945, Colonel Guenther, WDGAP, subj.: "Racial Incidents at Freeman Field, Indiana, and Fort Huachuca, Arizona," File 291.2, NARG 18.

98. Ibid.

99. Rpt., Gibson to McCloy, 14 May 1945, carton 1 of 1, Accession 68A 1137, National Records Center, Suitland, Md.

100. Agenda for meeting of McCloy Comm., 18 May 1945, File 23-290, NARG 18.

101. Memo for the Secretary of War, subj: "Report of Meeting of Advisory Committee on Special Troop Policies," 4 June 1945, File 291.2, NARG 18. A memo to the inspector general from the War Department General Staff, undated, states that the violation had been "called to the attention of the Commanding General, First Air Force." See also a letter from Maj. Gen. Philip E. Brown, acting inspector general, to Arnold. It called the AAF commander's attention, "for appropriate action, to the nonconformance in this case with Army Regulations and War Department policies." File 291.2, NARG 18.

102. Ltr., Owens to McCloy, 31 May 1945, File 23-290, NARG 18.

103. Undated memo, Giles to McCloy, File 291.2, NARG 18.

104. This comment was appended to the bottom of the Summary Sheet, 5 May 1945, "Racial Incidents at Freeman Field, Indiana, and Fort Huachuca, Arizona," File 291.2, NARG 18.

105. Container 326, NAACP Papers.

106. Staff Judge Advocate Brief, 11 Apr. 1945, in "Training, Documents," App. E.

107. Memo, Max F. Schneider, Acting Air Inspector to Chief of Staff, File 291.2, NARG 18. This shows a specification of charges drafted with a blank for the names of those who failed to sign the regulation on club segregation.

108. Official Summary of Roger C. Terry trial, in "Training, Documents," App. E.

109. "Review of the Staff Judge Advocate on Record of Trial by General Court Martial," 23 July 1945, in "Training, Documents," App. E.

110. Indorsement to Terry's sentence by Hunter, 30 July 1945, in "Training, Documents," App. E.

111. Memo, Brig. Gen. William W. Welsh to Commanding General, Continental Air Force, 24 May 1945, File 23–290, NARG 18.

112. *Pittsburgh Courier,* 23 June 1945, 1, and 30 June 1945, 1, 4, 5, 23; *Chicago Defender,* 23 June 1945, 1; and *Baltimore Afro-American,* 23 June 1945, 1, and 30 June 1945, 1, 3.

113. Ltr., General Eaker to Gen. J. T. McNarney, 2 June 1945 (AGC).

114. Memo, Eaker to Arnold, 19 June 1945, File 23–290, NARG 18.

115. Msg., Kenney to Arnold, 19 June 1945, Decimal File, 1938–46, H. H. Arnold Papers, Library of Congress, Washington, D.C.

116. "History of the 477th Bombardment Group (Medium)," 16 Apr.–15 July 1945, 1.

117. Undated Report of First Air Force Liaison Party, in "Training, Documents," App. E.

118. "Training, First Air Force," 86, 87. Lyon recorded this entire conversation verbatim.

Chapter 2: Marking Time

1. AAF documents containing reports from all AAF units in the United States which employed blacks can be located in the National Personnel Records Center (NPRC), St. Louis, Mo., under File No. 114-528. Also in this file are materials on the MacDill riot in October 1946 (see below) as well as other reports of racial incidents. The studies titled "Participation of Negro Troops in the Post-War Military Establishment" are packaged in loose-leaf fashion, with the summary study of various large units on top. For example, the reports of the numbered air forces and other smaller, individual reports are attached to the summary report. Official distillation of all this material, which also included reports from overseas units, was not found in NPRC. The original of this report is in the H. H. Arnold Papers, with copies in the AFSHRC and the National Archives. Citation to the material in St. Louis is as follows: title of specific report, followed by File 114-528, NPRC. All reports were written in the summer of 1945; copies are in AGC.

2. Memo, John J. McCloy to members of Advisory Cmte, 1 Sept. 1944, File 114-528, NPRC.

3. Maj. Gen W. F. Tompkins to CG, Army Air Forces, et al., 23 May 1945, File 114-528, NPRC. Tompkins made reference to the McCloy memorandum in his letter. I Troop Carrier Command advised its people to "keep in mind that this project is SECRET. Therefore colored personnel are not to know this survey is being made." See appendices to "Utilization of Negro Personnel within I Troop Carrier Command," File 114-528, NPRC. Brig. Gen. William E. Hall sent a letter dated 15 Jan. 1945 to AAF Personnel for General Arnold, making reference to the McCloy memo of 1 Sept. 1944. Hall said that HQ AAF was "charged with the responsibility of furnishing information upon which to base a reply to the [McCloy] memorandum. . . . The results of the study will determine the MOS [Military Occupational Specialty] and the types of units in which Negroes can be best utilized in the Post War Military." Hall asked for references to the "degree of proficiency attained and the length of time required" to train blacks. Also information was needed on which jobs blacks were "best qualified" for. He set a deadline of 1 Sept. 1945 for the reports.

4. "Utilization of Negro Personnel within I Troop Carrier Command," App., rpt, from George Field, Ill., File 114-528, NRPC.

5. "Training and Utilization of Negro Personnel in the Second Air Force," 1–5, 8, File 114-528, NPRC. This material was culled from reports from Alamogordo, Dalhart, Fairmont, Harvard, and Biggs Army Air Fields.

6. Ibid.; see attached report from Dalhart Army Air Field.

7. Ibid.; see attached report from Harvard Army Air Field.

8. "Training of Negroes within Third Air Force," 3–7, 8, File 114-528, NPRC.

9. "Training and Utilization of Negro Personnel in the Second Air Force." See also attached report from Smoky Hill Army Air Field.

10. Western Signal Aviation Unit Training Center, "Participation of Negro Troops in the Post-War Military Establishment," 5, File 114-528, NPRC. Second Air Force, in its summary report, noted that race prejudice hampered black morale and, in turn, proficiency. See specially 1–5.

11. "Training and Utilization of Negro Personnel in the Second Air Force," 1–5, 8–10, 12–15, File 114-528, NPRC.

12. Ibid. Second Air Force, like most other units, also noted blacks' higher venereal disease rate, which occasionally was ten times greater than the rate for whites. See supporting documents for this report, File 114-528, NPRC.

13. "Utilization of Negro Personnel within I Troop Carrier Command," 6–8, 9, 11–15, 17, File 114-528, NPRC.

14. Ibid., 15. Compare attached rpt. from Bergstrom Army Air Field. Unrelated to the washrack episode, but included in the same package of material from I Troop Carrier Command, was a vignette from Stout Field, Indiana, which demonstrated why black morale was fragile. Once during the war a black airman was chosen as "Soldier-of-the-Month," but he received none of the rewards in the civilian community which previous (white) recipients got. "Previously, soldiers selected as 'The-Soldier-of-the-Month' for a given month were rewarded by the citizenry with free passes to leading theaters, membership privileges for a month in a leading Athletic Club and various other incidental and monetary rewards. Upon selection of a colored 'Soldier-of-the-Month' such rewards were promptly withdrawn by the citizenry."

15. Ibid. See attached report from Bergstrom Army Air Field.

16. "Utilization of Negro Personnel within I Troop Carrier Command," 52, 53, 68–71, 75, File 114-528, NPRC, italics in original.

17. Andersen to Commanding General, Army Air Forces, 20 July 1945, File 114-528, NPRC.

18. Hunter to Commanding General, Continental Air Forces, 20 July 1945, File 114-528, NPRC. Hunter's letter was an endorsement to and accompanied the First Air Force report: "Participation of Negro Troops in the Post-War Military Establishment," 19 July 1945.

19. "Training, Documents," App. B. Lyon finds the Selway report "factually inaccurate. . . . It makes uncritical and tendentious use of statistics."

20. Hunter's letter, 20 July 1945, File 114-528, NPRC.

21. First Air Force, "Participation of Negro Troops in the Post-War Military Establishment," 1–4, File 114-528, NPRC.

22. Ibid., 19–20. Note the following: "The 477th Bombardment Group (M) activated on 15 January 1944. The main factor which retarded the training of this group was the slowness of the individuals in attaining the minimum standards of proficiency which would permit the organization to enter the final phases of training." Selway told the reader that it took only three to four months to train white medium bombardment units, and even allowing three to four times the training time for the 477th, blacks came only up to the level of the "poorest of white units." For the first nine months, however, three times the normal training period for white units, the 477th did not have navigators—it could not possibly have been checked out. In November (the 11th month of training), the 477th received bombardiers, but these did not have the necessary training to be navigators, further delaying the final check-out. All this time the unit was functioning on a base that was too small for its purposes; and therefore it made frequent, upsetting unit moves. All these facts were known by Selway, and all of them were omitted from his study.

23. Ibid., 1–4, 40.

24. Ibid., 42.

25. Ibid.

26. "Training, First Air Force," 30–31, 43–48.

27. Louis Nippert, "Memo for the Chief of Staff: Participation of Negro Troops in the Post-War Military Establishment," 17 Sept. 1945 (AFSHRC), 1–10 (hereafter cited as Nippert, "Participation"). A copy of the memo can also be found in the H. H. Arnold Papers and in the National Archives. A stanine score is a separate rating or score for each of certain air force specialties, indicating the predictive aptitude of a person.

28. The Selway report seems to have been effective in making this comparison.

29. Nippert, "Participation," 1–10.

30. Ibid. One research study cited by Lyon in "Training, First Air Force" showed that AGCT scores were influenced more by geographical location than by race. Blacks from the North scored higher than whites from the South. "The rejection rate for substandard intelligence was impressively higher for white men who came from North Carolina, Texas, and Arkansas than for Negroes who came from Massachusetts, Illinois, and New York City." In fact, the rejection rate for whites in southern states was three to four times higher than for blacks from the northern areas mentioned. Lyon cited Martin D. Jenkins, Charles Thompson, Francis A. Gregory, Howard H. Long, and Jane E. McAllister, *The Black and White of Rejection for Military Service: A Study of Rejections of Selective Service Registrants, by Race on Account of Educational and Mental Deficiencies* (Montgomery, 1944). Lyon suggested that the question should have been asked in 1944 how impoverished people, not blacks, could best be employed, since educational advantages determined the AGCT. Blacks from the South scored lower than whites from the same region, and their rejection rate for "substandard intelligence" was higher also. Lyon also explored the possible reasons for excess trouble in the 477th. He concluded that the unwillingness of the blacks to accept segregation and their tendency to fight back stemmed from the fact that most of them were northerners who would not submit easily to such humiliation. See "Training, First Air Force," 13–32.

31. Nippert, "Participation," 16–17.

32. Ibid., 1–4.

33. Ibid., 1–4, 21–33. Nippert's remarks might be compared with Selway's on the same subject. Selway found that blacks at Selfridge Army Air Field were adversely affected by blacks in Detroit. "Since May of 1943, the Negro press has repeatedly attacked the white personnel who were charged with the command and supervision of these programs [at Selfridge Army Air Field]. These newspaper articles made it difficult for the Commanding Officers to maintain strict discipline, and after each article, it was found that the Negro personnel were more indolent in their performance of their duties, and they would use the race issue with accusations of discrimination in attempting to excuse their own failures. On many occasions, it was apparent that the constant pressure from the black press, and the National Association for the Advancement of Colored People, resulted in organized insubordination and disobedience, which materially affected the training of these units." Compare Nippert's remarks with the following taken from First Air Force, "Participation of Negro Troops in the Post-War Military Establishment," 19 July 1945: "Indications point to the fact that these racial irritations and disorders were prompted and fostered by the Negro Press Association and the Association for the Advancement of Colored People, for the sole purpose of advancing the race, and they used these military units as vehicles on which to conduct their crusade" (1–4, File 114-528, NPRC).

34. Lee, *Negro Troops,* 397–401. See also *Chicago Defender,* 12 Aug. 1944, 1, for an indication of how cordially the black press welcomed this move.

35. Nippert, "Participation," 1–4.

36. Parrish's recommendations are not contained in the body of data stored at the St. Louis Records Center, and they may not have been included in the material given to Nippert.

37. Parrish to Brig. Gen. William E. Hall, n.d., "History of the 2143d AAF Base Unit Pilot School, Basic, Advanced and Tuskegee Army Air Field, Tuskegee Alabama," 1 Sept. 1945–31 Oct. 1945, App.

38. Ibid.

39. General Gillem, Maj. Gen. Lewis A. Pick, Brig. Gen. Allan D. Warnock, and Brig. Gen. Winslow C. Morse.

40. Memo to the Chief of Staff, 17 Nov. 1945, Alvan C. Gillem Board Papers, Army War College,

Carlisle Barracks, Pa. This is the cover sheet of the report. A similar letter from the chief of staff was found in the Gillem Board Papers, and in the margin was a handwritten note: "Add: The plan for implementation of same." This was marked approved by Secretary Robert Patterson. Chief of Staff to Gillem Board, 4 Oct. 1945, Gillem Board Papers.

41. See *Chicago Defender,* 1 Dec. 1945, 1, which headlined: "Army to End Jim Crow." "Future War Department policy on the utilization of the nation's manpower resources is expected to be one of complete integration and an end to Jim Crow in the Army." There appeared additional page-one stories in the *Defender* for the next two weeks. The *Pittsburgh Courier,* 9 Mar. 1946, also headlined the Gillem Board report. It said that this signified an end of Jim Crow in the army. On page 12 of the issue, Truman Gibson, in the first of a long series of articles, called the report a "significant step forward in the building of a truly democratic Army." He said the ultimate Gillem recommendation was integration.

42. Memo to the Chief of Staff, 17 Nov. 1945, Gillem Board Papers. The clause concerning qualified individuals in overhead units (such as administrative, finance, personnel, housekeeping, and other noncombatant organizations) was actually a call for on-the-job integration. As will be seen, this provision was carried out, but to a far lesser extent than the Gillem Board wanted. Certain highly qualified individuals were allowed to work as technicians and specialists in overhead organizations, but they continued to live, mess, and recreate in all-black units. This limited integration, it will be shown, influenced the air force decision to desegregate in 1949.

43. The Gillem Board considered extremely important the participation of blacks within white companies in the final days of fighting in World War II in Europe. This subject is discussed below; however, the board's emphasis is significant.

44. This reflected War Department orders on nonsegregation of recreational facilities as reinforced by the decisions taken after the Freeman Field affair.

45. Memo to the Chief of Staff, Gillem Board Papers.

46. Ibid.

47. Ibid., italics in original.

48. Ibid.

49. Ibid.

50. Ibid.

51. Ibid. These remarks appear in a summary of black service from the Revolutionary War to World War II. The short service of blacks in white units at the end of World War II received disproportionate prominence.

52. The 92d commander, Maj. Gen. Edwin Almond, testified before the board and said that blacks did "much good work when not in immediate danger, but freeze up under fire." He told the board: "[The] Negro division is a failure. Try combat platoons and expand gradually or stick to service and support units." See the "Briefs of Testimony" found in the Gillem Board Papers. While valuable, these briefs are difficult to use, since some are direct quotes and others are merely summaries of the testimony. Some 52 people appeared before the board, and their recommendations spanned the spectrum—from continued segregation and worse to complete integration. Their testimony will be discussed below.

53. Lee, *Negro Troops,* 688–700.

54. TAB A, List of Documents, Gillem Board Papers. This is a compilation of those documents the Gillem Board studied while deliberating. It also lists the 52 interviewees. There were several reports on the success of the black platoons within white companies as well as the results of the survey discussed below.

55. Information and Education Division, Army Service Forces, "Opinions about Negro Infantry Pla-

toons in White Companies of Seven Divisions, Based on a Survey Made in May–June 1945," Report No. B-157, Washington, D.C., 3 July 1945. Not everybody was impressed with the survey. Gen. Brehon Somervell, commander of the Army Service Forces, advised McCloy not to publish it. He wrote: "An experiment conducted with something like one thousand volunteers can hardly be regarded as a conclusive test. Organizations such as NAACP might try to use pressure for similar experiments with troops training in the United States and operating in the Pacific. Many members of Congress, newspaper editors, and other leaders who have given strong support to the War Department are vigorously opposed to mixing Negro and white troops under any conditions. It is doubtful that the report would gain enough support for the Army to offset the support it would lose on account of its implications." See ltr., Somervell to McCloy, n.d., in Gillem Board Papers. General Marshall believed that the experiment should have been followed up, but he also agreed with Somervell that the survey should not be published. Marshall wrote: "I agree [that] the practicability of integrating Negro elements into white units should be followed up. It is further agreed that the results of the survey of the Information and Education Division should not be released for publication at this time, since the conditions under which the platoons were organized and employed were the most unusual." Memo, Marshall to McCloy, 25 Aug. 1945, Gillem Board Papers. Maj. Gen. F. H. Osborne recommended declassification and dissemination. See cover letter on the report, Gillem Board Papers.

56. Information and Education Division, "Opinions about Negro Infantry Platoons."
57. William H. Hastie, "Briefs of Testimony," Gillem Board Papers.
58. Truman Gibson, ibid.
59. Brig. Gen. B. O. Davis, Sr., ibid.
60. Col. B. O. Davis, Jr., ibid.
61. Frederick Patterson, Charles Houston, and Walter White, ibid.
62. Noel Parrish, ibid.
63. Charles Dollard, ibid.
64. Walter L. Wright, ibid.
65. Bell I. Wiley, ibid.
66. Gen. Carl Spaatz, ibid. His views were important because he succeeded Arnold as commander of the AAF and later became the first chief of staff of the newly established independent air force. Under his leadership, pilot training was quietly integrated, and the first firm commitment to complete integration was made. His testimony before the board, however, reveals contradictions. Blacks could not have been carefully selected if they were taken with very low aptitude scores.
67. Lt. Gen. Ira Eaker, ibid. Parrish's testimony refuted Eaker's last two points, as did his letter to General Hall, previously cited. Another air force witness, Lt. Col. Louis Nippert, echoed Eaker's testimony. Nippert's entire testimony centered on a segregated AAF.
68. Brig. Gen. Dean Strother, ibid. The 322d, however, had been decorated.
69. Brig. Gen. Edwin W. Chamberlain, ibid.
70. Lt. Col. George L. Weber, ibid. See also General Almond's testimony.
71. Unsigned true copy of letter, 25 June 1945, Gillem Board Papers.
72. Hull to Gillem Board, 4 Jan. 1946, Supp. to the Gillem Report Memo, Gillem Board Papers.
73. Edwards to Gillem Board, 2 Jan. 1946, Supp. to the Gillem Report Memo, Gillem Board Papers. Edwards's statement is significant because he implemented integration in 1949. In fact, the rapid and complete desegregation by the air force is due more to Edward than to any other uniformed individual.
74. Noce to the Gillem Board, n.d., Supp. to the Gillem Report, Gillem Board Papers.
75. Commanding General, Army Air Forces (but signed by Eaker), to Gillem Board, n.d., Supp. to the Gillem Report, Gillem Board Papers.

76. Gibson to Robert P. Patterson, 28 Nov. 1945, Supp. to the Gillem Report Memo, Gillem Board Papers. This and the next letter must have been forwarded to Gillem for consideration. Italics in original.

77. McCloy to Patterson, 24 Nov. 1945, Supp. to the Gillem Report Memo, Gillem Board Papers. Noel Parrish did not believe that piecemeal—on-the-job—integration and the breaking up of the larger units was significant. He quoted George S. Schuyler of the *Pittsburgh Courier* on the subject: "Jim Crowism does not lose its vicious character when administered in homeopathic doses. A jim-crow company is just as bad as a jim-crow division because it emphasizes a phony racial difference which invites invidious comparisons and leaves the doors open for discrimination against Negroes." Parrish, "Segregation," 51, 52.

78. WD Circular 76, 1947; and *Army Talk 170*, 1.

79. *Army Talk 170*, 1.

80. Overhead units included headquarters support personnel engaged in housekeeping activities, accounting, and finance, etc.

81. *Army Talk 170*, 2–8.

82. Ibid., 12–20.

83. Ibid., 20–30, italics in original. I have never met a veteran from that period who remembers discussing the pamphlet or who even recalls it. Allowing for poor memories, the pamphlet must not have made a great impression. The *Pittsburgh Courier* (17 May 1947, 20), in an article titled "Brasshats Find Loophole," stated that *Army Talk 170* was "still just talk to tan GIs. . . . There have been repeated charges that in some southern camps, notably Fort Benning, Georgia, Army commanders have refused to issue *Army Talk 170* to the troops." The *Pittsburgh Courier* accused some army commanders in the South of preventing distribution of the pamphlet and barring all discussion of it. Since the Gillem recommendations were never implemented, suppression of the pamphlet would appear to have been in line with the general army intransigence. See below.

84. The Fahy Committee was formally called the President's Committee on Equality of Treatment and Opportunity in the Armed Services. "Report on Gillem Board Policy and Implementation," [1949], Fahy Committee Papers, Harry S Truman Library, Independence, Mo. (HSTL), 78–80, 81–85, 88, 89, 92, 112, 117. Dalfiume and Lee Nichols stress the Gillem Board's failure on a lack of a clear-cut proposal for ending segregation. Dalfiume, *Desegregation*, 149–54; and Lee Nichols, *Breakthrough on the Color Front* (New York, 1954), 74, 75. Dalfiume criticizes the language of WD Circular 124. He believes it did not denote a clear policy ending segregation; thus, it created confusion and did not end segregation. According to Dalfiume, some War Department officials believed in 1946 that segregation was to be ended, but others must not have. He also criticizes the board for establishing a maximum quota of 10 percent while simultaneously calling for the maximum utilization of blacks. In addition to the fuzzy language, the failure to implement the creation of a staff agency determined to effect integration doomed Gillem Board policy to failure. Dalfiume writes that many theater commanders, months after the circular was published, had never heard of the policy or had any guidance on its implementation. I do not believe that the Gillem Board should be criticized too harshly for its imprecise language, since the Truman executive order in 1948 was even more generalized. The insistence on a quota was probably invoked more to help blacks than to hurt them, since blacks never approached the 10 percent figure in the interwar military. The army feared inundation, and Truman later had to promise the army a 10 percent quota if black enlistment got out of hand. On the matter of the special staff organization to implement the policy, the Gillem Board really sought this, knowing the army would oppose integration. The Gillem Board should not, then, be criticized for recommending a cautious program in the 1940s,

one that was far in advance not only of the army policy in the early 1950s but also of civilian race relations. The army failed to carry out the policy because it did not want to, not because the policy contained fuzzy language. When Truman issued Executive Order 9981 in 1948, the army did nothing for three years, and Truman made it clear that his vague language meant integration, and he appointed an agency to carry it out (the Fahy Committee). Dalfiume probably did not have access to the documents contained in the Gillem Board Papers, which were classified at the time of his research. All his notes come from the published WD Circular 124. The Gillem Board would have changed the whole racial face of the army if permitted; it knew that its program was radical, and it wanted the program enforced. The board's choice of language in the memorandum to the chief of staff and to its detractors made this abundantly clear. See especially the supplement to the original report in the Gillem Board Papers.

85. Discussion of Responsibilities of the Commander, Supporting Documents, Gillem Board Papers. Dalfiume probably never saw this document.

86. Lee, *Negro Troops,* 348–79.

87. Memo from the Central Intelligence Group to Military Units, n.d. [probably 1942], Document Number 1458190 (AFSHRC).

88. *Intelligencer,* Sept. 1944, 10–13 (AFSHRC). The counterintelligence pages of these journals, required reading for command intelligence officers, were filled mainly with material on blacks. The implication generally was that there was something artificial about the claim of discrimination and something other than "civil rights" was behind the agitation.

89. Nippert, "Participation," App. U. In this portion of his report, Nippert listed, base by base, the major racial altercations the AAF suffered.

90. *Chicago Defender,* 27 Apr. 1946, "Weekly Magazine," 2.

91. "Mutiny in the Colored Area, 27 Oct. 1946," Headquarters, Fifteenth Air Force, Colorado Springs, Colo., File 114-528, NPRC. In this file, which also included the "Participation" study, is a folder on racial incidents in 1946 and 1947. Full reports on the MacDill and Fort Worth riots (see below) are in the folder, as well as fragmentary reports on other altercations. The MacDill material cited here was categorized "sedition." It is a counterintelligence report.

92. Ibid.

93. Ibid.

94. Ibid. See also Report of the Air Inspector of the Deputy Commander Strategic Air Command, "Investigation of Incident at MacDill Field on 27 October 1946," 2 Nov. 1946, File 114-528, NPRC. This report agrees with that previously cited in all details but adds items the other lacked. These quoted statements were corroborated by witnesses at the trials and were confessed to by Treadwell.

95. Col. J. K. Fogle, "Estimate of the Racial Situation," 8 Nov. 1946, File 114-528, NPRC. He recommended a "firm and uncompromising policy of dealing with Negro troops."

96. "Mutiny in the Colored Area." Harris's complete report is also in the file.

97. "Communist Party Programs as Related to Its Activities against the Armed Forces," n.d., File 114-528, NPRC. Attached to this estimate are clippings provided for the chief of staff of SAC by Colonel Fogle concerning the Communist menace. Some of the clippings are about MacDill; one was about a Russian investigation of racism in South Africa; another was a *Pittsburgh Courier* editorial that opposed colonialism; one was a *Pittsburgh Courier* editorial that described Jesus as a black. Attached was also a summary of a racial incident at Geiger Field, Washington, where some blacks seized arms and fled into the hills near the base. Fogle's comment: "Intelligence reports reveal unquestionably that condition No. 4 of the twenty-one conditions cited as requisites for admission to the Communist International, the duty of spreading communist ideas includes the special obligation to carry on a vigorous and systematic propaganda in the Army."

98. "History of MacDill Army Air Field," Dec. 1946, 14–36; "Mutiny in the Colored Area"; and *New York Amsterdam News*, 21 Dec. 1946, 1, 2, 35. The newspaper also claimed that the riot occurred when blacks tried to break into a white dance, which was also false. According to the official MacDill history, there had been attempts after the Harris report to improve the conditions in the "colored area." A letter in the MacDill file at NPRC from the acting adjutant general at MacDill to the commander in chief of SAC, 19 Dec. 1946, complained that the situation at MacDill was made worse because of desperate overcrowding in the black area. MacDill had facilities for only 1,330 blacks in their area, and already 1,825 lived there, and the number was soon to be increased to 3,395. The adjutant requested immediate funds to add more living quarters and to upgrade recreational facilities.

99. Report of the SAC Inspector General to Deputy Commander, SAC, signed by Lt. Col. Charles F. Fultin, n.d., File 114-528, NPRC. The *Pittsburgh Courier* of 11 Jan. 1947, 1, 4, reported that 300 blacks had rioted in October and that blacks had served as officers at the court-martial.

100. *Pittsburgh Courier,* 26 Oct. 1946, 11.

101. "Investigation of Fort Worth Racial Incident," 10 Feb. 1947, MacDill file, File 114-528, NPRC. The investigation and report were accomplished by Eighth Air Force. In this unsigned report the recorder referred to the blacks as boys and the whites as men.

102. Fogle to Deputy Chief of Staff, SAC, n.d., MacDill file, File 114-528, NPRC, italics in original.

103. "Investigation of Possible Racial Incident at Fort Worth and Dallas Air Force Base, Texas, 1946," File 114-528, NPRC.

104. "History of the Fifteenth Air Force," 1947, 48–61.

105. Ibid.

106. Ibid.

107. Ibid.

108. Maj. Gen. S. G. Henry to Army Personnel, 13 June 1945, File 23–290, NARG 18. Notes on the map indicate that the Civilian Aide's office prepared the map.

109. Between December 1945 and December 1946, AAF strength declined from 2,282,259 military personnel to 455,515.

110. Army Air Forces (AAF) Ltr. 3-100, Mar. 1946. See attached ltr. from Army Adjutant General, 4 Feb. 1946.

111. AAF Ltr 35-268, 11 Aug. 1945, by command of General Arnold.

112. AAF Ltr. 35-130, 21 June 1946.

113. *Pittsburgh Courier,* 8 Feb. 1947, 8.

114. Memo from the secretary of war: "War Department Policies and Practices Regarding Civil Rights," 15 May 1947, President's Committee on Civil Rights Papers, HSTL.

115. "History of Tactical Air Command," Mar. -Dec. 1946, vol. I, 116, 133–36, italics in original.

116. "History of Tactical Air Command," 1 Jan.–30 Nov. 1948, 82, 97.

117. Ibid., 88–91.

118. Ibid. See also the staff study itself: Tactical Air Command, "Utilization of Negro Manpower," 18 Mar. 1948, Langley Air Force Base, Va. (AFSHRC).

119. "History of Tactical Air Command," 1 Jan.–30 Nov. 1948.

120. Ibid., 93–95. Paszek, "Negroes and the Air Force," 8, 9, citing a contemporary air force leader, states that purely political pressures prevented the air force from substituting whites for blacks in the 332d, for to do so would "invite 'violent reactions of the Negro press.'" Paszek also indicates that the commander of the Ninth Air Force refused to let the unit die on the vine for political reasons. The TAC inspector reported after an Operational Readiness Inspection that "Officer promotion has been 'overlooked,' the personnel at Lockbourne cannot be considered in any overall AF policy

as they are completely isolated by their color from utilizing the overages in field grade ranks now existing in the Air Force." The inspector cited the group commander, squadron commanders, and operations officers as "fulfilling their duties in a manner warranting promotions." See the report of the TAC inspector on his visit to Lockbourne from 6 to 8 Apr. 1948 in "History of Tactical Air Command," 1 Jan.–30 Nov. 1948.

121. "History of Strategic Air Command," 1948, vol. VI, 87–90.

122. Ibid.; the complete text of the letter is in the SAC history.

123. Ibid. See also vol. VIII of the 1948 SAC history: *Supporting Documents,* 112–22. Aviation engineers were construction workers. One unit in Europe built control towers, hard stands, taxiways, and winterized living areas in addition to grading new roads and repairing old ones. Another unit constructed "1,500 feet of 8-inch water line," patched the "air strip with asphalt," performed road maintenance, and improved the "drainage system" of the airstrip. This unit later helped build gasoline-storage tanks and pipelines. See "History of the 837th Engineering Aviation Battalion," Nov. 1945, 1; and the "History of the 811th Engineering Aviation Battalion," 1 Jan.–31 Dec. 1947, 1, 2. Similar units without a military mission were the aviation squadrons, referred to in the TAC histories. One of these supplied men to other base functions to work as laborers, warehousemen, vehicle drivers, billeting attendants, and cooks. See "History of the 385th Aviation Squadron," 1947, 1. The AAF Transport Command complained about the conduct of such blacks. The War Department, they said, forced the command to maintain "separate housing and messing, separate orderly rooms and day rooms." And while the command had done all it could to make blacks comfortable, "they have not earned a very enviable record by themselves." Most disconcerting was their "disproportionately high percentage of infractions and violations of military and civil law." While there were four times as many whites in the command as blacks, blacks committed about 30 percent more offenses than whites. While blacks constituted one-fifth of the military personnel, they committed 57 percent of the violations. See "History of the Pacific Division AAF Transport Command," 1 June–31 Dec. 1946, 120–26.

124. "History of the 2143d AAF Base Unit," 1 Sept.–31 Oct. 1945, 1, 2.

125. Ibid., 34–39.

126. Ibid., 1 Jan.–14 Apr. 1946, 3, 4.

127. Ibid., 9–12.

128. *Pittsburgh Courier,* 12 July 1947, 1. The newspaper identified five blacks at Randolph.

129. "History of the 2143d AAF Base Unit," 1 Sept.–31 Oct. 1945, 10, 11; and clippings at the end of the history from the *Pittsburgh Courier,* 15 Sept. 1945, 29 Sept. 1945, and 5 Oct. 1945, and from the *Norfolk Journal and Guide,* 6 Oct. 1945.

130. "History of the 477th Composite Group," 15 Sept. 1945–15 Feb. 1946, 1, 2.

131. Ibid., 15 Feb.–31 Mar. 1946, 1; *Chicago Defender,* 9 Feb. 1946, 18, and 16 Feb. 1946, 1; and "History of the 477th Composite Group," 1 Mar.–15 July 1946, 37.

132. "History of the 477th Composite Group," 1 Mar.–15 July 1946, App., ltr. from Davis to the Group, 24 June 1946.

133. Ibid., 1 Mar.–15 July 1946, 15–18, 16 July–15 Oct. 1946, 8–11, 15, 16, 31 Oct.–31 Dec. 1946, 1, 2.

134. Ibid., 16 July–15 Oct. 1946, 3, 17–24.

135. *Pittsburgh Courier,* 7 Dec. 1946, 1, 5.

136. Ibid., 27 July 1946, 1, 4.

137. Ibid., 31 Aug. 1946, 5.

138. Ibid., 30 Aug. 1947, 5.

139. Ibid., 20 July 1946, 1, 4.

140. "History of the 477th Composite Group," 1 Jan.–31 Mar. 1947, 5, 6, 1 Apr.–30 June 1947, 1, 2. Williams's ltr., dated 6 May 1947, is appended to the end of this latter volume.

141. "History of the 332d Fighter Group (SE)," 1 July–14 Aug. 1947, 1–3.
142. Ibid., 15 Aug.–31 Dec. 1947, 1–4, 21–25; and ltr., Lt. Gen I. H. Edwards to Eugene Zuckert, 5 Dec. 1947, Special Interest File, 1948–1949, 34A-35, NARG 340. Specifically, the figures Edwards uses are 15,473 black airmen, of which 1,862 were at Lockbourne, and 257 total black officers, with 192 of these at Lockbourne.
143. *Baltimore Afro-American,* 24 July 1948, 1, 2.
144. "History of the 332d Fighter Wing," 1 Jan.–31 Mar. 1948, 7, 1 Apr.–30 June 1948, 2.
145. Rodgers intvw.
146. *Pittsburgh Courier,* 22 May 1948, 1, 5; *Pittsburgh Courier,* 29 May 1948, 1, 4.
147. "History of the 332d Fighter Wing," 1 Apr.–30 June 1948, 16, 17, 18–20, 1 July–30 Sept. 1948, 1, 12, 1 Oct.–30 Nov. 1948, 16, June 1949, 5; and *Air Force Times,* 21 May 1949, 1, 18. The only mention of this unit in the *Air Force Times* (before articles about integration) covered athletics, e.g., Whitfield's Olympic victory, except for this story on the gunnery meet.
148. Memo from Vandenberg to H. H. Arnold, 16 Oct. 1945, Official Decimal File, 1938–1946, H. H. Arnold Papers.
149. Ibid.

Chapter 3: "Unbunching"

1. This is Lee Nichols's term for integration. It refers to the fact that concentrated numbers of blacks produced weak units and that to improve the unit, one had to "unbunch" it. There is a difference between unbunching and integration; it is the difference between desegregation and integration. Unbunching was the former, and that, not the latter, was what the air force leadership intended. See Nichols, *Breakthrough,* 221–26.
2. Nichols, *Breakthrough,* 77–81; and Dalfiume, *Desegregation,* 177–78. It may be that the seminal idea for the air force to investigate this problem came from James C. Evans, the civilian aide to the secretary of defense. In several memoranda written after 1948, he made oblique references to his 1947 suggestion that the air force investigate segregation. Evans was always a behind-the-scenes fighter, and it is almost impossible to gauge his influence. In any case, everybody who has researched this problem knows of Evans. See especially Memo, Evans to Marr, 7 June 1950, which mentions previous contacts on this subject. Another memo, Evans to Assistant Secretary of the Air Force Zuckert, June 1948 (AGC), called upon the air force to show independence in racial matters. Jack Marr told Morris MacGregor that Evans instigated the original study which Marr completed; Marr to MacGregor, 19 June 1970 (AGC). Marr also told MacGregor that there was "no sociology involved," just a routine personnel action. Marr found that despite official segregation, numerous competent blacks were working alongside whites in a frictionless atmosphere. Ibid.; and Jack Marr, "A Report on the First Year of Implementation of Current Policies Regarding Negro Personnel," 9 July 1950 (AGC). See also General Edwards's remarks to the Commanders' Conference, Apr. 1949; Lt. Gen. I. H. Edwards, "Remarks—Major Personnel Problems," 12 Apr. 1949, in AFSHRC. In two other statements (14 Oct. 1947 and 9 Jan. 1950) to the Air War College on personnel problems, Edwards did not mention blacks. Unfortunately no copy of the Marr study has survived. Marr has confirmed, however, that he worked on such a study and recommended an end to segregation before Truman directed it. See Marr intvw. In Marr's 1950 report, he said: "Shortly after the Air Force was designated one of the Departments of the National Military Establishment, the Office of the Deputy Chief of Staff, Personnel, undertook a review of the Air Force situation as it pertained to Negro personnel and Negro units. The tangible considerations of sound management indicated that it would be in the best interests of effective air power to consider all individuals on the basis of merit and ability."

3. Intvw., author with Idwal Edwards, Arlington, Va., Feb. 1973.

4. Edwards's remarks to the Commanders' Conference, Apr. 1949.

5. Spaatz to Graves, 5 Apr. 1948, in Special File 35, Negro Affairs, 1948, Secretary of the Air Force, NARG 340. The *Pittsburgh Courier* reported on 12 June 1948 that the air force was planning "drastic changes." It predicted that the air force would have trouble integrating Lockbourne, considering the mood in the Pentagon (pp. 1, 5).

6. Testimony before the National Defense Conference on Negro Affairs, 26 Apr. 1948, Zuckert Testimony, Special File 35, Negro Affairs, 1948, Secretary of the Air Force, NARG 340.

7. Royall testimony, ibid.

8. Edwards testimony, ibid.

9. Royall to Forrestal, 9 Apr. 1948, ibid.

10. Dalfiume, *Desegregation*, 178; and Nichols, *Breakthrough*, 70, 79. See especially Marr intvw. The *Pittsburgh Courier* blamed Royall for the air force delay in the implementation of its program. According to the *Courier:* "What is described as a 'progressive forward-looking' Air Force plan for gradually integrating Negroes in that branch of the service is currently on the desk of Secretary of Defense James Forrestal. . . . Although approved and signed by Secretary Stuart Symington and Air Force Chief of Staff Hoyt Vandenberg, details of the plan cannot be released until Secretary Forrestal okays the release. . . . Purpose of the delay, it is learned . . . is to try to give the Army time to consider the plan in the hope that Secretary . . . Royall, can be persuaded to bring the Army into line." The newspaper reported that Royall was "emphatic" in his desire to hold up release, and the *Pittsburgh Courier* tied this to his aspirations to become governor of North Carolina. See *Pittsburgh Courier,* 5 Feb. 1949, 1, 4.

11. Dalfiume discovered, after extensive research in the Forrestal papers at Princeton, that Forrestal was actively seeking the desegregation of the navy when he was its secretary during and shortly after the war. Forrestal hired Lester Granger to help him unbunch the navy. In 1945, the navy had the most progressive program because of Forrestal. See Dalfiume *Desegregation*, 101–3; and oral history intvw with Marx Leva, Dec. 1969 and June 1970, HSTL. Leva was Forrestal's special assistant and general counsel, 1947–49 and later was an assistant secretary of defense (1949–51). Leva asserted that Truman "felt strongly" about integration and Forrestal "drove like the very devil."

12. Nichols, *Breakthrough*, 10; and intvw, author with Eugene Zuckert, Washington, D.C., Apr. 1973. Zuckert said Symington was enlightened about race and had been a "pioneer in race-mixing in industry."

13. Nichols, *Breakthrough*, 75, 76, 78.

14. Dalfiume, *Desegregation*, 77, 78.

15. See for example, Memo, Royall to Forrestal, 2 Dec. 1948, in Special Interest File 35, Negro Affairs, 1948, Secretary of the Air Force, NARG 340. Royall, who had earlier rejected the idea of an experimentally integrated unit, now offered an army post for such a venture but required all decisions on integration to be delayed until the results of such an experiment had been examined. On 22 December 1948, Symington sent a memorandum to Forrestal rejecting the Royall plan. He stated that the air force planned to integrate anyway. Attached to Symington's response was a memorandum from Edwards to Vandenberg recommending integration. In early January, Symington again told Forrestal he rejected Royall's delaying tactics and told the secretary of defense, "We propose to adopt a policy of integration." See Memo, Symington to Forrestal, 6 Jan. 1949, Special Interest File 34A–35, Secretary of the Air Force, NARG 340.

16. Nichols, *Breakthrough*, 78, 79.

17. Dalfiume, *Desegregation*, 177, 178.

18. Nichols, *Breakthrough*, 98–99.

19. Zuckert intvw.

20. Even Jack Marr, whom Zuckert called a "crusader" for integration, refused to go on record on this subject, although he was most candid off the record. He did identify Gen. Muir Fairchild, on the record, as an opponent but not as an obstructionist. Marr intvw. Zuckert, Symington's project officer for integration, told the author that Marr "wrote the paperwork, rode herd on this thing for General Edwards," and did a "terrific job." According to Zuckert, Marr was "interested; he was bright; he could write; and without him, we wouldn't have been able to do the job." Zuckert intvw.

21. Zuckert intvw.

22. Parrish intvw.

23. Intvw., author with Dean Strother, Colorado Springs, Colo., June 1974.

24. Nichols, *Breakthrough*, 78.

25. Intvw., author with Stuart Symington, Washington, D.C., Mar. 1973. Symington also told me that Zuckert carried out the program.

26. Nichols, *Breakthrough*, 78.

27. Edwards intvw.

28. Symington intvw.

29. Edwards's remarks to the Commanders' Conference, Apr. 1949, italics in original.

30. Ibid.

31. Ibid. These were most of the officers and about 60 percent of the enlisted men at Lockbourne Army Air Field.

32. Ibid.

33. Ibid.

34. Ibid.

35. Jack Marr disagrees with this interpretation and said that I (Gropman) am "a veritable gold mine of misinformation." Token integration was never in Marr's mind, and he is sure Edwards never expected it. He also told me that if "recalcitrant white commanders had been found," they would have been "summarily relieved of their commands." Ltr., Marr to author, 1 Oct. 1973 (AGC).

36. Edwards's remarks to the Commanders' Conference, Apr. 1949.

37. Ibid., italics in original.

38. Another explanation for the timing of air force integration was the need to eliminate some air groups during the fiscal year for budgetary reasons. This may have been a major reason to integrate the 332d in the first place, since no one in the Pentagon really believed that the unit would be effective in war. Symington sent a memorandum to Forrestal on 17 Feb. 1949 telling him that the air force needed rapid approval of the integration plan if it was going to make successful its "necessary cutback programming." Symington said the "Air Force is committed" to disbanding Lockbourne as a "part of the new 48 group program." He also said this would increase the efficiency of the air force. Copies of this memorandum were sent to Generals Eisenhower and Vandenberg, as well as to Zuckert. See Memo, Symington to Forrestal, 17 Feb. 1949, National Archives folder OPD 291.2 (14 Nov. 1948). These plans were leaked to the *Air Force Times*, which announced, "Segregation in AF to Be Ended Soon." It was a positive article that described Colonel Davis as a man with "natural authority and commanding presence." It also pointed out the apprehensions that blacks might have over the potential damage that could be inflicted by individual bigots. *Air Force Times*, 2 Apr. 1949, 7.

39. Air Force Ltr. 35-3, 11 May 1949. Attached to the drafts of AFL 35-3 and the accompanying implementing letter was a staff summary sheet Edwards sent Vandenberg telling him there was sufficient evidence to indicate that the number of blacks who would qualify for assignment to white units would be approximately "1% of the white strength." Edwards told Vandenberg that segregation

had "debilitating aspects" and must go. His policy was similar to the navy's, and he planned to keep only "qualified" blacks. To solve the "barracks problems," he suggested "separate sleeping facilities in the barracks." Vandenberg approved the letters and the solution to the barracks problem. To support the recommendations on the staff summary sheet, Edwards exposed the inefficiency of segregation in the weaknesses in the 332d and in the underutilization of skilled blacks such as former navigators who had become unusable under segregation. To convince Vandenberg that the air force would not become flooded with blacks, he told Vandenberg that James C. Evans had shown him statistics that proved that when "relatively high initial standards of qualification" were maintained, "blacks would only receive one percent of the appointments." According to Edwards, blacks accounted for only 1 percent of civil service appointments, 1 percent of pilot's license-holders, and 1 percent of those serving with whites in the navy. Edwards also told Vandenberg that they could always institute an administrative quota if blacks flooded into the air force in numbers too large to assimilate. See Staff Summary Sheet, attachments, Edwards to Vandenberg, 29 Dec. 1948, in Special Interest File 35, Secretary of the Air Force, NARG 340. Vandenberg wrote a letter to Symington on 12 Jan. 1949 to defend separate facilities in the barracks, although he did not consider this to be the "ultimate solution." He did consider separate facilities just a "progressive" step toward eventual integration. See ltr., Vandenberg to Symington, 12 Jan. 1949, Special Interest File 34A-35, Secretary of the Air Force, NARG 340. The record indicates that Edwards aimed too low and that his motivations were mainly (though certainly not solely) to rid himself of the inadequate 332d and get to the talented 1 percent. The reason the air force escaped the navy's tokenism while trying to imitate it is that the air force was not deliberately aiming at tokenism, and the Fahy Committee took from the air force's local commanders the right to keep blacks segregated. The barracks problem was also solved (see below).

40. Ibid.

41. See Special Interest File 35, Negro Affairs, 1949, NARG 340, for this draft and others. Jack Marr prepared these versions.

42. HQ USAF, to Major Commands, subj.: "Implementation of AF Letter 35-3," n.d., Fahy Committee Papers.

43. Draft of implementing letter, 31 Dec. 1948, Special Interest File 35, Negro Affairs, 1949, NARG 340.

44. Donald R. McCoy and Richard T. Ruetten, *Quest and Response: Minority Rights and the Truman Administration* (Lawrence, Kans., 1973), 221–23. See also President's Committee on Equality of Treatment and Opportunity in the Armed Services, *Freedom to Serve* (Washington, D.C., 1950), 34–70.

45. Zuckert intvw. Lem Graves claimed in February 1949 that Zuckert removed the proposed partitions from the barracks because Colonel Davis suggested that not to do so would be unwise. See *Pittsburgh Courier*, 5 Feb. 1949, 1, 4. Zuckert wrote to Symington on 5 Jan. 1949 mildly complaining of the barracks segregation, stating that the plan "admittedly . . . only goes part of the way." A week later, on 12 Jan. 1949, Zuckert wrote to him again outlining the policy but omitting the paragraph that provided for separation in the barracks. Zuckert to Symington, 5 and 12 Jan. 1949, Special Interest File 34A-35, NARG 340.

46. Morris MacGregor, "Armed Forces Integration, Forced or Free," unpublished paper delivered to the 1972 U.S. Air Force Academy Military History Symposium, 1–15.

47. Memo, "Utilization of Colored Bombardiers and Navigators," unsigned, n.d., to Director of Military Personnel, National Archives folder OPD 291.2 (15 Apr. 1948). The *Army Navy Journal*, 12 Feb. 1949, 693, reports that there were seven black navigators at Lockbourne.

48. President's Committee on Civil Rights, *To Secure These Rights* (Washington, D.C., 1947).

49. McCoy and Ruetten, *Quest and Response*, 14. The authors deny that Truman ever joined the Ku

Klux Klan, although they admit he may have "flirted" with it. These authors have written the most positive account of Truman's motivations in inspiring civil rights actions.

50. William C. Berman, *The Politics of Civil Rights in the Truman Administration* (Columbus, Ohio, 1970), x, xii. Berman has the most cynical scholarly account of Truman's motivations. His treatment should be contrasted with Dalfiume, *Desegregation,* 139–40, who criticizes Berman for his negative judgments.

51. Berman, *Politics,* 237–40. Contrast Berman with Dalfiume, *Desegregation,* especially 139, 140, and with McCoy and Ruetten, *Quest and Response,* 1–25, 249–50; the latter authors (p. 221) label military integration as "the most stunning achievement of the Truman era in the field of civil rights."

52. Barton J. Bernstein, "The Ambiguous Legacy: The Truman Administration and Civil Rights," paper delivered before the American Historical Association, 1966, also printed in Barton J. Bernstein, ed., *Politics and Policies of the Truman Administration* (Chicago, 1970), 271–96. Bernstein has been taken to task by Alonze L. Hamby of Ohio University in his unpublished comment on the Bernstein paper at the American Historical Association meeting; both papers are at HSTL. Hamby finds Bernstein less than generous to Truman in his Kansas City days and cites Roy Wilkins as pro-Truman even while Truman was a local politician. Hamby also believes Truman went further than he had to go if he were as ambivalent and reluctant as Bernstein thinks. As for the importance of rhetoric, Federal Judge Waites Waring, on overturning South Carolina's white primary, quoted extensively from Truman's Lincoln Memorial speech to the NAACP. After quoting Truman to the effect that the times required action on civil rights and an immediate attack upon "prejudice and discrimination," Waring told South Carolina, "It is time . . . to rejoin the Union." Memo, Robert C. Carr to George Elsey, 28 July 1948, file on "President's NAACP Speech 6/29/47," George Elsey Papers, HSTL.

53. See Monroe Billington, "White Southern Response to President Truman's Civil Rights Legislation," unpublished paper read at the Southern Historical Association meeting, Memphis, Tenn., Nov. 1966, copy in HSTL.

54. Berman, *Politics,* 44–51; and Bernstein, "Ambiguous Legacy," 296. Berman reminds the reader that Truman had unwittingly and "inadvertently" built up political pressure that could spell trouble for him in the future, by creating a committee that might develop an unacceptable program politically. Bernstein would not disagree. Berman says that the committee report, *To Secure These Rights,* was a "political bombshell" which had to be either "detonated or defused." See Berman, *Politics,* 72; and Bernstein, "Ambiguous Legacy," 278–82. Berman also argues that Truman's main motivation for appointing the committee in the first place was to offset the congressional losses suffered by the party in Nov. 1946; see Berman, 77–78.

55. Nichols, *Breakthrough,* 74; and Harry S Truman, *Memoirs of Harry S Truman,* vol. II, *Years of Trial and Hope* (New York, 1956), 210–13.

56. President's Committee on Civil Rights, *To Secure These Rights,* vii.

57. Ibid., ix.

58. Ibid., 41. This chapter is called "The Record: Short of the Goal," and the subchapter is titled "The Right to Bear Arms."

59. Ibid., 40–47.

60. Ibid., 82–87.

61. Memo, Robert K. Carr to the President's Committee, subj: "Negroes in the Armed Forces," prepared by Milton D. Stewart and Joseph Murtha, 10 June 1947, President's Committee on Civil Rights Papers.

62. President's Committee on Civil Rights, *To Secure These Rights,* 162–63.

63. Ibid.

64. Ibid.

65. Ibid.

66. This was confirmed by committee member Rabbi Roland B. Gittelsohn, intvw with author, Boston, Mass., Apr. 1970. This was not to be the last time somebody wanted to use the military to destroy segregation. See chapter 5.

67. *Public Papers of the Presidents of the United States: Harry S Truman* (Washington, D.C., 1947), 479–80.

68. Gittelsohn intvw.

69. Berman, *Politics,* 79–85.

70. *Newsweek,* 7 June 1948, 28, 29. See also Richard J. Stillman, *Integration of the Negro in the U.S. Armed Forces* (New York, 1968), 4, 5.

71. *Pittsburgh Courier,* 27 Mar. 1948, 1, 4.

72. Ibid., 10 Apr. 1948, 1, 4. The headline read, "Blast at Army Jolts Entire Nation."

73. Ibid. See also *Chicago Defender,* 24 Apr. 1948, 2.

74. *Newsweek,* 7 June 1948, 28–29.

75. Confidential Memo, Clifford to the President, Nov. 1947, 11–13, Clark M. Clifford Papers, HSTL.

76. Ibid., 39–40. Later he told Truman that the "negro vote in the crucial states will more than cancel out any votes the President may lose in the South." This was a remarkably accurate prediction. See Confidential Memo, 17 Aug. 1948, Clifford M. Papers.

77. Memo, William L. Batt to Gael Sullivan, "The Negro Vote," 20 Apr. 1948, Batt File, Clark M. Clifford Papers. A copy of this was sent to Clifford. Batt was research director of the Democratic National Committee.

78. Berman, *Politics,* 103, 105, 106, 112.

79. On 26 June 1948 the *Pittsburgh Courier* (pp. 1, 4), on the eve of its formal endorsement of Dewey, noted with some gloom that the "Republican dominated eightieth Congress closed shop early Sunday without passing a single piece of civil rights legislation—despite the party's platform pledges of 1940 and 1944, and which at this moment are piously being rewritten into the 1948 platform."

80. *Public Papers of the Presidents* (Truman, 1964), 279. See front-page headlines and related stories in the *Chicago Defender,* 31 July and 7 Aug. 1948.

81. *The Nation,* 28 Aug. 1948, 279.

82. Confidential Memo, Clifford to Truman, 17 Aug. 1948, Clark M. Clifford Papers.

83. *Baltimore Afro-American,* 28 Oct. 1944, 1. See also *New York Amsterdam News,* 28 Oct. 1944, 6A.

84. Rep. John E. Rankin (Miss.), Sen. Thomas T. Connally (Tex.), Rep. Edward E. Cox (Ga.), Sen. Theodore G. Bilbo (Miss.), and Sen. James C. Eastland (Miss.) were all ardent segregationists.

85. *Pittsburgh Courier,* 28 Oct. 1944, 1.

86. Ibid., 21 Oct. 1944, 1, 4.

87. Ibid., 4 Nov. 1944, 4.

88. Ibid., 28 October 1944, 1.

89. Ibid., 5 July 1947, 1, 4.

90. Ibid., 1 Nov. 1948, 5, and 8 Nov. 1948, 1, 4, 6. See 15 Dec. 1946 for the coverage of the creation of the President's Committee on Civil Rights (pp. 1, 4).

91. Ibid., 17 Jan. 1948, 7, and 3 Jan. 1948, 1, 4, and 8 Mar. 1947, 5, in which Truman was saluted for praising the black press.

92. Ibid., 14 Feb. 1948, 1, 4.

93. Ibid., 31 July 1948, 1, and 7 Aug. 1948, 1, 4. See also *Baltimore Afro-American,* 31 July 1948, 1, 2, 8.

94. *Pittsburgh Courier,* 25 Sept. 1948, 1, 5.

95. Ibid. For a contrary point of view, see *Chicago Defender,* especially 30 Oct. 1948, 1, and 2 Oct. 1948,

1, and any issue approaching the election of 1944, all of which opposed the editorials in the *Pittsburgh Courier* and the *Baltimore Afro-American*.

96. *Pittsburgh Courier,* 28 Feb. 1948, 1, 4. On 21 Feb, the paper had identified the following 15 states: New York, Pennsylvania, Illinois, Ohio, Michigan, California, Kentucky, New Jersey, Indiana, Kansas, Maryland, Missouri, West Virginia, Tennessee, and Delaware (p. 1). Adding Massachusetts and Connecticut to these would give a candidate 277 electoral votes, with 266 needed to win.

97. Ibid., 13 Nov. 1948, 3.

98. Ibid., 5 Feb. 1949, 3.

99. Berman, *Politics,* 129–33. Berman said that Truman climaxed his campaign with a civil rights speech on 29 Oct. in Harlem. This was a master stroke, and Dewey had ignored the black vote. This election, Berman says, meant that civil rights had become "institutionalized" on the national level, and blacks had become the "balance of power" in national politics.

100. *Pittsburgh Courier,* 20 Nov. 1948, 8. The newspaper very rarely printed letters to the editor in those days.

101. Stillman, *Integration,* 44.

102. McCoy and Ruetten, *Quest and Response,* 221–22.

103. When it first met, the committee was given a banner headline by the *Pittsburgh Courier* (22 Jan. 1949, 3): "Committee Begins Work on Ending Service Bias." This was one of many articles on the work of the Fahy Committee. The members who were active were Charles Fahy, Dwight Palmer, William Stevenson, John Sengstacke, and Lester Granger. The last two were black. Two other men on the committee did not actively participate in its work.

104. "Meeting of the President and the Four Service Secretaries with the President's Committee on Equality of Treatment and Opportunity in the Armed Services," Cabinet Room, the White House, 12 Jan. 1949, Official File 1285, 1948–Apr. 1950, Harry S. Truman Papers, HSTL.

105. John H. Sengstacke, "An Outline Discussion of the President's Executive Order 9981," n.d., Fahy Committee Papers.

106. McCoy and Ruetten, *Quest and Response,* 222, 223. See also Fahy to Truman on the progress of the committee to date, 27 July 1949, Enclosure E: The Air Force, Official File 1285, Harry S Truman Papers.

107. Fahy to Truman, 27 July 1949, Enclosure E: The Air Force, Official File 1285, Harry S Truman Papers.

108. Ibid.; and McCoy and Ruetten, *Quest and Response,* 223–24.

109. See, for example, Dalfiume, *Desegregation,* 180–200.

110. Ibid.; and McCoy and Ruetten, *Quest and Response,* 226–50. See also Army Regulation 600-629-1, 16 Jan. 1950: "Utilization of Negro Manpower in the Army." This called for "equality of treatment and opportunity . . . without regard to race, color, religion, or national origin" but did not end, or intend to end, segregation. It called for all occupational specialties to be opened to blacks and for all assignments to be made without regard to color; yet segregation continued for more than a year and was not completely eliminated for another four years.

111. Thomas Reid to Richard Dalfiume, 12 Feb. 1965, copy in Evans Military Correspondence File, James C. Evans Papers, Army War College, Carlisle Barracks, Pa. See also Dalfiume, *Desegregation,* 183, in which he describes the function of the Reid Board.

112. Testimony before the President's Committee on Equality of Treatment and Opportunity in the Armed Services, Afternoon Sessions, 28 Mar. 1949, Pentagon, 5, 30–34, NARG 341. Earlier in the afternoon General Edwards said that he had been "involved in this Negro problem even during the war." Proposals had been in the wind since 1943, but the climate had not been right until after the war. Edwards told Fahy that if integration proved damaging to efficiency, it would have to be abandoned. See pp. 28, 29, and 30–34, for Edwards's testimony.

113. *Air Force Times,* 2 Apr. 1949, 7. See also the story on 14 May 1949, 1. In an interview, Spann Watson said that he was responsible for the paragraph in the *Air Force Times* that suggested some blacks had fears. Watson intvw.

114. *Army Navy Journal,* 31 July 1948, 1321, 1329. See also the editorial page. On the Bradley issue, letters exchanged between the general and Truman in July and August reveal that Bradley had not known that the executive order had been released and that he believed he was being baited by reporters when he made his statement. No one should imply, he told Truman, that the "Army would stubbornly resist integration." See ltrs., Bradley to Truman, 30 July 1948, and Truman to Bradley, 4 Aug. 1948, in Negro Pamphlet File, Army War College, Carlisle Barracks. At least the *Air Force Times* and the *Army Navy Journal* reported integration. Two other air force–oriented journals ignored the event entirely. *Air Force Magazine* ("The Official Journal of the Air Force Association") made only one brief mention of the breakup of Lockbourne in August 1949. The *Air University Review,* devoted to stimulating "healthy discussion of Air Force problems which may ultimately result in improvement of our national security," also failed to report the change in racial policy.

115. Ltr., The Interested People of Lockbourne Air Force Base to Robert L. Carter, Assistant Special Counsel, 16 Mar. 1949, Countainer 405, NAACP Papers. See the earlier memo of 10 Mar. 1949 regarding Lockbourne. Carter disagreed with the men at the base and recommended no NAACP action.

116. Ibid.

117. Ibid. See the Lockbourne personnel memo which was attached to the 16 Mar. 1949 ltr. to Carter. A copy in the NAACP files has no names on it, but Spann Watson showed me the original (AGC), and it indicates that Watson wrote it with the collaboration of George Iles, Silas Jenkins, Andrews McCloy, and Samuel Lynn. Watson said that he had flown all over the East protesting the air force plan and that he had spoken to the *Air Force Times,* the *Pittsburgh Courier,* the NAACP, and the Urban League. Watson intvw. A letter to the editor in the *Pittsburgh Courier* two years earlier (21 June 1947, 13) demonstrates that at least one enlisted man found the officers to be selfish: "It was everyone for himself and God for all. If we don't help ourselves when we have the authority, we should not expect help from someone else. Until we learn unity and cooperation, we will forever be the white man's foot stool."

118. Ltr., The Interested People of Lockbourne Air Force Base to Robert L. Carter.

119. Wilkins to "Branch Officers," 6 Nov. 1949, Container 395, NAACP Papers. At about the same time, James C. Evans wrote to Roy Wilkins that he had expected "negative reactions" from some blacks expressing the arguments that "we would rather be together," or "we could advance better in our own group," or "we can make a better record for the race in racial units." Evans, moreover, was pleased to say that the "preponderance of expressions" were not negative but, rather, "positive and affirmative." Evans to Wilkins, 16 Nov. 1949, Container 395, NAACP Papers.

120. "History of the Ninth Air Force," 1 Dec. 1948–1 Jan. 1950, vol. II, Supporting Documents.

121. Memo, E. H. Underhill, Deputy Director of Military Personnel, to Director of Personnel Planning, DCS/P, "Status of Implementation of AFL 35-3," n.d. (AGC); this was the cover sheet on a memo that Zuckert was to take to the Fahy Committee on the progress of September 1949. All the men were given a three-part examination for aptitude, and all were interviewed. A "small" number were eliminated because they were "marginal" or "extraordinary" cases. The report notes, "Upon reporting to his new station, each airman is assigned to the performance of the duty recommended in the original screening process at Lockbourne."

122. Testimony before the Fahy Committee on 28 Mar. 1949: Idwal H. Edwards's testimony, 28–34, NARG 341.

123. Rpt., HQ 2260th Air Base Squadron, Lockbourne Air Force Base, Ohio, to Air Force DCS/P, Personnel Plans, "Personnel Progress as of 20 September 1949" (AGC).

124. *Air Force Times,* 23 July 1949, 7.

125. Records on Racial Policies 1944–1950, appended to a report on "Racial Integration of the Air Force," 6 Feb. 1950, NARG 341. Edwards missed his 1 percent estimate of black qualifications by 500 percent. Zuckert admitted that the screening boards might have been a mistake because of their impact on black morale. The eight bases reported in the results of screening were Lockbourne, Lackland, Barksdale, Randolph, Waco, Mather, Williams, and Goodfellow Air Force Bases. See Zuckert intvw. See also the appendix to this book, tables 1, 2, 4, and 11.

126. *Pittsburgh Courier,* 21 May 1949, 1, 4.

127. Ibid., 28 May 1949, sec. 2, 1.

128. Ibid., 6 Aug. 1949, 2, and 18 June 1949, 1, 4, and 22 Oct. 1949, 1, 4.

129. "History of the Ninth Air Force," 1 Dec. 1948–1 Dec. 1950, vol. II, Supporting Documents.

130. Kuter to Military Air Transport Service Commanders, 1 May 1949, File 250.1 to 291.2, NARG 340.

131. Edwards to Lt. Gen. Ennis Whitehead, Commanding General, Continental Air Command, 29 July 1949, Whitehead Correspondence (AFSHRC). In the same file are letters from Whitehead to Edwards reporting that all was going reasonably well. See, for example, his letter of 2 Mar. 1950.

132. LeMay to Edwards, 27 Sept. 1949, "History of Strategic Air Command," 1950, Supporting Documents.

133. LeMay briefing to SAC unit commanders, ibid.

134. LeMay to Ramey, 10 Oct. 1949, ibid. In this history, there is a report of a white sergeant who tried to force newly arrived blacks to bunk together at one end of the barracks. He was disciplined. The incident convinced the blacks that the air force was in "earnest about its policy of non-discrimination." See Supporting Documents.

135. [E. W. Kenworthy], "A First Report on the Racial Integration of the Air Force," 6 Feb. 1950, Records on Racial Policies 1944–1955, NARG 341.

136. Ibid.

137. Ibid.

138. Ibid.

139. Ibid. Members of the President's Committee on Religion and Welfare in the Armed Forces demonstrated no great willingness to come to grips with this type of problem. In their report on Keesler AFB, the problem is ignored; in their report on Maxwell AFB they commented only on the fact that the base was integrated. But blacks were not allowed to play on the base athletic teams. See "Community Organizations," President's Committee on Religion and Welfare in the Armed Forces Papers, HSTL. See also data on Biloxi, Miss., and Montgomery, Ala.

140. [Kenworthy], "First Report," section on Keesler AFB. Nichols wrote that if there were provocations by whites in Biloxi, "plans were in readiness to spirit the Negroes away from the area instantly." Nichols, *Breakthrough,* 100.

141. [Kenworthy], "First Report," section on Lackland AFB. Joseph H. B. Evans, Kenworthy's assistant and a black, also visited Lackland "unannounced" and was favorably impressed. Blacks were very pleased with their treatment. He noted that there were blacks in supervisory positions over whites. He also noted that the Officers Candidate School club was in a hotel in downtown San Antonio and was therefore segregated, neglecting the black cadets socially, but he observed that the whites were as upset over this as were the blacks. See Memo, Joseph H. B. Evans to the Fahy Committee, subj.: "Treatment of Negroes at Lackland Air Base," 3 Nov. 1949, Fahy Committee Papers.

142. [Kenworthy], "First Report," section on Maxwell AFB. More will be said about Maxwell AFB in this and the next chapter. General Edwards told me in an interview that he personally disbanded

the 3817th. The fact that the men worked in 29 organizations is a reflection of the Gillem policy. When black officers, however, tried to force the municipal buses to integrate while on the base, Maxwell officials refused to support the blacks and permitted continued segregation. See *Pittsburgh Courier,* 12 July 1949, 5.

143. [Kenworthy], "First Report," main body of the report.

144. Project Clear, *Summary Preliminary Report on Utilization of Negro Manpower* (Baltimore, [1951]), copy in Maxwell AFB Library (AFSHRC). The report was compiled during the Korean War and before the army decision to integrate. The air corps polled 5,872 whites in 1942 and found that most wanted blacks to receive the same training they got but wanted blacks to be segregated. See Research Branch, Special Services Division, Services of Supply, *Attitudes of Enlisted Men towards Negroes for Air Force Duty,* 30 Nov. 1942, Maxwell AFB Library.

145. Department of Defense, I&E Division, Attitude Research Branch, *Morale Attitudes of Enlisted Men, May–June 1949: Attitude toward Integration of Negro Soldiers in the Army,* Mar. 1949, Maxwell AFB Library, italics in original.

146. Parrish, "Segregation," 54, 59–60, 66, 93, 95, 100, 101.

147. Lt. Col. Solomon Cutcher, "Effective Utilization of Negro Personnel in the Armed Forces," Air Command and Staff College research study, Mar. 1948, Maxwell AFB Library, 22, 23. A complete perusal of all catalogues, indexes, and bibliographies at Maxwell and in the AFSHRC reveals that after integration in 1949, no other reports were compiled on this subject until the 1960s. The students' research subjects probably demonstrate their belief that the race problem had been solved in 1949.

148. Lt. Col. John B. Gaffney, "Application of Personnel Management as Applied to Negro Troops in the Air Forces," Air Command and Staff College research study, Oct. 1948, Maxwell AFB Library, 14–15.

149. Maj. Hugh D. Young, "Effective Utilization of Negro Manpower in the United States Air Force," Air Command and Staff School research study, Dec. 1948, Maxwell AFB Library, 22–26.

150. Economic Mobilization Course, "Training and Utilization of Manpower," Industrial College of the Armed Forces, Washington, D.C., 1948, Maxwell AFB Library, v. The committee members were all lieutenant colonels or colonels or the Navy equivalent.

151. Ibid., 52.

152. Ibid., 56–63, 64.

153. Ibid., 66–69.

154. Ibid., 73.

155. Ibid., 77.

156. Ibid., 81.

157. Ibid., 82–83.

158. Ibid., 84.

159. Ibid., 86.

160. Ibid., 106.

161. Col. Lester L. Kunish, "Utilization of Negro Airmen on Air Force Bases," Air War College research study, Feb. 1949, Maxwell AFB Library, 8, 10, 11, 12. Although Kunish recommended no real advance for blacks, he believed there were no jobs that blacks could not hold. See pp. 26–32. Also note a similar study at the War College by Col. Phillip B. Klein, "Utilization of Negro Personnel in the Air Force," Air War College research study, Mar. 1949, Maxwell AFB Library, especially 25–26, and a study by Col. W. E. Covington, Jr., "The Utilization of Negro Personnel," Air War College thesis, Mar. 1949, Maxwell AFB Library, especially 13, 14. Covington had commanded blacks. See also Lt. Col. Rollen H. Anthis, "Utilization of Negro Personnel in the Armed Forces," Air Command and Staff College research study, Mar. 1949, Maxwell AFB Library, 13–15.

162. Maj. John J. Pesch, "Should Negroes and Whites Be Integrated in the Same Air Force Units?," Air Command and Staff College research study, Apr. 1949, Maxwell AFB Library, 12–14.

163. Maj. James D. Catington, "Sociological Factors Concerned with the Segregation of Negro Troops in the Armed Forces," Air Command Staff College research study, May 1949, Maxwell AFB Library, 12, 13. See also Lt. Col. Orville C. Tangen, "Negro Personnel Management in the United States Air Force," Air Command and Staff College research study, May 1949, Maxwell AFB Library, especially ii, iii, 20–23. Tangen commanded blacks and blamed all the problems on segregation and recommended its immediate abandonment.

164. Lt. Col. Jack E. Cunningham, "Non-Segregation vs. Prejudice" Air Command and Staff College research study, Nov. 1949, Maxwell AFB Library, 13, 14. See also Lt. Col. Fidelis A. Link, "Determination of Policies for Utilization of Negro Manpower in the U.S. Air Force," Air Command and Staff College research study, Nov. 1949, 13–14. He said that the "Air Force will profit by leading in social reform." Also see Lt. Col. D. B. Avery, "The Negro and the Air Force," Air Command and Staff College research study, Nov. 1949, especially 3, 4, 17, 18, 19.

165. Inspector General Report on Racial Affairs, San Antonio, Tex., 13 Oct. 1949, Secretary of the Air Force, File 291.2, NARG 340.

166. Ibid. A wholesome reaction to racial integration was expected, according to David Mandelbaum. He drew on his knowledge of in-group sociology and suggested that "esprit de corps" would be the adhesive that would bind blacks and whites in the same unit together. Citing Ardant du Picq, Mandelbaum said that the cohesion du Picq wrote of in combat was no less important an influence during "training and in [the] garrison." Morale is dependent upon social relations within the soldiers' primary group or unit. Segregation would work against unit effectiveness by increasing a lack of confidence. He believed that integration would overcome adverse racial attitudes. In the unit, color would make little difference. See David G. Mandelbaum, *Soldier Groups and Negro Soldiers* (Berkeley, 1952), 1, 2, 9, 55, 88, 90, 131, 132.

167. "A Report of the First Year of Implementation of Current Policies Regarding Negro Personnel." See also ltr., General Edwards to Kuter 17 Oct. 1949, File 291.2, NARG 340. Edwards said that the expression "scarcely a ripple" described the situation "throughout the Air Force."

168. "History of Strategic Air Command," 1949, 43–45. Orlando AFB reported that two NCO clubs and two service clubs were established upon the suggestion of black personnel who believed that both blacks and whites would be more at home in a group "where the majority of their race congregate." Although the policy of separate clubs was unstated, white personnel gravitated to one club and blacks to the other, although either race was "welcome" at social events at either club. This history took note of Ku Klux Klan hostility, some of it physical, to air force integration in the Orlando, Florida, area. "History of 14th Air Force," 1 Jan.–30 June 1951, vol I, 61–66.

169. "History of the Air Training Command," 1 July–31 Dec. 1949, 29–31.

170. Gen. Robert Old to Whitehead, 19 Sept. 1949, "History of the Ninth Air Force," 1 Dec. 1948–1 Jan. 1950, vol. II, Supporting Documents.

171. "History of the Ninth Air Force," 1 Jan.–31 July 1950, 92–94. Brig. Gen. H. W. Bowman described the visit in a letter to the author. Bowman was deputy chief of staff for Ninth Air Force. He had been ordered by Maj. Gen. Willis Hale to "insure complete" integration well before Johnson's visit in February 1950. Hale had met Mordecai Johnson and found him to be critical of air force integration, though he had never seen an active air base. Hale asked Johnson to visit Langley to look for himself, and he accepted. Johnson was free to do what he wanted and go where he wished, "all out, no holds barred, all day." As Johnson boarded his plane to return to Washington, D.C., he was asked by Bowman to comment and responded: "Well, I don't believe it's that way everywhere." H. W. Bowman to the author, personal correspondence, 15 May 1973. The *Pittsburgh Courier* also

commented on Johnson's visit. It quoted him as saying: "The Air Force is making a genuine effort at Langley Air Force Base to deal with Negro airmen stationed there on a strict basis of individual merit. . . . The evidence is clear and substantial." The newspaper did note Johnson's disappointment with the small number of black aviators. *Pittsburgh Courier,* 4 Mar. 1950, 6.

172. President's Committee on Equality of Treatment and Opportunity in the Armed Services, *Freedom to Serve,* 6, 7, 17–26, 49–60. Lee Nichols wrote that air force integration worked as a lever on the army. Nichols, *Breakthrough,* 139, 140. The *Army Navy Journal* covered the release of the Fahy report, in a piece that was sympathetic toward integration, while the army still had not really budged. The journal noted that the committee had to battle on the basis of justice while their opponents argued for "efficiency," but the article came down on the side of justice. "The integrity of the individual, his equal worth in the sight of God, his equal protection under law, his equal rights and obligations of citizenship, and his equal opportunity to make constitutional use of his endowment—these are the very foundation of the American system of values. The President's Committee throughout its deliberations shaped its course constantly with these principles." *Army Navy Journal,* 3 June 1950, 1091.

173. *Pittsburgh Courier,* 30 Apr. 1949, 1, 4, and 30 July 1949, 5, and 8 Oct. 1949, 1, 5, and 12 Nov. 1949, 1, 4, and 9 June 1951, 1, 10.

174. Ibid., 25 June 1949, 1, 4.

175. Ibid., 28 July 1951, 2.

176. Ibid., 25 Aug. 1951, 2. There were four black flight instructors at Williams training white pilot trainees.

177. Ibid., 14 Apr. 1951, 1, 4. The unit George wrote of was the same 3817th that Kenworthy had seen in 1950.

178. The history of the 3817th Air University Wing is unique for the fact that the reader is never informed that it is a black unit. It describes low morale and makes vague statements about the unit's dwindling size. Finally, the unit disbanded without a trace, and no acknowledgment is made as to why it no longer existed. See "History of the 3800th Air University Wing, Maxwell AFB," Apr.–June 1949, 21–22, July–Sept. 1949, 22, Oct.–Dec. 1949, 19, Jan.–June 1950, 46–47, 1 Jul–31 Dec. 1951, App. C, 6 and 7, and Jan.–Mar. 1952, unpaged. James L. Hicks of the *Baltimore Afro-American* severely criticized discrimination at Shaw AFB, South Carolina, because blacks there had been barred from using the base swimming pool, service club, and NCO club. Blacks coming from integrated basic training at Lackland AFB had their morale lowered severely by their treatment at Shaw. Base personnel worked and lived in a frictionless atmosphere, "but at five o'clock in the evening, the integration ends." *Baltimore Afro-American,* 9 June 1951, 5. There apparently was some hesitant integration at Eglin AFB, Florida, for there is a communication between a senior and a junior military historian concerning the issue. The junior complained that the service squadron took too long to dissolve; the senior called for patience and told him to dig into the fact that the base commander had complaints from whites over integrating base housing. The senior seemed to recall that the swimming pool and officers' club policy has changed after integration. This is a draft with comments of July to Dec. 1950 "History of the 3203d Installations Group," Eglin AFB, Fla.; it was given to me by a historian in the Office of the Chief of Military History (AGC). The work shows that historians wrestled with this problem.

179. Report on Incidents at Brookley AFB, Ala., Secretary of the Air Force, Decimal File 291.2 (1951–1953), NARG 340 (AGC). One nearby base commander wanted to turn in the complainant, a Mr. LeFlore, because he was an NAACP official while working for the post office. The officer was told that such activities did not violate the law. The black press covered the Brookley incidents, believing they demonstrated the federal government's seriousness about integration. See *Chicago De-*

fender, 6 Oct. 1951, 1. The air force, furthermore, required barbers employed by the base exchange to cut everyone's hair or to quit. See unsigned memorandum to James Goode, 13 Oct. 1951, File 291.2, NARG 340.

180. "Assignment to Overseas Area for Negroes," Decimal File 291.2 (1948–1949), NARG 340. See numerous letters from Eugene Zuckert and others in the Department of the Air Force, Secretary of Defense Johnson, and members of the Department of State. Letters are from the fall of 1949 to the spring of 1950.

181. A.G.K. to Louis Johnson, 21 Aug. 1950, Decimal File 291.2, NARG 330. "A.G.K." was judge of probate in Union, South Carolina. Johnson employed a soft answer to turn away his wrath. See also in same file Johnson to A.G.K., 29 Aug. 1950.

182. Telegram, Gov. J. Strom Thurmond to Sen. Burnet Maybank, July 1949, forwarded to Symington, whose answer is clipped to the telegram, Decimal File 250.1 to 291.2, NARG 340.

183. Colonel Bell to Congressmen Allen of Louisiana incorporating Zuckert's reply, Decimal File 250.1 to 291.2, NARG 340.

184. Secretary of Defense, 1950, Decimal File 291.2, NARG 330.

185. Memo for General Vandenberg on "Activity within the Office of Inspector General during the Current Calendar Year," n.d., in "History of the Office of the Inspector General," 1 July–31 Dec. 1950 (AFSHRC).

186. *Air Force Times,* 25 Oct. 1952, 1, 25. See also "History of the Deputy Chief of Staff," vol. I, *Directorate of Personnel Planning, DCS/P,* 11. Marr worked in this agency, which had been charged with overseeing racial affairs since 1948. In the next decade it had to be reintroduced to its responsibilities. One might have anticipated that the history of integration would be told in these volumes, but it is a very disappointing source. The office engaged in many activities, and its history devotes little space to integration. For example, the page of the history covering the first full year of integration is devoted to generalizations on the subject. Although "Plans" initiated, planned, controlled, and implemented integration, they were involved in all manner of other activities including promotion, procurement, separation, utilization, and all major personnel projects not under the control of any one operating agency. They had many special projects. See "History of the Deputy Chief of Staff/Personnel," July 1949–30 June 1950, 1033 (AFSHRC).

187. Nichols, *Breakthrough,* 100, 101, 102, 104, 105.

188. Ibid., 156.

189. Ibid., 165–68.

190. Ibid., 168–70.

191. Ibid. See also Alice M. Yohalem, "Growing Up in the Desegregated Air Force," Columbia University, 1973, manuscript. This study demonstrates that black children of air force noncommissioned officers have higher aspirations than do black children of the same age growing up in segregated neighborhoods. They are also more likely to go to college. "The military environment appears to provide young dependents of black Air Force sergeants with more extensive interracial experiences than are available to their civilian peers. . . . Greater exposure to interracial experiences, while not a key factor in their goal formulation, appears to have placed these blacks in a better position to further their career objectives." See esp. 233–42.

192. Nichols, *Breakthrough,* 223–25.

193. Ibid., 166–67.

194. AFR 35-78, 4 Sept. 1950, and 15 Sept. 1955. See App. 2-4 and 2-5.

Chapter 4: Benign Neglect

1. See, for example, "Experiment in Democracy," *Baltimore Afro-American,* 17 June 1950, 13, about Selfridge Army Air Field, Michigan. The men were "lavish in their praise" of the air force because

personnel were "integrated at all levels." Also on 1 July 1950, the magazine section (pp. 3, 4) shows photos of one of the black jet pilots at Selfridge Army Air Field. There is no mention of any off-base problems. See the *Pittsburgh Courier,* 29 Mar. 1952, 1, 4, in which the USAFE was held up as a model of "democracy" for the army. The three previous weeks of articles by Collins George struck at army discrimination (8, 15, and 22 Mar.). This message was repeated in the 5 Apr. edition with a headline on p. 13, which read: "Air Force Integration Shames Army in Europe." The 16 June 1952 *Baltimore Afro-American* crowed on p. 3 that "Everybody's Mixed at Robins Air Force Base," and it marvelled at the lack of segregation deep in the "heart of Georgia." A black, it said, would not have known he was in Georgia "once inside the base." The paper had no criticism about the failure of the air force to provide for its men off the post. See similar articles in the *Chicago Defender,* 5 Aug. 1950, magazine section, 1, and 24 Feb. 1950, 2. The *Baltimore Afro-American* expressed its attitude in a front-page headline which stated: "Air Force Best Deal." In an article written by James Hicks, the newspaper pointed out that 30,000 airmen were training in "harmony" at Lackland AFB, Texas, that 6,000 blacks were totally integrated with 24,000 whites, and that air force policy was to totally "ignore race." Hicks reported that he had not received a single complaint from blacks at Lackland. It would seem that engaging in activities outside the base gates required a heightening of consciousness on everybody's part.

2. With minor exceptions, the black press seldom criticized the military after integration in the early 1950s. The *Chicago Defender,* 16 Nov. 1957, 1, said that military integration was complete, without a single complaint or mention of any problem, save the lack of assignments of blacks to the attache corps outside of Africa. The *Baltimore Afro-American,* 23 May 1960, magazine section, in the midst of a burgeoning tide of racial protest, spoke only of the "great strides" in the military since 1948, giving a listing of those who had achieved rank and responsibility in the integrated service, complete with photos. There is not a hint of the job left to be done.

3. *Pittsburgh Courier,* 8 July 1950, 1. See also the *Chicago Defender,* 15 July 1950, 8; and *Baltimore Afro-American,* 8 July 1950, 1, 2. The *Baltimore Afro-American* had an article on 29 Sept. 1951, 9, on a black fighter bomber squadron commander, Maj. Charles McGee, who was cited in the *Pittsburgh Courier,* 29 Nov. 1951, 3. The *New York Amsterdam News* picked up the Korean story last, and on 15 July 1950 it buried the war on page 3.

4. *Pittsburgh Courier,* 27 Jan. 1951, 3. In the 1970s, James rose to four-star rank, serving as commander of the North American Air Defense Command (NORAD). No other black airman has received the attention paid James, except for Benjamin Davis, Jr. See also the *Chicago Defender,* 26 Apr. 1955, 3, and 2 Apr. 1955, 20; and *Baltimore Afro-American,* 26 Apr. 1955, 5. Here James was cited as a fighter squadron commander, one of the first to have such a position in the integrated era. See also *Chicago Defender,* 2 Feb. 1957, 10.

5. *Baltimore Afro-American,* 8 Dec. 1951, 1; *Chicago Defender,* 8 Dec. 1951, 1; and *Pittsburgh Courier,* 29 Dec. 1951, 5.

6. *Baltimore Afro-American,* 19 Aug. 1950, 1, 2.

7. *Pittsburgh Courier,* 25 Nov. 1950, 2.

8. See numerous copies of the four major members of the black press during the war. For example, the *Chicago Defender,* 3 Feb. 1951, 1, 2, and 4 Aug. 1951, 1, 2; and *Pittsburgh Courier,* 12 July 1951, 2, and 9 Sept. 1951, 1 and 4. See also Dalfiume, *Desegregation,* 201–19.

9. Gen. E. E. Partridge, "Diary of Korea," vol. 3, entry 22 Jan. 1951 (AFSHRC). A photo published in the *Baltimore Afro-American,* 20 Nov. 1964, 5, shows General Partridge pinning stars on newly promoted Brig. Gen. B. O. Davis, Jr.

10. *Pittsburgh Courier,* 1 Nov. 1951, 1, 4, 5. A *Pittsburgh Courier* poll in mid-1952 found that Truman was the most popular candidate among blacks: 7 June 1952, 2.

11. *Baltimore Afro-American,* 16 Feb. 1952, 5, and 14 June 1952, 1, 4.

12. Ibid., 4 Oct. 1952, 5. The covenant had been signed in July 1951. The Nixon California home was also covered by a covenant; see the *Baltimore Afro-American,* 25 Oct. 1952, 7.

13. The *Chicago Defender* supported the Democratic ticket, as it usually did, and it often criticized Eisenhower after he took office. See 2 Aug. 1952, 10, and 6 Sept. 1952, 1, and 20 Sept. 1952, 1, informing its readers that the "NAACP Gives OK to Stevenson." After Eisenhower was inaugurated, headlines proclaimed: "Ike Put on Spot by Powell" (12 Apr. 1953) and "Ike Stumbles over FEPC—Dashes Hopes of Liberals—Dixiecrats Laud General's Views" (14 June 1953, 1, 2).

14. Dwight D. Eisenhower, *The White House Years: Mandate for Change* (New York, 1963), 285–87. Eisenhower claimed too much credit for himself on military integration. See pp. 292–96.

15. *Pittsburgh Courier,* 3 Nov. 1956, 1, 3.

16. *Baltimore Afro-American,* 3 Nov. 1956, 1, 4. The *Chicago Defender* supported Stevenson (3 Nov. 1956, 4).

17. Robert J. Donovan, *Eisenhower: The Inside Story* (New York, 1956), 154–55. See Merlo J. Pusey, *Eisenhower the President* (New York, 1956), for a complete absence of material on blacks. Eisenhower's primary assistant, Sherman Adams, tried to put Ike in the best light in his book, *First Hand Report: The Story of the Eisenhower Administration* (New York, 1961). Adams found that Eisenhower had been "surprised" by the Warren Court decision and believed it would require an evolutionary process to succeed (pp. 331–32). Eisenhower earns Adams's praise for appointing blacks to key government positions, but Adams fails to mention what these were (p. 333). Adams stumbles hardest over the military. He wrote: "Meanwhile, the administration was making big strides in removing segregation from the armed services . . . where the previous administration had accomplished little" (p. 334). When Eisenhower completed the second volume of his memoirs, he devoted an entire chapter to civil rights, perhaps because of interest generated in the subject by the Kennedy-Johnson administrations (Eisenhower's book was published in 1965). Eisenhower covered all of his moves bordering on civil rights, even though the material belonged in his first volume of memoirs. The former president wrote that he had agonized over signing a weakened civil rights bill in 1957, agreeing to sign it because a half loaf was better than none. See Eisenhower, *The White House Years: Waging Peace, 1956–1961* (New York, 1965), 148–76.

18. Executive Order 10590, 18 Jan. 1955. This committee did not look into the military other than to examine the lot of the civilians in the Department of Defense. See Official File 103-U, White House Central Files, Eisenhower Library, Abilene, Kans.

19. Eisenhower, *Waging Peace,* 148–76; and Adams, *First Hand Report,* 335. This act established the Civil Rights Commission; John Hannah was its first chairman and Father Theodore Hesburgh its vice chairman. The act also provided the Justice Department with a Civil Rights Division and new authority to investigate voting fraud and discrimination. It was followed by the Civil Rights Act of 1960, which made it illegal to use force or threats to obstruct court orders, required states to preserve voting records for 22 months and open them for inspection by the attorney general, and authorized the armed services to educate children of servicemen when local schools near military bases closed rather than integrated. The Civil Rights Act of 1957 is P.L. 85-135, 85th Congress, H.R. 6127, 9 Sept. 1957, 71 *Statutes at Large* 634. The act of 1960 is P.L. 86-449, 86th Congress, H.R. 8601, 3 May 1960, 74 *Statutes at Large* 86. See also Richard Bardolph, ed., *The Civil Rights Record: Black Americans and the Law, 1949–1970* (New York, 1970), 399–405; Franklin, *Slavery to Freedom,* 624; and Harry Golden, *Mr. Kennedy and the Negroes* (New York, 1964), 136–38.

20. Adams, *First Hand Report,* 331–59; and Eisenhower, *Waging Peace,* 148–76. This was Eisenhower's finest hour, if his most reluctant one, in the civil rights epoch. Harry Golden is especially critical of Eisenhower for his lack of leadership, lack of courage, and overall poor record in assisting blacks. He condemns Eisenhower for repeating over and over that "you can't legislate morality," and

Golden believes Eisenhower played politics with the issue, to his everlasting shame. See Golden, *Kennedy and the Negroes,* 100–108. Another man who found Eisenhower's actions at Little Rock insufficient was the man Ike appointed to the White House staff but waited five years to swear in, E. Frederick Morrow, Ike's "Black Man in the White House." It is not difficult to read the heartbreak in Morrow's words: "President Eisenhower's luke-warm stand on civil rights made me heartsick . . . it was obvious that he would never take any positive giant step to prove that he unequivocally stood for the right of every American to walk this land in dignity and peace, clothed with every privilege . . . accorded a citizen of our Constitution. His failure to clearly and forth rightly respond to the Negro's plea for a strong position on civil rights was the greatest cross I had to bear in my eight years in Washington . . . . During his presidency, he had generalized on the whole question of civil rights. At no time had he made any overt gesture that would encourage Negroes to believe that he sympathized with, or believed in, their crusade for complete and immediate citizenship." See E. Frederick Morrow, *Black Man in the White House: A Diary of the Eisenhower Years by the Administrative Officer for Special Projects, the White House, 1955–1961* (New York, 1963), 298–300. See also Emmet John Hughes, *The Ordeal of Power: A Political Memoir of the Eisenhower Years* (New York, 1963). Hughes, an insider with keen political perceptions, found Eisenhower "profoundly reticent" on civil rights and claims that the president acted with the "most conservative caution." He also quoted Eisenhower negatively on the *Brown* decision, claiming that it would set back progress in the "South at least fifteen years. . . . Feelings are deep on this." Hughes believes that Eisenhower's lukewarm support of the Civil Rights Act of 1957 almost invited the confrontation at Little Rock. See Hughes, *Ordeal of Power,* especially 200, 201, 242.

21. Wilson to Eisenhower, 29 May 1953, Secretary of Defense, 1953, File 291.2, NARG 330 (AGC). The air force had 10 of the 21 schools. See *Pittsburgh Courier,* 11 July 1953, 1, 5.

22. *Pittsburgh Courier,* 4 Apr. 1953, 1, 4; and *Chicago Defender,* 4 Apr. 1953, 11.

23. Memo, Oveta Culp Hobby to Wilson, 13 Apr. 1953, with a confidential memorandum to Eisenhower attached (AGC).

24. Draft dated 6 June 1953, Official Files, White House Central Files, Eisenhower Library. This can be said with certainty: the sum total of the material on race in the Eisenhower Library can be housed in a very few boxes. There are literally hundreds of times more material in the Truman and Kennedy libraries.

25. Shivers to Eisenhower, 16 July 1953, ibid.

26. *Air Force Times,* 26 Sept. 1953, 3, and 5 Dec. 1953, 3.

27. Memo, Wilson to the service secretaries, 12 Jan. 1954, in unlabled box of correspondence, James C. Evans Papers. See also the *Army Navy Air Force Journal,* 6 Feb. 1954, 647.

28. Harold Talbott to C. M. Dannely, 12 Jan. 1955, Air Force, File 291.2, NARG 340. The *Air Force Times,* 3, reported on 2 July 1955 that the air force was taking over the operation of "eight more on-base schools this fall to meet Defense orders against racial segregation in dependent schools. . . . With that eight they will now be operating 10 in all, taken over because local school boards would not cooperate." These were schools in Maryland, Florida, Virginia, Alabama, and Texas.

29. Dalfiume, *Desegregation,* 4. His evidence is a letter from Lee Nichols to the U.S. Information Agency, January 1963, copy in the possession of James C. Evans. When Evans was asked for the letter, he said he could not locate it.

30. Ltr., Earl Warren to the author, 9 Feb. 1973 (AGC), and intvw, author with Earl Warren, Washington, D.C., Apr. 1973.

31. Intvw., author with Thomas Clark, Washington, D.C., Mar. 1973. Clark had some interesting things to say about the decision: (1) it did not come out of the blue but was one of many decisions moving in that direction for several years; (2) the Court had not delayed making the decision to

avoid difficulties but to gather several cases together to make as broad a decision as possible; (3) integration had not worked as it should because certain politicians failed to provide the leadership demanded of them by the times; (4) Clark truly regretted the "deliberate speed" qualification on implementing the decision, saying that he favored then a year-at-a-time program beginning with kindergarten; (5) the decision would have been made in 1954 even if Warren had not come to the bench, and Chief Justice Vinson would have voted with the majority had he been alive; (6) Justice Hugo Black and he had strenuously objected to using Gunnar Myrdal anywhere in the written opinion because sociology had nothing to do with a decision based entirely on law.

32. Thurgood Marshall to the author, 5 July 1973 (AGC).

33. Accession 68A 1006, carton 2 of 6, National Records Center: see several folders, one which is full of letters from objecting parents.

34. *Air Force Times,* 8 Feb. 1958, 3. P.L. 815 provided funds to build schools, and P.L. 374 provided operating funds.

35. *Chicago Defender,* 18 Oct. 1958, 2, and its issues both before and after that date.

36. *Army Navy Air Force Journal,* 30 Aug. 1958, 8.

37. Memo for the Record, James Goode, 24 Nov. 1958, subj: "Little Rock Air Force Base School." This was attached to a memo to the secretary of the air force from Charles Finucane, 10 Oct. 1958; and Goode Memo for the Record, 17 Oct. 1958, after meeting with Finucane and Steve Jackson (AGC).

38. *Air Force Times,* 20 Dec. 1958, 1, 33, and 1 Jan. 1959, 14.

39. Ltr., Maxwell M. Rabb to Joan Bopp, 18 Jan. 1954, General Files, White House Central Files, Eisenhower Library. When Rabb resigned in 1958, E. Frederick Morrow assumed his responsibilities.

40. Ltr., Powell to Wilson, 24 Feb. 1954, ibid.

41. Draft of a letter from Rabb's office, Oct. 1954, ibid.

42. See series of correspondence on the 1957 Tulane–West Point game, ibid..

43. These are segments of annual reports of the Secretary of Defense, Official Files, White House Central Files, Eisenhower Library.

44. James C. Evans, "Integration in the Armed Services: A Progress Report," Washington, D.C., 1955.

45. The term "a captive of deep southern prejudices" is used by David Sutton in "The Military against Off-Base Discrimination," in Charles Moskos, ed., *Public Opinion and the Military Establishment* (Beverly Hills, Calif., 1971), 149–79. Commanders tended to become members of the establishment and therefore listened sympathetically to the town leaders. Sutton claims that civilian leaders would advance the military career of cooperative commanders or would provide for them in retirement with a job. Recalcitrant commanders might be punished by powerful southerners in the Congress. These were offered by Sutton as reasons for the failure of the Gesell Committee recommendations (see below) to modify southern practices, but assuredly they also applied in the era before Gesell.

46. Capt. Emmet S. Walden, Jr., "Maxwell Air Force Base: An Equal Opportunity Case Study," Air Command and Staff College research study, 1964, iii, iv.

47. Ibid., 9–11.

48. Ibid., 11–18. When I was stationed at Maxwell in 1965, I was told clearly not to entertain blacks in my home. I was asked not to make waves and spoil the good relationship the base had with the town. If there was trouble, if the police were to invade homes to prevent violence, whites would be on their own, and police visits were often violent, the base warned.

49. Ibid., 18–25. The quoted message, dated 21 June 1961, was sent by Lt. Gen. Walter E. Todd, Air University commander, and is repeated in its entirety in the thesis. The message was in response to queries for information by the deputy chief of staff/personnel about a controversy that began with the withdrawal of an invitation for 400 white Boys State attendees to have lunch on the base.

The withdrawn invitation provoked the sponsor, the Alabama American Legion, to react with rage. The base had forbidden the segregated group the use of base facilities because of an interpretation of a Kennedy Executive Order (10925, 6 Mar. 1961) which required "immediate and specific action . . . to assure that no use is made of the name, sponsorship, facilities, or activity of any executive department or agency by or for any employee recreational organization practicing discrimination based on creed, color, or national origin." A message from the secretary of the air force required all commanders to certify in writing that they understood and were in full compliance with the order. See msg., Dir/Personnel Planning to All Major Commands (ALMAJCOM), 22 May 1961. Maxwell's commander had stipulated that no facility would be available in the future to segregated organizations. Earlier, Todd suggested in a letter to Lt. Gen. Truman Landon that these types of prohibitions would destroy community goodwill. He added: "Many of these activities are long standing, have been built up over the years, and have been extremely valuable in the fine relationships with the local community of Montgomery. These and other functions that will be closed down entirely or modified to exclude joint participation with Montgomery organizations will severely strain, if not completely destroy, a workable relationship with the local community. This relationship is among the finest that exists in the Air Force and is the result of years of close cooperation and good will." See ltr., Todd to Landon, 25 May 1961, quoted in Walden, "Maxwell Air Force Base."

50. Walden, "Maxwell Air Force Base," 18–25.

51. Ibid., 51–54. Of course, all schooling was segregated except for a single elementary school on the base.

52. Ltr., with attachments from Legislative Liaison to Diggs, 1 July 1960, "History of the Office of the Inspector General," 1 July–31 Dec. 1960, 49–60.

53. Ibid.

54. Ibid.

55. Ibid.

56. [George N. Dubina], "Air University History," Maxwell AFB, 1971, 42–50 (AFSHRC).

57. Alfred E. McEwen, "Permanent Change of Station: A Continuing Problem for Negro Airmen," Air Command and Staff College research study, June 1966, 1–7, 23, 24.

58. Ibid., 46–49, 50–56.

59. Folder on Lt. Titus A. Saunders, Jr., James C. Evans File, carton 13 of 15, Accession 68A 1033, National Records Center. There is a long loose-leaf on Saunders from which this section is taken. It shows that ultimately Saunders received an honorable discharge. See ltr., Saunders to Evans, 14 Feb. 1957, and Memo for the Record by Evans, 27 Nov. 1956. See clipping from *New York Times*, 2 Dec. 1956, for the Quarles quote. Saunders was supported in his claims against Mississippi by a chaplain at the Columbus base. See also ltr., Chaplain Pilcher to Governor Lausche, 29 May 1956. The file includes a resume of the court transcript of the Lowndes County trial, 5 May 1955. The *Baltimore Afro-American*, 8 Dec. 1956, 1, 2, blasted the air force in an article titled "The Ugly Truth: Air Force Bowed to Miss. Bigotry," by Louis Lomax. He accused the Air Force of giving Saunders a "second-rate discharge" to appease Mississippi politicians. The *Air Force Times*, 28 Nov. 1953, 29, reported a similar incident involving a black lieutenant who was discharged under a reduction-in-force after being reprimanded by his superiors for refusing to sit in the rear of the bus on a trip from Florida to Alabama. The NAACP publicized the incident and accused the air force of knuckling under to southern discrimination; the *Air Force Times* merely reported the facts of the incident.

60. Hist. of the Inspector General, Inquiries and Complaints, 1 July 1962 to 31 Dec. 1962, 22–29. A ltr. from the NAACP, 11 Apr. 1962, to the inspector is included in this history. This was not the first time someone requested the use of off-limits sanctions.

61. Ibid., 18–21.

62. Ltr., Maj. Gen. Joe Kelly to Diggs, 29 Aug. 1956, Diggs Folder, carton 8 of 15, Accession 68A 1033, National Records Center.

63. Ltr., Kuter to Edwards, 13 Dec. 1948, File 291.2 35(50), NARG 340.

64. Ltrs., James L. Flaherty to Vandenberg, 20 Sept. 1949, and Vandenberg to Flaherty, 20 Oct. 1949, File 291.2 34(40), NARG 340.

65. Ltr, Edwards to Kuter, 11 Jan. 1950, File 291.2 35(50), NARG 340.

66. Memo by the Office of Community Services, Military Personnel Division, Air Force Finance Center, Denver, Colo., n.d., File 291.2 36(50), NARG 340.

67. Ibid. Collins George reported in the *Pittsburgh Courier*, 14 July 1951, that he investigated Great Falls and found the base integrated but the town hostile. A week earlier, 7 July 1951, 1, George had called for legislation to protect black servicemen from laws and customs that harmed their morale.

68. Memo, Brig. Gen. John Ives to the Assistant Secretary of the Air Force (Management), subj.: "Racial Discrimination in Great Falls, Mont.," 7 July 1953, File 291.2 36(50), NARG 340. The *Chicago Defender*, 23 May 1953, 12, complained that blacks in Great Falls received the silent treatment.

69. Ltr., Hart to the Secretary of the Air Force, 28 Dec. 1961, Pohlhaus Folder, carton 11 of 15, Accession 68A 1033, National Records Center. The folder contains numerous items on discrimination at Glasgow.

70. *Pittsburgh Courier*, 1 Sept. 1953, 1, 4.

71. James A. Madison, "Summary of Services to the United States Air Force for the Period September 1, 1952, to December 31, 1954," N.Y. National Recreational Association (AGC). Madison's report does not seem to have sparked any response from the air force. The *Air Force Times*, summarizing Madison's findings, stated that it was air force policy to "conform to local community practices." See *Air Force Times*, 2 Apr. 1955, 2. Some Madison recommendations were not adopted until the advent of the Kennedy administration.

72. Housing Folder, Accession 68A 1033, carton 15 of 15, National Records Center. Nearly half of the folder is concerned with the Bunker Hill problem. See also carton 2 of 15 for other materials. Evans is an interesting figure in all of this. Basically a conservative, he had as his goal equality of opportunity. The *Baltimore Afro-American*, 28 May 1960, p. 8 of the magazine section, stated that Evans was the "man most responsible for carrying out integration in the armed forces." Although one finds this assessment difficult to document, the general reaction of those involved in black issues supports such a claim. An article in the *Army Navy Air Force Register* and in *Defense Times*, 28 Nov. 1959, 9–11, by John Wiant, shows what Evans thought about the problems confronting blacks. Evans was quoted: "A Negro with a college degree still has to know how to speak clearly, write clearly and understand that there is more to day-to-day existence than knowing the theory that goes with a college degree." An example was cited of a black forced out of the service, even though he held a degree, because he could not communicate effectively. The separated officer claimed that he was the victim of racial discrimination because he had married a white woman, but Evans believed his education at a black college in Alabama was the major factor. Evans said: "The day of military integration has arrived. There is no discrimination—or so little that it is unimportant—on the basis of race. The white military man, officer and enlisted, has accepted the idea that the skin color of the man working or sleeping next to him is unimportant." Whites, however, do "not have to accept as equal a man he considers educationally or socially inferior. It doesn't matter if this man has white, brown or purple skin. What does matter is his ability to pull his share of the load." Evans's office found virtually "no cases of discrimination." It is not surprising that Evans showed little enthusiasm for the Kennedy administration's approach to the problem. After 1961, Evans's views appear less frequently in the documents.

73. Folder 350 on Schools, Accession 68A 1033, carton 4 of 15, National Records Center. The main plaintiff is "Staff Sgt. A. L.," who wrote often and was able to provide Evans with affidavits. See ltrs., A. L. to Evans, 6 Sept. 1963, and Evans to A. L., 17 Sept. 1963. Also ltr., A. L. to Evans, 26 July 1963, italics in original.

74. Ltr., S. L. to Jack Greenberg, 3 Nov. 1957. Folder OASD(m) CR & IR Division, Personnel Complaints and Investigations, carton 10 of 15, Accession 68A 1033, National Records Center. Greenberg forwarded the letter to Evans.

75. Ltr., David S. Smith to Powell, 19 Dec. 1957, ibid. This letter included a ten-page, single-spaced investigation of S. L.'s claims. See also ltrs., S. L. to Evans, 23 July 1957, 28 Oct. 1957, and 17 Dec. 1957, and Evans to Senator Harrison A. Williams, Jr., 2 Mar. 1961, ibid.

76. *Air Force Times,* 30 Apr. 1955, 29.

77. *Pittsburgh Courier,* 14 Aug. 1954, 1, 4. Three years earlier, Ollie Stewart reported in the *Baltimore Afro-American,* 20 Oct. 1951, 5, that there was "no color problem" at Chateauroux Air Base, France. But Powell was most critical of Chateauroux later.

78. *Chicago Defender,* 29 Aug. 1959, 1.

79. Ltr., Diggs to Dudley Sharp, 7 July 1960 (AGC).

80. *Chicago Defender,* 28 Apr. 1961, 1, 2.

81. "History of the 6139th Air Base Group, Misawa Air Base, Japan," 1963, 31–34 (AFSHRC).

82. Memo, Nichols to Robert S. McNamara, 13 May 1963, Folder on Lee Nichols, carton 5 of 15, Accession 68A 1033, National Records Center.

83. Memo, William Gorman to Norman Paul, 16 July 1963, ibid. The memo is a distillation of the statistics given to the Gesell Committee. See the appendix to this book, tables 3–15, for data on the slow progression of promotion.

Chapter 5: The Kennedy Era

1. Memo by E. Frederick Morrow, 7 Mar. 1960, in Staff Files, Eisenhower Library. It is not known if Eisenhower saw the memo. The sit-in movement was launched at Greensboro, North Carolina, when black college students insisted on being served at a local lunch counter. The students forced desegregation of department stores, supermarkets, libraries, and movies. By September 1960 more than 70,000 students were participating; 3,600 were arrested. John Hope Franklin begins his chapter "The Negro Revolution" with the Greensboro sit-ins. He believed the sit-ins inaugurated "the most profound, revolutionary changes in the status of Negro Americans that had occurred since emancipation." See Franklin, *Slavery to Freedom,* 624–25.

2. Enacted on 9 September 1957, this act provided for protection of the constitutional right of all citizens to vote, regardless of race or color. It also provided for a program of assistance in efforts to protect other constitutional rights of U.S. citizens and established a bipartisan presidential commission to study and recommend further steps to protect those constitutional rights.

3. *Pittsburgh Courier,* 5 Mar. 1960. The first three pages are devoted to the sit-ins. Consecutive issues were devoted to the "sit-down front." The *Baltimore Afro-American* picked up the story a week earlier and ran with it for the next several months. See the 27 Feb. 1960 issue and others over several months. This story flowed into the Freedom Rides, Birmingham, the legislation, Selma, and beyond.

4. Intvw., John Stewart with Clarence Mitchell, Feb. 1967. Mitchell had favored Stuart Symington or Hubert Humphrey until the nominating convention. He did not find Kennedy committed to civil rights even after the election. Roy Wilkins believed Kennedy to be unknowledgable about the subject in 1957, although he saw in Kennedy a man with a "keen sense of the morality of the question." According to Wilkins, Kennedy in office made it "no longer fashionable to be prejudiced."

Intvw., Berl Bernhard with Wilkins, Aug. 1964. Bernhard also interviewed Thurgood Marshall in Apr. 1964. Marshall found Kennedy more aware than either Mitchell or Wilkins, but there is a tone of trying to say something good about the assassinated president in all of these interviews. The Mitchell, Wilkins, and Marshall interviews are at the John F. Kennedy Library, Boston, Mass.

5. *Chicago Defender,* 29 Oct.–4 Nov. 1960, 1, 2; *Baltimore Afro-American,* 23 July 1960, 2, and 15 Oct. 1960, 4, and 5 Nov. 1960, 1, 4. In 1964 all three papers supported Lyndon Johnson; the *Pittsburgh Courier,* thereby, broke a tradition (only twice broken previously in the century) by endorsing a Democrat, 10 Oct. 1964, 1. See also the *Baltimore Afro-American,* 17 Oct. 1964, 4, and *Chicago Defender,* 10–16 Oct. 1964, 1, 2.

6. *Pittsburgh Courier,* 19 Nov. 1960, 1, 3. Harry Golden agrees and says that Kennedy received 85 percent of the black vote. Golden, *Kennedy and the Negroes,* 70, 154.

7. *Chicago Defender,* 19–25 Nov. 1960, 1. Arthur Schlesinger would agree that the margin of victory came from black voters. "Had only white gone to the polls in 1960," Schlesinger wrote, "Nixon would have taken 53 percent of the vote." See Arthur M. Schlesinger, Jr., *A Thousand Days: John F. Kennedy in the White House* (Boston, 1965), 928–30.

8. *Baltimore Afro-American,* 19 Nov. 1960, 1, 2. Theodore Sorensen would agree with this general analysis. See Sorensen, *The Kennedy Legacy: A Peaceful Revolution for the Seventies* (New York, 1969), 218–19, and Sorensen, *Kennedy* (New York, 1965), 243, 250.

9. Like the motivations of his Democratic predecessor, Kennedy's seem to be open to question. Although this subject is as fruitless to examine as it was with Truman, the parallel is worth following for a moment. Father Theodore M. Hesburgh was a man in a position to know from his vantage point on the Civil Rights Commission. In his interview by Joseph O'Connor in Mar. 1966 for the Kennedy Library, Hesburgh praised, faintly, the dead president, making a direct comparison to Eisenhower, believing that both men had equally "very good basic instincts." When interviewed by Paige Mulholland for the Johnson Library in Feb. 1971, Hesburgh was more candid. He stated that Johnson was more active and sincere than Kennedy on civil rights. "My general impression," Hesburgh said, "is that while the Kennedy administration got very high marks on civil rights because of the personal attractiveness of the President, and his rather outspoken manner, the simple fact is that the performance I thought was rather miserable as far as legislation." Hesburgh claimed that none of the Johnson legislative achievements were possible during the Kennedy administration. The Kennedy attitude was "don't do anything until you absolutely have to." Hesburgh claimed that there was a strong Kennedy "myth" in civil rights and that the president who was described in the Schlesinger and Sorensen biographies was not the "guy that I had to do business with." See Schlesinger, *A Thousand Days,* 924–77, and Sorensen, *Kennedy,* 528–69, for opposing views. Harry Golden is even more pro-Kennedy in *Mr. Kennedy and the Negroes.* For a balanced view and an objective treatment of Eisenhower too, see James L. Sundquist, *Politics and Policy: The Eisenhower, Kennedy, and Johnson Years* (Washington, D.C., 1968), 221–86.

10. Executive Order 10925, 6 Mar. 1961. See Inspector General, USAF, *United States Air Force TIG Brief,* 26 May 1961. This weekly publication, issued by the air force inspector general, contained a brief of selected items that were of special interest to commanders, their inspectors general, and other staff officers. Often these items dealt with "soft areas" which could become trouble spots, management oversights, and various other subjects.

11. Memo, Dep. Secy. of Defense Roswell Gilpatric to the Service Secretaries, 19 June 1961 (AGC). In keeping with the executive profile, Kennedy appointed a President's Committee on Equal Employment Opportunity, which first met on 27 July 1961 with Vice President Johnson as its chairman and Arthur Goldberg as its vice chairman. This group was to oversee civilian equal opportunity in government and to extend protection to those who worked for employers servicing

government contracts. See Memo for the Record, by James C. Evans, 31 July 1961, carton 1 of 15, Accession 68A 1033, National Records Center. Earlier, Kennedy had created a civil rights subcabinet group, which first met on 14 Apr. 1961 and was scheduled to meet once a month in the White House. This group saw itself as a "service committee" trying to ensure "close coordination" within the administration and the cabinet. It was composed of men at the assistant secretary level. See unsigned memorandum, Civil Rights Sub-Cabinet Group, the minutes of the first meeting, 14 Apr. 1961 (AGC).

12. Members of the Gesell Committee were Joseph O'Meara, South Bend, Indiana; Nathaniel Colley, Sacramento, California; Abe Fortas, Washington, D.C.; Benjamin Muse, Manassas, Virginia; John Sengstacke, Chicago, Illinois; and Whitney Young, New York City, New York.

13. Intvw., author with Adam Yarmolinsky, Boston, Mass., July 1973. Yarmolinsky comments about military race relations in his book, *The Military Establishment: Its Impact on American Society* (New York, 1971), 340–54.

14. Ltr., Diggs to McNamara, 12 Feb. 1962, Diggs Folder, carton 8 of 15, Accession 68A 1033, National Records Center.

15. Committee on Equal Opportunity in the Armed Forces, 24 June 1962 (Gesell Committee) Folder, Accession 68A 1033, carton 15 of 15, National Records Center. See especially James Evans's Memo for the Record, 26 Oct. 1961.

16. Ltr., Kennedy to Chairman, President's Committee on Equal Opportunity in the Armed Forces, 24 June 1962, in *Public Papers of the Presidents of the United States: John F. Kennedy* (Washington, D.C., 1963), 257. The *Air Force Times* noted the formation of the Committee (3 June 1962, 24) and had earlier commented on the fact that blacks faced enormous troubles off base, noting especially housing difficulties. See *Air Force Times,* 21 Apr. 1962, 25. An internal White House staff memorandum shows that the creation of a committee was decided upon before mid-November 1961. Carlisle Runge of Defense Manpower wrote to Harris Wofford, Kennedy's first special assistant for civil rights, on 15 Nov. 1961 indicating that the "Deputy Secretary of Defense has approved the establishment of an advisory committee comprised of distinguished citizens to look into problems of discrimination affecting servicemen." Sub-Cabinet Group on Civil Rights, Harris Wofford Papers, Kennedy Library. It still took six more months to appoint the committee. The black press still did not consider off-post discrimination a special problem outside of the larger one of general segregation and discrimination. The Gesell Committee appointment received scant mention in the press. The *Pittsburgh Courier* noted its formation on 7 July 1962 but gave it only half a column on pp. 1 and 4.

17. John Horne, Memo for the Record, 20 Nov. 1962, Second meeting of the President's Committee on Equal Opportunity in the Armed Forces (AGC). There was great reluctance in the air force to appear to be gathering data on the South for the Kennedy administration. In 1962 the Defense Department required each base with a population of more than 500 to supply Manpower with an equal opportunity survey. This was kept out of the press for almost a year because it probably embarrassed the military. All of these surveys are marked "For Official Use Only," which means that no one in the service could release the information. The hope was to gather data about each particular situation for Defense planners and, perhaps, entirely as a by-product, to open the eyes of the post commanders to the situation confronting blacks. All facets of community life—from public accommodations to private housing—were to be covered. See Alfred B. Fitt to White, 8 Jan. 1963, Civil Rights File, Lee White Papers, Kennedy Library. The *Army Navy Air Force Journal,* 23 Oct. 1963, 1, 38–39, took up the military point of view and begged McNamara to "stop or slow down the mimeograph machines which are clacking in the sensitive area of civil rights and the Armed Forces." See related in the *Air Force Times:* 15 Jan. 1964, 18; 11 Mar. 1964, 3; 22 Apr. 1964,

26; 9 Sept. 1964, 4. These surveys would surprise no one, especially white leaders in southern communities. In the case of the South, all facilities were segregated. The Commission on Civil Rights was created by the Civil Rights Act of 1957 (71 Stat. 634).

18. James P. Goode, Memo for the Record, 14 Nov. 1962, with copies to Benjamin Fridge and John Horne (AGC). James P. Goode claimed that there was no air force policy which excluded blacks from Maxwell. While it is well known that there were black enlisted personnel at Maxwell during all eras, no one the author interviewed could ever remember a black officer being stationed at Maxwell unless he was attending one of the professional schools. It would appear that it was not until the 1970s that Maxwell received black officers in other than a student's role.

19. Ltr., Gesell to Zuckert, 8 Oct. 1962 (AGC). The answers came on 30 November and 4 April the following year. The first set of answers covered 19 of the questions in no set order. The staff summary sheet was signed by Maj. Gen. Albert Clark of Military Personnel. Goode sent the answers to the remaining 11 questions to Gesell in April 1963 (AGC). The key to the air force attitude was demonstrated in its answer to the first question on the method of dealing with discrimination: "While we abhor discriminatory laws and customs, Air Force commanders have extremely limited powers to alleviate undesirable off-base situations." The air force did not have a program. It had a policy as expressed in AFR 35-78, which is not a substitute for a program.

20. President's Committee on Equal Opportunity in the Armed Forces, "Initial Report: Equality of Treatment and Opportunity for Negro Military Personnel within the United States," 13 June 1963. See also *Congressional Record*, House, 1963, 14358–69.

21. President's Committee on Equal Opportunity in the Armed Forces, "Initial Report," 5–8, 25, 26.

22. Ibid., 10.

23. Ibid., 48–49.

24. Ibid., 52.

25. Ibid., 69–71, italics in original. As indicated in sections of the previous chapter, the use of off-limits sanctions to encourage integration was not a totally new idea in 1963. Symington told me that he had used such a threat successfully in 1949. Blacks in Alaska had complained to him of segregation in local taverns. Symington called the mayor of the town and told him, "If I hear one complaint like this again from anybody on this base, I'll declare the entire town off-limits to every member of the base." The former air force secretary said it worked. Symington intvw.

26. President's Committee on Equal Opportunity in the Armed Forces, "Initial Report," 69–71.

27. Ibid.

28. Ibid., 27–31.

29. Ibid., 61–64.

30. Ibid.

31. Ibid., 34–35.

32. Ibid., 65. But who in the southern white power structure would agree to sitting down with blacks on such a commission?

33. Ibid., 85–88.

34. Ibid., 39–41.

35. Ibid., 38, 39. Nearly all these recommendations were echoed in a study published by the U.S. Commission on Civil Rights in October 1963. The commission had begun work on its report at about the same time the Gesell Committee had begun its work. The commission published its findings in a well-prepared book, titled *Civil Rights '63* (Washington, D.C., 1963). The specific chapter is titled "The Negro in the Armed Forces," 171–224. Commission Chairman John Hannah notified Robert McNamara that the commission would investigate the military. See ltr., Hannah to McNamara, 26 Mar. 1962 (AGC). In the investigative process, the commission staff found that blacks stationed in

the South were bitter over the lack of support from the military in their interactions with civilian communities. The staff also found that none of the base commanders interviewed had ever heard of the Gilpatric memorandum and that southern commanders had done little to improve the life of black servicemen within the civilian community. (See U.S. Commission on Civil Rights, "Summary of Staff Reports," Nov. 1962 [AGC].) In its formal report, the commission catalogued black grievances and recommended an end to all military encouragement of civilian segregation and discrimination. It sought an end to ROTC at segregating institutions, an end to all vestiges of segregation and discrimination on base, a total ban on participation in segregated athletic contests or events, an upgrading of housing opportunities, the removal of impact funds from segregating school systems, and the use of off-limits sanctions to force civilian businesses to integrate. See *Civil Rights '63*, 174, 179–80, 186–89, 191, 197, 204–9, 215–17. The commission also published a separate pamphlet, *Family Housing and the Negro Serviceman* (Washington, D.C., Oct. 1963) (AGC). This outlined the severe problems black servicemen have in finding decent homes. See especially pp. 1–10.

36. *Civil Rights '63*, 92–93. Copies of the Gesell Committee's final report, are very difficult to find. The report dealt with overseas discrimination and segregation in the National Guard. The report echoes Congressmen Diggs and Powell's findings that whites had infected Europeans and Asians with bias and in the process made life hard on blacks. It recommended the rapid application of corrective measures as indicated in the initial report. The report pointed out that the National Guard had still not been brought under the provisions of Executive Order 9981 and that since nearly all of the guard's money came from the federal government, it should be integrated immediately. See President's Committee on Equal Opportunity in the Armed Forces, "Final Report: Military Personnel Stationed Overseas, and Membership and Participation in the National Guard," Nov. 1964 (AGC).

37. *Public Papers of the Presidents* (Kennedy, 1963), 495.

38. McNamara sent a memo to Kennedy summarizing the report and telling the president, "Military effectiveness is unquestionably reduced as a result of civilian discrimination against men in uniform." McNamara told Kennedy that he was about to create a civil rights staff within his office, and he included a draft of a Department of Defense directive on equal opportunity. See Memo, McNamara to Kennedy, 24 July 1963, Office of Civil Rights Folder, carton 2 of 6, Accession 68A 1006, National Records Center.

39. Memo, Fitt to Marshall, 19 July 1963, Burke Marshall Papers, Kennedy Library. There are two attached memoranda, one addressed to the president and one to McNamara. The one to the president is similar to the memo sent to him by McNamara. The Fitt memo to McNamara is in great detail. Fitt became the director of the Civil Rights Division within Defense Manpower, working in Norman Paul's office. It can be assumed that Fitt wrote the Department of Defense directive on equal opportunity, although no drafts have surfaced with his name on them.

40. Ibid.

41. *Congressional Record*, House, 1963, 14369–80.

42. Yarmolinsky intvw. Yarmolinsky found Kennedy committed to civil rights before the election, but Kennedy became more educated as time went on. He stated, "Kennedy was not a crusader on the issue, although he came across that way."

43. Robert S. McNamara, *The Essence of Security: Reflections in Office* (New York, 1968), 122–40.

44. Zuckert intvw.

45. *Army Navy Air Force Journal*, 21 Sept. 1963, 8, 30.

46. Congressman Watkins Abbit, extension of remarks from Lynchburg, Va., news editorial of 10 Oct. 1963, *Congressional Record*, House, 109:A6370.

47. Congressman F. Edward Hébert, extension of remarks, ibid., A5637–38. Hébert inserted more remarks than any other individual. He also added editorials from northern newspapers.

48. Congressman Hébert, extension of remarks from the New Orleans newspaper editorial of 30 July 1963, ibid., A4950.

49. Smith to Gesell, 5 Aug. 1963, Civil Rights File, Lee White Papers.

50. Hébert to Gesell, 9 Aug. 1963, ibid.

51. Congressman Abbit, extension of remarks, *Congressional Record*, House, 109:A4575–78. Almond appears not to have changed his estimate of the ability of black servicemen since World War II and the Korean War.

52. Congressman John J. Flynt, extension of remarks from an editorial in the *Georgia Free Press* (Thomaston), 21 Aug. 1963, ibid., A5350–51. Earlier, Flynt had another editorial inserted, from the same paper, which claimed that the report would so demoralize the troops that "we could fall to the Russians without so much as firing a weapon" (6 Aug. 1963 editorial, A5038).

53. Congressman Strom Thurmond, extension of remarks, ibid., A5422. The newspaper platform for editorialist Truman Sensing was not identified.

54. *Air Force Times*, 25 Sept. 1963, 5. Hébert supported this legislation, which was not successful, by reading into the *Congressional Record* an editorial from the *Norfolk Ledger-State*. See *Congressional Record*, House, 109:A6467.

55. Intvw., Larry Hackman with Harris Wofford, May 1968, Kennedy Library.

56. Memo, Goode to Zuckert, 9 Nov. 1963 (AGC).

57. Ibid., 5 Dec. 1962, Folder on President's Committee on Equal Opportunity in the Armed Forces, 1963, Burke Marshall Papers.

58. Memo from Office of the Secretary of the Air Force to Special Assistant (Manpower, Personnel, and Reserve Forces), 10 Apr. 1963 (AGC).

59. Air Force Committee on Equal Opportunity, Minutes of the Fourth Mtg, 8 July 1963 (AGC). The civil rights bill went to Congress in June 1963.

60. Ltr., Zuckert to Norman Paul, 10 July 1963 (AGC). This included an attached memo titled "Air Force Comments on Reports by the President's Committee on Equal Opportunity in the Armed Forces." In the memo, the air force promised vigorously to attract blacks and reaffirmed its color-blind promotion policy. It promised fair assignments, a review of the promotion process, and adoption of antidiscrimination policies. The air force, however, wanted to delay action on off-base discrimination until the civil rights bill had been acted upon.

61. Memo to the Joint Chiefs of Staff, 27 July 1963 (AGC), italics in original.

62. Intvw., author with Gen. William F. McKee, Washington, D.C., May 1973.

63. *Air Force Times*, 10 July 1963, 12. It also pointed out that if the air force prevented school buses from segregating children, the air force might not be able to afford replacing such buses with its own resources.

64. Ibid., "Family Magazine," 21 Aug. 1963, 3, 8.

65. *Air Force Times*, 24 July 1963, 16, and the letters on the same page. Some whites praised the report, but not many.

66. Ibid.: 17 July 1963, 18; 7 Aug. 1963, 18; 14 Aug. 1963, 18; 24 July 1963, 16; 18 Sept. 1963, 26; and 28 Aug. 1963, 22.

67. Ibid., 31 July 1963, 16, and 28 Aug. 1963, 23.

68. Ibid., 7 Aug. 1963, 12, 18.

69. Memo, Charyk to Chief of Staff, 8 Dec. 1962 (AGC).

70. Memo, Hester to Secretary of the Air Force, 26 Feb. 1963 (AGC).

71. Memo, Gesell to Marshall, 7 Mar. 1963, Burke Marshall Papers.

72. "History of the Directorate of Personnel Planning," 1 July–31 Dec. 1963, 177–91. Koontz was the first secretary of the Air Force Committee on Equal Opportunity. This history demonstrates that

the air force opposed the Gesell Committee recommendations, which it called "highly controversial and sensitive." The history also indicated that AFR 35-78 was being revised. Several black organizations had asked for off-limits sanctions, but "these requests were all denied." The Equal Opportunity Group tried to get children who lived at Columbus AFB, Mississippi, into integrated schools but ended by getting the children banned from all schools temporarily until the air force dropped its demand.

73. Memo, Koontz to Jones, 10 Dec. 1963, in Dir. of Personnel Planning, Read File, July–Dec. 1963 (AGC).

74. Memo, Moore to Commander, Tactical Air Command, 10 Dec. 1963, ibid.

75. Memo for Record by Koontz, 27 Dec. 1963, ibid.

76. Memo, Dir. of Personnel Planning to SAC, 1 Oct. 1963, ibid.

77. Memo, Koontz to W. K. Williams, 7 Nov. 1963, and Moore (written by Farris) to J. F. Pohlhaus, 10 Dec. 1963, ibid.

78. Msg, Koontz to SAC, 12 Dec. 1963, ibid.

79. Memo, Koontz to Stone, 14 Oct. 1963, ibid.

80. Intvw., author with Brig. Gen. Richard L. Ault, Washington, D.C., May 1973. Zuckert told the author that Ault's splendid performance at Craig earned him a star. Zuckert intvw.

81. "History of the Directorate of Personnel Planning," 1 Jan.–30 June 1964, 177–84, 1 July–31 Dec. 1964, 174–83.

82. Memo, Fitt to McNamara, 9 Mar. 1964, in Folder on Eglin AFB, carton 2 of 6, Accession 68A 1006, National Records Center. Fitt asked for comments on his proposal from the services. This was discussed at the tenth meeting of the Air Force Committee on Equal Opportunity, 13 Apr. 1964—see minutes (AGC). The senior members of the staff were present, and they disapproved.

83. Col. L. T. Seith to All Major Commands, 24 May 1964 (AGC). This implemented a Defense Department ruling on school attendance. The *Air Force Times* broadcast this new move, telling its readership that the effect of the directive would be massive because 100,000 servicemen were enrolled in courses that were paid in part or wholly by the Defense Department. See Ltr., 15 Apr. 1964, 3, and Ltr., 6 May 1964, 2 (AGC).

84. Ltr., Stone to All Major Commands, 15 July 1964 (AGC). This was also publicized in the *Air Force Times,* which told its readers that henceforth air force speakers would have to "shun segregated audiences." As in all of these changes, the impetus for the new direction came from the Department of Defense. McNamara issued a directive requiring the military to refrain from sponsoring, supporting, "or financially assisting, directly or indirectly, any conference or meeting held under circumstances where participants are segregated or treated unequally because of race." For the defense policy, see the *Air Force Times,* 2 July 1964, 8. The air force echo was Stone's letter.

85. Of course, the Civil Rights Act was far more than a public accommodations bill, but as far as the air force was concerned, this title was the one of significance, since it would lend the weight of law to any actions that base commanders might take to force integration on segregating communities. The Civil Rights Act (P.L. 88-352, 88th Congress, H.R. 7152, 2 July 1964, *Statutes at Large* 241) has been called by John Hope Franklin "the most far-reaching and comprehensive law in support of racial equality ever enacted by Congress" (Franklin, *Slavery to Freedom,* 635). The bill contained ten titles dealing with voting, public accommodations, public facilities, public education, the Commission on Civil Rights, federally assisted programs, equal employment opportunity, voting statistics, intervention and removal in civil rights cases, and community relations service. See also Bardolph, *Civil Rights Record,* 405–10.

86. Talking Paper for the Chief of Staff, n.d., in Dir. of Personnel Planning, Read File, July–Dec. 1964 (AGC).

87. *Air Force Times,* 22 July 1964, 1, 4. The newspaper also advertised the fact that blacks were now "encouraged" to file bias suits and that bases were "urged" to assist them. See also *Air Force Times,* 12 Aug. 1964, 2.

88. Office of the Secretary of the Air Force, *Supplement to the Air Force Policy Letter for Commanders,* Aug. 1964 (AGC).

89. *Air Force Times,* 1 July 1964, 10.

90. See minutes of the ninth meeting of the Air Force Committee on Equal Opportunity, 15 Jan. 1964 (AGC). By then the regulation had been submitted and was awaiting approval. *Air Force Times,* 1 Jan. 1964, 8, has an outline of the essential parts of what became AFR 35-78. Unfortunately, unlike the first drafts of AFL 35-3, no early drafts of this regulation have surfaced.

91. AFR 35-78, 19 Aug. 1964, Equal Opportunity and Treatment of Military Personnel. The impact of the Gesell Committee is reflected in the emphasis on off-base problems and the fact that off-post problems cover half of the regulation. The other services also produced new equal opportunity regulations similar to 35-78. Titles II, III, and IV of the Civil Rights Act dealt with public accommodations, public facilities, and public education.

92. Ibid.

93. Ibid.

94. Ibid.

95. Ibid.

96. Ibid.

97. Ibid.

98. Ibid.

99. *Air Force Times,* 26 Aug. 1964, 1, 10; see also 12 Aug. 1964, 2.

100. There are numerous documented cases of servicemen taking complaints to the judge advocate and gaining his support in desegregating communities which were in violation of the new law. In most cases, once the base commander and the judge advocate told the community that legal action was being taken, the facilities desegregated. See Request for Suits by Servicemen, folder on the Civil Rights Bill, carton 15 of 15, Accession 68A 1003, National Records Center. This is a folder of dozens of cases filed under AFR 35-78 and similar army and navy regulations. Also see Memo for Assistant Secretary of Defense (Manpower), unsigned, 27 Nov. 1964, in Dir. of Personnel Planning, Read File, July–Dec. 1964 (AGC). This is a cover sheet for a request for a suit by an airman at Keesler Air Force Base, Mississippi. It stated that after suits had been threatened in the past, "in each instance, voluntary assurances have been given by the establishments concerned that future practices would provide for nondiscriminatory treatment of military personnel and their dependents."

101. The Watts riot left 34 dead, 1,032 injured, and 3,952 arrested. Although it was not the first race riot of the new era, it was probably the most violent, and it certainly caught the world's attention. See Franklin, *Slavery to Freedom,* 642–43. The Travis AFB riot was the worst the air force has ever experienced. It continued for three days, 22–24 May 1971, and resulted in 1 dead, 30 injured, and 135 arrested. The Travis riot reoriented the entire air force way of looking at the race problem. See *Air Force Times,* "Family Magazine," 18 Aug. 1971, 4–7, 19.

102. Fred C. Shapiro and James W. Sullivan, *Race Riots New York, 1964* (New York, 1964).

103. Ltr, Koontz to Ellender, 7 Apr. 1964, in Dir. of Personnel Planning, Read File, Jan.–June 1964 (AGC).

104. Ltrs, Dir. of Personnel Planning to Diggs, 30 Jan. 1964, Saltonstall, 15 Oct. 1964 (AGC).

105. For example, see Memo for the Record, telephone conversation between Koontz and Ault, 16 Jan. 1964, memo to General Martin on Craig AFB, 16 Jan. 1964, and memo to General Martin on 14 Apr. 1964 (AGC).

106. Ault intvw. This victory occurred in April 1964. There were 200 units in the Nathan Bedford Forrest Homes. See memo to General Martin, 14 Apr. 1964 (AGC).

107. Ault intvw. Ault had received a tongue-lashing from Robert Kennedy after the air force colonel tried to explain to the attorney general that his mission was to train pilots at Craig, not to shut down Selma. After the Civil Rights Act, the town got "with the program." Ault threatened off-limits sanctions, and the threat opened facilities. Throughout his four years at Selma, he could not remember any advice from the Equal Opportunity Group, although he was in constant communication with the group. He said, however, that he appreciated the lack of guidance because this gave him wide latitude to solve his own problems.

108. "History of the Directorate of Personnel Planning," 1 July–31 Dec. 65, 8–14. In the history for the previous six months, Equal Opportunity was still listed as "Group."

109. Intvw., author with C. S. Doane, Washington, D.C., May 1973. Doane said that Farris proposed the downgrading of the group, believing the problem was in hand. At the time of the Travis riot, the director of the equal opportunity section was Lt. Col. Hughie Mathews. In an interview, Mathews related that the air force had no program until after the Travis riot. Mathews claimed that his predecessors back to Colonel Farris were serious but were hamstrung by the lack of air staff interest. The man Mathews succeeded was called "nigger lover" by some of his co-workers in the air staff. Mathews said that this was somebody's "poor idea of a sick joke." After the Travis riot, the office staff rose from one officer to six, plus a corresponding number of clerks to make the office efficient. Mathews believes that the air force made more progress after the Travis riot than in the 23 years of air force history before it. "After Travis," he said, "the Air Force got serious." Intvw., author with Hughie E. Mathews, Washington, D.C., Apr. 1973.

110. Memo, J. William Doolittle to the Chief of Staff, subj.: "Racial Relations within the Air Force," 17 Sept. 1968 (AGC). Who would have thought to look for equal opportunity in the flying pay and entitlements branch? Doolittle was in the secretary's office in Manpower and Reserve Affairs. He believed the air force was doing well in racial affairs, but he pointed out the lack of a program, saying that a policy—as written in air force regulations—was not a substitute for a program.

111. Memo, Civil Rights Office to Norman Paul, 21 Sept. 1965, subj.: "Policy Formulation, Planning and Action in the Office of the Deputy Assistant Secretary of Defense (Civil Rights)," 26 July 1964–26 Sept. 1965 (AGC). This memorandum shows that all of the air force equal opportunity efforts preceding publication of AFR 35-78—such as a ban on housing listings which specified race and a ban on official attendance at segregating institutions of higher learning—had come as initiatives from the Department of Defense. The air force, like the other services, had been ordered to produce a new equal opportunity regulation by November 1963, but these were all held up until after passage of the important legislation. The memo, furthermore, pointed out a growth in the black officer corps and the advance of blacks into positions of command and into the senior service and joint schools. Between the time Benjamin Davis had attended the War College in 1949 and the time Col. Frederick E. Davison entered the Army War College in 1962, no black officers had attended these important schools. When the memorandum was written, there were two blacks at the Naval War College, one black at the Army War College (and only three graduates in the history of the school), one black at the National War College, two blacks at the Air War College, and none at the Industrial College of the Armed Forces. The memo noted that between 1950 and 1965, only 26 blacks had achieved command of air force tactical units.

112. Vergil M. Bates, "The Commander's Role in the Problem of Equal Opportunity," Air War College thesis, 1965, 48–49.

113. Don G. Harris, "A Conflict of Responsibilities: Community Relations—Off-Base Equal Opportunities for Negroes," Air Command and Staff College research study, June 1965, 68–71.

Epilogue

1. AFR 35-11, "Equal Opportunity for Military Personnel in Off-Base Housing Programs," 14 Apr. 1969. Personnel who rent or lease housing in violation of this regulation can be penalized under the Uniform Code of Military Justice and, at a minimum, would jeopardize their housing allowance.

2. Headquarters, U.S. Air Forces in Europe, *Commanders Notebook on Equal Opportunity and Human Relations,* [1970]. See the foreword by Brig. Gen. Brian Gunderson.

3. Ibid., 2, 3, 4, 5–7.

4. Ibid., 8–11.

5. Ibid., 12–21, 22–34, 39–41.

6. AFR 35-78, Change B., 14 Dec. 1970. Change A called for regular "Off-Base Equal Opportunity Status Reports." This had been published on 8 Apr. 1965.

7. Ibid.

8. AFR 35-78, "Equal Opportunity and Treatment of Military Personnel," 18 May 1971. See App. 2–7.

9. *Air Force Times,* "Family Magazine," 18 Aug. 1971, 4–7, 19. An example of complacency is provided in an Air War College thesis produced by an air force colonel, Charles W. Kinney, in 1970. Kinney determined that the race problem in America was a civilian problem and that the air force had solved its racial issues. See his "The Other War," Air War College research study, Apr. 1970, 1. Eight months earlier, a Marine lieutenant colonel, George B. Crist, had produced a paper that came to the opposite conclusion—that the military was not ahead of society at all and that the services were bringing on serious race problems because of complacency. See his "Black Is Beautiful and the Military Establishment," Air War College thesis, Dec. 1970, 1, 2. After the Travis riot the solutions became more radical than those suggested in the past. See, for example, Walter A. Collins, "The Race Problem in the United States Air Force," Air Command and Staff College research study, May 1972, 96–97; and William T. Fuller, Jr., "An Analysis of Racial Discrimination in the U.S. Air Force," Air Command and Staff College research study, May 1972, vii, 11, 33, 53–66, 61.

10. *Air Force Times,* "Family Magazine," 18 Aug. 1971, 4–7, 19.

11. Ibid. This analysis of the causes for in-service riots is corroborated in part by Jack D. Foner, *Blacks and the Military in American History: A New Perspective* (New York, 1974), 201. Foner believed that the Pentagon tried to avoid racial friction but that it was frustrated by bigots at lower levels. On pp. 201–60, he examined the Vietnam period and demonstrated that continuous race rioting was brought about by bigotry and residual institutional racism. Although the Travis riot is discussed, the problems of the air force are regarded as much less severe than those of the other services. Foner believed that blacks encountered the same problems a decade earlier but now would no longer put up with discrimination. He concluded that blacks were changing faster than the services could improve. This view is shared by Robert W. Mullen, *Blacks in America's Wars: The Shift in Attitudes from the Revolutionary War to Viet Nam* (New York, 1973), 83–85.

12. *Air Force Times,* "Family Magazine," 18 Aug. 1971, 4–7, 19.

13. The first Air Force Social Actions Directorate was Col. David L. Thompson. He supplied me with this information and gave other assistance, including permission to duplicate the files of the Equal Opportunity Office, which date back to Jack Marr's time. Intvw., author with David Thompson, Jan. 1973, Washington, D.C.

14. AFR 50-26, "Education in Race Relations," 2 Dec. 1971.

15. Intvw., author with with Gen. Lucius Theus, Washington, D.C., Jan. 1973. I taught the race relations course for one year as an additional duty and am familiar with the curriculum. Richard Dalfiume wrote that Benjamin O. Davis, Sr., recommended race relations training for all personnel as early as September 1942. See Dalfiume, *Desegregation,* 76. For an example of how one major com-

mand implemented the new air force policy, see Pacific Air Forces Manual 35-1, "Equal Opportunity and Treatment of Military Personnel," 15 Apr. 1972. This manual instructs social actions personnel not to direct their energies toward changing attitudes. Efforts "directed toward the re-education of attitudes produces few results, as only behavior is measurable."

16. Air Force Manual 36-10, "Officer Evaluation Reports," 25 Nov. 1974.

17. Department of Defense, *Report of the Task Force on the Administration of Justice in the Armed Forces,* 4 vols. (Washington, D.C., 30 Nov. 1972), 1:2. 17. There were fourteen members on this task force: 5 blacks and 9 whites; 1 woman and 13 men. Among its members were civilian and military lawyers, the judges advocate general of all the services; and the commander of the First Army and the general counsel of the NAACP (who served as cochairman). Five (white) members disagreed with the main thrust of the report and were permitted to express their objections in a minority section of the text. The dissenters believed that the report overemphasized the depth of systemic discrimination in the military and also found fault with the panel's conclusion that race discrimination was the primary reason for the differences between court-martial and promotion rates. They did not object to the facts—blacks had a higher court-martial rate and a lower promotion rate than whites—but they did not believe prejudice explained the entire differential. They hastened to state, however, that they were in complete "accord that racial and minority discrimination is present in the military establishment, just as it is in the civilian society. Its presence in any degree denigrates the individual, reflects adversely on the service, and makes the military mission more difficult of accomplishment." Ibid., 1:129.

18. Ibid., 1:25–32, 39–41. The task force surveyed 19 air force bases but had less than 60 courts-martial to work with. Reversing the trend elsewhere, the task force found that 16 percent of the blacks received counseling short of punishment while less than 3 percent of the whites did. Whites had a higher court-martial rate, but blacks had a higher nonjudicial punishment rate. As in the army, more blacks than whites submitted "not guilty" pleas and more blacks than whites received acquittals. In another part of the report, the task force gathered some data from 1,299 air force court-martial cases over a period of years from all bases. While whites and blacks generally had the same court-martial rates when considered by specialty, this study proved that men in the more menial career fields were far more likely to fall afoul of the system and receive a court-martial than men in the more technological or mission-oriented career fields. More than 66 percent of the courts-martial were shown to occur in four menial specialties, and the blacks were concentrated in these fields: 39.7 percent of the whites worked in the technological or operational specialties, while only 25 percent of the blacks did. Ibid.: 3:8, 9, 71, 87, 228, 229; 4:25, 27.

19. Ibid., 1:112–17.

Glossary

AAF	Army Air Forces
AFB	Air Force Base
AFL	Air Force Letter
AFR	Air Force Regulation
AFSHRC	Albert F. Simpson Historical Research Center
AGC	Alan Gropman Collection
AGCT	Army General Classification Test
App.	appendix
AR	Army Regulation
ATC	Air Training Command
CCTS	Combat Crew Training Squadron
DCS/P	Deputy Chief of Staff for Personnel
DRRI	Defense Race Relations Institute
E-1	Private (to 1953); thereafter, Airman, Basic
E-2	Private, First Class (to 1953); thereafter, Airman, Third Class
E-3	Corporal (to 1953); thereafter, Airman, Second Class
E-4	Sergeant (to 1953); thereafter, Airman, First Class
E-5	Staff Sergeant
E-6	Technical Sergeant
E-7	Master Sergeant
E-8	Senior, Master Sergeant (since 1958)
E-9	Chief, Master Sergeant (since 1958)
FEPC	Fair Employment Practices Committee

GI	Government Issue
G-3	Operations
HQ	headquarters
HSTL	Harry S Truman Library
ICAF	Industrial College of the Armed Forces
M	Medium
MP	military policeman
NAACP	National Association for the Advancement of Colored People
NARG	National Archives Record Group
NCO	noncommissioned officer
NPRC	National Personnel Records Center
OASD	Office of the Assistant Secretary of Defense
OD	officer of the day
O-1	Second Lieutenant
O-2	First Lieutenant
O-3	Captain
O-4	Major
O-5	Lieutenant Colonel
O-6	Colonel
O-7	Brigadier General
P.L.	Public Law
ROTC	Reserve Officer Training Corps
SAC	Strategic Air Command
TAC	Tactical Air Command
USAF	U.S. Air Force
USAFE	U.S. Air Forces in Europe
WD	War Department

Bibliography

Manuscript Collections

In addition to archival collections, I was fortunate to obtain access to several unusually fruitful sources. I not only was allowed to duplicate the material in the files of active offices but also was permitted to copy material previously obtained by other researchers. Several working historians also sent me copies of documents they thought would prove useful for this narrative. Such material has been cited as the Alan Gropman Collection (AGC), located in the Albert F. Simpson Historical Research Center (AFSHRC), Maxwell AFB, Alabama, adding to the center's growing body of material on blacks in the air force. Future scholars who want to work in this area will find several offices in the Pentagon most useful for their purposes. The Office of the Deputy Assistant Secretary of the Air Force for Manpower Policy was very generous and helpful. The Equal Opportunity Division within the Deputy Chief of Staff/Personnel Deputate had material going back to the 1940s. If these files have been thinned to make room for current business, the record manager for the division should be able to provide information as to the location of the extant files. Most noncurrent files in the Pentagon are moved to the National Records Center in Suitland, Maryland.

Adjutant General Decimal File, 1945. Record Group 18. National Archives, Washington, D.C.

H. H. Arnold Papers. Library of Congress, Washington, D.C.

Clark M. Clifford Papers. Harry S Truman Library, Independence, Mo.

Director of Personnel Planning, USAF, Papers. Record Group 561. National Archives, Washington, D.C.

George Elsey Papers. Harry S Truman Library, Independence, Mo.

James C. Evans Papers. Army War College, Carlisle Barracks, Pa.

Alvan C. Gillem Board Papers. Army War College, Carlisle Barracks, Pa.

Lyndon B. Johnson Papers. Lyndon B. Johnson Library, Austin, Tex.

Burke Marshall Papers. John F. Kennedy Library, Boston, Mass.

National Association for the Advancement of Colored People (NAACP) Papers. Library of Congress, Washington, D.C.

Negro Pamphlet File. Army War College, Carlisle Barracks, Pa.

Office of Civil Rights. Office of the Deputy Assistant Secretary of Defense (CR & IR) OASD(m). Accession 68A 1066. National Records Center, Suitland, Md.

Office of the Assistant Secretary of War, Civil Aide to the Secretary. Record Group 107. National Archives, Washington, D.C.

Office of the Deputy Assistant Secretary of Defense (CR & IR) Counselor, OASD(m). Accession No. 68A 1033. National Records Center, Suitland, Md.

President's Committee on Civil Rights Papers. Harry S Truman Library, Independence, Mo.

President's Committee on Equality of Treatment and Opportunity in the Armed Services (Fahy Committee) Papers. Harry S Truman Library, Independence, Mo.

President's Committee on Religion and Welfare in the Armed Forces Papers. Harry S Truman Library, Independence, Mo.

Secretary of Defense Papers. Record Group 330. National Archives, Washington, D.C.

Secretary of the Air Force Papers. Record Group 340. National Archives, Washington, D.C.

Staff Files. Dwight D. Eisenhower Library, Abilene, Kans.

Harry S Truman Papers. Harry S Truman Library, Independence, Mo.

Hoyt S. Vandenberg Papers. Library of Congress, Washington, D.C.

Lee White Papers. John F. Kennedy Library, Boston, Mass.

Ennis C. Whitehead Papers. Albert F. Simpson Memorial Archives, Maxwell AFB, Ala.

White House Central Files. General Files, Official Files. Eisenhower Library, Abilene, Kans.

Harris Wofford Papers. John F. Kennedy Library, Boston, Mass.

File 114-528. National Personnel Records Center, St. Louis, Mo.

Public Documents

This section lists the numerous regulations and other directives issued by the army and the air force. The files of the Office of the Chief of Military History, Washington, D.C., contain the most complete collection of army regulations. The Air University Library, Maxwell AFB, Ala., contains the air force collection. The directives are listed chronologically, followed by an alphabetical listing of the other public documents used.

"War Department Policies Governing the Employment of Negro Personnel upon Mobilization," G-3/6541-527. 3 June 1940.

AG 291.2 (10-9-40). 16 Oct. 1940.

Army Regulation 210-10, Posts, Camps, and Stations Administration. 20 Dec. 1940.

War Department Pamphlet No. 20-6, Command of Negro Troops. 29 Feb. 1944.

War Department Memo 600-45. 14 June 1945.

Army Air Forces Letter 35-100, Utilization of Negro Personnel. 1 Mar. 1946.

War Department Circular 124, Utilization of Negro Manpower in the Postwar Army Policy. 27 Apr. 1946.

Army Air Forces Letter 35-101, Utilization of Negro Manpower in Postwar Army. 10 June 1946.

Army Air Forces Letter 35-130, Enlistments and Reenlistments in the Regular Army. 21 June 1946.

War Department, Adjutant General's Office, Enlisted Branch (War Department) 342.06. Enlistment of Negroes. 27 Aug. 1946.

War Department. *Army Talk 170.* 12 Apr. 1947.

Air Force Letter 39-8, Assignment of Air Force Enlistees, Reenlistees, and Returnees. 14 Feb. 1949.

Air Force Letter 35-3, Air Force Personnel Policies. 11 May 1949.

Army Regulation 600-629-1, Utilization of Negro Manpower in the Army. 16 Jan. 1950.

Air Force Regulation 35-78, Air Force Personnel Policies. 14 Sept. 1950.

Air Force Regulation 35-78, Air Force Personnel Policy Regarding Minority Groups. 15 Sept. 1955.

Department of Defense Directive 5120.36, Equal Opportunity in the Armed Forces. 26 July 1963.

Air Force Regulation 35-78, Equal Opportunity and Treatment of Military Personnel. 19 Aug. 1964.

Air Force Regulation 35-11, Equal Opportunity for Military Personnel in Off-Base Housing Programs. 24 Sept. 1969.

Air Force Regulation 35-78, Equal Opportunity and Treatment of Military Personnel. 18 May 1971.

Pacific Air Forces Manual 35-1, Equal Opportunity and Treatment of Military Personnel. 15 Apr. 1972.

Department of Defense. *Integration and the Negro Officer in the Armed Forces of the United States of America*. Washington, D.C., 1962.

Department of Defense, I&E Division, Attitude Research Branch. *Morale Attitudes of Enlisted Men, May–June 1949: Attitude toward Integration of Negro Soldiers in the Army*. Washington, D.C., Mar. 1949.

Department of Defense. *Report of the Task Force on the Administration of Military Justice in the Armed Forces*. 4 vols. Washington, D.C., 30 Nov. 1972.

Headquarters, U.S. Air Forces in Europe. *Commanders Notebook on Equal Opportunity and Human Relations*. [1970]. Mimeographed.

Information and Education Division, Army Service Forces. *Opinions about Negro Infantry Platoons in White Companies of Seven Divisions, Based on a Survey Made in May–June 1945*. Washington, D.C., 3 July 1945.

Inspector General, USAF. *United States Air Force TIG Brief*. 26 May 1961.

Office of Statistical Control. *Army Air Forces Statistical Digest: World War II*. Dec. 1945.

President's Committee on Civil Rights. *To Secure These Rights*. Washington, D.C.: U.S. Government Printing Office, 1947.

President's Committee on Equal Opportunity in the Armed Forces. "Initial Report: Equality of Treatment and Opportunity for Negro Military Personnel within the United States." 13 June 1963. Mimeographed.

———. "Final Report: Military Personnel Stationed Overseas, and Membership and Participation in the National Guard." Nov. 1964. Mimeographed.

President's Committee on Equality of Treatment and Opportunity in the Armed Services. *Freedom to Serve*. Washington, D.C.: U.S. Government Printing Office, 1950.

Project Clear. *Summary Preliminary Report on Utilization of Negro Manpower*. Baltimore: Operations Research Office, Johns Hopkins University, [1951]. Mimeographed.

Public Papers of the Presidents of the United States: Harry S Truman. Washington, D.C.: U.S. Government Printing Office, 1947, 1948.

Public Papers of the Presidents of the United States: John F. Kennedy. Washington, D.C.: U.S. Government Printing Office, 1962, 1963.

Research Branch, Special Service Division, Services of Supply. *Attitudes of Enlisted Men toward Negroes for Air Force Duty*. 30 Nov. 1942.

Slonaker, John. *The U.S. Army and the Negro*, Army War College, Carlisle Barracks, Pa. 1971. Mimeographed.

Statistical Control Division. *Army Air Forces Statistical Digest: 1946*. June 1947.

Statistical Services. *United States Air Force Statistical Digest: 1948, Jan. 1949–June 1950, Fiscal 1951, 1952, 1953, 1954*.

Strickland, Patricia. *The Putt-Putt Air Force: The Story of the Civilian Pilot Training Program and the War Training Service (1939–1944)*. Washington, D.C.: Federal Aviation Administration, [1971].

U.S. Commission on Civil Rights. *Civil Rights '63.* Washington, D.C.: U.S. Government Printing Office, 1963.

———. *Family Housing and the Negro Serviceman.* Washington, D.C.: U.S. Government Printing Office, Oct. 1963.

U.S. Congressional Record. House, 1963.

Newspapers

Air Force Times, 1944–64.
Army Navy Journal, 1948–50.
Army, Navy, Air Force Journal, 1941–64.
Baltimore Afro-American, 1944–64.
Chicago Defender, 1944–64.
The Crisis, 1940, 1942.
New York Amsterdam News, 1944–57.
Pittsburgh Courier, 1944–64.

Personal Correspondence

H. W. Bowman to the author. 15 May 1973.
Jack Marrw to the author. 1 Oct. 1973.
Thurgood Marshall to the author. 5 July 1973.
Earl Warren to the author. 9 Feb. 1973.

Interviews

I have included here all interviews consulted, including those in the oral history collections, those conducted by colleagues and forwarded to me, and those in which I participated. Interviews that can be found in the Oral History Collection at Columbia University are marked (CU).

Personal Interviews

Richard L. Ault. Washington, D.C., May 1973.
Thomas Clark. Washington, D.C., Mar. 1973.
Benjamin O. Davis, Jr. Washington, D.C., Jan. 1973. (CU)
Mr. and Mrs. Benjamin O. Davis, Jr. (joint interview). Colorado Springs, Colo., May 1973. (CU)
C. S. Doane. Washington, D.C., May 1973.
Idwal Edwards. Arlington, Va., Feb. 1973. (CU)
James C. Evans. Washington, D.C., Jan. 1973. (CU)
Roland Gittelsohn. Boston, Mass., Apr. 1970.
James P. Goode. Washington, D.C., Feb. 1973.
Daniel James, Jr. Washington, D.C., Jan. 1973.
William F. McKee. Washington, D.C., May 1973.
Jack Marr. Cobbs Creek, Va., Feb. 1973. (CU)
Hughie E. Mathews. Washington, D.C., Apr. 1973. (CU)
Noel F. Parrish. San Antonio, Tex., Mar. 1973. (CU)
Marion R. Rodgers. Colorado Springs, Colo., Jan. 1973.
Dean Strother. Colorado Springs, Colo., June 1974.
Stuart Symington. Washington, D.C., Mar. 1973.
Lucius Theus. Washington, D.C., Jan. 1973. (CU)
David Thompson. Washington, D.C., Jan. 1973.
Earl Warren. Washington, D.C., Apr. 1973.

Spann Watson. Washington, D.C., Apr. 1973. (CU)

Adam Yarmolinsky. Boston, Mass., July 1973.

Eugene Zuckert. Washington, D.C., Apr. 1973.

Interviews Conducted by Others

Richard Nugent, by Alan Osur. Indian Harbor Beach, Fla., June 1973.

Interviews in Oral History Collections

Theodore Hesburgh, by Joseph O'Connor. Mar. 1966. John F. Kennedy Library, Boston, Mass.

Theodore Hesburgh, by Paige Mulholland. Feb. 1971. Lyndon B. Johnson Library, Austin, Texas.

Marx Leva. Washington, D.C., Dec. 1969 and June 1970. Harry S Truman Library, Independence, Mo.

Thurgood Marshall, by Berl Bernhard. Apr. 1964. John F. Kennedy Library, Boston, Mass.

Clarence Mitchell, by John Stewart. Feb. 1967. John F. Kennedy Library, Boston, Mass.

Roy Wilkins, by Berl Bernhard. Aug. 1964. John F. Kennedy Library, Boston, Mass.

Harris Wofford, by Larry Hackman. May 1968. John F. Kennedy Library, Boston, Mass.

Unpublished Studies

The extensive collection of unit histories and other studies available at the Albert F. Simpson Historical Research Center at the Air University Library form the spine of this narrative. Everything listed in this section can be found in the Simpson Center or the Air University Library.

Professional School Studies and Special Reports

Anthis, Rollen H. "Utilization of Negro Personnel in the Armed Forces." Air Command and Staff College research study, Mar. 1949.

Avery, D. B. "The Negro and the Air Force." Air Command and Staff College research study, Nov. 1949.

Bates, Vergil M. "The Commander's Role in the Problem of Equal Opportunity." Air War College thesis, 1965.

Catington, James D. "Sociological Factors Concerned with the Segregation of Negro Troops in the Armed Forces." Air Command and Staff College research study, May 1949.

Collins, Walter A. "The Race Problem in the United States Air Force." Air Command and Staff College research study, May 1972.

Covington, W. E., Jr. "The Utilization of Negro Personnel." Air War College thesis, Mar. 1949.

Crist, George B. "Black Is Beautiful and the Military Establishment." Air War College thesis, Dec. 1970.

Cunningham, Jack E. "Non-Segregation vs. Prejudice." Air Command and Staff College research study, Nov. 1949.

Cutcher, Solomon. "Effective Utilization of Negro Personnel in the Armed Forces." Air Command and Staff College research study, Mar. 1948.

Economic Mobilization Course, "Training and Utilization of Manpower." Industrial College of the Armed Forces, Washington, D.C., 1947–48.

Fuller, William T., Jr. "An Analysis of Racial Discrimination in the U.S. Air Force." Air Command and Staff College research study, May 1972.

Gaffney, John B. "Application of Personnel Management as Applied to Negro Troops in the Air Forces." Air Command and Staff College research study, Oct. 1948.

Harris, Don G. "A Conflict of Responsibilities: Community Relations—Off-Base Equal Opportunities for Negroes." Air Command and Staff College research study, June 1965.

Kinney, Charles W. "The Other War." Air War College research study, Apr. 1970.

Klein, Phillip B. "Utilization of Negro Personnel in the Air Force." Air War College research study, Mar. 1949.

Kunish, Lester L. "Utilization of Negro Airmen on Air Force Bases." Air War College research study, Feb. 1949.

Link, Fidelis, A. "Determination of Policies for Utilization of Negro Manpower in the U.S. Air Force." Air Command and Staff College research study, Nov. 1949.

McEwen, Alfred E. "Permanent Change of Station: A Continuing Problem for Negro Airmen." Air Command and Staff College research study, June 1966.

Nippert, Louis. "Memo for the Chief of Staff: Participation of Negro Troops in the Post-War Military Establishment." 17 Sept. 1945.

Office of the Commandant, Army War College. "Memorandum for the Chief of Staff: The Use of Negro Manpower in War." 30 Oct. 1925.

Parrish, Noel F. "The Segregation of Negroes in the Army Air Forces." Air Command and Staff School research study, May 1947.

Pesch, John J. "Should Negroes and Whites Be Integrated in the Same Air Force Units?" Air Command and Staff College research study, Apr. 1949.

Report of the War Department Special Board on Negro Manpower. "Policy for Utilization of Negro Manpower in the Post-War Army with Recommendations for Development of Means Required and a Plan for Implementation of the Same." Nov. 1945.

Tangen, Orville C. "Negro Personnel Management in the United States Air Force." Air Command and Staff College research study, May 1949.

Walden, Emmet S., Jr. "Maxwell Air Force Base: An Equal Opportunity Case Study." Air Command and Staff College research study, 1964.

Young, Hugh D. "Effective Utilization of Negro Manpower in the United States Air Force." Air Command and Staff School research study, Dec. 1948.

Unit Histories and Miscellaneous Studies

"History of the First Bomb Wing." 1 July–31 Dec. 1943.

"History of the Ninth Air Force." 1 Dec. 1948–1 Jan. 1950, 1 Jan.–31 July 1950.

"History of 14th Air Force." 1 Jan.–30 June 1951.

"History of the Fifteenth Air Force." 1947.

"History of 90th Food Service Squadron." Feb. 1952.

"History of the 332d Fighter Group (SE)." 1 July–14 Aug. 1947, 15 Aug.–31 Dec. 1947, 1 Apr.–30 June 1948, July–Sept. 1948, Oct.–Nov. 1948.

"History of the 332d Fighter Wing." 1 Jan.–31 Mar. 1948, 1 Apr.–30 June 1948, 1 July–30 Sept. 1948, 1 Oct.–30 Nov. 1948, June 1949.

"History of the 385th Aviation Squadron." 1947.

"The Composite History of the 477th Composite Group, Godman Field, Kentucky." Jan. 1944–Sept. 1945.

"History of the 477th Bombardment Group (Medium)." 15 Jan.–5 May 1944, 6 May–15 July 1944, 16 July–15 Oct. 1944, 16 Oct. 1944–15 Jan. 1945, 16 Jan.–15 Apr. 1945, 16 Apr.–15 July 1945.

"History of the 477th Composite Group." 15 Sept. 1945–15 Feb. 1946, 15 Feb.–31 Mar. 1946, 1 Mar.–15 July 1946, 16 July–15 Oct. 1946, 31 Oct.–31 Dec. 1946, 1 Jan.–31 Mar. 1947, 1 Apr.–30 June 1947.

"History of the 811th Engineering Aviation Battalion." 1 Jan.–31 Dec. 1947, Jan. 1950.

"History of the 837th Engineering Aviation Battalion." Nov. 1945.

"History of the 2143d AAF Base Unit Pilot School, Basic, Advanced and Tuskegee Army Air Field, Tuskegee, Alabama." 1 Jan.–14 Apr. 1945, 1 Sept.–31 Oct. 1945, 1 Nov.–31 Dec. 1945, 1 Jan.–14 Apr. 1946.

"History of the 2164th AAF Base Unit, Tuskegee Institute." 1 Jan.–31 Oct. 1945.

"History of the 2500th ABG, Mitchell AFB." Oct., Nov. 1949.

"History of the 3800th Air University Wing, Maxwell AFB." Apr.–June 1949, July–Sept. 1949, Oct.–Dec. 1949, Jan.–June 1950, July–Dec. 1950, 1 July–31 Dec. 1951, Jan.–Mar. 1952.

"History of the 3904th Air Base Group, Stead AFB, Nevada." May 1952.

"History of the 6139th Air Base Group, Misawa Air Base, Japan." 1963.

[George N. Dubina.] "Air University History." Air University, Maxwell AFB, Ala., 1971.

"History of Continental Air Command." Dec. 1948–Dec. 1949.

"History of Far East Air Forces." Jan.–June 1955.

"History of Hondo Army Air Field." 1 Jan.–28 Feb. 1945.

"History of MacDill Army Air Field." Dec. 1946.

"History of Strategic Air Command." 1948, 1949, 1950.

"History of Tactical Air Command." Mar.–Dec. 1946, 1 Jan.–30 Nov. 1948.

"History of the Air Training Command." 1 July–31 Dec. 1949.

"History of the Directorate of Personnel Planning." 1 July 1949–30 June 1950, 1 July–31 Dec. 1963, 1 Jan.–30 June 1964, 1 July–31 Dec. 1964, 1 Jan.–30 June 1965, 1 July–31 Dec. 1965.

"History of the Office of the Inspector General." 1 July–31 Dec. 1950, 1 July–31 Dec. 1960, 1 July–31 Dec. 1962.

"History of the Pacific Division AAF Transport Command." 1 June–31 Dec. 1946.

[Lyon, Earl D.] "The Training of Negro Combat Units by the First Air Force." 2 vols. May 1946.

Madison, James A. "Summary of Services to the United States Air Force for the Period September 1, 1952, to December 31, 1954." New York Recreational Association.

Partridge, E. E. "Diary of Korea." 1950–51.

Tactical Air Command. "Utilization of Negro Manpower." 18 Mar. 1948.

Yohalem, Alice M. "Growing Up in the Desegregated Air Force." Columbia University, 1973. Manuscript.

Books

Adams, Sherman. *First Hand Report: The Story of the Eisenhower Administration.* New York: Harper, 1961.

Bardolph, Richard, ed. *The Civil Rights Record: Black Americans and the Law, 1849–1970.* New York: Crowell, 1970.

Berman, William C. *The Politics of Civil Rights in the Truman Administration.* Columbus: Ohio State University Press, 1970.

Bernstein, Barton J., ed. *Politics and Policies of the Truman Administration.* Chicago: University of Chicago Press, 1970.

Bogart, Leo, ed. *Social Research and the Desegregation of the U.S. Army: Two Original 1951 Field Research Reports.* Chicago: Markham Publishing Co., 1969.

Carisella, P. J., and James W. Ryan. *The Black Swallow of Death.* Boston: Marlborough House, 1972.

Cornish, Dudley Taylor. *The Sable Arm: Negro Troops in the Union Army, 1861–1866.* New York: Longmans, Green and Co., 1956.

Craven, Wesley Frank, and James Lea Cate, eds. *The Army Air Forces in World War II.* Vols. II and VI. Chicago: University of Chicago Press, 1949, 1955.

Dalfiume, Richard M. *Desegregation of the U.S. Armed Forces: Fighting on Two Fronts, 1939–1953.* Columbia: University of Missouri Press, 1969.

Donovan, Robert J. *Eisenhower: The Inside Story.* New York: Harper, 1956.

Eisenhower, Dwight D. *The White House Years: Mandate for Change, 1953–1956.* New York: Signet Books, 1963.

———. *The White House Years: Waging Peace, 1956–1961.* New York: Doubleday, 1965.

Foner, Jack D. *Blacks and the Military in American History: A New Perspective.* New York: Praeger, 1974.

Fowler, Arlen Lowery. *The Negro Infantry in the West, 1869–1891.* Westport, Conn.: Greenwood, 1971.

Francis, Charles E. *The Tuskegee Airmen: The Story of the Negro in the U.S. Air Force.* Boston: Bruce Humphries, 1955.

Franklin, John Hope. *From Slavery to Freedom: A History of Negro Americans.* 3d ed. New York: Vintage, 1969.

Golden, Harry. *Mr. Kennedy and the Negroes.* New York: World, 1964.

Grant, Madison. *The Passing of the Great Race in America.* 4th ed. New York: Scribners, 1923.

Hughes, Emmet John. *The Ordeal of Power: A Political Memoir of the Eisenhower Years.* New York: Atheneum, 1963.

Jones, Maldwyn A. *American Immigration.* Chicago: University of Chicago Press, 1960.

Leckie, William H. *The Buffalo Soldiers: A Narrative of the Negro Cavalry in the West.* Norman: University of Oklahoma Press, 1967.

Lee, Irvin H. *Negro Medal of Honor Men.* 3d ed. New York: Dodd, Mead and Co., 1969.

Lee, Ulysses. *The Employment of Negro Troops.* Washington, D.C.: U.S. Government Printing Office, 1966.

McCoy, Donald R., and Richard T. Ruetten. *Quest and Response: Minority Rights and the Truman Administration.* Lawrence: University of Kansas Press, 1973.

McNamara, Robert S. *The Essence of Security: Reflections in Office.* New York: Harper and Row, 1968.

Mandelbaum, David G. *Soldier Groups and Negro Soldiers.* Berkeley: University of California Press, 1952.

Morrow, E. Frederick. *Black Man in the White House: A Diary of the Eisenhower Years by the Administrative Officer for Special Projects, the White House, 1955–1961.* New York: Coward-McCann, 1963.

Moskos, Charles, ed. *Public Opinion and the Military Establishment.* Beverly Hills, Calif.: Russell Sage, 1971.

Mullen, Robert W. *Blacks in America's Wars: The Shift in Attitudes from the Revolutionary War to Viet Nam.* New York: Monad Press, 1973.

Nichols, Lee. *Breakthrough on the Color Front.* New York: Random House, 1954.

Polenberg, Richard. *War and Society: The United States, 1941–1945.* Philadelphia: Lippincott, 1972.

Pusey, Merlo J. *Eisenhower the President.* New York: Macmillan, 1956.

Quarles, Benjamin. *The Negro in the American Revolution.* Chapel Hill: University of North Carolina Press, 1961.

———. *The Negro in the Civil War.* Boston: Little Brown and Co., 1953.

Roberts, Kenneth L. *Why Europe Leaves Home.* New York: Bobbs Merrill, 1922.

Schlesinger, Arthur M., Jr. *A Thousand Days: John F. Kennedy in the White House.* Boston: Houghton Mifflin, 1965.

Shapiro, Fred C., and James W. Sullivan. *Race Riots New York, 1964.* New York: Crowell, 1964.

Sorensen, Theodore C. *Kennedy.* New York: Bantam Books, 1965.

———. *The Kennedy Legacy.* New York: Macmillan, 1969.

Stillman, Richard J. *Integration of the Negro in the U.S. Armed Forces.* New York: Praeger, 1968.

Sundquist, James L. *Politics and Policy: The Eisenhower, Kennedy, and Johnson Years.* Washington, D.C.: Brookings Institution, 1968.

Truman, Harry S. *Memoirs of Harry S Truman.* 2 vols. New York: Signet, 1956.

Wolseley, Roland E. *The Black Press and U.S.A.* Ames: Iowa State University Press, 1971.

Yarmolinsky, Adam. *The Military Establishment: Its Impact on American Society.* New York: Harper and Row, 1971.

Articles and Pamphlets

Finkle, Lee. "The Conservative Aims of Militant Rhetoric: Black Protest during World War II." *Journal of American History* 60 (Dec. 1973): 692–713.

Hastie, William H. "On Clipped Wings: The Story of Jim Crow in the Army Air Corps." NAACP Pamphlet, 1 July 1943.

Paszek, Lawrence J. "Negroes and the Air Force, 1939–1949." *Military Affairs,* spring 1967, 1–10.

"Racial Troubles Increasing." *Intelligencer* (Stout Field, Ind.), Sept. 1944.

Wiant, John. "Integration a Fact in Services, but—." *Army-Navy-Air Force Register & Defense Times,* 28 Nov. 1959.

Index